Latin Is Fun

BOOK II

Lively Lessons for Advancing Students

Second Edition

John C. Traupman, Ph.D.
Emeritus Professor of Classics
St. Joseph's University
Philadelphia, Pennsylvania

Thomas A. Burgess, M.A.
Southern Westchester BOCES High School
Valhalla, New York

AMSCO SCHOOL PUBLICATIONS, INC.
315 Hudson Street / New York, N.Y. 10013

Cover Photo: www.istockphoto.com, Wall of Ara Pacis Augustae building. Rome, Italy.
Cover Design by: Meghan J. Shupe/Tony D'Adamo
Book Design and Composition by: Progressive Information Technologies
Illustrations by: Tom O'Sullivan and Ed Malsberg
Chapter Openers by: Tony D'Adamo
Colorization by: Progressive Information Technologies

Please visit our Web site at *www.amscopub.com*

When ordering this book, please specify
either **R 605 W** *or* LATIN IS FUN, BOOK II, SECOND EDITION

ISBN: 978-1-56765-439-4 / *NYC Item 56765-439-3*

Preface

Quintilian, the foremost ancient Roman educator, said: "Be sure to make learning fun lest the youngsters get to hate the subject before they learn it." That principle is the basis of this book. At the same time, this book also uses genuine Latin structure and idioms in the exercises, readings, and conversations so that students will be prepared to read and comprehend Latin writers upon completion of this course.

LATIN IS FUN, BOOK II continues the natural, personalized, enjoyable, and rewarding program of language acquisition begun in the first course. BOOK II provides all of the elements of a full second course. It aims at oral proficiency, as well as listening, writing, and reading competence, thereby meeting the requirements of the national proficiency standards for this level of Latin.

LATIN IS FUN, BOOK II will broaden students' levels of achievement in basic skills, with emphasis on realistic, meaningful communication. Through topical contexts, students will also expand their vocabularies, their control of structure, and their ability to communicate about their daily lives in task-oriented and social situations.

LATIN IS FUN, BOOK II consists of four parts. Each part contains five lessons followed by a *recognitiō* (review) unit, in which various *āctivitātēs* (activities) recapitulate structures for students to practice. These *āctivitātēs* include games and puzzles as well as conventional exercises.

Each lesson includes a step-by-step sequence of the following student-directed elements. The design of these lessons makes materials directly accessible and helps students have fun learning and practicing Latin.

Culture

Each lesson begins with a *modicum cultūrae,* an illustrated essay on a specific topic of Roman culture, that serves as the context for the chapter. This feature is particularly important for students who are learning about a culture quite different from their own. The *modicum cultūrae* is not a "cultural extra" but, rather, an integral part of the unified lesson that helps students better understand cultural concepts in the rest of the lesson. Integrated with the cultural essay are vocabulary, structures, and readings.

Vocabulary

Unlike traditional Latin textbooks that introduce each chapter with vocabularies in isolation, each lesson presents topically and thematically related vocabulary through sets of drawings that convey the meanings of new words and expressions in Latin without recourse to English. This device—sometimes individual vignettes, sometimes composite scenes—enables students to make direct and vivid associations with the Latin terms and their meanings. The *āctivitātēs* that immediately follow also use pictures to help students practice words and expressions.

To produce interesting, realistic readings and conversations from the very outset, the book provides additional vocabulary side-by-side with the readings.

Structure

LATIN IS FUN, BOOK II introduces new structural elements one at a time in small learning components that are followed directly by appropriate *āctivitātēs*. This simple, straightforward, guided presentation helps students make their own discoveries, formulate their own conclusions, and gain a sense of accomplishment. This book's aim is not simply to cover specified elements of grammar. Instead, grammatical concepts are incorporated within the context of the readings and conversations.

Conversation

To encourage students to use Latin to communicate, each lesson includes a conversation and a dialog exercise. All conversations, illustrated in cartoon-strip fashion, contain a "punch line" to emphasize a message and add a touch of humor. Dialog exercises repeat the conversations but with gaps that students fill based on the original conversation. Students can achieve oral proficiency by reading and practicing the conversations multiple times.

Reading

Each lesson contains a short narrative or playlet that features the new structures and vocabulary and reinforces previously acquired vocabulary. Each selection presents these elements but also addresses a topic of intrinsic interest by relating real, everyday experiences of ancient Romans to those of people today. The extensive use of cognates and near-cognates underscores the relationship between English and Latin language and culture.

Personal Information

One goal of this program is to enable students to personalize language by relating lesson situations to their own lives. The "personal questions" at the end of each lesson give students an opportunity for personal connections.

The Latin Connection

Since many, if not all, students study Latin to enhance their command of English vocabulary, each lesson ends with an exercise in English derivatives based on the Latin words that occurred in the lesson. These exercises are more elaborate than those presented in LATIN IS FUN, BOOK I. To understand some of the derivatives, students probably will have to consult an English dictionary or get help from the teacher.

Teacher's Manual with Answers; Testing

A separate *Teacher's Manual with Answers* includes suggestions for teaching all elements in this book, additional oral practice, bibliographic information for further study, suggestions for activities and student projects, and a complete key for all exercises and puzzles.

The *Manual* also includes a quiz for each lesson, a unit test for each part, and two achievement tests. These tests are purposely simple so that ALL students finish with a sense of accomplishment. The tests use various techniques to evaluate mastery of structure, vocabulary, and comprehension. Teachers may use these tests as they appear or modify them to fit particular needs. Keys are provided for all test materials.

Contents

PARS TERTIA

PARS QUĀRTA

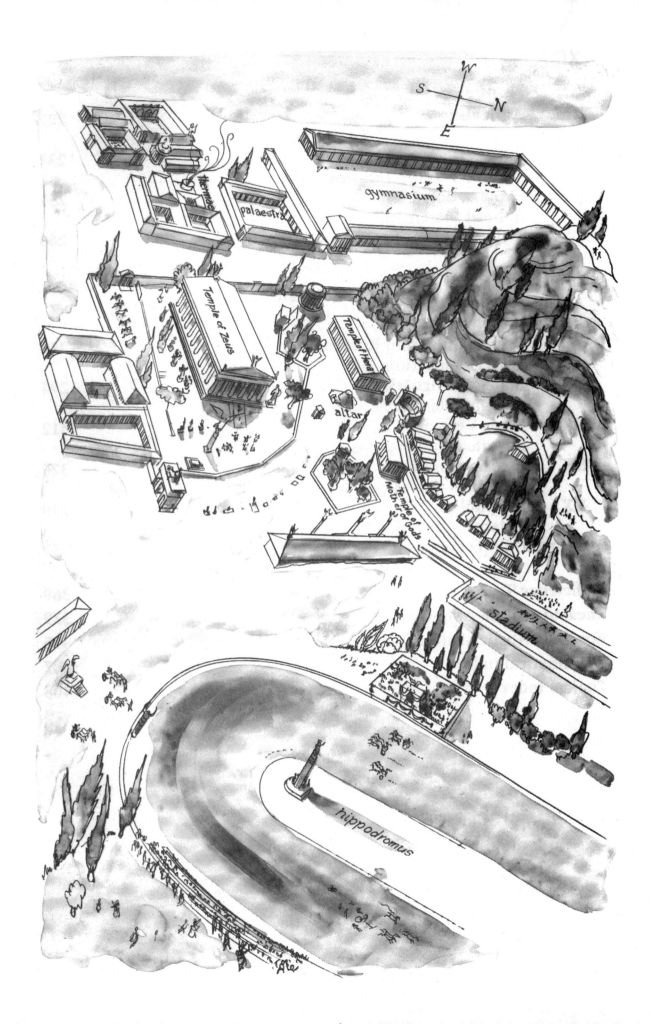

PARS PRĪMA

I Lūdī Olympicī

Demonstratives

 1 Modicum cultūrae

The Olympic Games, which began in 776 B.C., included only Greek athletes until the Romans, who conquered Greece in 146 B.C., forced Greece to let them compete. Although the Games continued at the original Greek site of Olympia, the Roman people soon caught "Olympic fever." Even Rome's Emperor Nero entered an event! Although he fell out of his chariot during the chariot race, other drivers allowed him to win. After all, who would be bold (or foolish) enough to defeat mad Emperor Nero knowing the winner would lose his head for the honor?

The Games, which lasted five days, included running, jumping, discus throwing, javelin throwing, boxing, wrestling, and chariot racing. These skills were important for success in ancient warfare. Participants belonged to one of two age groups: boys to the age of 18, and men over the age of 18. Girls could not participate. In fact, no females could attend the Games except the priestess of the goddess Demeter.

Athletes trained in two buildings: a smaller, square building called a **palaestra,** which means "wrestling place" (although boxers also trained there), and the **gymnasium,** a much longer building that contained a track under a covered portico for runners and space for discus and javelin throwers. Some sports popular in today's Olympic Games, such as swimming, diving, basketball, and gymnastics, were not part of ancient Olympic Games.

The Olympic grounds were divided into three parts. The first was the space in which the athletes practiced. In it were the **palaestra,** the **gymnasium,** and the baths. The second and central area was the sacred precinct housing the temple of Zeus (called Jupiter by the Romans), the temple of Hera (Juno), and the temple of the Mother of the Gods. The Greeks held the Games to honor Zeus, whose temple contained a 45-foot-high ivory and gold statue of the god. This statue was one of the Seven Wonders of the Ancient World. Near the temple was a huge, 32-foot sacrificial altar to Zeus. The central area also contained buildings to house the Olympic officials. Throughout the sacred precinct were hundreds of statues to the gods and to successful Olympic heroes. The third area contained the horse race track (**hippodrom*us* –*ī m***) and the stadium, in which all other events took place. (*See illustration on page xi.*)

In July or August (a month before the Games began), cities throughout Greece declared a truce in any ongoing wars so that all those who wished to attend the Games could travel safely to Olympia. Before the Games began, all athletes took a solemn oath that they had trained hard for at least ten months and that they would not cheat in the competitions. At the end of the Games, the winner of each event received a crown of wild olive branches cut from a tree near the temple of Zeus. When the hero returned to his hometown, he received both high honors and a substantial amount of money.

The ancient Olympic Games lasted over a thousand years until Emperor Theodosius ended them in A.D. 394. Theodosius, a Christian, objected to the Games because he felt they honored pagan gods.

auriga -ae m

curriculum -ī n

iaculum -ī n

discus -ī m

cursor -ōris m

iaculātor -ōris m

discobolus -ī m

caestus -ūs m

gymnasium -ī n

luctātor -ōris m

palaestra -ae f

pugil -is m

ĀCTIVITĀS

A. Quid id est? Write the correct Latin name for each picture. Give the genitive case and the gender of each:

3 As you read the following story about Ajax and Claudius at the Olympic Games, notice the demonstrative adjectives **hīc, haec, hoc** (*this*) and **ille, illa, illud** (*that*). Demonstrative adjectives point out someone or something. As you will see, these adjectives are declined much like the adjective **bonus, bona, bonum.** The demonstrative adjectives are printed in bold type. **Note**: For a full explanation of a reflexive verb like **sē exercēre**, see Lesson II, p. 24.

Erat aestās. Erat prīmus diēs lūdōrum Olympicōrum. Āthlētae ubīque sē exercēbant. Magna turba circumstābat et āthlētās spectābat.

Āiāx, puer Graecus ex Spartā, et amīcus suus, Claudius, ex Campāniā, modo ad Olympiam pervēnērunt. Āiāx semel anteā Olympiam vīsitāvit. Claudius autem numquam anteā Olympiam vīsitāvit.

"Estne grandis statua Iovis in hōc templō?" rogāvit Claudius. "Nōn est," respondit Āiāx. "**Hōc** templum est templum Iūnōnis, sed **illud** est templum Iovis. **Illa** statua est ūna ex septem mīrāculīs mundī. Sed **illud** templum posteā vīsitāre possumus. Prīmō ad palaestram eāmus."

Duo amīcī palaestram intrāvērunt. "Ecce," inquit Āiāx, "**hī** āthlētae sunt pugilēs et **illī** sunt luctātōrēs. **Hī** pugilēs caestūs gestant."

"Certantne pugilēs et luctātōrēs in **hāc** palaestrā?" rogāvit Claudius. "Minimē," respondit Āiāx. "In **hōc** locō āthlētae sē exercent et palaestricus **illōs** attentē observat. Āthlētae in stadiō ultrā **illa** templa certant."

"Suntne āthlētae etiam in **illō** aedificiō proximō?" rogāvit Claudius.

"Sānē. **Illud** aedificium est gymnasium. In **illō** aedificiō cursōrēs sē exercent, discobolī discōs conīciunt, iaculātōrēs iacula conīciunt. Quamobrem **illud** aedificium tam longum est."

"Licetne observāre **illōs** āthlētās?" rogāvit Claudius.

"Licet," respondit Āiāx. "**Illī** āthlētae sunt amīcissimī, sed **hīc** palaestricus est strictissimus. Vīsne vidēre aurīgās et equōs et curricula in hippodromō?"

"Minimē, Āiāx. Ego aurīgās et equōs et curricula in Circō Maximō saepe vīdī."

---

ubīque *everywhere*
  sē exercēre *to train, exercise*
turba *–ae f crowd*
  circumstō –stāre –stetī –status *to stand around*
Āiāx, Āiācis *m boy's name*
Campānia *–ae f Campania (a district south of Rome)*
  modo *just*
perveniō –venīre –vēnī –ventus *to arrive*
  semel *once*
  anteā *before*
autem *adv however*
  numquam *adv never*
grandis –is –e *large, huge*
mīrāculum –ī *n wonder*
  mundus –ī *m world*
prīmō *first*
  eāmus *let's go*
intrō –āre –āvī –ātum *to enter*
inquit *(he) says*

locus –ī *m place*
palaestricus –ī *m coach*

attentē *closely*
ultrā *prep (+ acc) beyond, on the other side of*
  certō –āre –āvi *to compete*
aedificium –ī *n building*
proximus –a –um *nearby, next*

conīciō –īcěre –iēcī –iectus *to hurl, throw*
quamobrem *that's why*
  tam *so*

licet *it is allowed, we are allowed*
amīcus –a –um *friendly*
  strictus –a –um *strict*
vīsne? *do you want?*
hippodromus –ī *m race track, hippodrome*

"Bene!" inquit Āiāx. "Nunc eāmus ad gymnasium, deinde ad templum Iovis, ubi **illam** statuam grandem vidēre possumus. Deinde certāmina in stadiō spectāre possumus."

eāmus *let's go*

deinde *then, next, after that*
certāmen –inis *n contest, competition*

ĀCTIVITĀS

B. Respondē ad quaestiōnēs:

1. Ubi est domus Āiācis?
2. Ubi est domus Claudī?
3. Quotiēns (*how often*) Āiāx Olympiam anteā vīsitāvit?
4. Quotiēns Claudius Olympiam anteā vīsitāvit?
5. Quid est ūnum ex septem mīrāculīs mundī?
6. Quis sē exercet in palaestrā?
7. Certantne āthlētae in palaestrā?
8. Ubi certant āthlētae?
9. Quis pugilēs et luctātōrēs attentē observat?
10. Quid conīciunt discobolī?

4 You have just met some of the forms of **hīc, haec, hōc,** which mean *this.* They either modify nouns as demonstrative adjectives, or they stand alone as demonstrative pronouns and mean *this one* or simply *he, she,* or *it.* Let's look at the entire declension:

	MASCULINE	FEMININE	NEUTER
SINGULAR			
NOMINATIVE	hīc	haec	hōc
GENITIVE	hūius	hūius	hūius
DATIVE	huic	huic	huic
ACCUSATIVE	hunc	hanc	hōc
ABLATIVE	hōc	hāc	hōc
PLURAL			
NOMINATIVE	hī	hae	haec
GENITIVE	hōrum	hārum	hōrum
DATIVE	hīs	hīs	hīs
ACCUSATIVE	hōs	hās	haec
ABLATIVE	hīs	hīs	hīs

In the singular, the genitive has the same form for masculine, feminine, and neuter. This is also true of the dative case. Did you notice that all plural endings except two are the same as the plural endings of **bonus, bona, bonum?** Which two endings are different?

Make sure you understand the difference between the demonstrative ADJECTIVE and the demonstrative PRONOUN. Look at these two examples:

Hīc **pugil est rōbustus.**	*This boxer is strong.*
Hīc **est rōbustus.**	*This one (He) is strong.*

In the first example, **hīc** describes **pugil** and is, therefore, a demonstrative *adjective*. In the second example, **hīc** stands alone; as such, it is a demonstrative *pronoun*.

PITFALL: Hīc can be an adjective (*this*), a pronoun (*this one*), or an adverb (*here, in this place*). Another adverb—**hūc**—means *here, to this place*. Note the difference:

Venī hūc!	*Come here!*
Āiāx est hīc.	*Ajax is here.*

In the first sentence, *here* implies motion; in the second sentence, *here* implies position.

ĀCTIVITĀTĒS

C. Write the correct form of the demonstrative adjective for each of the following:

1. _____ pugil

2. _____ pugilēs

3. _____ palaestra

4. in _____ palaestrā

5. per _____ palaestram

6. contrā _____ luctātōrem

7. contrā _____ luctātōrēs

8. cum _____ luctātōribus

9. _____ gymnasium

10. sine _____ discīs

D. Read the sentences carefully. Then write the correct forms of the demonstrative adjectives represented by the blanks:

1. _____ gymnasium est magnum.

2. Āthlētae in _____ gymnasiō sē exercēbant.

3. Templum Iovis est proximum _____ gymnasiō.

4. Columnae _____ templī sunt altae.

5. _____ turba hūc venit ex omnibus partibus Graeciae.

6. In _____ palaestrā omnēs āthlētae sunt robustī.

7. Lūdī Olympicī _____ virō et _____ feminae nōn placent.

8. _____ palaestricus est iūstus.

9. _____ pugilēs sunt robustī.

10. Quis timet _____ luctātōrēs?

11. _____ virī sunt pugilēs excellentēs.

12. Sine _____ caestibus pugil vincĕre nōn potest.

5 The other demonstrative adjective in the story of Ajax and Claudius was **ille, illa, illud** (*that*). Its endings are very similar to those of **bonus, bona, bonum** in all but a couple of cases. Here is the entire declension:

	MASCULINE	FEMININE	NEUTER
SINGULAR			
NOMINATIVE	ille	illa	illud
GENITIVE	illīus	illīus	illīus
DATIVE	illī	illī	illī
ACCUSATIVE	illum	illam	illud
ABLATIVE	illō	illā	illō
PLURAL			
NOMINATIVE	illī	illae	illa
GENITIVE	illōrum	illārum	illōrum
DATIVE	illīs	illīs	illīs
ACCUSATIVE	illōs	illās	illa
ABLATIVE	illīs	illīs	illīs

As you can see, the genitive and dative singular have the same form throughout. Although the forms are irregular, they are easy to remember. The plural is regular throughout. **Ille** sometimes means *that famous*.

E. Supply the correct form of **ille, illa, illud:**

1. Quid est _____ aedificium?

2. Iaculātor _____ discum longissimē (*very far*) coniēcit.

3. _____ discobulī hūc veniunt ex Graeciā.

4. Quis in _____ curriculō stat?

5. Vīsne spectāre _____ equōs?

6. Āiāx _____ puerō discum novum dedit.

7. _____ templum est antīquum.

8. _____ āthlētae sunt cursōrēs ex Campāniā.

9. Tēctum _____ templī est aurātum (*gold-plated*).

10. Caestūs _____ pugilis sunt gravēs.

11. Rotae _____ curriculōrum sunt fractae (*broken*).

12. _____ discobolus nōn procul ab Olympiā habitat.

F. In each of the following sentences, decide which form of **hīc, haec, hōc** correctly replaces the first blank. Then decide on the appropriate form of **ille, illa, illud** to replace the second blank:

1. _____ templum est novum, sed _____ est antīquum.

2. _____ statua est grandis, sed _____ est parva.

3. _____ āthlētae sunt cursōrēs, sed _____ sunt iaculātōrēs.

4. In _____ gymnasiō sunt iaculātōrēs; in _____ sunt pugilēs.

5. Caesar _____ gladiātōrī pecūniam dedit, sed _____ gladiātōrī nihil dedit.

6. _____ aurīgae sunt victōrēs, sed nōn _____ .

7. _____ discobolus ūnum discum habet; _____ duōs habet.

8. _____ pugil cum _____ pugile certāre potest.

9. In _____ hippodromō sunt aurīgae, sed in _____ hippodromō sunt curricula.

10. _____ iaculum mihi placet sed _____ iaculum nimis (*too*) longum mihi est.

11. Discus _____ discobolī nōn longē (*far*) volat, sed discus

_____ discobolī longissimē volat.

12. In _____ gymnasiō āthlētae certant sed nōn in _____ gymnasiō.

6 Another demonstrative that means *that* is **iste, ista, istud,** which is declined exactly like **ille, illa, illud.** When the word modifies a noun, it is a demonstrative adjective; when it stands alone, it is a demonstrative pronoun. This word is sometimes used to express contempt:

Quis timet istum gladium?   *Who is afraid of that sword of yours?*
Iste senātor pecūniam accēpit.   *That (disgraceful) senator accepted money.*

Sometimes, though, **iste** simply means *that* without implying any feeling of contempt.

ĀCTIVITĀTĒS

G. Supply the correct form of **iste, ista, istud:**

1. _____ pugil

2. _____ iaculum

3. in _____ gymnasiō

4. _____ cursōrēs

5. cum _____ aurīgā

6. sine _____ iaculātōribus

7. contrā _____ luctātōrem

8. ab _____ palaestrā

H. In each sentence below, select the correct form of **hīc, haec, hōc** to replace the first blank and the correct form of **iste, ista, istud** to replace the second blank:

1. _____ cursor est rapidus, sed _____ est lentus.

2. _____ pugilēs sunt Graecī, sed _____ sunt Rōmānī.

3. Ego saepe cum _____ luctātōre pugnō sed numquam cum

_____ luctātōre.

4. Exspectā mē in _____ locō, nōn in _____ palaestrā.

5. _____ palaestricī sunt benignī sed _____ sunt strictī.

6. Praefersne (*Do you prefer*) _____ discum an _____ discum?

7. _____ āthlētae discōs conīciunt, sed _____ conīciunt iacula.

8. Palaestricus aquam _____ pugilī dedit sed nōn _____ pugilī.

9. Cūr _____ luctātōrem timēbās sed nōn _____?

10. Ego in _____ domō habitābam, nōn in _____.

Dialogus

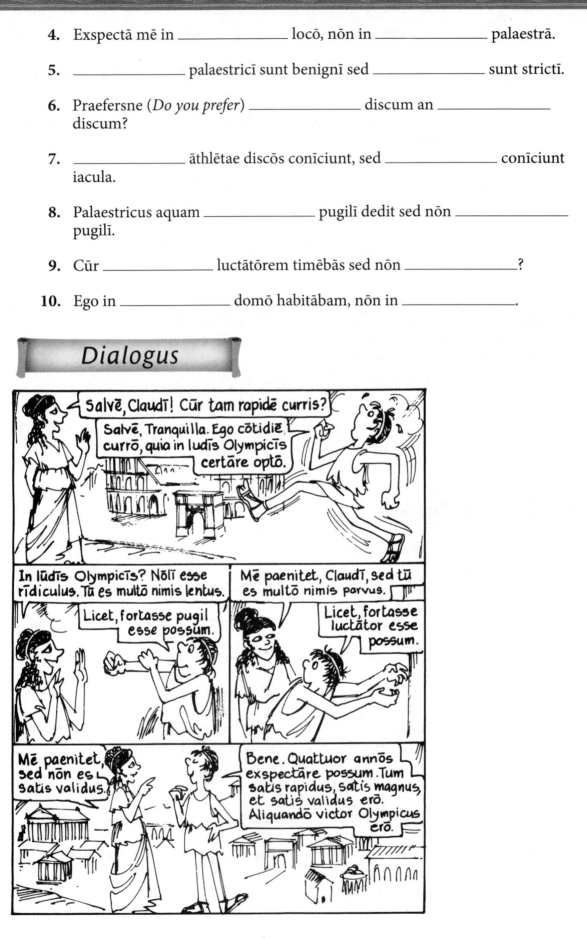

VOCĀBULA

optō *–āre –āvī to want*
nōlī esse *don't be*
multō nimis *much too*
lentus –a –um *slow*
licet *well, o.k.*
mē paenitet *I am sorry*

satis *adv enough*
validus –a –um *strong*
exspectō –āre –āvi *to wait*
tum *then*
erō *I will be*
aliquandō *adv someday*

Quaestiōnēs Persōnālēs

1. Potesne currĕre rapidē?

2. Potesne salīre (*to jump*) longē?

3. Vīsne certāre in lūdīs Olympicīs?

4. Vīsne vidēre lūdōs Olympicōs?

5. Praefersne pugilēs an (*or*) luctātōrēs an cursōrēs?

6. Praefersne vidēre lūdōs Olympicōs in Graeciā an in patriā tuā?

7. Ubi erunt (*will be*) proximī (*the next*) lūdī Olympicī?

8. Exercēsne tē cōtīdiē?

Compositiō

You have participated in previous Olympic Games in Greece. Your friends are eager to attend the next Games. Explain to them what various athletes do or where they complete.

Colloquium

Complete this conversation with original expressions or expressions from the previous conversation:

THE LATIN CONNECTION

1. Did you know that a **gymnasium** was not only a place for exercise but also a lecture hall for philosophers? This explains why some countries in Europe use the word "gymnasium" for high school. Yet another connection between the Olympics and school exists. **Curriculum** in Latin means *chariot* or *racetrack*. What is this word's meaning in English?

2. What is a *cursor* on a computer screen? Why might this word have been chosen?

3. Can you give another English word for each of the following as well as the Latin word from which the word comes?

   (a) turbulent

   (b) circumstance

   (c) ubiquitous

   (d) approximate

   (e) miracle

4. The verb **conīciō** consists of the prefix **con–** and the verb **iacĕre**. The principal parts of **conīciō** (*to throw*) are:

conīciō	**conīcĕre**	**coniēcī**	**coniectus**

The last principal part is a past participle that means *thrown* or *having been thrown*. You will see in a later lesson just how the past participle functions. Right now notice that the English verb *conjecture* derives from the last principal part. Write the principal parts of the following verbs and give the English derivatives from the last principal parts:

   EXAMPLE: **ēiciō ēicĕre ēiēcī ēiectus** *to eject; ejection*

1. inīciō

2. interīciō

3. obīciō

4. prōiciō

5. reīciō

6. subīciō

II | Thermae

Volō/nōlō; Reflexive Verbs

1 Modicum cultūrae

Roman public baths were much more than simply shower stalls and bathtubs. Remember that most people in Rome lived in apartments that had no toilets or bathrooms. In place of toilets, people used chamber pots (**matella** *–ae f*). Only the homes of the rich contained a toilet (**lātrīna** *–ae f*) and a bath (**balneum** *–ī n* or **balnea** *–ae f*). Public baths (**balnea** *–ōrum npl*), therefore, became one of the most important centers of Roman life. Citizens of every class enjoyed their use. The Romans did not use soap for the first thousand years.

In earlier historical periods, Romans seldom used the bath and then only for cleanliness and health, not as a luxury. The Roman author Seneca tells us that, in the old days, Romans washed their legs and arms daily and bathed their whole bodies once a week. Of course, people enjoyed swimming in the Tiber river as much for fun as for cleanliness. The earliest public baths were simple and often dingy; they were used by the lower classes. In addition to public baths, private owners ran commercial bathhouses and charged a small fee. Every town had at least one public bath, and many larger towns had several. By the year A.D. 300, Rome had 856 such baths.

Gradually the baths became more pleasant and elaborate. The term **thermae** (*-ārum fpl*), which originally meant *hot springs,* applied to magnificent structures erected by various Roman emperors to win popularity. These huge establishments contained, in addition to bathing facilities, lounges in which Romans could chat with their friends, libraries (**bibliothēca** *-ae f*), reading rooms, and lecture halls, as well as snack shops (**popīna** *-ae f*), barbershops (**tōnstrīna** *-ae f*), and places to exercise (**palaestra** *-ae f*). The first barber came to Rome in 300 B.C.

Rome could boast of several lavish **thermae.** The emperor Diocletian ordered the construction of the largest in the whole Roman Empire. Located in the heart of Rome, this bath was dedicated in A.D. 306. Requiring the efforts of 40,000 builders, this structure could hold 30,000 bathers. The admission fee was a fraction of a cent. The **thermae** were the poor people's country clubs. There they could forget about their shabby apartments and enjoy exercising, swimming, a massage, reading books they could not afford at home, and catching up on the latest gossip. Men and women had different hours—women in the morning and men in the afternoons. An aqueduct built 400 years earlier brought water 57 miles from the Sabine Mountains to the **thermae** of Diocletian. The huge reservoir used to store the water outside the baths was about the size of a football field. From this reservoir, lead pipes of various sizes distributed water to all of the pools, tubs, basins, and fountains.

The chief rooms of the **thermae** were the pickpocket-friendly dressing rooms (**apodytērium** *-ī n*), the hot bath (**caldārium** *-ī n*), the warm bath (**tepidārium** *-ī n*), and the cold bath (**frīgidārium** *-ī n*). The facility also contained a massage room (**ūnctōrium** *-ī n*), sauna (**lacōnicum** *-ī n*), toilets (**lātrīna** *-ae f*), and equipment storerooms (**cella** *-ae f*). The Baths of Diocletian even featured a full-size theater as well as several large swimming pools (**piscīna** *-ae f*)!

Visitors can see the remains of the Baths of Diocletian today. Now, however, the facility contains two churches (one large, one smaller), a museum, a planetarium, and a movie theater instead of bathing facilities.

The general plan of the Baths of Diocletian will give you an idea of what these **thermae** included. It is impossible today to identify all of the smaller rooms.

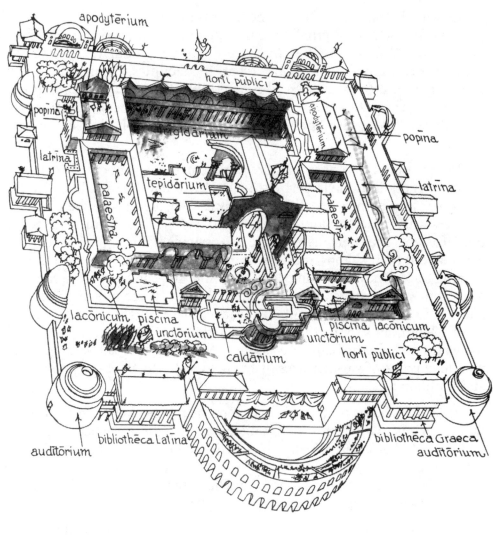

ĀCTIVITĀS

A. Here and on the next page are some typical scenes in a Roman bath. Match the sentences with the pictures they describe:

Puer in piscīnam salit   (*jumps*).
Puellae in palaestrā pilā lūdunt.
Puer vestēs in apodytēriō exuit
   (*takes off*).
Puellae ante fontem in tepidāriō stant.
Virī librōs in bibliothēcā legunt.
Philosophus in audītōriō docet.
Virī in laconicō sedent et sūdant
   (*sweat*).

Duo virī in palaestrā halterēs
   levant   (*lift*).
Trēs puellae in piscīnā in
   frīgidāriō natant   (*swim*).
Puerī ē piscīnā in caldāriō exeunt.
Multae fēminae thermās intrant.
Puer tomāclum et pānem in popīnā
   emit.

2 Now read this conversation between Marcus, his older brother Lucius, and their cousin Rufus who is visiting Rome from the small town of Ardea in the district of Latium. Pay special attention to the forms of **volō** (*I want*) and **nōlō** (*I don't want*) that appear in bold type. Although the present tense of these verbs is irregular, you should have no trouble identifying and understanding them:

MARCUS: **Vīs**ne, Rūfe, īre cum frātre meō et mēcum ad thermās novās?

RŪFUS: Ad thermās? Quae sunt "thermae"? Numquam dē thermīs audīvī.

quae? *What?*

LŪCIUS: Numquam dē thermīs audīvistī? Thermae sunt balneum grande ubi piscīnae et palaestrae et bibliothēcae et audītōria sunt. Multī librī

grandis *–is –e big, huge*
audītōrium *–ī n lecture hall*

boni sunt in bibliothēcā. In audītōriō philosophī docent.

philosophus *–ī m philosopher*

Rūfus: Omitte bibliothēcam et audītōrium. Neque librōs legĕre **volō** neque philosophōs audīre **volō**. Quid tū et frāter tuus facĕre **vultis?**

omittō *–ĕre* **omīsī omissus** *to skip, forget about*

Marcus: In palaestrā pilā lūdĕre possumus aut trochōs volvĕre.

pila *–ae f ball* (Note: The Romans said "play *with* a ball.")
trochus *–ī m hoop*
volvō *–ĕre –ī* **volūtus** *to roll*
  parvulus *–ī m little boy*
fortasse *perhaps*

Rūfus: Trochum volvĕre **nōlō**. Nōn parvulus sum. Sed fortasse pilā lūdĕre possumus.

Lūcius: Et sī tū **vīs**, discum aut iaculum conīcĕre possumus. Omnēs amīcī nostrī pilā lūdĕre **volunt**.

Rūfus: Bene! Post exercitātiōnem, in piscīnā in frīgidāriō natāre **volō**. Postquam sūdāvī, aquam frīgidam, nōn tepidam amō.

bene! *fine*
  exercitātiō *–ōnis f exercise*
natō *–āre –avi to swim*
  sūdō *–āre –āvi to sweat*
tepidus *–a –um lukewarm, warm*
quidnī? *why not?*

Marcus: Quidnī? Ego quoque in piscīnā frīgidā natāre **volō**. Deinde, sī **vīs**, in piscīnam in tepidāriō salīre possumus. Frāter meus in piscīnā in frīgidāriō natāre **nōn vult**.

Rūfus: Estne ūnctōrium in thermīs?

ūnctōrium *–ī n massage room*

Marcus: Sānē. Est ūnctōrium cum optimīs ūnguentīs in tōtō orbe terrārum. Et post natātiōnem, ūnctiō est vērum oblectāmentum!

ūnguentum *–ī n perfumed oil, perfume*
natātiō *–ōnis f swim*
  ūnctiō *–ōnis f massage*
  oblectāmentum *–ā n delight, pleasure*
bellus *–a –um nice, cute*
occurrō *–ĕre –ī* **occursum** *(+ dat) to meet*
licet *it is allowed*
hortī publicī *–ōrum mpl park*
frequenter *adv often*
deambulō *–āre to stroll, walk around*
eō casū *in that case*
  omnīnō *completely*
petō *–ĕre –īvī –ītus to chase (after)*

Rūfus: Post ūnctiōnem, fortasse puellīs bellīs in tepidāriō occurrĕre possumus!

Lūcius: Mē paenitet, sed nōn licet puellīs in thermīs cum puerīs natāre. Sed in hortīs publicīs extrā thermās multae puellae bellae frequenter deambulant.

Rūfus: Eō cāsū, cūr nōn istās thermās omnīnō omittimus et statim . . .

Marcus: Nōn, nōn, Rūfe. Prīmum ad thermās eāmus; posteā puellās petĕre possumus.

ĀCTIVITĀS

B. Respondē ad quaestiōnēs:

1. Quae sunt "thermae"?
2. Ubi in thermīs puerī pilā lūdunt?
3. Quid faciunt Rōmānī in bibliothēcā?

4. Ubi in thermīs philosophī docent?

5. Cūr Rūfus trochum volvĕre nōn vult?

6. Ubi in thermīs puerī natāre possunt?

7. Quid est vērum oblectāmentum post natātiōnem?

8. Ubi sunt hortī pūblicī?

3 In the conversation between Rufus, Marcus, and Lucius, you saw the present tense forms of **volō.** Now let's review the entire present tense of **volō** (*I want*) and **nōlō** (*I don't want*):

ego	volō	nōlō
tū	vīs	nōn vīs
is/ea/id	vult	nōn vult
nōs	volumus	nōlumus
vōs	vultis	nōn vultis
eī/eae/ea	volunt	nōlunt

The principal parts (first person present, present infinitive, first person perfect) of the two verbs are:

volō	velle	voluī
nōlō	nōlle	nōluī

The imperfect forms are **volēbam, volēbās,** etc. and **nōlēbam, nōlēbās,** etc.

ĀCTIVITĀTĒS

C. Substitute the appropriate forms of **nōlle** in place of the forms of **velle:**

1. In hāc piscīna natāre [volō].

2. Illae puellae in flūmine natāre [volunt].

3. Ad thermās īre [volumus].

4. Cūr tū Rōmam aestāte vīsitāre [vīs]?

5. Ubi tū et amīcus tuus natāre [vultis]?

6. Marcus in hanc piscīnam salīre [vult].

7. Nōs nunc ūnctiōnem habēre [volumus].

8. Cūr tū in hortīs pūblicīs deambulāre [vīs]?

D. Supply the correct form of **velle** in the following sentences:

1. Rūfus puellīs occurrĕre _____.

2. Post ūnctiōnem, fēminae in hortīs pūblicīs deambulāre _____.

3. Ego et pater meus āthlētās in palaestrā spectāre _____.

4. Lūcius in hōc lacōnicō sedēre et sūdāre _____.

5. Sī tū et Marcus tomācla emĕre _____, eāmus ad illam popīnam.

6. Simul atque (*as soon as*) ego piscīnam videō, in eam salīre

   _____.

7. Lūcius et ego Ardeam et alia oppida in Latīo vīsitāre _____.

8. Virī in palaestrā halterēs levāre _____.

E. Read the following sentences carefully. Then supply the correct form of **nōlle:**

1. Quamquam bene natāre possum, hodiē natāre _____.

2. Quia hodiē calidum est, hī puerī in caldāriō sedēre _____.

3. Virī Rōmānī ante merīdiem ad thermās īre _____.

4. Antequam in piscīnam saliō, in lacōnicō sūdāre _____.

5. Sī tū in audītōrium īre _____, philosophum audīre nōn potes.

6. Vōsne in bibliothēcā librōs legĕre _____?

7. Multī ē Campāniā thermās novās Rōmae vidēre _____.

8. Postquam ego thermās vīsitāvī, ista balnea intrāre _____.

F. As we saw earlier, the imperfect tense endings are regular. Substitute the correct form of **nōlle** for **velle:**

1. Ego herī ad thermās īre [volēbam].

2. Quis in hāc piscīnā natāre [volēbat]?

3. Amīcī meī mē in tepidāriō exspectāre [volēbant].

4. [Volēbāsne] mēcum in hortīs pūblicīs deambulāre?

5. Senātōrēs cum populō in lacōnicō sedēre [volēbant].

6. Puer cum āthlētīs pilā lūdĕre [volēbat].

4 In Lesson I, you met the expression **Āthlētae sē exercent** (*The athletes are training*). The verb **sē exercent** is termed REFLEXIVE because, instead of the action transferring from subject to object, it *reflects* back to the subject. The sentence **Āthlēta sē lavat** means *The athlete is washing* or *The athlete is washing himself. Himself* is a reflexive pronoun.

A reflexive verb uses regular simple accusative pronouns in the first and second persons, singular and plural, but it uses **sē** in the third person, singular and plural:

mē lavō	*I wash/am washing (myself)*
tē lavās	*you wash/are washing (yourself)*
sē lavat	*he/she washes/is washing (himself/herself)*
nōs lavāmus	*we wash/are washing (ourselves)*
vōs lavātis	*you wash/are washing (yourselves)*
sē lavant	*they wash/are washing (themselves)*

In Latin sentences, the reflexive pronoun is often separated from the reflexive verb by other words in the sentence.

ĀCTIVITĀS

G. Complete the sentences with the correct reflexive (*mirror*) pronouns:

1. Puella _____ in speculō videt.

2. Vidēsne _____ in speculō?

3. Marcus _____ in speculō videt.

4. Āthlētae _____ ante certāmen exercēbant.

5. Ego et amīcī in hāc palaestrā _____ exercēbāmus.

6. Quamobrem tū et frāter tuus _____ nōn exercēbātis?

7. Quamquam multī in palaestrā erant, cum istīs _____ exercēre nōluī.

8. Amīcī meī _____ in caldāriō lavābant.

5 Certain verbs, as you may recall, take the dative rather than the accusative case, such as **noceō –ēre –uī** (*to harm*), **cōnfīdō –ere –ī** (*to trust*), and **diffīdō –ere –ī** (*to distrust*). When these verbs are used reflexively, they require the dative of the reflexive pronoun. Again, the reflexive pronoun in the dative case is the same as the simple dative pronoun in the first and second persons singular and plural; in the third person singular and plural, the reflexive pronoun is **sibi:**

mihi noceō	*I hurt/am hurting myself*
tibi nocēs	*you hurt/are hurting yourself*

sibi nocet	he/she/it hurts/is hurting himself/herself/itself
nōbīs nocēmus	we hurt/are hurting ourselves
vōbīs nocētis	you hurt/are hurting yourselves
sibi nocent	they hurt/are hurting themselves

ĀCTIVITĀTĒS

H. Complete the following sentences with the correct reflexive pronouns:

1. Ille āthlēta _____ nocuit.

2. Quōmodo _____ nocuistī?

3. Hī āthlētae _____ diffīdunt.

4. Quandō ego et Claudius pilā lūdēbāmus, _____ nocuimus.

5. Hīc discobulus _____ nocuit.

6. Quia ego timidus sum, in perīculō numquam _____ cōnfīdō.

I. Some of the following verbs take the accusative case while others take the dative case of the reflexive pronoun. Complete the sentences with the correct reflexive pronouns:

1. Claudius _____ in tepidāriō lavābat.

2. Quamobrem Claudius _____ nōn confīdit?

3. Claudī, sī _____ lavāre vīs, remanē in caldāriō.

4. Amīcī meī, sī _____ lavāre vultis, salīte in hanc piscīnam.

5. Quot āthlētae _____ in palaestrā nocuērunt?

6. Puerī, nōlīte nocēre _____.

7. Rūfe, nōlī nocēre _____.

8. Propter timōrem _____ saepe diffīdimus.

Quaestiōnēs Persōnālēs

1. Habetne familia tua piscīnam?

2. Praefersne natāre in flūmine an in piscīnā?

3. Praefersne natāre in frīgidāriō an tepidāriō an caldāriō?

4. Natāvistī umquam in oceanō?

5. Potesne natāre bene an male?

6. Lūdisne pilā cum amīcīs tuīs?

Dialogus

VOCĀBULA

tant*us* –*a* –*um* *such big*
nē ... quidem *not even*
balneol*um* –ī *n little bath*
Miserum Rūfum! *Poor Rufus!*
dēsīderō –āre –āvī –ātus *to miss*
quotiēns? *how often?*

licet tibi *are you allowed*
semel aut bis *once or twice*
addūcō –ĕre addūxī adductus *to take to*
stagn*um* –ī *n pond*

Compositiō

Assume that you live in ancient Rome. Your cousin in Ardea has never seen the baths. Write your cousin four statements that will describe the **thermae.**

⟳ THE LATIN CONNECTION

A. Perhaps you have heard the expression "She was the *belle* of the ball." From which Latin word is *belle* derived?

B. People might say of a smart girl: "She is a *fount* of knowledge." From which Latin word does the word *fount* come?

C. For each of the following words, give another English word that means the same. Then give the Latin word from which each listed word comes.

  1. tepid

  2. stagnant

  3. licit

  4. grand

  5. legible

  6. omit

  7. disc

  8. frigid

  9. latrine

  10. puerile

Complete the dialog with original answers or with ideas taken from the previous conversation:

III | Superstitiō

Future Tense

1 Modicum cultūrae

If you had unexpectedly dropped in on the ancient Romans, you might have been amazed at the strange methods they used to try to predict the future. Priests called **harūspicēs** (**harūsp*ex* –*icis* m**) tried to interpret the will of the gods by examining the internal organs of sacrificial animals. The slightest abnormality of the liver, for instance, could indicate doom. **Harūspicēs** also marked off a section of the sky (called a **templum** –*a* n) and divided it into sections with an augural staff (**litu*us* –*ī* m**). Depending on the section in which lightning was seen, **harūspicēs** made various predictions. Another group of priests called augurs (**aug*ur* –*uris* m**) also divided the sky into sections; these people made predictions according to the directions birds flew through the **templum.** Augurs even made predictions by watching chickens eat. If the chickens refused to eat, the priests foretold disaster. Augurs also interpreted the sounds and moves chickens made as they ate.

Romans often retold the story of a navy commander named Appius Claudius the Handsome. Just before a naval battle off Sicily, he asked an augur to observe the chickens he had carried in a coop aboard ship. When the seaman learned that the chickens would not eat (Oh-oh!), he flung them into the sea and said, "If they won't eat, then they will drink." When he then lost the naval battle, everyone blamed him for not believing the bad omen the chickens gave.

The Romans saw an omen in any event that was the least bit unusual. Dreams, natural phenomena (such as thunder, hail, and floods), and the birth of deformed animals were all omens to the Romans. They even regarded left-handed people with suspicion!

Astrologers were very influential in Rome. Emperor Augustus and those rulers that came after him regularly consulted astrologers. Today people still believe certain items bring good or bad luck. How many of these items can you name? How do people today try to find out what the future holds?

 ## 2 Vocābula

Ariēa *–etis m*

**Taur*us* *–ī m*

Geminī *–ōrum mpl*

zōdiacus (circulus) *–ī m*

Cancer *–crī m*

Leō *–ōnis m*

Virgō *-inis f*

Lībra *-ae f*

Scorpiō *-onis m*

Sagittārius *-ī m*

Capricornus *-ī m*

Aquārius *-ī m*

Piscēs *-ium mpl*

augur *-uris m*

astrologus *-ī m*

harūspex *-icis m*

NOTE: The Romans believed that the whole world consisted of four elements: fire (**ignis *-is m***), water (**aqua *-ae f***), air (**āër *-is m***), and earth (**terra *-ae f***).

3 Hōroscopium

Learn to read this horoscope. Pay attention to the verbs in bold type. These verbs are in the future tense:

Sī tū inter vīcēsimum prīmum diem Martiī et vīcēsimum diem Aprīlis nātus(–a) es, tuum signum zōdiacī est Ariēs. Elementum tuum est ignis. Tū es persōna līberālis, benīgna, fidēlis, sed interdum audāx et violenta. Amīcōs tuōs semper **iuvābis** et inimīcōs tuōs nōn **timēbis.**

elementum –ī n
element
ign*is –is* m *fire*
līberāl*is –is –e*
generous
interdum *adv*
sometimes
iuvō *–āre –ī iūtus*
to help
inimīcus *–ī* m *enemy*
terr*a –ae* f *earth*
fort*is –is –e brave*
valid*us –a –um*
strong
īrācund*us –a –um*
quick-tempered

Sī tū inter vīcēsimum prīmum diem Aprīlis et vīcēsimum prīmum diēm Māiī nātus(–a) es, tuum signum zōdiacī est Taurus. Elementum tuum est terra. Tū es persōna patiens et fortis et valida, sed interdum arrogāns, tarda, īrācunda, superstitiōsa. Post multa perīcula, magnum successum **habēbis.** Aliī tibi **invidēbunt** propter successum tuum.

aliī *–ōrum* m *pl*
others
invideō *–ēre* **invīsī**
(+ *dat*) *to envy*

Sī inter vīcēsimum secundum diem Māiī et vīcēsimum prīmum diem Iūniī nātus(–a) es, signum tuum zōdiacī est Geminī. Tuum elementum est aër. Tū es persōna sincēra et astūta et iūsta sed etiam mūtābilis et avāra et inquiēta. Dīligenter **labōrābis,** sed mentem tuam saepe **mūtābis.**

aër aëris m *air*
astūt*us –a –um*
clever, astute
mūtābil*is –is –e*
fickle
avār*us –a –um greedy*
inquiēt*us –a –um*
restless
mens mentis f *mind*
mūto *–āre –āvī*
–ātus to change

Sū tū inter vīcēsimum secundum diem Iūniī et vīcēsimum diem Iūliī nātus(–a) es, tuum signum zōdiacī est Cancer. Elementum tuum est aqua. Tū es persōna cum sensū commūnī. Memoriam excellentem et cor bonum habēs. Animālia parva amās. Tū es persōna prūdens et intellegēns sed interdum nimis cauta et timida. Quia tū persōna cauta es, vītam longam **habēbis.**

nimis *too*
caut*us -a -um*
cautious

Sī tū inter vīcēsimum tertium diem Iūliī et vīcēsimum tertium diem Augustī nātus(–a) es, signum tuum zōdiacī est Leō. Elementum tuum est ignis. Es persōna audāx et ambitiōsa et fortis sed interdum superba et arrogāns et nimis audāx. Corpus validum habēs. Rapidē currĕre potes. Nihil tē **terrēbit.** Aliquandō domum magnam et pecūniam multam **habēbis.**

superbus *-a -um*
proud

validus *-a -um*
strong
nihil *nothing*
  terrēo *–ēre –uī*
  –ītus to frighten

Sī tū inter vīcēsimum quārtum diem Augustī et vīcēsimum tertium diem Septembris nātus(–a) es, signum tuum zōdiacī est Virgō. Elementum tuum est terra. Es persōna studiōsa et astūta et industria, sed interdum fastīdiōsa et trīstis et nimis cauta. Vestēs pulchrās amās. Antequam aliquid facis, singula dīligenter cōnsīderās. Quia līberālis ergā omnēs es, multōs amīcōs semper **habēbis.**

fastīdiōsus *-a –um*
  picky
  trīstis *–is –e sad*
singula *–ōrum npl*
  details
cōnsīderō *–āre to*
  consider
ergā (+ *acc*) *toward*

Sī tū inter vīcēsimum quārtem diem Septembris et vīcēsimum tertium diem Octōbris nātus(–a) es, signum tuum zōdiacī est Lībra. Elementum tuum est aër. Es persōna polīta et ēlegāns et obēdiēns, sed etiam fastīdiōsa et irrītābilis et interdum difficilis. Vēr et autumnus tibi placent, sed aestās tibi praecipuē placet. Quia tū persōna iūsta es, aliquandō advocātus aut iūdex **eris.**

polītus *–a –um*
  polite, refined

fastīdiōsus, *–a, –um*
  snobbish
vēr vēris *n spring*
aestās *–ātis f summer*
  praecipuē
  especially
advocātus, *-ī m*
  lawyer
  iūdex *–icis m judge*

Sī tū inter vīcēsimum quārtum diem Octōbris et vīcēsimum secundum diem Novembris nātus(–a) es, signum tuum zōdiacī est Scorpiō. Elementum tuum est aqua. Tū es persōna neque dīves neque pauper, neque nimis audāx neque nimis timida. Multōs labōrēs in vītā **habēbis,** sed eōs facile **superābis.**

scorpiō, *–ōnis m*
  scorpion
dīves *–itis rich*
  neque ... neque
  neither ... nor
  pauper *–eris poor*
labōrēs *–um mpl*
  troubles
superō *–āre –āvī*
  –ātus to overcome

Sī tū inter vīcēsimum tertium diem Novembris et vīcēsimum diem Decembris nātus(–a) es, signum tuum zōdiacī est Sagittārius. Elementum tuum est ignis. Quia tū persōna ambitiōsa es, labōrem numquam **timēbis.** Semper dīligenter **laborābis.** Multam pecūniam **merēbis.** Sed persōna obstināta et impatiens et cerebrōsa es. Forsitan aliquandō mīles aut āthlēta aut senātor **eris.** Multās terrās **vīsitābis** in Eurōpā et Asiā et Āfricā. Nomen tuum **erit** clārum.

labor –ōris m *work*

mereō –ēre–ītus –uī
to earn
cerebrōsus –a –um
hot-headed
forsitan *perhaps*

clārus –a –um
famous

Sī tū inter vīcēsimum prīmum diem Decembris et vīcēsimum diem Iānuāriī nātus(–a) es, signum tuum zōdiacī est Capricornus. Elementum tuum est terra. Tū es persōna cauta et sēria et dīligēns, sed interdum obstināta et mūtābilis et frīgida ergā aliēnōs. Quia tū persōna sēria et dīligens es, forsitan aliquandō **eris** magister (magistra) aut medicus(–a). Parentēs viam ad successum tibi **mōnstrābunt.**

sērius –a –um
serious
mūtābilis –is –e *fickle*
frīgidus –a –um
cool
aliēnus –ī m
stranger, foreigner
mōnstrō –āre –āvī
–ātus *to show*

Sī tū inter vīcēsimum prīmum diem Iānuāriī et duodēvīcēsimum diem Februāriī nātus(–a) es, signum tuum zōdiacī est Aquārius. Elementum tuum est aër. Tū es persōna honesta et līberālis et studiōsa. Sed interdum tū es rebellis et difficilis. Apud condiscipulōs semper populāris **eris.** Aliquandō theātrum tē **vocābit** et tū **eris** actor clārus (actrix clāra). Vītam fortūnātam **habēbis.**

honestus –a –um
*honorable,
respectable*
rebellis –is –e
rebellious
apud (+ acc)
among
condiscipulus –ī m
classmate

Sī tū inter undēvīcēsimum diem Februāriī et vīcēsimum diem Mārtiī nātus(–a) es, signum tuum zōdiacī est Piscēs. Elementum tuum est aqua. Es persōna tenera et amābilis et artifex sed etiam timida et mūtābilis et interdum trīstis. Sed tū es fidēlis amīcīs tuīs. Tū habēs mentem sānam in corpore sānō. Ergo tū **eris** bonus negōtiātor aut āthlēta. Multa praemia **merēbis.**

tener –era –erum
tender
artifex –ficis *artistic*
sānus –a –um *sound*
negōtiātor –ōris m
business person
praemium –ī n
award

A. Now that you have learned about zodiac signs, see if you can identify them on sight. Then write their Latin names. How about writing the genitive ending and the gender as well?

B. Read the following descriptions carefully. Then identify the sign of the zodiac:

1. Ego sum animal magnum et ferōx. Dentēs longōs et acūtōs habeō. Iuba longa mihi est. Cum ego rugiō, omnia animālia in silvīs timent, quia ego sum rēx bēstiārum.

   ferōx –ōcis *wild, ferocious*
   acūtus –a –um *sharp*
     iuba –ae *f mane*
   cum *when* **rugiō –īre –iī** *to roar*

   Ego sum _____.

2. Ego sum animal grande. In fundō habitō. Herbam multam cōnsumō, sed ego lac agricolīs nōn dō, sed vaccae lac agricolīs dant. Duo cornua habeō, et cum vexillum rubrum videō, ego oppugnō.

   cornu –ūs *n horn* **cum** *adj*
     when **vexillum –ī** *n flag*
   oppugnō –āre –āvī –ātus *to*
     charge

   Ego sum _____.

3. Nos sumus frātrēs. Eōdem diē nātī sumus. Eāsdem vestēs saepe gestāmus. Vultūs nostrī simillimī sunt. Diem nātālem eundem celebrāmus.

   īdem eadem idem *the same*
   gestō –āre –āvī –ātus *to wear*
     vultus –ūs *m looks, expression*
   diēs nātālis *m birthday*

   Nōs sumus. _____.

4. Nōs duo neque manūs neque crūra habēmus. Dīcĕre nōn possumus, quia vox nobīs nōn est. Caudam habēmus. Cum in aquā sumus, respīrāre possumus sed extrā aquam respīrāre nōn possumus. Pinnās habēmus. Flūmina et stāgna nobīs placent.

   dīcō –ĕre dīxī dictus *to speak*
     vox vōcis *f voice*
   cauda –ae *f tail*
   respīrō –āre *to breathe*
     extrā *(+ acc) outside of*
   pinna –ae *f fin*

   Nōs sumus _____.

5. Animal parvum sed perīculōsum sum. In dēsertīs habitō. In harēnā calidā rēpĕre amō. Tria crūra in dextrā parte corporis meī habeō et tria in sinistrā parte. Etiam duo bracchia mihi sunt. In caudā meā habeō acūleum venēnātum. Ictus meus magnum dolōrem facit.

   dēserta –ōrum *npl desert*
     harēna –ae *f sand*
     rēpō –ĕre rēpsī *to crawl*
   dexter –tra –trum *right*
     pars partis *f side*
   sinister –tra –trum *left*
     bracchium –ī *n arm, claw*
   acūleus –ī *m sting*
   venēnātus –a –um *poisonous*
     ictus –us *m bite, sting*
   faciō –ĕre fēcī factus *to cause*

   Ego sum _____.

4 Until now, the verbs you have encountered have been in either present or past tense. How do you describe actions and events that will happen in the future? The horoscope told you some things that will happen in the future. Let's look at some examples:

Virgō benīgna multās amīcās **habēbit.**	*A kind girl will have many friends.*
Quid Rōmānī dē astrologīs **cōgitābunt?**	*What will the Romans think* *about astrologers?*
Quid crās in forō gestābimus?	*What will we wear in the forum tomorrow?*

If you compare the imperfect forms of the verbs of the first and second conjugations with their future-tense forms, you will see how simple it is to form the future tense. The imperfect tense is formed as follows:

		–bam
		–bās
I	**portā**	*–bat*
II	**tenē**	*–bāmus*
		–bātis
		–bant

To form the future tense, use the same stem and add the future personal endings:

		–bō
		–bis
I	**portā**	*–bit*
II	**tenē**	*–bimus*
		–bitis
		–bunt

What is the typical vowel in the imperfect endings?

What is the usual vowel in the future endings?

ĀCTIVITĀTĒS

C. Write the future tense of the following verbs:

	portāre	tenēre	dare
ego	_____	_____	_____
tū	_____	_____	_____
is, ea, id	_____	_____	_____
nōs	_____	_____	_____
vōs	_____	_____	_____
eī, eae, ea	_____	_____	_____

D. Read the following sentences carefully so that you understand each sentence. Then convert the verb from the imperfect to the future tense:

1. Astrologī caelum frequenter observābant.
2. Augustus astrologōs cōnsultābat.
3. Cūr tū mentem tuam sine causā mūtābās?
4. Ego consīderābam scorpiōnēs esse periculōsōs.

5. Tiberius virginem Rōmānam amābat.

6. Vidēbāsne multōs cancrōs in ōrā maritimā?

7. Agricola vaccās et taurōs in fundō habēbat.

8. Augurēs lituum in manū sinistrā tenēbant.

9. Vidēbātisne capricornum cum ūnō cornū?

10. Aquāriī aquam leōnibus in amphitheātrō dābant.

E. Provide the correct future-tense forms of the verbs for the sentences below:

1. (observāre) Astrologī astra et planētās _____.

2. (vīsitāre) Cūr Augustus astrologum _____?

3. (celebrāre) Quis diem nātālem crās _____?

4. (dēmōnstrāre) Astrologusne Sagittārium _____?

5. (cōnsultāre) Omnēs Rōmānī astrologōs _____.

6. (manēre) Ego et pater in urbe _____.

7. (merēre) Quantam pecūniam astrologus _____?

8. (placēre) Nōnne hōroscopium tuum tibi _____?

9. (vidēre) Augurēs avēs nōn _____.

10. (habēre) Tū et frāter sānam mentem et corpus sānum _____.

5 The endings of the future tense of **īre** (*to go*) are regular; that is, they are the same as the endings of verbs such as **portāre** and **tenēre.** The entire stem is simply **ī–.** The stem of **abīre** (*to go away*) is **abī–,** the stem of **exīre** (*to go out*) is **exī–;** the stem of **adīre** (to go to, approach) is **adī–.**

ĀCTIVITĀTĒS

F. Write the future-tense forms of **īre** (*to go*) and **abīre** (*to go away, leave*):

	īre	abīre
ego	_____	_____
tū	_____	_____
is, ea, id	_____	_____

nōs   _____   _____

vōs   _____   _____

eī, eae, ea   _____   _____

G. Change the verbs from the imperfect to future tense:

1. Post cēnam omnēs amīcī meī abībant.
2. Quis ē domō astrologī exībat?
3. Augurēs aram ante templum adībant.
4. Quandō tū ē pīstrīnā cum pāne exībās?
5. Ego et avia mea ad bibliothēcam redībāmus.

H. Change the verbs from present to future tense:

1. Multī mīlitēs in bellō pereunt.
2. Āthlēta ad stadium cōtīdiē it.
3. Augurēs et harūspicēs templum ineunt.
4. Astrologus aliēnōs numquam adit.
5. Ego et Titus astrologum adīmus.

6 Do you want to know what your future holds? How does astrology work? Ancient Romans often called astrologers **mathēmaticī**, probably because astrologers had to do a lot of computing. Suppose you were strolling through the Roman forum and stopped to listen to an astrologer trying to drum up business. Listen!

Ego sum mathēmaticus aut astrologus, quia ego astra in caelō cōtīdiē observō et mōtiōnēs astrōrum dīligenter dēnotō. Itaque futūra praedīcĕre possum, quoniam astra in caelō omnia in terrā afficiunt, perinde āc lūna aestūs ōceanī afficit. Lūna plēna multōs hominēs afficit. Nōs omnēs sub ūnō ex duodecim signīs zōdiacī nātī(–ae) sumus. Ergō diēs nātālis noster est maximī mōmentī.

Nōlīte dēcernĕre dē rēbus magnīs nisi prius hōroscopium vestrum consultātis. Crēde mihi, astrologia est scientia vēra, nōn superstitiō! Sī mē cōnsultābitis, ego vōs iuvābō. Nīmīrum, pensitābitis multam pecūniam prō meō cōnsiliō.

mōtiō –ōnis f movement
dēnotō –āre –āvī –ātus to mark down
  futūra –ōrum npl future
praedīcō –ĕre **praedīxī praedictus** to predict
afficiō –ĕre **affēcī affectus** to influence
  perinde āc just as
  aestus –ūs m tide
plēnus –a –um full
momentum –ī n importance
dēcernō –ĕre **decrēvī decrētus** to decide
  magnus –a –um important
  nisi prius unless first
scientia –ae f science
nīmīrum of course
pensitō –āre –avi –atus to pay
  cōnsilium –ī n advice

I. Now that you have heard the astrologer's "sales pitch," see if you can answer the following questions:

1. What is the first thing the man does as an astrologer?

2. What does he record?

3. What do the stars influence?

4. What does the moon influence?

5. What does the full moon influence?

6. Which day in our lives determines our future?

7. What should we do before we decide on anything important?

8. According to him, what is astrology?

9. What will he do if you consult him?

10. What does he say in the end that may make you question his sincerity?

7 In the description of the horoscope, you saw some instances of the future tense of **esse** (*to be*). Were you able to figure them out? The stem of the future tense (**er–**) is the same as the stem of the imperfect tense, but the personal endings are different. Note the imperfect and future of **esse**:

	IMPERFECT	FUTURE
ego	eram	erō
tū	erās	eris
is, ea, id	erat	erit
nōs	erāmus	erimus
vōs	erātis	eritis
eī, eae, ea	erant	erunt

8 Do you remember how you formed the present tense of **posse** (*to be able*)? Do you recall that **posse** is a combination of the root **pot–** (which means *able*) and **esse** (*to be*)? Do you remember when the letter *t* changed to *s* in the present tense? To form the future, add the future forms of **esse** to the root **pot–**:

ego _____

tū _____

is, ea, id _____

nōs _____

vōs _____

eī, eae, ea _____

ĀCTIVITĀTĒS

J. Change the verb in the following sentences from the imperfect to the future:

1. Bona fortūna tibi erat.
2. Cūr tam līberālis erās?
3. Condiscipulī meī erant studiōsī.
4. Nōs erāmus āthlētae clārī.
5. Astrologus ante templum hodiē erat.

K. Provide the correct future-tense forms of **posse**:

1. Astrologī nōn semper futūra praedīcĕre _____.
2. Nōs astra noctū vidēre _____.
3. Ego hōroscopium tuum legĕre nōn _____.
4. Tū et soror tua astrologum consultāre _____.
5. Augurēs Rōmānī futūra per avēs praedīcĕre _____.
6. Lūna aestūs ōceanī afficĕre _____.
7. Omnēs discipulī signa zōdiacī circulī discĕre _____.
8. Num ego fēlīx esse _____ sine hōroscopiō?
9. Augurēs Rōmānī gallīnās crās observāre _____.
10. Ego multam pecūniam astrologō pensitāre nōn _____.

Quaestiōnēs Persōnālēs

1. Quandō est tuus diēs nātālis?
2. Quid est tuum signum Zōdiacī circulī?
3. Quandō est diēs nātālis mātris tuae?
4. Quid est ēius signum?
5. Quandō est diēs nātālis patris tuī?
6. Quid est ēius signum?
7. Potestne hōroscopium praedīcĕre futūra tua?

VOCĀBULA

quod *which*
fēlīx *–īcis lucky*
dēbeō *–ēre –uī –itus to owe*

dēnārius *–ī m dollar*
īnfēlīx *–īcis unlucky*

Pretend that you are the astrologer in this dialog. Complete it by answering the questions:

Astrologe, quōmodō futūra mea praedīcěre poteris?

_____
_____
_____

(Say that you will observe the stars and the signs of the zodiac.)

Quot signa sunt in zōdiacō circulō?

_____
_____

(Answer the question and then ask what his sign is.)

Signum meum est Sagittārius. Estne signum meum fēlix an infēlix?

_____
_____

(Respond affirmatively and give your opinion of the sign.)

Num multōs labōrēs in vītā habēbō? Vītam bonam et secūram habēbō?

_____
_____

(Give your opinion and then ask for 200 dollars.)

Rēs Persōnālēs

Imagine that you have consulted a Roman astrologer. He says that any of the following can be yours in the future, but you have to choose only three. Write your three choices, listing the most important first and the least important last.

longa vīta   multī amīcī

multa pecūnia   familia amābilis

fēlīx vīta   successus in vītā

lībertās   corpus sānum

Compositiō

Find out the zodiac signs of three of your friends. Then, using ideas from the horoscope in this lesson, tell each friend what the stars say about their futures. For each person, list his or her first name, the sign, and the prediction.

⟳ THE LATIN CONNECTION

A. One of the signs of the zodiac is Lībra, which means either "a pair of scales" (such as those used to weigh things) or "a pound." What English abbreviation meaning "pound" comes from **lībra?**

B. Can you give the Latin words for these English derivatives?

1. superstition
2. dexterity
3. astronaut
4. circle
5. mutant
6. ignite
7. fortitude
8. sinister
9. mental
10. corporal
11. memorial
12. superb
13. judicial
14. alien
15. vocal
16. reptile
17. predict
18. artifact

IV | Spectācula Rōmāna

Future Tense (continued); Ablative of Means

1 Modicum cultūrae

The Romans did not have organized sports teams representing cities, towns, and schools. Instead, wealthy citizens, public officials and, later on, the emperors, provided games and entertainment to celebrate military victories, religious festivals, election campaigns, or even public funerals.

Until amphitheaters were built, the Roman Forum and the Circus Maximus were home to boxing and wrestling matches, as well as circus acts (jugglers, tightrope walkers, acrobats). By far the most popular events were the gladiatorial shows and wild-animal hunts (**vēnātiō** *–ōnis f*).

Gladiators were usually slaves, prisoners of war, or condemned criminals. Occasionally free-born citizens became gladiators for the excitement of the sport. Gladiators lived and trained in the gladiatorial school (**lūd***us* *–ī m*) under the watchful eyes of their trainers (**lanist***a* *–ae m*). Some won many victories, gained freedom and popularity, and even became rich. But most lived and died miserably.

To add variety to the show, organizers grouped gladiators into various classes according to the type of armor they wore or their method of fighting. For example, a net man (**rētiāri***us* *–ī m*) had only a trident and a fishing net (which he tried to throw over his opponent) as weapons. The arms of a Thracian (**Thrāx** *–ācis m*) were a helmet, shin guards, small round shield, and curved dagger. Others fought on

45

horseback and looked very much like medieval knights. Most gladiators had their right arms wrapped to the shoulder in leather straps. For the amusement of spectators, one class of gladiators wore holeless visors so they fought, in essence, blindfolded. Some animal fighters (**bēstiārius –ī m**) went into combat with a spear against wild animals; others, mostly criminals, were simply thrown unarmed to wild beasts that had been brought to Rome from Asia and, more commonly, North Africa.

On the morning of the show (**spectāculum –ī n**), the blare of trumpets announced gladiators who paraded around the arena to the cheers of the crowds before saluting the producer of the games. Then the gladiators paired off to fight; often, several pairs fought at the same time. The contests, which continued until noon, had musical accompaniments.

During the lunch break, jugglers, magicians, clowns, and animal trainers entertained the crowd. The afternoon performance was sometimes a battle with wild animals. Some 5,000 animals met violent deaths during the hundred-day holiday marking the dedication of the Colosseum by the emperor Titus in A.D. 80.

Spectators also thrilled to the spine-tingling chariot race in the Circus Maximus. As if the excitement of watching chariots careening around curves were not enough, Emperor Augustus ordered the construction of an artificial lake near the Tiber river—large enough to host mock naval battles. Although the ships were smaller than seagoing vessels, the battles were dangerous and even deadly.

2 The equipment gladiators wore may be new to you. Examine it carefully, and try to remember the name of each item:

hasta. -ae f

lanista -ae m

gladius -ī m

sīca -ae f

galea -ae f

scūtum -ī n

ocrea -ae f

parma -ae f

tridēns -entis m

gladiātor -ōris m

rēte -is n

ĀCTIVITĀS

A. See if you can identify the equipment these gladiators wear:

3 In Lesson III, you learned how to form the future tense of verbs of the first and second conjugations and of **sum** and **possum**. Now it's time to learn the future tense of the remaining conjugations. Read the following story of the gladiator rebellion led by Spartacus in 73 B.C. Pay special attention to the verbs in bold type. These are verbs of the *–ĕre, –īre* and *–iō* conjugations in the future tense:

In urbe Capuā erat amphitheātrum magnum. Nōn procul ab amphitheātrō erat lūdus gladiātōrius, ubi multī gladiātōrēs ex omnibus partibus orbis sē exercēbant. Servī erant. Lanistae eōrum erant crūdēlissimī et saepe mīserōs gladiātōrēs ferulīs verberāvērunt.

Quōdam diē, ūnus ē gladiātōribus, nōmine Spartacus, amīcōs suōs convocāvit et dixit: "Amīcī meī, quōusque ad dēlectāmentum populī Rōmānī pugnābimus? Quōusque ad glōriam dominōrum nostrōrum vītās nostrās **āmittēmus?** Quōs timēmus? Lanistās nostrōs? Sed gladiōs, sīcās, scūta, parmās habēmus. Ītalia patria vestra nōn est. Vōs ex Asiā et Graeciā et Germāniā et Galliā et longinquā Britanniā ad Ītaliam vēnistis. Nunc est tempus redīre ad patriās vestrās.

"Nōndum inter nōs **contendēmus.** Nōndum contrā bēstiās in arēnā **contendēmus.** Nōn prō dominīs nostrīs sed prō lībertāte nostrā **contendēmus.** Contrā legiōnēs Rōmānās bellum **gerēmus.** Sī vōs fortiter **contendētis, vincētis.** Numquam mīlitēs Rōmānī nōs vīvōs **capient.**

nōn procul ab (+ abl) *not far from*
  lūdus –ī *m school*

orbis –is *m world*
  servus –ī *m slave*
miser –era –erum *poor, miserable*
ferula –ae *f whip*
  verberō –āre *to beat*
quōdam diē *one day*
convocō –āre *to call together*
quōusque *how long*
  ad (+ acc) *for*   **dēlectāmentum**
  –ī n entertainment
dominus –ī *m owner, master*
  āmittō –ĕre āmīsī āmissus *to lose*
quōs *whom*
sīca –ae *f dagger*
longinquus –a –um *distant*
nōndum *no longer*
  inter nōs *with each other*
  contendō –ĕre –dī –tum *to fight*
bellum gerĕre *to fight a war*
vincō –ĕre vīcī victus *to win, defeat*
vīvus –a –um *alive*
  capiō –ĕre cēpī captus *to take, capture*

Ad montem Vesuvium **fugiēmus.** Servī undique ad nōs **fugient** et ūnā cum nōbīs contrā Rōmānōs **contendent.** Victōria nōbīs **erit!** Superābimus!"

Ūnus ē gladiātōribus clāmāvit: "Sī tū, Spartace, nōs **dūcēs** et **dēfendēs,** certē **vincēmus.** Nūllus Rōmānus nōs **vincet."**

Spartacus respondit: "Crēdite mihi, ego vōs **dūcam** et **dēfendam.** Nōbīs **erit** victōria, nōbīs **erit** lībertās."

Spartacus et gladiātōrēs duōs annōs contrā Rōmānōs fortiter pugnāvērunt sed dēnique Rōmānī Spartacum necāvērunt.

fugiō –ĕre fūgī fugitus *to flee*
undique *from everywhere*
ūnā cum (+ *abl*) *together with*
superō –āre -āvī –ātus *to overcome, win*

certē *adv certainly*
nūllus –a –um *no*

necō –āre *to kill*

4 If you review this story very carefully, paying particular attention to the words in bold type, you will find the personal endings of the future tense for all persons singular and plural. Can you now write those personal endings?

SINGULAR	PLURAL
_____	_____
_____	_____
_____	_____

Let's compare the forms of the future tense of **dūcĕre** to the the verb's present-tense forms:

	PRESENT	FUTURE
ego	dūc*ō*	dūc*am*
tū	dūc*is*	dūc*ēs*
is, ea, id	dūc*it*	dūc*et*
nōs	dūc*imus*	dūc*ēmus*
vōs	dūc*itis*	dūc*ētis*
eī, eae, ea	dūc*unt*	dūc*ent*

You can see how easy it is to confuse the present and future tenses. What vowel typically appears in the personal endings of present-tense verbs? Which vowel is common in the personal endings of future-tense verbs? In which two forms does the accent shift in the future tense?

Now you can easily form the future of *–īre* verbs such as **audīre** and of *–iō* verbs such as **accipĕre.** Notice that the letter *i* is part of the stem:

	audiō	**accipiō**
ego	audi _____	accipi _____
tū	audi _____	accipi _____

is, ea, id	audi _____	accipi _____
nōs	audi _____	accipi _____
vōs	audi _____	accipi _____
eī, eae, ea	audi _____	accipi _____

ĀCTIVITĀTĒS

B. How good are you at making predictions? Can you predict the future forms of verbs? Which verbs in the following list will use *–ābō* to form the future tense?

1. praedīcĕre
2. pugnāre
3. habēre
4. superāre
5. exercēre
6. convocāre

C. The verbs in the next list will present a greater challenge as you decide which verbs will form the future with *–ēbō*. Although the infinitive of each verb ends in *–ere,* some end in *–ēre* while others have *–ĕre* endings.

1. placēre
2. merēre
3. dīcĕre
4. tenēre
5. timēre
6. crēdĕre
7. legĕre
8. movēre

D. You may need to resort to augury to predict correctly in this exercise, because all of the following verbs have exactly the same infinitive. Some belong to the *–ĕre* conjugation and form the first person future with the ending *–am,* such as **dēfendam.** Others form the future with the ending *–iam,* such as **fugiam** (*I will flee*). Here's the trick. Remember the ending of the first-person singular of the present tense. Does it end in *–ō,* as in **dēfendō,** or in *–iō,* as in **perficiō?** Spot the verbs that use *–iam* to form the future tense:

1. accipĕre
2. dīcĕre
3. currĕre
4. capĕre
5. afficĕre
6. dēfendĕre

5 Before continuing with exercises that practice the future tense, let's first see how the Romans used the ABLATIVE OF MEANS or INSTRUMENT. Compare the following sentences:

Gladiātor *gladiō* contendet.   *The gladiator will fight WITH A SWORD.*

Gladiātor *cum Rōmānīs* contendet.   *The gladiator will fight WITH (AGAINST) THE ROMANS.*

In the first example, **gladiō** is the means or instrument; therefore, no preposition is necessary. The form **gladiō** is called the ablative of means or the instrumental ablative. The second example, however, does not contain the ablative of means or instrument. **Rōmānīs** are persons so the preposition **cum** is used. Let's test the difference in some sentences.

ĀCTIVITĀTĒS

E. As you read the following sentences, decide if the preposition **cum** is needed with the noun in the ablative. Write the correct expression. Notice that all verbs in this activity are in the future tense:

1. Astrologus futūra (stellīs/cum stellīs) praedīcet.

2. Gladiātor crūra sua (cum ocreīs/ocreīs) prōteget.

3. Bēstiāriī (bēstiīs/cum bēstiīs) contendent.

4. Mīlitēs patriam suam (vītīs suīs/cum vītīs suīs) dēfendent.

5. Rētiārius (cum tridente/tridente) crās pugnābit.

6. Bēstiārius panthērās (sīcā/cum sīcā) occīdet.

F. Read the following sentences carefully. Then change the verb to the future tense. To draw your attention, the nouns in the ablative of means or instrumental ablative are in bold type:

1. Ego et Syrus **gladiīs** contendimus.

2. Quōmodo sine **scūtō** contendis?

3. Gladiātōrēs glōriae causā contendunt.

4. Ego aut **scūtō** aut **parmā** contendō.

5. Quis palmam (*palm*) victōriae accipit?

6. Gladiātōrēs nunc galeās induunt.

7. Bēstiārius tigrēs et ursōs **hastā** occīdit.

8. Cūr tū et frāter tuus **cum aliēnō** contenditis?

G. You have a choice of two verbs for each of the sentences below. Careful! Only one verb makes sense. Write the future tense of the verb that correctly completes each sentence:

1. (accipĕre/fugĕre) Rētiārius palmam victōriae _____.

2. (prōtegĕre/occidĕre) Galea caput gladiātōris _____.

3. (contendĕre/capĕre) Nōs mox in arēnā _____.

4. (accipĕre/dēfendĕre) Mīlitēs urbem fortiter _____.

5. (prōtegĕre/contendĕre) Cūr tū sine parmā _____.

6. (fugĕre/capĕre) Servus ā lūdō gladiātōriō _____.

H. Be alert for this next activity. The verbs represent *all* conjugations. Change each to the future tense. Be sure to use the correct future ending:

1. Gladiātōrēs lanistās semper timent.

2. Post proelium rētiārī ocreās exuunt.

3. Ego et avus meus stadium intrāmus.

4. Lanista gladiātōrem ferulā verberat.

5. Multī spectātōrēs in stadium veniunt.

6. Quid in lūdō gladiātōriō invenīs?

7. Potestne Thrāx rētiārium vincĕre?

8. Caesar palmam victōrī dat.

9. Quot gladiātōrēs in arēnā pugnant?

10. Nōs omnēs ob glōriam contendimus.

I. A **lanista** is asking a young trainee some questions. The poor trainee is too nervous to answer. Can you supply complete-sentence answers to the following questions?

1. Gestābisne scūtum an parmam?

2. Contendēsne cum Thrāce an cum rētiāriō?

3. Nōnne galeam gestābis?

4. Pugnābisne sīcā an gladiō?

5. Num bēstiae tē terrēbunt?

6. Contendēsne prō pecūniā an lībertāte?

7. Necābisne adversārium (*opponent*) tuum sī vincēs?

8. Accipiēsne palmam victōriae sī vincēs?

1. Praefersne pugnam inter gladiātōrēs an inter bestiās et bestiāriōs?

2. Praefersne animālia prōtegĕre an occīdĕre?

3. Praefersne vidēre bēstiās in amphitheātrō an in vīvāriō *(zoo)*?

4. Cōnsiderāsne pugnās gladiātōriās esse bonās an malās?

5. Quot animālia domestica habēs domī tuae?

Dialogus

Study this conversation between Davus, a young trainee, and Thrax, a big, seasoned gladiator:

mī amīce *my friend*
facile *adv easily*
vincō *–ĕre* vīcī victus *to defeat*
quam *how*
validus *–a –um strong*
audeō *–ēre to dare*
abhinc *ago*
leō *–ōnis m lion*
ursus *–ī m bear*

vīsne? *do you want?*

taberna vīnāria *–ae f wine shop*
sērus *–a –um late*

uxor *–ōris f wife*
irātus *–a –um (+ dat.) angry with*

Colloquium

Complete the dialog based on the model of the conversation, but substitute your own words wherever you can:

Your friend from abroad has come to visit you in Rome and to see his or her first gladiatorial show in the amphitheater. Tell your friend some things about the gladiators and the weapons they will use.

⟲ THE LATIN CONNECTION

A. Can you supply the Latin words from which these English words derive?

1. spectacle
2. servile
3. invincible
4. contentious
5. audacious
6. nullify
7. vivacious

B. At this point, you have met the word **occīdĕre** (*to kill*) several times. This word combines the prefix **ob–** and **caedĕre.** When a prefix is added to **caedere,** the verb becomes **–cīdere.** The *b* of the prefix **ob–** changes to *c,* the first letter in **–cīdere,** to form the new word **occīdĕre.** From this verb we get the noun **cīdium,** which means *killing.* **Cīdium** is the base for many words. For instance, **homicīdium,** meaning "the killing of a human being," gives us the English word *homicide.* Write the meaning of the following Latin words; then list their English derivatives:

EXAMPLE:	MEANING	DERIVATIVE
homicīdium	*killing of a man*	*homicide*

1. fungicīdium
2. genocīdium
3. germicīdium
4. herbicīdium
5. īnsecticīdium
6. pesticidium

V | Animālia

Comparative Degree

1 Modicum cultūrae

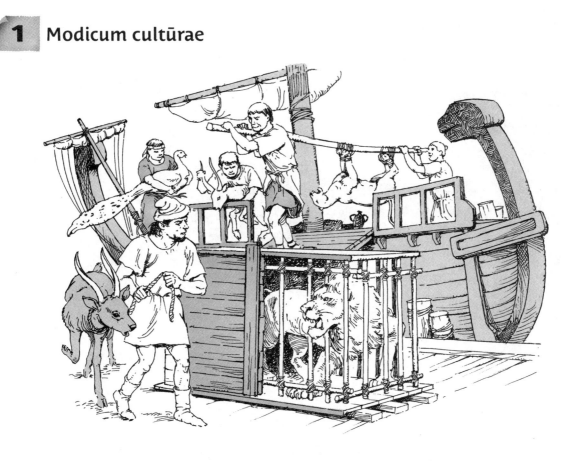

As the Roman Empire spread, Romans imported animals from all over the world. As we learned in Lesson IV, great numbers of these animals met their deaths in the amphitheater simply to entertain spectators. The Romans called these performances "hunts" (**vēnātiōnēs**), an inaccurate term since the animals had no chance of escape. These "hunts" were popular for some 400 years.

Animals were also important in the religion of the time. Augurs and sooth-sayers used animals to predict the future. In addition, you may remember that Romans associated certain animals with the gods. For instance, the eagle (**aquila** **–ae** *f*) was sacred to Jupiter, and the peacock (**pāvō –ōnis** *m*) was sacred to Juno. When they saw these animals, the Romans believed that the gods had sent the animals as messengers. Other animals became sacrifices to gain the favor of the gods.

In a practical sense, animals played a crucial role in war. Donkeys and mules were beasts of burden that hauled heavy loads. Horses provided mounts for cavalry soldiers. Elephants were the nearly unstoppable "tanks" of ancient warfare. Hannibal used elephants to carry supplies across the Alps from Spain into Italy in the Second Punic War.

Finally animals were, in Roman as in modern times, pets. For instance, family goats hitched to little chariots or wagons often gave children a fun ride.

2 Vocābula

sciūrus -ī m

apis - is f

mūlus - ī m

mannus - ī m

pāpiliō -ōnis m

arānea -ae f

cervus -ī m

caper, caprī m

panthēra -ae f
leopardus -ī m

castor -is m

crocodīlus -ī m

formīca -ae f

serpens -entis m

ĀCTIVITĀTĒS

A. Below are pictures of animals in cages (**cavea** *–ae f*) in a zoo (**vīvārium** *–ī n*). The names of the animals are missing. Some words you just met; others you've already learned. Identify the name of each caged animal. If one animal is pictured, use the singular form of the noun; use the plural form to refer to two animals:

B. Study this list of animals. Can you group them according to their usual habitat (Farm, Air, Fields/Woods, Jungle)?

apis	castor	mūlus	sciūrus
aquila	cervus	panthēra	sīmia
ariēs	crocodīlus	pāpiliō	taurus
cancer	elephantus	serpēns	tigris
caper	mannus		

3 First you learned Latin adjectives in the simple form, or *positive degree* (**clārus** *–a –um*). Next you learned adjectives in the highest, or *superlative,* degree. Do you remember the superlative degree of **clārus?** If you responded **clārissimus,** congratulate yourself!

Do you remember the superlative endings of adjectives that end in *–er*, such as **pulcher, pulchra, pulchrum?** If you do, you have a *superlative* memory! What are the superlative endings of adjectives that end in *–ilis, –ilis, –ile,* such as **facilis?**

Now meet the COMPARATIVE DEGREE (English examples: *faster, easier, more beautiful*). Similar to the superlative degree, which means *most*, the comparative degree indicates *more*. In Latin, the adverb for *more* is **magis.** The Latin comparative ending *–ior* is similar in sound and spelling to the English comparative ending *–ier*.

(arbor) **alta**

altior

altissima

(serpens) **longus**

longior

longissimus

(sīca) **brevis** or **curtus**

brevior or **curtior**

brevissima or **curtissima**

(crocodīlus) **ferōx**

ferōcior

ferōcissimus

(puella) **fēlīx**

fēlīcior

fēlīcissima

How observant are you? Did you notice that the comparative ending of the adjectives is the same for the masculine and feminine? What is that ending?

The neuter ending of the comparative is different, however, as we will learn later. Right now, let's study the last two examples: **ferōx** and **fēlīx**. These words are single-ending adjectives of the third declension. The full stem of such adjectives can be seen in the genitive case: **ferōx, ferōcis; fēlīx, fēlīcis.**

What is the full stem of **ferōx?** What is the full stem of **fēlīx?**

Notice that the full stem is used in the comparative and superlative degrees.

ĀCTIVITĀTĒS

C. Try a few comparisons of your own. Study the sentence beneath each picture below. Rewrite the sentences by changing the adjectives first to comparative and then to superlative. Be sure to note the gender of each noun:

EXAMPLE:

Hīc serpēns est longus. Ille serpēns est longior. Iste serpēns est longissimus.

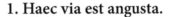

1. Haec via est angusta.

2. Hīc porcus est pinguis.

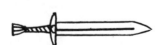 

3. Hīc gladius est curtus.

D. Provide the masculine/feminine comparative form and the superlative form of the following adjectives:

POSITIVE

1. tard*us –a –um* (*slow*)

2. aud*āx –ācis* (*bold*)

3. ēleg*āns –antis* (*elegant*)

4. simil*is –is –e* (*similar*)

5. vēl*ōx –ōcis* (*fast*)

6. facil*is –is –e* (*easy*)

7. mīt*is –is –e* (*tame, mild*)

4 Let's consider the mystery of the disappearing letter *e* in some adjectives. How does it affect the comparative degree? Analyze the following adjectives:

miser misera miserum (*poor, miserable*)
pulcher pulchra pulchrum (*beautiful*)
tener teneris tenere (*tender, soft*)
ācer ācris ācre (*sharp, keen*)

List the adjectives that drop the letter *e* in the feminine and neuter forms. The same adjectives drop this letter in the comparative form. What is the comparative form of **miser? Pulcher? Tener? Ācer?** List them.

ĀCTIVITĀS

E. Identify the following pictures. Then complete the sentences by providing the proper form of the adjective in the comparative degree:

EXAMPLE:

Apis est pulchra.　　　　Pāpiliō est pulchrior.

1. _____ est dīligēns. _____ est _____.

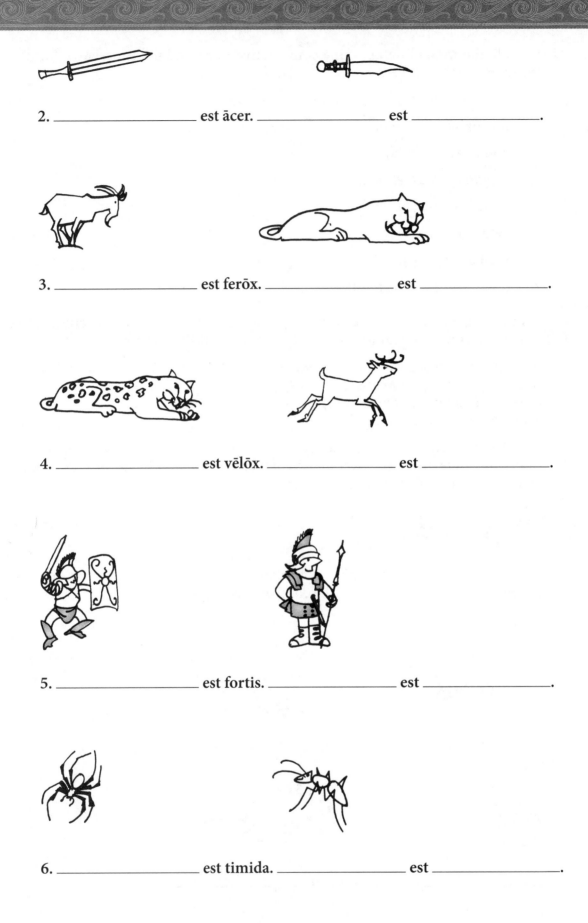

2. _____ est ācer. _____ est _____.

3. _____ est ferōx. _____ est _____.

4. _____ est vēlōx. _____ est _____.

5. _____ est fortis. _____ est _____.

6. _____ est timida. _____ est _____.

5 So far we have seen only the masculine/feminine forms of comparative adjectives. The neuter form ends in **–ius.** This neuter form is *also* the form of the comparative adverb. The usage of the word in the sentence will tell you whether, for example, **velōcius** is the neuter comparative adjective or the comparative adverb. The following sentences demonstrate this difference:

Aquila est animal *velōcius* quam pāpiliō.	*An eagle is a faster animal than a butterfly.*
Aquila volat *velōcius* quam pāpiliō.	*An eagle flies faster than a butterfly.*

In the first sentence, **velōcius** is an *adjective* that describes the noun **animal.** In the second sentence, **velōcius** is an *adverb* modifying the verb **volat.**

> **CAUTION:** Don't confuse an adjective in the positive degree such as **sērius** (*serious*) or **medius** (*central*) with a comparative neuter adjective such as **velōcius** (*faster*).

ACTIVITĀS

F. In the following sentences, be sure you identify the gender of the noun modified by the comparative adjective before you write the correct form of the missing adjective:

1. Domus est aedificium altum. Templum est aedificium _____.

2. Parma est gravis. Scūtum est _____.

3. Hasta est ācris. Gladius est _____.

4. Arānea est insectum dīligēns. Apis est animal _____.

5. Rētiārius est fortis. Bēstiārius est _____.

6. Mannus est timidus. Cervus est _____.

7. Medicīna est amāra. Acētum (*vinegar*) est _____.

8. Castor est bellus. Sciūrus est _____.

9. Leopardus est ferōx. Crocodīlus est _____.

10. Astrologus est astūtus. Augur est _____.

6 To this point, we have addressed comparative adjectives in the nominative case only. Of course, these adjectives are declined like any adjective of the third declension EXCEPT that the ablative singular of comparative adjectives ends in **–e** exactly like a noun of the third declension. To refresh your memory, the adjective gravis (*heavy*) is fully declined in the table below. Some of the comparative forms are also listed. Which words will complete the table? Take care! Remember that a neuter adjective, just like a neuter noun, has the same form in both accusative and nominative cases.

	POSITIVE		COMPARATIVE	
	MASC./FEM.	NEUTER	MASC./FEM.	NEUTER
SINGULAR				
NOM.	gravis	grave	gravior	gravius
GEN.	gravis	gravis	graviōris	graviōris
DAT.	gravī	gravī		
ACC.	gravem	grave		
ABL.	gravī	gravī	graviōre	graviōre
PLURAL				
NOM.	gravēs	gravia		graviōra
GEN.	gravium	gravium		
DAT.	gravibus	gravibus		
ACC.	gravēs	gravia		
ABL.	gravibus	gravibus		

ĀCTIVITĀS

G. Each of the following sentences has an adjective in the positive degree. Write its corresponding comparative degree:

1. Gladiātor tunicam longam gestāvit.

2. Lanista cum illīs servīs miserīs vēnit.

3. Castor caudam curtam habēbat.

4. Numquam crocodīlōs ferōcēs vīdī.

5. Astrologus hōroscopium fēlix mihi praedixit.

6. Ego in urbe pulchrā diū habitāvī.

7. Puella illum mannum mītem amat.

8. Sciūrī in arbore altā sedēbant.

9. Ego leōnēs ferōcēs in vīvāriō vīdī.

10. Aliēnus ē terrā longinquā venit.

7 In English, we generally use the adverb *than* to compare two or more things. Latin uses the word **quam:**

Crocodīlus est perīculōsior *quam* **serpēns.**	*A crocodile is more dangerous than a snake.*

The Romans, however, often skipped **quam** and simply placed the noun in the ablative case directly after the comparative:

Crocodīlus est perīculōsior serpente.	*A crocodile is more dangerous than a snake.*

The word **quam** is helpful in another type of comparison, too. Use this word when you compare two things and want to indicate that they are equal or similar:

Leō est *tam* **ferōx** *quam* **panthēra.**	*A lion is as ferocious as a panther.*

ĀCTIVITĀS

H. Rewrite the following sentences using **quam** and the nominative instead of the ablative:

1. Porcus est pinguior ove.
2. Cervus est mītior leōne.
3. Leopardī sunt vēlōciōrēs elephantīs.
4. Mūlī sunt tardiōrēs equīs.
5. Formīcae sunt industriōrēs apibus.

8 We know that certain adjectives in English have irregular forms in the comparative and superlative degrees: *good, better, best; bad, worse, worst.* Similarly, some Latin adjectives (and adverbs) have irregular comparatives and superlatives. Listed below are some of the most common irregular adjectives and adverbs:

	M/F	NEUTER	
bonus *–a –um* *good*	**melior** *better*	**melius**	**optimus** *–a –um* *best*
malus *–a –um* *bad*	**pēior** *worse*	**pēius**	**pessimus** *–a –um* *worst*
magnus *–a –um* *big*	**māior** *bigger*	**māius**	**maximus** *–a –um* *biggest*
parvus *–a –um* *small*	**minor** *smaller*	**minus**	**minimus** *–a –um* *smallest*
superus *–a –um* *high, on high*	**superior** *higher*	**superius**	**suprēmus** *–a –um* **summus** *–a –um* *highest*

CAUTION: Don't confuse the superlative **summus** (*highest*) with the verb **sumus** (*we are*). Note that the first has a double *m,* while the second has a single *m.*

I. Rewrite the following sentences, substituting the ablative of comparison for **quam** and the nominative:

1. Mūs est minor quam castor.

2. Equus est māior quam mannus.

3. Hiems est pēior quam autumnus.

4. Aestās est melior quam hiems.

5. Arbor est superior quam domus.

6. Elephantī sunt māiōrēs quam leopardī.

7. Līlium est melius quam viola.

8. Scūtum est māius quam parma.

J. Compare the animals using the clues that have been provided. First state the comparison using **quam** and the nominative; then repeat the comparison using the ablative:

EXAMPLE: **PARVUS**

Fēlēs est minor quam porcus.

Fēlēs est minor porcō.

1. vēlōx

2. intellegēns

3. ferōx

4. bonus

5. perīculōsus

9 Let's read a story about a girl whom a goddess changed into a spider (**arānea** –*ae f*) because of the girl's excessive pride:

In Lȳdiā erat puella, nōmine Arachnē. Vestēs pulcherrimās texēbat. In vestibus pictūrās admīrābilēs pīnxit. Puellae ex omnibus partibus Lȳdiae vēnērunt et opus admīrābile spectāvērunt. Omnēs puellae invidēbant Arachnae. "Minerva certē tē hanc artem docuit," dīcēbant puellae. Arachnē autem magnā cum īrā respondit: "Nūgās! Minerva nōn est, nōn erat et nōn erit mea magistra. Ego eam ad certāmen prōvocābō! Facile eam vincam, quamquam dea est!"

Minerva verba superba audīvit et dīxit: "Arachnē est puella superba et audāx. Ad ēius casam ībō et eam monēbō." Iam stetit Minerva ante casae iānuam, nōn ut dea sed ut anus. "O, Arachnē," ait Minerva, "certā cum aliīs puellīs sed nōlī prōvocāre deās! Minerva erit īrāta."

"Misera anus," respondit Arachnē, "nūgās dīcis. Deās nōn timeō. Nulla puella et nulla dea texĕre et pingĕre potest melius quam ego. Sī dea ipsa veniet, eam ad certāmen prōvocābō."

Tum Minerva formam anūs exuit et suam formam vēram induit. Omnēs puellae deam adōrāvērunt. Arachnē sōla nōn erat territa, et iterum deam ad certāmen prōvocāvit. Sine morā Minerva et Arachnē certāmen incipiunt. Minerva in purpureō veste beneficia deōrum deārumque ergā hominēs pingit. Contrā, Arachnē maleficia Iovis pingit. Nē Minerva quidem pulchrum opus carpĕre potuit. Minerva autem magnā cum īrā dīxit: "Tū certē splendidē texĕre et pingĕre potes. Sed Iovem et omnēs deōs arrogantiā tuā offendistī. Itaque tē in arāneam mūtābō. Nōn iam pulchrās vestēs texēs; ex hōc tēlās texēs." Subitō Arachnē minor atque minor fīēbat. Prō crūribus et manibus, nunc octō crūra habēbat. Arachnē nunc arānea fīēbat.

Lȳdiā –*ae f ancient kingdom (now a part of Turkey)*
texō –*ĕre* –*uī* –*tum to weave*
admīrābilis –*is* –*e wonderful*
　pingō –*ĕre* **pīnxī pictus** *to embroider*
opus –*ĕris n work*
invideō –*ĕre* **invīdī** (+ dat.) *to envy*
certē *surely*　**ars artis** *f skill*
īra –*ae f anger*
nūgae –*ārum f pl nonsense*
certāmen –*ĭnis n contest*
　prōvocō –*āre* –*āvī* –*ātus to challenge*
quamquam *although*
superbus –*a* –*um proud*
moneō –*ēre* –*uī* –*itus to warn*
ut *as*
　anus –*ūs f old lady*
īrātus –*a* –*um angry*

ipsa *herself*
exuō –*uĕre* –*uī* –*ūtus to take off*
adōrō –*āre to adore, worship*
　solus –*a* –*um alone*
　territus –*a* –*um scared*
iterum *again*
　mora –*ae f delay*
incipiō –*ĕre* **incēpī inceptus** *to begin*
purpureus –*a* –*um crimson*
ergā (prep. + acc.) *to, toward*
beneficium –*ī n kindness, good deed*
contrā *on the other hand*
　maleficium –*ī n evil deed*
nē ... quidem *not even*
carpō –*ĕre* –*sī* –*tus to find fault with, carp at*
offendō –*ĕre* –*ī* **offensus** *to offend*
　nōn iam *no longer*
tēla –*ae f web*
　ex hōc *from now on*
　subitō *suddenly*
fīēbat (*she*) *became*
　prō (+ *abl*) *instead of*

ĀCTIVITĀS

K. Respondē ad quaestiōnēs:

1. Ubi habitābat Arachnē?
2. Quid Arachnē texēbat?
3. Quid in vestibus pīnxit?
4. Quis Arachnae invidēbat?
5. Quem Arachnē ad certāmen prōvocāvit?
6. Quam formam Minerva assūmpsit?
7. Ubi Minerva vēram formam iterum induit, quid aliae puellae fēcērunt?
8. Quis sōla nōn erat territa?
9. Quid Minerva in veste pīnxit?
10. Quid pīnxit Arachnē in veste?

Compositiō

You are a childcare provider in a day-care center filled with various stuffed animal playthings. Write five questions that children might ask about animals. For example, children might want to know: "Is a fox faster than a rabbit?" "Can a peacock fly?" "Is a bear bigger than a pig?"

VOCĀBULA

quaesō *please*
quod *which?*
nesciō *I don't know*
incertus −a −um *unsure*

orbis (−is m) terrārum *world*
nimium *too*
interrogātum −ī n *question*
pōnō −ĕre posuī positus *to put, ask*

Supply the Latin animal names that make each of the following statements true of you. Notice that the first four answers must be in the accusative case:

1.   Ego amō mannōs magis quam _____.

2.   Timeō arāneās magis quam _____.

3.   Amō sciūrōs magis quam _____.

4.   Amō columbās magis quam _____.

5.   Pāpiliōnēs mihi placent magis quam _____.

Think of all the students you know. Compare five pairs of students using the adjectives in the list below or others from the general vocabulary at the end of the book. Feel free to use the students' English names:

EXAMPLES: līberālis   Thomas est tam līberālis quam Jennifer.
Thomas is as generous as Jennifer.
Thomas est līberālior quam Jennifer.
Thomas is more generous than Jennifer.

altus (*tall*)	**crūdus** (*crude*)	**sērius** (*serious*)
amābilis (*lovable*)	**curtus** (*short*)	**sincērus** (*sincere*)
bellus (*cute*)	**fēlīx** (*lucky, happy*)	**studiōsus** (*studious*)
benignus (*kind*)	**fidēlis** (*loyal*)	**superbus** (*proud*)
cārus (*dear*)	**honestus** (*honorable*)	**timidus** (*shy*)
clēmēns (*gentle*)	**īnsānus** (*crazy*)	**vēlōx** (*fast*)

Your little brother is very curious. Supply answers to his questions:

VOCĀBULA

mel, mellis *n honey*
colligō –ĕre collēgī collectus *to gather*
nux, nucis *f nut*
macula –ae *f spot*

niger nigra nigrum black
pellis –is *f hide, skin*
tantus –a –um *so much*
sciō scīre scīvī scītus *to know*
quōmodo *adv how*

THE LATIN CONNECTION

Answer the following questions. Then enclose in parentheses the Latin word that inspired the English derivative.

> **EXAMPLE:** What is a *maladjusted* child?
>
> A maladjusted child is a badly adjusted child. **(malus –a –um)**

1. What is a *serpentine* road?
2. What is the *velocity* of a bullet?
3. What type of person is an *optimist?*
4. What kind of person is a *pessimist?*
5. What is a *minor* mistake?
6. What is a *major* blunder?
7. What is a *supreme* sacrifice?
8. What is the *summit* of a mountain?
9. What happens when two statements *contradict* each other?
10. What are *textiles?*
11. What type of person is a *malefactor?*
12. What are royal *vestments?*
13. What is a *mellifluous* voice?
14. What winged animals might live in an *apiary?*
15. If a girl has *pulchritude,* what does she possess?
16. When you *abbreviate* a word, what do you do?
17. What is a *moratorium?*
18. When a situation *ameliorates,* how does it change?

Recognitiō I

(Lēctiōnēs I–V)

LĒCTIŌ I

a. Demonstrative adjective/pronoun meaning *this (one)*, *these*:

SINGULAR			
NOMINATIVE	hīc	haec	hoc
GENITIVE	hūius	hūius	hūius
DATIVE	huic	huic	huic
ACCUSATIVE	hunc	hanc	hōc
ABLATIVE	hōc	hāc	hōc
PLURAL			
NOMINATIVE	hī	hae	haec
GENITIVE	hōrum	hārum	hōrum
DATIVE	hīs	hīs	hīs
ACCUSATIVE	hōs	hās	haec
ABLATIVE	hīs	hīs	hīs

b. Demonstrative adjective/pronoun meaning *that (one)*, *those*:

SINGULAR			
NOMINATIVE	ille	illa	illud
GENITIVE	illīus	illīus	illīus
DATIVE	illī	illī	illī
ACCUSATIVE	illum	illam	illud
ABLATIVE	illō	illā	illō
PLURAL			
NOMINATIVE	illī	illae	illa
GENITIVE	illōrum	illārum	illōrum
DATIVE	illīs	illīs	illīs
ACCUSATIVE	illōs	illās	illa
ABLATIVE	illīs	illīs	illīs

c. The demonstrative **iste, ista, istud** [*that (one)*], which has the same endings as **ille, illa, illud,** is sometimes used to express contempt.

LĒCTIŌ II

a. The conjugation of **volō** (*I want, I wish*) and **nōlō** (*I do not want, I do not wish*):

ego	volō	nōlō
tū	vīs	nōn vīs
is/ea/id	vult	nōn vult
nōs	volumus	nōlumus
vōs	vultis	nōn vultis
eī/eae/ea	volunt	nōlunt

b. The principal parts of these two verbs are:

volō	**velle**	**voluī**
nōlō	**nōlle**	**nōluī**

c. A reflexive verb uses the regular simple pronoun in the first and second persons singular and plural and **sē** in the third person singular and plural:

mē lavō	*I wash/am washing (myself)*
tē lavās	*you wash/are washing (yourself)*
sē lavat	*he/she washes/is washing (himself/herself)*
nōs lavāmus	*we wash/are washing (ourselves)*
vōs lavātis	*you wash/are washing (yourselves)*
sē lavant	*they wash/are washing (themselves)*

LĒCTIŌ III

a. To form the future tense of the first two conjugations (*–āre* and *–ēre*), add the future personal endings to the stem:

		–bō
		–bis
I	portā	*–bit*
II	tenē	*–bimus*
		–bitis
		–bunt

The formation of the future tense of the remaining conjugations follows a different pattern.

b. The future endings of the verb **īre** (*to go*) are regular; that is, the endings are identical to those of verbs such as **portāre** and **tenēre.** The entire stem is **ī–: ībō** (*I will go*), **ībis** (*you will go*), and so on.

c. The future tense of **sum** consists of the stem **er–** plus the personal endings:

ego	**erō**	*I will be*
tū	**eris**	*you will be*
is/ea/id	**erit**	*he/she/it will be*
nōs	**erimus**	*we will be*
vōs	**eritis**	*you will be*
eī/eae/ea	**erunt**	*they will be*

LĒCTIŌ IV

a. To form the future of verbs of the **–ĕre** (third) conjugation, add personal endings to the present stem. These endings are different from the personal endings of the first two verb families:

ego	**dūcam**	*I will lead*
tū	**dūcēs**	*you will lead*
is/ea/id	**dūcet**	*he/she/it will lead*
nōs	**dūcēmus**	*we will lead*
vōs	**dūcētis**	*you will lead*
eī/eae/ea	**dūcent**	*they will lead*

b. To form the future of the **–īre** (fourth) conjugation of verbs such as **audīre** and of the **–iō** verb family such as **accipĕre,** remember that the letter *i* is part of the stem. The future forms of **audiō** are **audiam** (*I will hear*), **audiēs** (*you will hear*), and so on. The future forms of **accipiō** are **accipiam** (*I will receive*), **accipiēs** (*you will receive*), and so on.

c. The ablative of means (also called the instrumental ablative) does not require a preposition in Latin. It is equivalent to the English prepositions *with* or *by.*

Rōmulus Remum *gladiō* necāvit.   *Romulus killed Remus with a sword.*

a. To form the comparative degree of adjectives, add *–ior* to the stem for the masculine and feminine genders and *–ius* for the neuter gender. Remember that the full stem of single-ending adjectives of the third declension (**ferōx, fēlīx**) are visible in the genitive case (**ferōcis, fēlīcis**): **ferōc–** and **fēlīc–**. The complete declension of the comparative degree of the adjective **fēlīx** follows:

	MASC./FEM	NEUTER
SINGULAR		
NOMINATIVE	**fēlīcior**	**fēlīcius**
GENITIVE	**fēlīciōris**	**fēlīciōris**
DATIVE	**fēlīciōrī**	**fēlīciōrī**
ACCUSATIVE	**fēlīciōrem**	**fēlīcius**
ABLATIVE	**fēlīciōre**	**fēlīciōre**
PLURAL		
NOMINATIVE	**fēlīciōrēs**	**fēlīciōra**
GENITIVE	**fēlīciōrum**	**fēlīciōrum**
DATIVE	**fēlīciōribus**	**fēlīciōribus**
ACCUSATIVE	**fēlīciōrēs**	**fēlīciōra**
ABLATIVE	**fēlīciōribus**	**fēlīciōribus**

b. Adjectives that drop the letter *e* in the feminine and neuter of the positive degree (**pulcher, pulchra, pulchrum**) also drop this letter in the comparative degree: **pulchrior, pulchrius.**

c. The comparative degree of the adverb has exactly the same form as the neuter of the adjective. For example, **fēlīcius,** meaning *more happily,* is the comparative degree of the adverb.

d. Because the comparative degree of certain adjectives is irregular, the forms must be memorized. Below are some of the most common irregular comparatives:

	MASC./FEM.		NEUTER
bonus *–a –um* *good*	**melior** *better*	**melius**	**optimus** *–a –um* *best*
malus *–a –um* *bad*	**pēior** *worse*	**pēius**	**pessimus** *–a –um* *worst*
magnus *–a –um* *big*	**māior** *bigger*	**māius**	**maximus** *–a –um* *biggest*

(continued)

	MASC./FEM.		NEUTER
parvus –a –um *small*	**minor** *smaller*	**minus**	**minim**us *–a –um* *smallest*
superus *–a –um* *high, on high*	**superior** *higher*	**superius**	**suprēmus** *–a –um* **summus** *–a –um* *highest*

e. To compare two items in Latin, the Romans either used **quam** (*than*), or they omitted **quam** and changed the noun that followed to the ablative case. This form is called the ablative of comparison:

Crocodīlus est perīculōsior *quam*   *A crocodile is more dangerous than*
   serpēns.   *a snake.*
Crocodīlus est perīculōsior serpente.

f. Quam also compares two things that are equal or similar:

Leō est *tam* **ferōx** *quam* **panthēra.**   *A lion is as ferocious as a panther.*

ĀCTIVITĀTĒS

A. Quis est augur? Read the following sentences. Then decide which of the five men each describes.

1. Togam gestat.
2. Comam in capite habet.
3. Barbam nōn habet.

4. Numquam rīdet.
5. Vēlum suprā caput gestat.
6. Lituum manū dextrā tenet.

B. Below are six pictures. Complete the description beneath each picture by using the correct form of the word **velle:**

1. Infans dormīre _____.

2. Āthlēta sē lavāre _____.

3. Ego et Claudia pilā lūdĕre _____.

4. Vōs in piscīnā natāre _____.

5. Tū iaculum conīcĕre _____.

6. Pugilēs pugnāre _____.

C. Study the following chart. In your notebook, write the Latin word that corresponds to each English word. Then locate each Latin word in the puzzle. Words can be read right to left, left to right, up, down, or diagonally.

1. statue
2. Olympia
3. boxing glove
4. helmet
5. beaver
6. here
7. goat
8. air
9. dagger
10. three
11. net

12. lion
13. snack shop
14. storeroom
15. shin guard
16. in front of
17. racing chariot
18. exercise place
19. games
20. earth
21. slave
22. gymnasium

M	U	I	S	A	N	M	Y	G	T
A	U	O	C	A	S	T	O	R	R
R	C	L	E	O	V	R	E	T	E
T	E	Y	U	S	U	V	R	E	S
S	L	M	I	C	A	P	E	R	U
E	L	P	D	S	I	C	A	R	T
A	A	I	U	O	C	R	E	A	S
L	G	A	L	E	A	E	R	S	E
A	N	T	E	S	T	A	T	U	A
P	O	P	I	N	A	V	H	I	C

D. Cruciverbilūsus:

HORIZONTĀLE

1. wrestling place
5. site of Olympic Games
10. snack shop
11. that one (*m*)
13. summer
15. his own
16. air
18. himself
21. then, at that time
23. net
24. play, school
26. I love
27. trip
28. temple
31. this (*f, abl.*)
33. to
34. she
35. fire
36. me
37. from, by
39. man
40. his, her, its
42. crowd
43. he is
44. I do not want
45. weight
47. ring
49. you love (*pl.*)
50. part

1.	boxers	14.	so many	29.	person
2.	in front of	17.	also, even	30.	ball
3.	often	19.	why	32.	certain
4.	king	20.	to change	38.	good (*n*)
6.	wolf	22.	apples	39.	it flies
7.	pony	24.	lion	41.	already
8.	spiders	25.	but	42.	your
9.	to compete	26.	friend	46.	or
10.	foot	27.	so	48.	as, when
12.	light				

E. When you consulted a Roman astrologer for your horoscope, he forgot to share some predictions with you. Use the secret numbers to break the code and learn what the stars have planned for you. The numbers tell you which letter to place above the lines:

CODE					
A_1	B_2	C_3	D_4	E_5	F_6
G_7	H_8	I_9	L_{11}	M_{12}	N_{13}
O_{14}	P_{15}	Q_{16}	R_{17}	S_{18}	T_{19}
U_{20}	V_{21}	X_{22}	Y_{23}	Z_{24}	

1.
$\overline{12}\ \overline{20}\ \overline{11}\ \overline{19}\ \overline{1}\ \overline{18}$ $\overline{19}\ \overline{5}\ \overline{17}\ \overline{17}\ \overline{1}\ \overline{18}$ $\overline{9}\ \overline{13}$
$\overline{5}\ \overline{20}\ \overline{17}\ \overline{14}\ \overline{15}\ \overline{1}$ $\overline{5}\ \overline{19}$ $\overline{9}\ \overline{13}$
$\overline{1}\ \overline{18}\ \overline{9}\ \overline{1}$ $\overline{21}\ \overline{9}\ \overline{18}\ \overline{9}\ \overline{19}\ \overline{1}\ \overline{2}\ \overline{9}\ \overline{18}.$

2.
$\overline{6}\ \overline{1}\ \overline{12}\ \overline{9}\ \overline{11}\ \overline{9}\ \overline{1}$ $\overline{19}\ \overline{20}\ \overline{1}$ $\overline{19}\ \overline{5}$
$\overline{18}\ \overline{5}\ \overline{12}\ \overline{15}\ \overline{5}\ \overline{17}$ $\overline{1}\ \overline{12}\ \overline{1}\ \overline{2}\ \overline{9}\ \overline{19}.$

3.
$\overline{19}\ \overline{20}$ $\overline{14}\ \overline{12}\ \overline{13}\ \overline{9}\ \overline{1}$ $\overline{15}\ \overline{5}\ \overline{17}\ \overline{9}\ \overline{3}\ \overline{20}\ \overline{11}\ \overline{1}$
$\overline{21}\ \overline{9}\ \overline{19}\ \overline{1}\ \overline{5}$ $\overline{18}\ \overline{20}\ \overline{15}\ \overline{5}\ \overline{17}\ \overline{1}\ \overline{2}\ \overline{9}\ \overline{18}.$

4.
$\overline{19}\ \overline{20}$ $\overline{21}\ \overline{9}\ \overline{19}\ \overline{1}\ \overline{12}$ $\overline{11}\ \overline{14}\ \overline{13}\ \overline{7}\ \overline{1}\ \overline{12}$
$\overline{5}\ \overline{19}$ $\overline{6}\ \overline{5}\ \overline{11}\ \overline{9}\ \overline{3}\ \overline{5}\ \overline{12}$
$\overline{8}\ \overline{1}\ \overline{2}\ \overline{5}\ \overline{2}\ \overline{9}\ \overline{18}.$

5.
$\overline{1}\ \overline{11}\ \overline{9}\ \overline{16}\ \overline{20}\ \overline{1}\ \overline{13}\ \overline{4}\ \overline{14}$ $\overline{5}\ \overline{17}\ \overline{9}\ \overline{18}$
$\overline{15}\ \overline{5}\ \overline{17}\ \overline{18}\ \overline{14}\ \overline{13}\ \overline{1}$ $\overline{3}\ \overline{11}\ \overline{1}\ \overline{17}\ \overline{9}\ \overline{18}\ \overline{18}\ \overline{1}\ \overline{12}\ \overline{1}$
$\overline{3}\ \overline{11}\ \overline{1}\ \overline{18}\ \overline{18}\ \overline{9}$ $\overline{19}\ \overline{20}\ \overline{1}\ \overline{5}.$

F. How many of these items do you remember? Provide the Latin words; then read down the boxed column of letters to discover where these items can be seen:

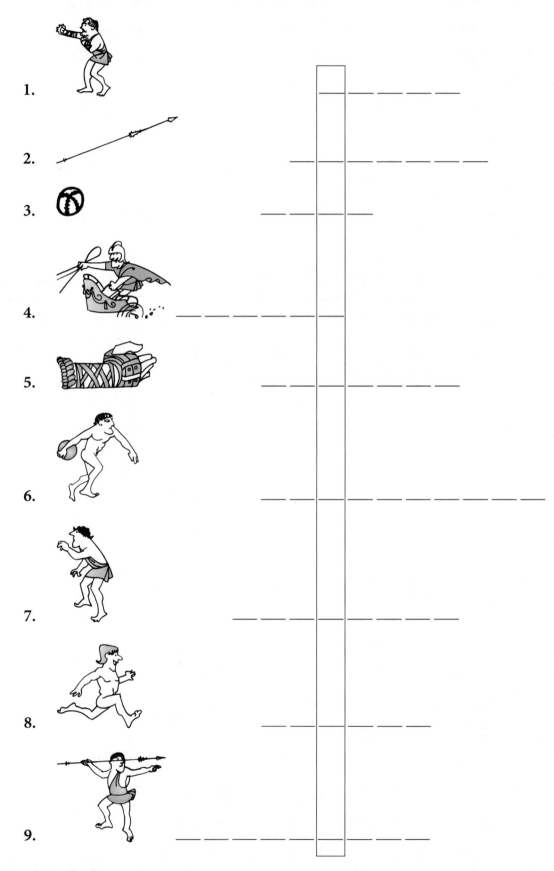

1. _ _ _ _ _ _

2. _ _ _ _ _ _

3. _ _ _ _

4. _ _ _ _ _ _ _

5. _ _ _ _ _ _

6. _ _ _ _ _ _ _ _ _

7. _ _ _ _ _ _ _

8. _ _ _ _ _

9. _ _ _ _ _ _

G. At the zoo, you notice that the zookeeper mixed up the letters on the labels for the animals. Unscramble the words to identify the animals. Next, unscramble the letters in the circles to learn what all animals have in common:

S I P A ⬡ ☐ ⬡ ☐

R E P A C ☐ ⬡ ☐ ☐ ☐

U M S U L ⬡ ☐ ☐ ☐ ☐

N E P T H A R A ☐ ☐ ⬡ ☐ ☐ ☐ ⬡

C L O R D O C I U S ☐ ☐ ☐ ☐ ☐ ☐ ⬡ ⬡ ☐ ☐

The secret word is: ☐ ☐ ☐ ☐ ☐ ☐ ☐ ☐ .

H. Picture story: You should have no trouble reading about this trip to Olympia. Whenever you see a picture, substitute the appropriate Latin word. Try to use the proper endings of the words you supply:

Marcus est [image] Rōmānus, tredecim annōs nātus.

Marcus et [image] Olympiam vīsitāre volunt.

Ab [image] ad [image] mense Augustō nāvigābunt.

Pater [image] et [image] spectāre vult. In Olympiā

nempe [image] nōn certant. Marcus autem [image]

et 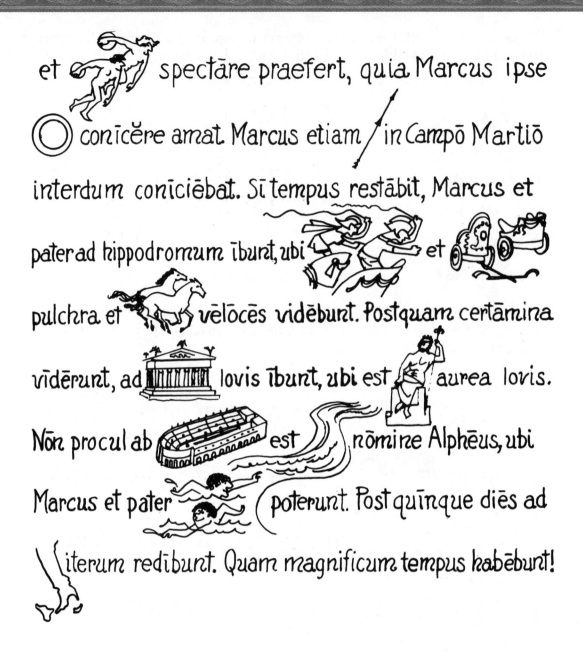 spectāre praefert, quia Marcus ipse

conīcĕre amat. Marcus etiam / in Campō Martiō

interdum conīciēbat. Sī tempus restābit, Marcus et

pater ad hippodromum ībunt, ubi et

pulchra et vēlōcēs vidēbunt. Postquam certāmina

vīdērunt, ad lovis ībunt, ubi est aurea lovis.

Nōn procul ab est nōmine Alphēus, ubi

Marcus et pater poterunt. Post quīnque diēs ad

iterum redībunt. Quam magnificum tempus habēbunt!

VOCĀBULA

nempe *of course*
autem *now*
ipse *himself*
restō –āre restitī *to remain, be left over*

hippodromus –ī *m racetrack,*
  hippodrome
iterum *again*

PARS SECUNDA

VI | Rōmulus et Remus

Relative Pronouns; Interrogative Adjectives

1 Modicum cultūrae

Some of the stories Roman children loved to hear told of the earliest days of Rome which, according to legend, was founded on April 21, 753 B.C. Although Rome was supposedly built on seven hills, the city began on the Palatine Hill, which the Romans called a mount (**mōns montis** *m*). Even Romans a mere 700 years later (in the time of Emperor Augustus) probably couldn't have imagined the vicinity of the Palatine, Capitoline, and Aventine hills without the buildings and paved roads that crowded the area.

The little valley at the foot of the Palatine and Capitoline hills began as a meadow, swampy much of the year. Later, this valley became the marketplace in which peasants set up booths (**taberna** *–ae f*) to sell their produce and wares. Later still, it became the Roman Forum, full of public buildings such as temples, courthouses (**basilica** *–ae f*), and the Senate building (**cūria** *–ae f*).

A second valley, between the Palatine and Aventine, became the Circus Maximus race track, the site of chariot races and a variety of other events. The cattle market (**forum boārium**) was established close to the Tiber River in the area between the Palatine and the Capitoline. Nearby, a simple wooden bridge spanned the Tiber.

Peasants and shepherds inhabited the Palatine Hill; their homes were primitive huts. Later this hill was the site of ancient Rome's most fashionable district, in which the rich built mansions and emperors, magnificent palaces. Today, tourists travel to see the ruins of these elaborate structures.

The Aventine Hill, later to become the residential quarter of poorer people, began as a grass-covered area dotted with clusters of trees.

The Capitoline Hill had two peaks. On one, Romans built the great temple to Jupiter. The other peak became a fortified citadel (**arx, arcis** *f*) in which people could take refuge in times of attack. Here was located the **augurāculum,** the official spot where the augur took auspices for the city. A dense cluster of trees filled the depression between the two peaks.

Beyond the Capitoline Hill, in a wide loop of the Tiber River, was a big open field called the **Campus Mārtius** (*Field of Mars*), which was used for military training and athletic exercise.

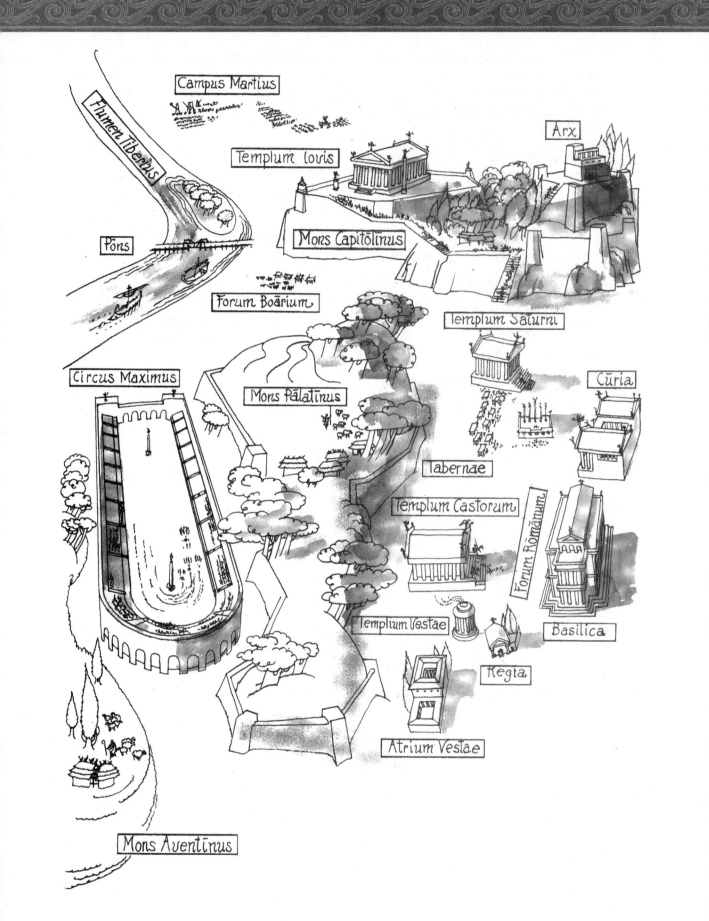

A. How many physical features of early Rome can you identify?

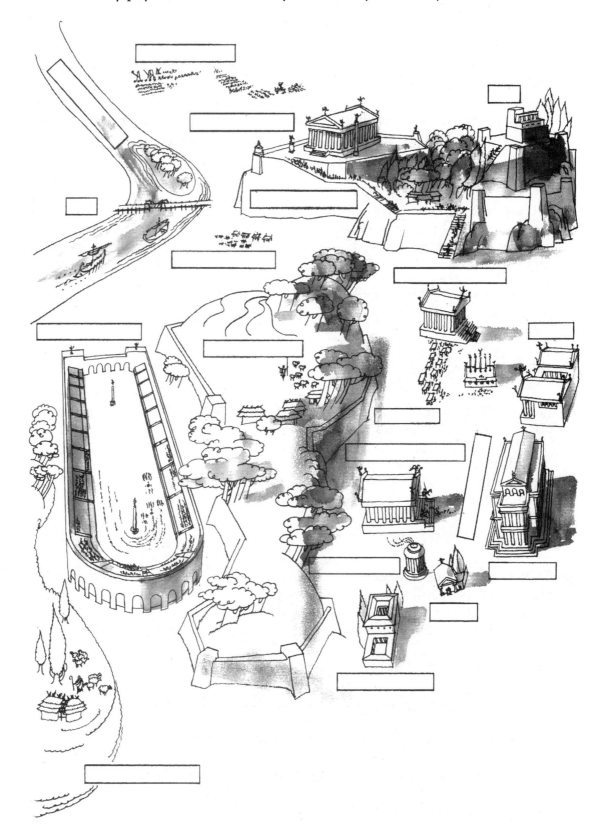

2 Before we read the legend of the founding of Rome, let's study RELATIVE PRONOUNS. A relative pronoun introduces a relative clause and relates back to a previous noun (the antecedent) in the sentence:

Gladiātor *quī fortiter pugnat* saepe victor est.

The gladiator who fights bravely is often the victor.

Quī is the relative pronoun; **gladiātor** is its antecedent. It's easy to tell where the relative clause begins and ends in Latin! It begins with the relative pronoun and ends with the verb. In English, we sometimes omit the relative pronoun: *Jason is the player* (*whom/that*) *I admire most.* That sentence still makes sense without the relative pronoun (*whom* or *that*). In Latin, though, the relative pronoun is *always* used; however, Romans sometimes omitted the *antecedent*!

Quī multam pecūniam habet multōs amīcōs habet.

(A person) who has a lot of money has a lot of friends.

Latin relative pronouns may be masculine (**quī** = *who/that*), feminine (**quae** = *who/that*), or neuter (**quod** = *which/that*). Remember, though, that in Latin things (to which we'd ordinarily refer as "it") can be masculine, feminine, or neuter (for example, **digitus** *m*; **coma** *f*; and **bracchium** *n*). Study the following sentence very carefully:

Gladiātor, quī in arēnā pugnāvit, rētiārium occīdit.

What is the relative pronoun in this sentence? Its antecedent? Its gender?

ĀCTIVITĀTĒS

B. Identify the gender of each of the following nouns before you write the relative pronoun you would use to refer to it:

1. gladius
2. lanista
3. hasta
4. scūtum
5. sīca
6. pater
7. māter
8. īnsectum
9. apis
10. castor

C. Copy the following sentences, inserting the appropriate relative pronouns. Then place brackets [ ] around each relative clause:

1. Bēstiāriī nōn timent leōnem _____ in arēnā est.

2. Apis est īnsectum _____ mel colligit.

3. Castor est animal _____ prope flūvium habitat.

4. Sciūrus _____ in arbore sedet nūcem edit.

5. Pāpiliō _____ in agrō nostrō est multōs colōrēs habet.

6. Ego numquam vīdī cervum _____ tam vēlōciter currĕre potest.

7. Amīcus meus in urbe habitat _____ prope flūmen sita est.

8. Gladiātor parmam gestāvit _____ gravissima erat.

9. Mihi nōn placet senātor _____ superbus est.

10. Arānea est īnsectum _____ tēlās texĕre potest.

3 The plural forms of relative pronouns are **quī, quae, quae.** Notice that the first two plurals (masculine and feminine) are identical to their singular forms. Only the neuter changes form. Remember that both the noun antecedent and the verb will indicate whether the pronoun is singular or plural.

ĀCTIVITĀS

D. Copy these sentences, inserting the correct forms of the plural relative pronouns. Then enclose the relative clauses in brackets [ ]:

1. Bēstiāriī _____ animālia timent in arēnā pugnāre nōn dēbent.

2. Formīcae sunt īnsecta _____ in cavernīs sub terrā habitant.

3. Vīdistīne umquam mannōs et equōs _____ in prātō sunt?

4. Sciūrī sunt animālia _____ arborēs facile ascendĕre possunt.

5. Pāpiliōnēs _____ veterrimī sunt volāre nōn possunt.

6. Pāpiliōnēs habent ālās _____ flāvae et rubrae et caeruleae sunt.

7. Ego mūlōs habeō _____ gravia onera portāre possunt.

8. Panthērae _____ in vīvāriō habitant nōn laetae sunt.

9. Bēstiāriī multa animālia occīdērunt _____ ex Āfricā vēnērunt.

10. Gladiātōrēs _____ ē lūdō Capuae fūgērunt contrā Rōmānōs pugnāvērunt.

4 Earlier, you learned about interrogative pronouns and often saw them in sentences. What is Latin word for the interrogative pronoun *who*? The pronoun *what*? Did you know that, as you learned the relative pronouns **quī, quae, quod,** you also learned the INTERROGATIVE ADJECTIVES?

Q*uī* vēnātor leōnem occīdit?	*Which hunter killed the lion?*
Q*uae* soror est maxima nātū?	*Which sister is the oldest?*
Q*uod* animal tēlās texit?	*Which animal spins cobwebs?*

Latin uses the plural interrogative adjectives (**quī, quae, quae**) in the same way.

ĀCTIVITĀS

E. Some of these sentences require singular interrogative adjectives, while some need the plural forms. Write the correct form of interrogative adjective for each of the following:

1. _____ senātor est iūdex?

2. _____ homō amīcum nōn adiuvat?

3. _____ animal per tōtam hiemem dormit?

4. _____ animālia in aquā habitant?

5. _____ fēmina novam vestem nōn amat?

6. _____ fundus equōs et vaccās nōn habet?

7. _____ augur futūra praedīcĕre nōn potest?

8. _____ urbs prope Tiberim Flūmen iacet?

9. _____ montēs prope forum sunt?

10. _____ pīstor pānem tuum facit?

5 So far, we've worked with relative pronouns in the nominative case. Let's see what these pronouns look like in the accusative case:

	SINGULAR	PLURAL
NOM.	**quī** (*who*), **quae** (*who*), **quod** (*which*)	**quī** (*who*), **quae** (*who*), **quae** (*which*)
ACC.	**quem** (*whom*), **quam** (*whom*), **quod** (*which*)	**quōs** (*whom*), **quās** (*whom*), **quae** (*which*)

As usual, the neuter accusative form is the same as the nominative. Did you also notice that some of the accusative endings are the same as noun endings you already know? Which three forms in the accusative case (singular or plural) have the same endings as their corresponding nouns?

ACTIVITĀTĒS

F. Nominative or accusative? Read the sentences carefully. Then write down the correct form of each relative pronoun:

1. Quis cēpit sciūrum (quī/quem) in hortō nostrō fuit?

2. Mannus (quī/quem) in prātō est vēlōciter currĕre potest.

3. Leopardus (quī/quem) vēnātōrēs in monte cēpērunt ferōcissimus est.

4. Medicus fēminam sānāvit (quae/quam) dolōrem dentis habuit.

5. Pars corporis (per quae/per quam) audīmus est auris.

6. Augur (quī/quem) senātōrēs cōnsultāvērunt est astūtus.

7. Nōs omnēs hominem amāmus (quī/quem) benignus est.

8. Urbs (per quae/per quam) Tiberis Flūmen fluit est Rōma.

9. Via (quae/quam) per Forum Rōmānum currit est Via Sacra.

10. Vir (quī/quem) ante Iovis templum in Monte Capitōlīnō vīdī est augur.

G. Singular or plural? First, copy these sentences, inserting the correct relative pronouns in the accusative case. Then, place brackets around each relative clause:

1. Astrologus _____ Augustus cōnsultāvit ex Graeciā vēnit.

2. Stellae _____ in caelō vīdimus sunt clārae et pulchrae.

3. Gladiātōrēs _____ Spartacus in arēnā occīdit geminī erant.

4. Scūtum _____ Spartacus gestāvit oblongum erat.

5. Vīdistīne tabernās _____ Rōmānī in forō aedificāvērunt?

6. Montēs inter _____ Circus Maximus iacet sunt Palātīnus et Aventīnus.

7. Templum _____ augurēs vīsitant in arce stat.

8. Pōns _____ Rōmānī fabricāvērunt trāns Tiberim in Etrūriam dūcit.

9. Numqam vīdī novam basilicam _____ Rōmānī aedificāvērunt.

10. Aedificium _____ senātōrēs cōtīdiē intrant est cūria.

Let's read one of the most popular legends of early Rome. As you read, pay particular attention to the relative pronouns. Some are in the ablative case. Although we haven't learned about this case yet, see if they cause you any problem. If they do, feel free to complain to your teacher!

Rōmulus et Remus geminī erant. Eōrum māter erat Rhea Silvia, et eōrum pater erat Mārs, quī deus bellī erat. Eōrum avus erat Numitor, quī rēx Albae Longae erat. Ēius frāter, Amūlius, autem Numitōrem ē rēgnō expulit et ipse rēgnum occupāvit.

Amūlius, quia filiōs Rheae Silviae timuit, eam Virginem Vestālem fēcit; geminōs autem in arcā inclūsit et in flūmen Tiberim iniēcit. Sed arca quae geminōs continēbat, ad rīpam fluitāvit. Iupiter enim, quī omnia videt, geminōs servāre voluit. Lupa, quae forte dē Monte Aventīnō dēscendit, īnfantēs invēnit et eōs lacte suō nūtrīvit. Lupa eōs sīcut catulōs suōs prōtēxit.

Post paucōs diēs Faustulus, quī pāstor erat et in Monte Palātīnō habitābat, ad illum locum vēnit in quō īnfantēs dormiēbant. Faustulus, quī vir benignus erat, īnfantēs ad casam suam in Montem Palātinum tulit. Faustulus īnfantēs Rōmulum et Remum nōmināvit. Faustulus et uxor ēius, Laurentia, geminōs libenter ēducāvērunt. Puerī vītam fēlīcem sine cūrīs dūcēbant. Modō in Monte Aventīnō, modō in Monte Capitōlīnō lūdēbant; et modō in valle, quae inter montēs iacet, lūdēbant. Saepe lupam vīdērunt quae īnfantēs nūtriēbat. Lupa autem semper amīca eīs fuit.

Post multōs annōs, geminī urbem novam condĕre volēbant in illō locō in quō Faustulus et Laurentia eōs ēducāvērunt. Sed prius necesse erat ōmen prosperum petĕre. Itaque Rōmulus in Monte Palātinō inaugurāvit. Remus autem in Monte Aventīnō inaugurāvit. Ōmen prīmum Remō ēvēnit, nam sex vulturēs per ēius templum in caelō volāvērunt. Remus exultāvit et clāmāvit: "Ego hīc in Monte Aventīnō novam urbem condam. Et populus faciet mē prīmum rēgem."

Tunc maximē Rōmulus, quī in Monte Palātīnō sedēbat, duodecim vulturēs in suō templō observāvit. "Ecce," inquit Rōmulus, "duplicem numerum vulturum observāvī; itaque ego urbem novam condam, et urbs nōmen meum accipiet. Ego prīmus rēx urbis erō. Circum

Alba Longa *–ae f hill town southeast of Rome*
rēgnum *–ī n kingdom, royal power*
  expellō *–ĕre* **expulī expulsus** *to expel*
  ipse *himself*
Virgō Vestālis *Vestal Virgin*
  arcā *–ae f chest*
includō *–ĕre* **inclūsī inclūsus** *to lock up, enclose*
  inīciō *–ĕre* **iniēci iniectus** *to throw into*
contineō *–ēre –ui* **contentus** *to contain*
  rīpa *–ae f bank*
  fluitō *–āre –āvī –ātus to float*
lupa *–ae f she-wolf*
  forte *by chance*
nūtriō *–īre –ī(v)ī –ītus to nourish, to nurse*
sīcut *just as*
  catulus *–ī m cub*
pāstor *–ōris m shepherd*
ferō ferre tulī lātus *to bring, take*
nōminō *–āre –āvi –ātis to name*
libenter *gladly*
ēducō *–āre –āvi –ātis to raise*
  vītam dūcere *to lead a life*
  cūra *–ae f care, worry*
modō ... modō *sometimes ... sometimes*
vallēs *–is f valley*
amīcus *–a –um friendly*
condō *–dĕre –didī –ditus to found*
prius *adv first*
prosperus *–a –um favorable*
inaugurō *–āre –āvī –ātus to look for an omen*
ōmen *–inis n omen*
eveniō *–īre* **ēvēnī eventum** *to occur*
nam *conj for*
  templum *–ī n a space in the sky marked off for taking omens*
exultō *–āre –āvī –ātus to jump for joy*
tunc maximē *just then*
ecce *look*
  inquit *(he, she) says*
duplex, duplicis *double*
circum *(+ acc) around*

Montem Palātīnum ego dūcam mūrum, quī urbem novam prōteget."

Sīc contrōversia amāra inter frātrēs geminōs exārsit, deinde īra, dēnique caedēs, nam Rōmulus frātrem gladiō necāvit et urbem ā sē nōmināvit. Rōmulus multōs annōs Rōmae rēgnāvit et post ēius mortem in caelum ascendit et fīēbat deus. Nōmen ēius in caelō est Quirīnus.

mūrum dūcĕre *to build a wall*
prōtegō –tegĕre –tēxī –tēctus
  to protect
amārus –a –um *bitter*
exārdēscō –ĕre exārsī *to flare up*
  caedēs –is *f murder*
ā sē *after himself*
rēgnō –āre –āvī –ātus (+ *dat*) *to*
  rule over
fīēbat *he became*
  caelum –ī *n heaven*

ĀCTIVITĀS

H. Respond in complete Latin sentences to these questions about the story you just read:

1. Quī erant parentēs geminōrum?

2. Quis erat Rōmulī et Remī avus?

3. Quis erat Numitōris frāter malus?

4. Cūr Amūlius geminōs occīdĕre voluit?

5. Quī deus geminōs servāre voluit?

6. Quis geminōs lacte suō nūtrīvit?

7. Quis Rōmulum et Remum ēducāvit?

8. In quō monte Remus inaugurāvit?

9. In quō monte Rōmulus inaugurāvit?

10. Quis erat prīmus rēx Rōmae?

 It's time to look at the ablative case of the relative pronouns. What is the ablative ending of a masculine noun of the second declension, such as **amīcus?** Of a first-declension feminine noun, such as **stella?** Of a second-declension neuter noun, such as **scūtum?**

These endings also appear in the ablative singular of relative pronouns. The ablative plural forms (masculine, feminine, and neuter) are the same: **quibus.** Below is a summary of what we know at this point about relative pronoun endings:

	MASCULINE	FEMININE	NEUTER
SINGULAR			
NOM.	**quī** (*who*)	**quae** (*who*)	**quod** (*which*)
ACC.	**quem** (*whom*)	**quam** (*whom*)	**quod** (*which*)
ABL.	**quō** (*whom*)	**quā** (*whom*)	**quō** (*which*)

(continued)

	MASCULINE	FEMININE	NEUTER
	PLURAL		
NOM.	quī (who)	quae (who)	quae (which)
ACC.	quōs (whom)	quās (whom)	quae (which)
ABL.	quibus (whom)	quibus (whom)	quibus (which)

A preposition often, but not always, precedes the ablative case. Remember that the ablative of means does not use a preposition:

Collis *in quō* Rōmulus vulturēs observāvit erat Palātīnus.
The hill on which Romulus observed the vultures was the Palatine.

Diēs *quō* Rōmulus Rōmam condidit est fēstus diēs.
The day on which Romulus founded Rome is a holiday.

Tēlum *quō* Rōmulus Remum necāvit erat gladius.
The weapon with which Romulus killed Remus was a sword.

Pars corporis *quā* vidēmus est oculus.
The part of the body with which we see is the eye.

How observant are you? Did you notice that the pronoun **quō** used no preposition in the second and third sentences? You probably realized that **quō** in both sentences was the ablative of means or instrument!

What is the gender of **quō** in the first sentence? In the second sentence? Third? Fourth? In sentence 4, what is the antecedent of **quā?**

ĀCTIVITĀTĒS

I. Copy these sentences, adding the correct forms of the relative pronouns in the ablative case:

1. Oppidum in _____ Numitor rēgnāvit (*ruled*), erat Alba Longa.

2. Parentēs ex _____ Rōmulus et Remus nātī sunt erant Mars et Rhea Silvia.

3. Arca in _____ Amūlius geminōs inclūsit ad flūminis rīpam fluitāvit.

4. Flūmen in _____ arca fluitāvit erat Tiberis.

5. Mōns in _____ Faustulus habitāvit erat Palātīnus.

6. Collis dē _____ lupa dēscendit erat Aventīnus.

7. Locus in _____ lupa geminōs nūtrīvit nōn procul ā Palātīnō aberat.

8. Casa in _____ Faustulus et Laurentia puerōs ēducāvērunt, in Monte Palātīnō erat.

9. Vallēs in _____ geminī lūdēbant nunc est Forum Rōmānum.

10. Casae in _____ pastōrēs habitābant erant parvae et simplicēs.

J. The antecedent doesn't always appear immediately before a relative pronoun in a Latin sentence. Carefully review the following sentences to identify the antecedents. Write each antecedent and the proper form of its relative pronoun:

> EXAMPLE: **Partēs** corporis **quibus** videmus sunt oculi nostri.
>
> *The parts of the body with which we see are our eyes.*

1. Gladiātor bracchium suum mihi exhibuit in _____ vulnus grave fuit.

2. Scīsne signum zōdiacī circulī sub _____ ego sum nāta?

3. Apēs aculeum habent _____ īcĕre (*to sting*) possunt.

4. Trēs puerī in Albā Longā erant cum _____ ego lūdēbam.

5. Pastōrēs arcam in flūmine vīdērunt in _____ geminī dormiēbant.

6. Rōmulus frātrem suum occīdit cum _____ contrōversiam habēbat.

7. Arachnē erat puella superba et arrogāns cum _____ Minerva certāvit.

8. Claudia digitum manūs sinistrae mihi exhibuit in _____ ānulum aureum gestābat.

8 Read to discover how Romulus doubled the population of his new city in record time:

Rōma, quae iam oppidum magnum et validum erat, perpaucōs cīvēs adhūc habuit. Itaque Rōmulus fugitīvōs undique in oppidum novum invītāvit et asȳlum eīs dedit in Monte Capitōlīnō. Multī agricolae pastōrēsque ex agrīs ad novum oppidum convēnērunt. Casās in Monte Capitōlīnō aedificāvērunt. Etiam ovīlia prō ovibus suīs aedificāvērunt in valle quae inter Capitōlīnum et Palātīnum iacēbat. Rōmulus eōs omnēs fēcit cīvēs Rōmānōs.

Sed nōndum uxōrēs habēbant. Ergo Rōmulus Sabīnōs quī in oppidīs vīcīnīs habitābant ad lūdōs invītāvit. "Venīte," inquit Rōmulus, "ad nostrum oppidum novum. Splendidōs lūdōs ēdam. Hospitālitātem Rōmānam vōbīs adhibēbō. Et adferte uxōrēs filiāsque vestrās."

iam *by now*
perpaucī –ae –a *very few*
  cīvis –is m *citizen*
  adhūc *till now*
undique *from all around*
asȳlum –ī n *refuge, asylum*
ex agrīs *from the countryside*
ovīle –is n *sheepfold*
ovis –is f *sheep*

nōndum *not yet*
Sabīnī –ōrum m pl *Sabines, a hill tribe near Rome*
  vīcīnus –a um *neighboring*
  lūdī –ōrum m pl *public games*
ēdō –ĕre ēdidī ēditus *to provide, put on*
adhibeō –ēre –uī –itus *to show*
adferō –ferre –tulī –lātus *to bring along*

Magna multitūdō Sabīnōrum ad lūdōs vēnit. Rōmānī eōs benignē excēpērunt. In valle quae inter Palātīnum et Aventīnum iacet cōnsīdēbant, in quā Circus Maximus nunc est. Rōmānī et Sabīnī lūdōs attentē aspiciēbant cum subitō Rōmulus signum dedit. Iuvenēs Rōmānī ex sēdibus exsiluērunt; virginēs Sabīnās rapuērunt; eās ad casās suās portāvērunt et eās in mātrimōnium dūxērunt.

Trīstēs parentēs virginum timōre in oppida sua refūgērunt. Sed post aliquot annōs, Sabīnī Rōmānīs bellum indīxērunt. Sabīnī cum Rōmānīs diū et ācriter pugnāvērunt in valle in quā nunc Forum Rōmānum est. Subitō fēminae Sabīnae inter īnfestās aciēs cucurrērunt. Hinc marītōs hinc patrēs suōs ōrāvērunt: "Marītī, nōlīte necāre patrēs nostrōs!" Et "Patrēs, nōlīte pugnāre cum vestrīs generīs!"

Repentīnum silentium fuit. Deinde dūcēs utrimque prōdiērunt. Nōn modō pācem fēcērunt, sed etiam ūnam cīvitātem ex duābus creāvērunt.

benignē *warmly* **excipiō –ĕre excēpī exceptus** *to welcome*
cōnsīdō –ĕre cōnsēdī cōnsessum *to sit down*
aspiciō –ĕre aspexī aspectus *to watch*
cum subitō *when suddenly*
iuvenis –is *m young man*
  sēdēs –is *f seat*
exsiliō –īre –uī *to jump up*
  virgō –inis *f girl*
  rapiō –ĕre –uī –tus *to seize, kidnap*
in mātrimōnium dūcĕre *to marry*
timōre *out of fear*
refugiō –ĕre refūgī *to flee back*
indīcō –ĕre indīxī indictus (+ *dat*) *to declare* (*war*) *on*
diū et acriter *long and hard*
īnfestus –a –um *hostile*
  aciēs –ēī *f battle line*
hinc ... hinc *on one side ... on the other side*
  marītus –ī *m husband*
  ōrō –āre –āvī –ātus *to beg*
gener –ī *m son-in-law*
repentīnus –a –um *sudden*
  silentium –ī *n silence*
utrimque *from both sides*
  prōdeō –īre –ii *to step forward*
  nōn modō ... sed etiam *not only. . . but also*
  pax pācis *f peace*
cīvitās –ātis *f state*
creō –āre –āvī –ātus *to create*

ĀCTIVITĀS

K. Respondē ad quaestiōnēs:

1. Quid Rōmulus fugitīvīs dedit?

2. Ubi Rōmulus asȳlum dedit?

3. Quid in valle inter Capitolīnum et Palātīnum aedificāvērunt?

4. Cūr Rōmulus Sabīnōs ad lūdōs invītāvit?

5. Ubi Rōmānī et Sabīnī lūdōs aspexērunt?

6. Quis signum iuvenibus Rōmānīs dedit?

7. Quis virginēs Sabīnās rapuit?

8. Quō (*where*) Rōmānī virginēs portāvērunt?

9. Quis bellum Rōmānīs īndixit?

10. Quis inter īnfestās aciēs cucurrit?

Faustulus and Laurentia might have had this conversation when the twins were found:

VOCĀBULA

mūnusculum –ī *n gift*
conīciō –ĕre **coniēcī coniectus** *to guess*
sit (*it*) *is*

fīliolus –ī *m baby boy*
aliquis *somebody*
cicōnia –ae *f stork*
afferō afferre attulī allātus
    to bring

Colloquium

Complete this dialog based on the conversation. Try to make small changes of your own:

1. In quā urbe habitās?

2. Estne urbs magna an parva?

3. Estne flūmen prope urbem tuam?

4. Quot scholae in urbe tuā sunt?

5. Quot hominēs in tuā urbe habitant?

6. Praefers habitāre in urbe vetere an novā?

7. Quae urbs est optima in tōtō orbe terrārum?

Compositiō

Some of the most interesting stories about Rome come from the time when the city was just a small town of farmers and shepherds. In your own words, retell something about Romulus and Remus.

THE LATIN CONNECTION

A. Which English word derives from **hospitālitās?** What is the genitive form of this feminine noun?

All Latin words ending in *–itās* are feminine abstract nouns. (Abstract nouns, such as *virtue* and *goodness,* cannot be seen with the eyes or felt with the hands; instead, they are concepts understood in the mind.) From Latin nouns ending in *–itās* come English nouns that end in *–ity.*

B. Write the English derivative of each of these Latin nouns:

1. **ūnitās** *–ātis f* (from **ūnus**)

2. **sānitās** *–ātis f* (from **sānus**)

3. **mortālitās** *–ātis f* (from **mortālis**)

4. **nōbilitās** *–ātis f* (from **nōbilis**)

5. **sēcūritās** *–ātis f* (from **sēcūrus**)

C. As shown above, each Latin abstract noun derives from a Latin adjective. Can you write the definitions of the following?

1. ūnus
2. sānus
3. mortālis
4. nōbilis
5. sēcūrus

D. Other words come from **ūnus**: unanimous (being of one mind), unison (being of one sound), universal (all turned to one). Can you write the definitions of the following English words that derive from **ūnus?**

1. unicorn
2. uniform
3. unify
4. union
5. uniparental
6. unique
7. unit
8. united

E. What does the phrase **ē plūribus ūnum** mean?

F. Write three other English words that end in –*ity*. Indicate their Latin sources.

G. What English derivatives come from these Latin words? (Some Latin words have more than one English derivative. List as many as you can.)

1. nūtrīre
2. ēducāre
3. inaugurāre
4. exultāre
5. nōmināre
6. creāre
7. continēre
8. indicāre

VII | Medicīna et valētūdō

Pluperfect Tense

1 Modicum cultūrae

You may be surprised to learn that Rome had no doctors for the first five hundred years of its existence. No public hospitals existed. The sick were cured with herbs, or they died. The ancients, always experimenting with herbs for their healing value, handed down knowledge of this herbal medicine, mixed with a bit of witchcraft and magic, from father to son. Anyone could practice medicine since there were no medical schools or regulatory organizations to oversee the sale of medicines and drugs. Quacks (medical frauds; those pretending to have extensive medical knowledge) often enjoyed great popularity in Rome.

Ancient Roman knowledge of the human body was primitive by our standards. Consider these widespread beliefs of the time about the human body: The liver is the seat of love. The heart is the seat of intelligence. Hatred finds its seat in bile, while pride comes from the lungs. Laughter stems from the spleen and anger from the brain. The Romans had no idea that blood circulated through the body. That discovery was made in the eighteenth century.

When doctors from Greece and the Near East finally arrived in Rome, they had little prestige. Many were slaves or men of lower classes. The first doctors to permanently reside in Rome came from Greece in 219 B.C. Many doctors quickly accumulated huge fortunes, but their wealth did not usually bring them respect and dignity. The Romans never completely lost their prejudice against doctors. The learned Roman scholar Marcus Terentius Varro, who was in charge of the library of Emperor Augustus, ranked doctors in the same category with dyers and blacksmiths.

Wealthy families with large numbers of slaves often had their own doctor in residence. Some had male and female medical slaves as well as an infirmary. Not until the fourth century did the state provide scientific training for those who would become public doctors. (The state, however, did not require these doctors to pass exams or get degrees.) Public doctors were required to try to heal all who consulted them; the poor received their services free of charge. Private doctors could practice as they pleased.

Yet, the Roman ideal was **"mēns sāna in corpore sānō"** (*"a sound mind in a sound body"*). Both the Roman people and their doctors believed that most illness could be overcome with proper diet and exercise, although they treated some sicknesses with medicinal herbs. The Romans stressed good health (**valētūdō** *–inis f*). Their usual expression for goodbye—**"Valē!"** or "Be in good health!"—was proof of their commitment to health. Truthfully, the old expression *farewell* more closely reflects what the Romans intended than the word *goodbye*.

Before you learn the new vocabulary in Section 2, see if you remember body part names from your first course in Latin:

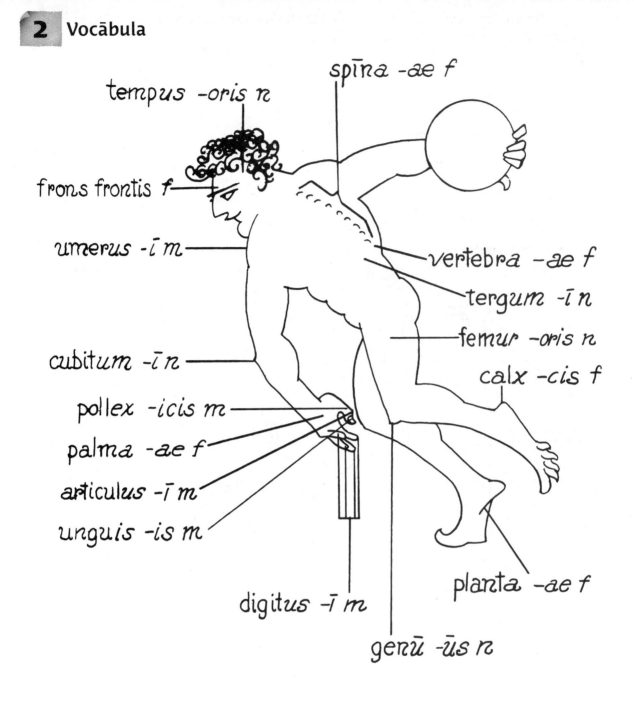

spīna -ae f

tempus -oris n

frons frontis f

umerus -ī m

vertebra -ae f

tergum -ī n

femur -oris n

cubitum -ī n

calx -cis f

pollex -icis m

palma -ae f

articulus -ī m

unguis -is m

digitus -ī m

genū -ūs n

planta -ae f

ĀCTIVITĀTĒS

A. What tool could ancient Romans use to measure things? It had to be something everyone had. It had to be convenient. They found just the thing: body parts! Can you write the Latin word for each of the following handy body parts?

1. finger
2. hand
3. elbow
4. foot

B. How good are you at recognizing the Latin words for body parts? In the following sentences you'll have to know the genitive case to identify the words:

EXAMPLE: Digitus est pars **manūs.**

1. Palma est pars _____.

2. Frōns est pars _____.

3. Vertebra est pars _____.

4. Femur est pars _____.

5. Pollex est pars _____.

6. Calx est pars _____.

7. Cubitum est pars _____.

8. Spīna est pars _____.

9. Genū est pars _____.

10. Unguis est pars _____.

11. Planta est pars _____.

12. Tempus est pars _____.

C. Using your knowledge of anatomy, write the word that completes each sentence:

1. Spīna est in _____.

2. Digitī sunt in _____.

3. Femur est in _____.

4. Frōns est in _____.

5. Pollex est in _____.

6. Labra sunt in _____.

7. Cubitum est in _____.

8. Oculī sunt in _____.

9. Calx est in _____.

10. Vertebrae sunt in _____.

11. Palma est in _____.

12. Tempora sunt in _____.

13. Aurēs sunt in _____.

14. Coma est in _____.

15. Dentēs sunt in _____.

D. As a Roman doctor, your task is to explain the parts of the body to a group of medical students. Write the names of the body parts to complete this chart:

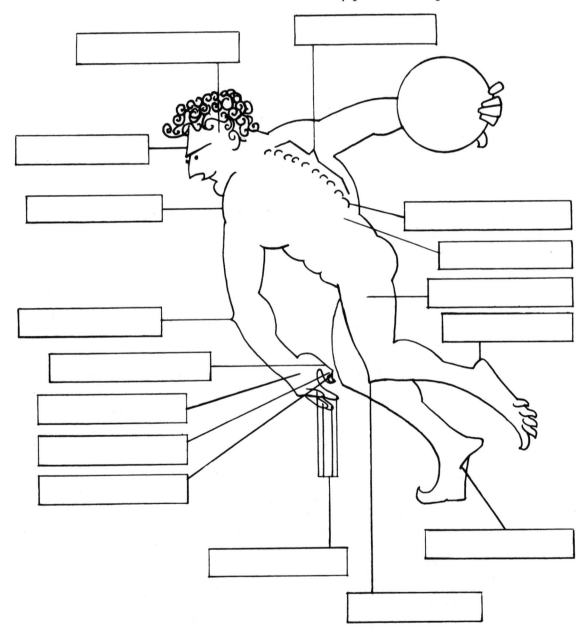

3 Most likely, you've seen a post-game TV interview of a winning athlete. Read this interview in the "locker room" (**cella** *–ae* f) of a Roman gladiator:

SCAENA: In cellā sub amphitheātrō. Vulnerātus gladiātor in lectō iacet post pugnam in arēnā. Nōmen gladiātōris est Thrāx. Medicus Graecus intrat.

MEDICUS: Quid est tibi, Thrāx?

THRĀX: In novissimā pugnā ego multa vulnera accēpī. Tōtum corpus meum dolet. Bracchia dolent; crūra dolent; tergum dolet. Crēde mihi, medice, fatīgātus sum.

MEDICUS: Exue tunicam tuam et exhibē mihi tua vulnera.

THRĀX: Multa vulnera in corpore meō sunt. Est ūnum vulnus in fronte meā, alium in tempore dextrō, quattuor vulnera in pectore. Ecce, tōtum corpus meum est cruentum!

MEDICUS: Ita, Thrāx. Et habēs alia vulnera: ūnum in femore, ūnum in umerō. Et ūnum in genū sinistrō videō.

THRĀX: Nōn vulnera sōlum habeō sed etiam tumōrēs.

MEDICUS: Tumōrēs in bracchiīs et umerīs videō. Tōtum quidem bracchium sinistrum tumidum est.

THRĀX: Poterisne mea vulnera sānāre? Habēsne remedia prō vulneribus et tumōribus meīs?

MEDICUS: Sānē. Vulnera et tumōrēs sānāre possum. Herbās et medicīnās et fasciās prō istīs vulneribus habeō. Vulnera in pectore tuō gravissima sunt. Sīc victō saepe contingit.

THRĀX: Medice, nōn sum victus; ego victor in certāmine eram. Vulnera et tumōrēs adversāriī meī vidēre dēbēs. Iste habet multō plūra vulnera quam ego. Habet vulnera ubīque, etiam in tergō!

vulnerātus *–a –um* wounded

Quid est tibi? *What's wrong with you?*
novissimus *–a –um* latest
vulnus *–eris* n wound
　tōtus *–a –um* whole
　doleō *–ēre –uī* to hurt
fatīgātus *–a –um* exhausted
exhibeō *–ēre –uī –itus* to show

pectus *–oris* n chest, breast
cruentus *–a –um* bloody

tumor *–ōris* m swelling, lump

quidem *in fact*
　tumidus *–a –um* swollen, puffed up
sānō *–āre –āvī –ātus* to heal

herba *–ae* f herb
　fascia *–ae* f bandage
gravis *–is –e* serious
sīc contingit (+ dat) *that's what happens*
　victus *–ī* m loser
certāmen *–inis* n contest
　adversārius *–ī* m opponent
iste *that guy*
　multō plūra *many more*
ubīque *everywhere*

E. Respondē ad hās quaestiōnēs:

1. Ubi est gladiātor?
2. Quandō gladiātor vulnera accēpit?
3. Quot vulnera gladiātor in capite habet?
4. Quot vulnera gladiātor in crūribus habet?
5. Ubi sunt tumōrēs?
6. Quae pars corporis est omnīnō (*entirely*) tumida?
7. Ubi sunt vulnera gravissima?
8. Quae remedia habet medicus?
9. Estne gladiātor victus an victor?
10. Quis habet vulnera in tergō?

F. As a Roman doctor, you must diagnose your patients by matching the statements with your patients' pictures:

Dolōrem tergī habet.

Pollex est fractus.

Sunt vulnera in femore et genū.

Planta et calx sunt īnflammātae.

Trēs vertebrae spīnae sunt īnflammātae.

Est vulnus in tempore dextrō.

Palma sinistrae manūs est tumida.

Oculī sunt īnflammātī.

Tumōrem in fronte habet.

Cubitum est tumidum.

8. 9. 10.

4 So far, you have learned about verbs in the present, imperfect, future, and perfect tenses. There is another verb tense that occurs from time to time: the PAST PERFECT (also called the PLUPERFECT). This tense is very easy to form! Simply add the past tense of **sum** to the perfect stem of any verb (that is, the third principal part of a verb minus the personal ending):

pugnāv- + **-eram**   *I had fought*   **pugnāv-** + **-erāmus**   *we had fought*
pugnāv- + **-erās**   *you had fought*   **pugnāv-** + **-erātis**   *you had fought*
pugnāv- + **-erat**   *he/she/it had fought* **pugnāv-** + **-erant**   *they had fought*

The pluperfect tense refers to a past action that happened *prior to* another past action:

Medicus sānāvit gladiātōrem quem rētiārius *vulnerāverat*.
The doctor healed the gladiator whom the net man had wounded.

In this sentence, which action took place first: the healing or the wounding?

If you answered *the wounding*, you are right. The verb **vulnerāverat** is in the pluperfect tense. You might say the pluperfect is the "double past" tense!

ĀCTIVITĀTĒS

G. Change the verbs in these sentences from the perfect to the pluperfect tense:

1. Cursor crūs frēgit.
2. Rētiāri tridentēs in umerīs portāvērunt.
3. Medicus vulnus in pectore sānāvit.
4. Avia dolōrem articulōrum (*arthritis*) habuit.
5. Nōs dolōrēs capitis habuimus.
6. Bēstiārī vulnera in pectore accēpērunt.
7. Nōnne magnōs clāmōrēs in arēnā audīvistis?
8. Puella avem in palmā manūs suae tenuit.
9. Geminī in Monte Palātīnō diū habitāvērunt.
10. Lupa geminōs nūtrīvit.

H. Complete the following sentences by writing the correct pluperfect form of each verb in parentheses:

1. (inīcĕre) Arca, quam Amūlius in flūmen _____, ad rīpam fluitāvit.

2. (esse) Amūlius Numitōrem expulit ex urbe, in quā multōs annōs

   _____ rēx.

3. (invenīre) Lupa nūtrīvit geminōs, quōs prope flūmen _____.

4. (portāre) Laurentia īnfantēs ēducāvit, quōs Faustulus domum

   _____.

5. (observāre) Mōns in quō Remus vulturēs _____ erat Aventīnus.

6. (lūdĕre) Rōmulus urbem condidit in colle in quō ut puer

   _____.

7. (servāre) Geminī nōn timuērunt lupam quae eōs _____.

8. (capĕre) Iuvenēs quī virginēs Sabīnās _____ erant Rōmānī.

9. (dare) Nōn sumpsī medicīnam quam medicus mihi _____.

10. (accipĕre) Medicus sānāvit vulnus quod Thrāx in certāmine

    _____.

11. (cūrāre) Medicus quī familiam meam _____ in Graeciam trānsiit.

12. (venīre) Ille gladiātor quī ex Thrāciā _____ fortiter in arēnā certāvit.

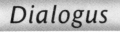

VOCĀBULA

tam *adv so*
pallidus –a –um *pale*
febris –is *f fever*

continuus –a –um *continuous*
gravēdō –inis *f a cold*
probātiō –ōnis *f test*

Compositiō

You are a doctor making hospital rounds. Ask three of your patients to describe why they're in the hospital. Be sure to record your questions and your patients' answers, as doctors always do. If, instead, you want to more thoroughly examine just one patient, ask that patient three questions and record his or her responses.

Quaestiōnēs Persōnālēs

1. Habēsne mentem sānam in corpore sānō?
2. Quot tempora habēs?
3. Quot umerōs habēs?
4. Quot digitōs pedis habēs?
5. Quot pollicēs habēs?
6. Quō tempore annī habēs gravēdinēs?
7. Quandō febrem continuam habēs, vīsitāsne medicum?
8. Praefersne dolōrem capitis dolōrī stomachī?
9. Nōnne scholam ob valētūdinem malam omīsistī?
10. Quotiēns (*how often*) omīsistī scholam annō novissimō ob valētūdinem malam?

Colloquium

Write your own Latin answers in the following conversation:

Salvē. Quid agis hodiē?

_____
_____
(Say that you are sick.)

Quid est tibi? Cūr tam tristis es? Habēsne dolōrem capitis?

_____
_____
(Respond negatively. Say that your stomach hurts.)

Ego medicīnam adferre possum aut medicum vocāre possum.

_____
_____
(Say that you don't need a doctor.)

Quōmōdo tē adjuvāre possum?

_____
_____
(Supply your own answer.)

THE LATIN CONNECTION

A. Answer these questions about words derived from Latin:

1. Where would you find the *pectoral* muscle?

2. Where is a *temporal* bone located?

3. When you *genuflect,* what part of the body do you bend?

4. With which part of the body do you indicate single *digits*?

5. What are *audio-visual* aids?

6. What is an *oral* examination?

7. Where would you find a *femoral* artery?

8. What kind of work is *manual* labor?

9. What is a *cordial* greeting?

10. From which part of the body does a *nasal* sound originate?

11. Which part of your body do you place on a *pedal*?

12. What kind of punishment is *corporal* punishment?

13. What is another word for *vertebral* column?

14. When two people *confront* each other, which body parts are facing?

15. Where would you find the *humeral* bone?

B. Many English adjectives that come directly from Latin are formed by adding the suffix *–al* (meaning "of or pertaining to") to the *stem* of a noun. (Remember: To find the complete stem of a Latin noun, drop the ending of the genitive.)

nātiō, nātiōnis *f* (*nation*)

The stem of this noun is **nātiōn–**. To make an English adjective from this Latin stem, we add the suffix *–al* to get the adjective *national,* which means "of or pertaining to a nation."

Copy the following table. For each Latin noun, write the *English* adjective derived by dropping the genitive ending and adding *–al*. Then write the meaning of each adjective. (Note: Although each noun in this table names a body part, *–al* adjectives can be formed from other Latin nouns, too. We just saw how *national* resulted from the addition of the suffix *–al* to the stem of **nātiō.**)

NOM.	GEN.	ENGLISH ADJECTIVE	ENGLISH MEANING
1. spīna	spīnae	spinal	of the spine
2. corpus	corporis		
3. mēns	mentis		
4. vertebra	vertebrae		

NOM.	GEN.	ENGLISH ADJECTIVE	ENGLISH MEANING
5. dēns	dentis		
6. pectus	pectoris		
7. frōns	frontis		
8. digitus	digitī		
9. nāsus	nāsī		
10. auris	auris		
11. faciēs	faciēī		
12. caput	capitis		

C. In Latin, all adjectives formed in this way have three endings. For example, **globus –ī m** (*globe*) gives us the adjectives **globālis –is –e** (*global*, "of or pertaining to the globe"). The word *oval* derives from the Latin **ōvālis –is –e**, which is the adjective form of the noun **ōvum –ī n** (*egg*). As a result, *oval* means "egg-shaped."

Because these adjectives are easy to recognize and translate from the previous discussion, this book will no longer give the meanings of these words in the margin.

Below are nouns you have already learned. Copy and complete the table by writing each Latin adjective and its endings as well as the corresponding English adjective derivative:

1. mūrus	mūrī	**mūrālis –is –e**	mural
2. bēstia	bēstiae		
3. parēns	parentis		
4. fīlius	fīlī		
5. locus	locī		
6. pastor	pastōris		
7. astrum	astrī		
8. verbum	verbī		
9. fīnis	fīnis		
10. medicus	medicī		
11. initium	initī		
12. rūs	rūris		
13. cultūra	cultūrae		
14. rēx	rēgis		
15. vōx	vōcis		

VIII Dominus et servus

Present Participles

1 Modicum cultūrae

The Romans, as indeed most of the ancient world, practiced slavery. The supply of slaves was seemingly endless: prisoners of war, people who had fallen into debt under laws that unjustly favored moneylenders, people (especially children) kidnapped by pirates, children of slave women, and criminals whose punishments involved the loss of liberty.

Slaves learned a wide range of trades and professions to increase the wealth of their masters. Cooks, blacksmiths, dyers, waiters, porters, carpenters, potters, tanners, farmers, gladiators, secretaries, accountants, architects, doctors, and dancers arrived in Rome from every quarter of the globe. Dealers sold as many as 10,000 slaves in a single day on the small Greek island of Delos. Caesar and Pompey reportedly captured as slaves over a million people in Gaul and Asia.

Slave dealers (**mangō –ōnis** *m*) brought their slaves to market in the Forum and elsewhere in the city of Rome. They displayed slaves on a revolving platform (**catasta** *-ae f*). Each slave had a sign (**titulus** *-ī m*) hanging from his or her neck bearing all information that potential buyers wanted to know: age, nationality, abilities, and personal qualities. Slaves with intelligence and learning brought the highest prices. Not owning at least one slave was a sign of embarrassing poverty.

Slaves belonging to an urban household (**familia urbāna**) generally had easier lives than those of slaves on a country estate (**familia rūstica**). Even more difficult were the lives of slaves who worked in flour mills, in the mines, or as oarsmen on Roman galleys (huge ships). The most wretched slaves, however, were those forced to serve as members of chain gangs (**compeditī** *-ōrum m pl*) that worked on prison farms (**ergastulum** *-ī n*). They worked, ate, and even slept in chains.

According to Roman law, slaves were the absolute property of their masters, who could do with them whatever they wished. Although many masters were kind and considerate, others were cruel and abusive. A slave could not own property, could not marry legally, and had no legal protection against his or her master's mistreatment. Runaway slaves, when caught, received a brand delivered with a red-hot iron to the forehead. For the most serious offenses, a slave could be crucified (put to death on a cross), sent unarmed into the arena to face wild beasts, or burned alive. Because of brutal conditions and treatment, it was not uncommon for resentful and frustrated slaves to murder their masters. Rome witnessed some very serious slave rebellions. You may recall that Spartacus led a rebellion that defeated several Roman legions and came close to overthrowing the government.

Can you imagine the feelings of the thousands of boys and girls who were sold into slavery by Roman conquerors and transported to far-off lands? Never again would they see their families, friends, or familiar surroundings. They could no longer practice their native religions or speak their native languages. One rule guided their lives: obey or be punished.

Usually slaves working on small family farms or in the city became, over the years, almost members of the family, sharing the family religion and allowed to use their meager savings (**pecūlium** *-ī n*) to buy their freedom or purchase small items that gave them pleasure. Many faithful slaves received their freedom in the last wills and testaments of their masters.

servus -ī m
serva -ae f
manicae -ārum fpl
catasta -ae f
dominus -ī m
domina -ae f
seruus -ī m
mola -ae f
frumentum -ī n
amphora -ae f
dominus -ī m
furnus -ī m
farīna -ae f
candēlābrum -ī n
armārium -ī n
valvae -ārum fpl
grabātus -ī m
pānis -is m
corbis -is f
situla -ae f

ĀCTIVITĀS

A. Match the sentences with the pictures they describe:

Servī ad molam (*flour mill*) labōrant.
Servus frūmentum in corbe fert
  (*carries*).
Servus manicās gestat.
Mangō servōs ad catastam dūcit.
Servus aquam ex amphorā fundit
  (*pours*).
Serva valvās armārī claudit.
Servus pānēs in furnum inserit.
Serva aquam in situlā portat.

Serva in grabātō sedet.
Domina duās servās in catastā
  observat.
Trēs servī in catastā stant.
Serva vestēs in armārium ponit.
Servus farīnam subigit (*kneads*).
Serva candēlābrum incendit (*lights*).

1.

2.

3.

4.

5.

6.

7.

8.

9.

10.

11.

12.

13.

14.

3 English adjectives ending in *-ing* (example: the *smiling* boy) are called "verbal" adjectives because they are formed from verbs. These adjectives are also called PARTICIPLES.

In Latin the present participles in the *-āre* conjugation end in *-āns* (genitive: *-antis*) and are declined like **ēlegāns**:

Servus aquam *portāns* est validus. *The slave carrying water is strong.*
Ego servum aquam *portantem* nōvī. *I know the slave carrying water.*

Notice that, in the first example, **servus** as well as the participle **portāns** (which modifies **servus**) are in the nominative case. In the second example, **servum** is the direct object and, therefore, in the accusative case; consequently, **portantem** must also be in the accusative case. Participles, like adjectives, agree in number, gender, and case with the nouns they modify.

Important announcement! In English, the participle usually directly precedes or follows the noun it modifies. Latin participles, however, sandwich modifiers between themselves and the nouns:

> **Servus *aquam in amphorā portāns* dominum strictum habet.**
> *The slave carrying water in a jar has a strict master.*

In Latin, it's easy to see exactly where the participial phrase ends and the rest of the sentence continues because the participle is positioned at the end of the phrase.

The participles of the other verb conjugations end in *-ēns* (genitive: *-entis*):

dēns *dolēns* *an aching tooth*
āthlētae in stadiō *currentēs* *athletes running in the stadium*
cum servīs *effugientibus* *with fleeing slaves*

The declension of these participles is just like that of **excellēns** or **intellegēns,** which you already know.

4 Read this letter from a young slave, Bassus, to his mother and father, who were sold to a different master. Pay attention to the participles in bold type. The letter begins with the typical Roman greeting:

Bassus parentibus suīs salūtem dat.

Mangō, vir crūdēlissimus, mē in manicīs in Forum Rōmānum dūxit. Nōn sōlus eram. Multī aliī servulī mēcum erant. Virī Rōmānī circumstābant, **spectantēs** et **rīdentēs.** Nōs servulī autem erāmus perterritī. Titulum circum cervīcēs gestābāmus. In titulō erant nōmen, aetās, patria et artēs nostrae. Ab sōle **oriente** ad sōlem **occidentem** in forō stābāmus. Neque cibus neque aqua nōbīs erat. Mangō nōs in catastā stāre coēgit. Virī Rōmānī, **circumstantēs,** nōs lustrāvērunt, **dīcentēs:** "Hīc servulus est nimis imbēcillus; ille servulus est nimis parvus; iste servus nullōs mūsculōs habet. Sed illī servulī sunt āthlēticī."

Dēnique pīstor ex oppidō Ōstiā **veniēns,** mē et duodecim servulōs ēmit, **dīcēns,** "Festīnāte, festīnāte, puerī! Ōstia est longinqua abhinc." Dominus noster nōn crūdēlis est sed sevērus. Numquam lūdĕre possumus. Labōrāmus ab sōle **oriente** ad sōlem **occidentem.**

Quattuor mēnsēs iam in pīstrīnā labōrāmus. Duo servī validī frūmentum in amphorīs portant et id in molam īnfundunt. Duo servī molam versant et hōc modō frūmentum molunt.

Ego farīnam ex molā in corbe excipiō et ad mēnsam adferrō. Trēs servulī ad mēnsam **stantēs** farīnam subigunt; hōc modō pānem ex farīnā faciunt. Dēnique ūnus servulus pānēs in furnum īnserit et pānēs coquit.

Interdiū ego sum admodum occupātus; sed noctū, in grabātō **iacēns,** saepe lacrimō. Ego vōs et avum aviamque, amīcos, patriam vehementer dēsīderō. Quam miser sum! Quam miseram vītam agō! Valēte.

Bassus

---

salūtem dare (+ *dat*) *to send greetings*

sōlus -a -um *alone*
servulus -ī *m young slave*
circumstō -stāre -stetī *to stand around*
  rīdeō -ēre rīsī rīsus *to laugh*
perterritus -a -um *scared stiff*
aetās -ātis *f age*
  ars artis *f skill*
  oriēns orientis *rising*
occidēns occidentis *setting*
cogō -ĕre coēgī coāctus *to force*
lustrō -āre -āvī -ātus *to look (someone) over*
imbēcillus -a -um *weak*
nullus -a -um *no*

dēnique *finally*
  pīstor -oris *m baker*
  Ōstia -ae *f seaport of Rome*
festīnō -āre -āvī -ātus *to hurry up*
  longinquus -a -um *far*
  abhinc *from here*

iam labōrāmus *we have been working*
  pīstrīna -ae *f bakery*
validus -a -um *strong*
  frūmentum -ī *n grain*
  amphora -ae *f (big) jar*
mola -ae *f millstone*
  īnfundō -fundĕre -fūdī -fūsus *to pour into*
  versō -āre -āvī -ātus *to turn*
molō -ĕre -uī -itus *to grind*
farīna -ae *f flour*
  excipiō -ĕre excēpī exceptus *to catch*
subigō -ĕre subēgī subactus *to knead*
  modus -ī *m way*
  pānēs *loaves of bread*
īnserō -ĕre -uī -tus *to put into; to insert*
  coquō -ĕre coxī coctus *to bake*
admodum *very*
iaceō -ēre -uī *to lie*
  lacrimō -āre -āvī -ātus *to cry*
vehementer *terribly*
dēsīderō -āre -āvī -ātus *to miss*
agō agĕre ēgi actus *to lead (a life)*
  valēte *good-bye*

B. Repondē ad quaestiōnēs:

1. Quis Bassum et aliōs servulōs in Forum Rōmānum dūxit?

2. Quid Bassus circum manūs habuit?

3. Quid faciēbant virī Rōmānī circumstantes?

4. Quid servulī circum cervīcēs gestābant?

5. Quid mangō in titulō īnscripsit?

6. Quamdiū (*how long*) servulī in forō stābant?

7. Ubi mangō servulōs stāre coēgit?

8. Quis dēnique Bassum et servulōs ēmit?

9. Quid facit Bassus in pīstrīnā?

10. Quem dēsīderat Bassus?

 Now that you have seen some present participles in action, let's look at the full declension of the participle.

	MASC./FEM.	NEUTER
	SINGULAR	
NOMINATIVE	dīcēns	dīcēns
GENITIVE	dīcentis	dīcentis
DATIVE	dīcentī	dīcentī
ACCUSATIVE	dīcentem	dīcēns
ABLATIVE	dīcentī, -e	dīcentī, -e

The alternative ablative singular ending *–e*, instead of the usual *–ī*, is used in special forms, such as the ablative absolute (a special use of the ablative case that you will learn later in Lesson XX). For now, just remember that the ending of the ablative singular can be either *–ī* or *–e.*

	MASC./FEM.	NEUTER
	PLURAL	
NOMINATIVE	dīcentēs	dīcentia
GENITIVE	dīcentium	dīcentium
DATIVE	dīcentibus	dīcentibus
ACCUSATIVE	dīcentēs	dīcentia
ABLATIVE	dīcentibus	dīcentibus

ĀCTIVITĀTĒS

C. Write the correct nominative form of the participle. Then give the English meaning:

1. (labōrāre) servulī

2. (occidĕre) sōl

3. (lacrimāre) puer

4. (dolēre) tergum

5. (ēsurīre) animal

D. Write the correct form of the participle for the indicated verb. Then write the English meaning of the phrase:

1. (amāre) cum _____patre

2. (vīvĕre) sine _____parentibus

3. (dormīre) ab _____servō

4. (currĕre) in _____equō

5. (dolēre) prō _____dente

6. (effugĕre) ad _____servum

7. (pugnāre) inter _____pugilēs

8. (rīdēre) ob _____virōs

E. Read the following sentences carefully. Then write the correct form of the present participle in each sentence:

1. Servus, molam (versāns/versantem), est validus.

2. Pīstor, in pīstrīnā (stāns/stantem), pānēs venditābat.

3. Duo servī, farīnam ex molā (excipiēns/excipientēs), sunt frātrēs.

4. Servī timent dominum domō (veniēns/venientem).

5. Ego prōtegam omnēs servōs (fugiēns/fugientēs).

6. Mangōnēs, servōs in catastrā (vēnditāns/vēnditantēs), sunt mōnstra.

7. Servulī, pānem in pīstrīnā (coquentī/coquentēs), sunt pīstōrēs bonī.

8. Servae, farīnam in mēnsā (subigēns/subigentēs), ex Asiā veniunt.

9. Ego et frāter meus lupum, dē Monte Aventīnō (dēveniēns/dēvenientem), vīdimus.

10. Potestne medicus meum tergum (dolēns/dolentem) cūrāre?

F. After you read the following sentences, write the participle form of the indicated verb that correctly completes each sentence:

1. (portāre) Servus amphoram _____ pīstrīnam intrāvit.

2. (stāre) Claudē valvās armārī in ātriō _____!

3. (vocāre) Audīsne dominam, servōs ad sē _____?

4. (versāre) Servī, molam _____, admodum fatigātī erant.

5. (labōrāre) Quis invidet servulō ad molam _____?

6. (sedēre) Ego cibum dedī miserīs virīs ante templum _____.

7. (iacēre) Dominus verberāvit servulum in grabātō _____.

8. (īnfundĕre) Serva, aquam in amphoram _____, est bellissima.

9. (labōrāre) Compeditī, in ergastulō _____, miserrimī sunt.

10. (coquĕre) Servī, pānem _____, pecūlium mox habēbunt.

VOCĀBULA

cōnsīdō –ĕre cōnsēdī cōnsessum *to sit down*
adsum *here I am*
admodum mē paenitet *I am very sorry*
iterum *again*

tumeō –ēre –ui *to swell;* **tumēns**
   swollen
mehercule! *by heaven!*
quidnam? *just what?*

Colloquium

Complete the dialog with expressions from the conversation and the chapter as a whole:

Compositiō

You are applying for a job in a Roman bakery. Tell the owner the various bakery tasks you can perform. Try to impress him with your skills. You might also mention some positive personal characteristics to help you get the job!

Rēs Persōnālēs

A. As a slave in Rome, you could not become a senator, lawyer, or soldier but you could be almost anything else if you had the ambition. If you were standing on the **catasta** in the Roman Forum and were asked to give your preference, name five jobs or careers that interest or suit you. Can you explain in Latin the reason for each choice? If not, you may use English to give your reasons:

> EXAMPLE: **Praeferō (volō) esse agricola, quia rūs amō.**

B. Name three professions or jobs that you would dislike. Begin with **Nōlō**:

🔄 THE LATIN CONNECTION

In Latin, the participle can act as an adjective—**amāns pater** (*loving father*)—or it can stand alone and act as a noun—**amāns** (*lover*) or **amāns patriae** *lover of country / patriot.*

An English derivative of a Latin participle may also be either an adjective or a noun. For example, the following derivatives come from the Latin participle **currēns, currentis:**

> *current* affairs (adjective)
>
> electrical *current* (noun)
>
> river *current* (noun)

Copy the following table. Write the nominative and the genitive of the participle of each verb. Then delete the genitive ending and write the English derivative. Remember that *–iō* verbs such as **faciō** keep the letter **i** in the participle: **faciēns, facientis.** Follow the pattern of the first verb in the list:

VERB	PARTICIPLE	ENGLISH DERIVATIVE
1. serpō *–ĕre* (*to crawl*)	**serpēns, serpentis**	**serpent**
2. agō *–ĕre* (*to act, do*)		

VERB	PARTICIPLE	ENGLISH DERIVATIVE
3. recipiō –ĕre (*to receive*)		
4. studeō –ēre (*to study*)		
5. accidō –ĕre (*to happen*)		
6. repugnō –āre (*to fight back*)		
7. cōnfīdō –ĕre (*to trust*)		
8. adiaceō –ēre (*to lie next to*)		
9. antecēdō –ĕre (*to go before*)		
10. praesideō –ēre (*to sit before; to preside*)		
11. cōnsultō –āre (*to consult*)		
12. dēficiō –ĕre (*to run low*)		
13. efficiō –ĕre (*to bring about*)		
14. fluō –ĕre (*to flow*)		
15. pertineō –ēre (*to belong to*)		
16. contineō –ēre (*to hold together*)		
17. conveniō –īre (*to come together, agree*)		
18. dēterreō –ēre (*to frighten away, prevent*)		
19. appareō –ēre (*to appear*)		
20. ardeō –ēre (*to burn, glow*)		

VERB	PARTICIPLE	ENGLISH DERIVATIVE

21. inhabitō *–āre*
    (*to inhabit*)

22. exspectō *–āre*
    (*to expect*)

23. observō *–āre*
    (*to observe*)

24. respondeō *–ēre*
    (*to answer*)

25. lateō *–ēre*
    (*to hide*)

26. sileō *–ēre*
    (*to be silent*)

A *spellbinding* spelling tip! Having trouble deciding if some English words end in *–ent* or *–ant*? English words derived from participles of the first conjugation end in *–ant* (*observant*). Those derived from any other conjugation end in *–ent* (*deterrent*). Although some exceptions to this rule exist, the general principle should help you spell well!

IX | Vehicula et viae

Locative Case; **īdem, eadem, idem**

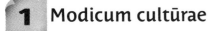 1 Modicum cultūrae

In the ancient world, an ordinary person's usual means of transportation was the donkey, which was used for hauling loads as well as for personal travel. You might say that the donkey was the poor man's pickup truck! In the cities, the wealthy traveled in a litter (**lectīca** *–ae f*) or a sedan chair (**sella gestātōria** *–ae f*). In a litter, passengers reclined on a couch; travelers sat upright in sedan chairs. Soft cushions ensured comfort while curtains (**vēlum** *–ī n*) gave passengers privacy. A team of strong, brightly dressed slaves of equal height carried the litters and chairs. The number of slave carriers varied from two to eight, depending on the size of the litter. Many cities (including Rome) banned vehicles during daylight hours to protect pedestrians in the narrow streets and to cut down on noise. Women of the highest rank and Vestal Virgins were allowed to travel in the city in a four-wheeled carriage (**pīlentum** *–ī n*) on special occasions, such as processions and public games.

For travel beyond the city, Romans used the chariot (**currus** *–ūs m*), in which the driver stood. Initially used for war the chariot, like today's Jeep, eventually became a civilian vehicle. A two-wheeled cart (**carrus** *–ī m*) often transported heavy loads. Oxen or horses drew heavier versions of the **carrus,** which often had solid wheels rather than the customary spoked wheels (**rota** *–ae f*). Men pushed or pulled smaller, lighter carts.

The most common Latin word for wagon was **plaustrum** (*–ī n*). Some wagons had two wheels made from solid drums (**tympanum** *–ī n*); oxen or mules drew these wagons. Other wagons had four wheels.

Long-distance travelers commonly used a four-wheeled carriage (**raeda** *–ae f*), which could carry baggage and as many as eight passengers. Some carriages were double-deckers, meaning that some passengers rode on an upper, open deck while others sat in the carriage's lower, curtain-enclosed deck. Just as we have luxury and economy cars today, the Romans could choose between fancy and basic models of carriages. Which model do you think wealthy Romans chose? Since most large-city residents didn't own a vehicle, they rented carriages (**raeda meritōria** *–ae f*) for travel outside the city gates. These vehicles came equipped with brakes (**sufflāmen** *–inis n*) and even tripometers, mileage gauges that kept track of the number of miles passengers traveled. Individuals and couples who wanted to travel fast and baggage-free chose a light, topless carriage (**cisium** *–ī n*) with two wheels. This carriage, designed in Gaul (now France), had a two-passenger maximum.

Another two-wheeled traveling chariot (**essedum** *–ī n*) followed the lines of the war chariots used by the Britons and Gauls. Travelers themselves drove the smaller ones; the larger ones generally required a driver. Although we can find many references to the **essedum** in literature of the time, we do not know its exact shape.

We do, though, know the shape of the two-wheeled buggy **carpentum** (*–ī n*) because its image appears on Roman coins. It held two or three passengers as well as a driver. Enclosed, this buggy had an arched, overhead cover. For grand occasions, owners richly adorned, or decorated, this small vehicle.

Unfortunately for their passengers, ancient vehicles did not have rubber tires or springs to cushion the ride. Iron wheel rims made traveling a bone-jarring experience. Flat volcanic stones, carefully fitted together, paved only the best streets and roads. Smaller stones filled any spaces between paving stones. Over the years, weathering and use made Roman roads very bumpy by modern standards. More than four hundred years passed before Romans built their first all-season highway (**via strāta,** literally *paved road*). Built in 312 B.C. under the direction of a grumpy old Roman named Appius Claudius Caecus (the Blind), Via Appia bears his name. Originally the highway ran south from Rome to Capua, a distance of 132 miles. Eventually the ancients extended the roadway to Brundisium on the Adriatic coast of southern Italy, a total distance of 360 miles. Another sixty years or so later, Romans finally set up milestones along the way to indicate distances; about two hundred years after that, they established mile markers every mile along main highways.

Because ancient Romans had not yet developed a system of hotels and motels along their highways, whenever possible travelers stayed along the way at the homes of friends and relatives. The few inns (**caupōna** *–ae f*) in existence were dismal, generally as unsanitary and noisy as they were unprotected from thieves and robbers. In all likelihood, travelers had to share a bed with lice and bedbugs and eat unappetizing food. Some slept in their carriages (**carrūca dormītōria** *–ae f*) to avoid the gloomy, dirty inns. Larger towns had more comfortable accommodations. Local officials arranged for visiting officials and soldiers to be billeted, or lodged, in private homes.

2 Vocābula

carrus -ī m

cisium -ī n

raeda -ae f

currus -ūs m

rota -ae f

sella gestātōria -ae f

lectīca -ae f

carpentum -ī n

mūlus -ī m

tympanum -ī n
plaustrum -ī m

bōs, bovis m

radius -ī m

A. Match the sentences with the pictures they describe:

Senātor in hāc sellā gestātōriā sedet.
Duo bovēs hōc plaustrum trahunt (*pull*).
Quattuor servī hanc lectīcam gestant.
Marītus et uxor in hōc cisiō sedent.
Vir hunc currum agit.
Duo mūlī hōc carpentum trahunt.

Ūnus radius (*spoke*) rotae est fractus.
Haec raeda rotās quattuor habet.
Hōc plaustrum onus magnum fert.
Haec rota radiōs octō habet.
Vir in hāc lectīcā librum legit.
Hōc plaustrum nōn rotās sed tympana habet.

1.

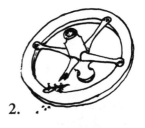

3.

4.

2.

5.

6.

7.   8.

9.   10.

11.   12.

3 The prepositions **ab** and **ad** are not used with the names of towns. A special case, called the LOCATIVE CASE, indicates *in* or *at* a town. (Most Latin names of Italian towns are feminine or neuter singular. Less common are feminine and masculine plural names.) Below are typical names of towns along the Via Appia:

NOMINATIVE	ACCUSATIVE		ABLATIVE		LOCATIVE	
Rōm*a* –*ae* f	**Rōmam**	*to Rome*	**Rōmā**	*from Rome*	**Rōmae**	*in/at Rome*
Lānuvi*um* –*ī* n	**Lānuvium**	*to Lanuvium*	**Lānuviō**	*from Lanuvium*	**Lānuviī**	*in/at Lanuvium*
Formi*ae* –*ārum* f pl	**Formiās**	*to Formiae*	**Formiīs**	*from Formiae*	**Formiīs**	*in/at Formiae*
Fund*ī* –*ōrum* m pl	**Fundōs**	*to Fundi*	**Fundīs**	*from Fundi*	**Fundīs**	*in/at Fundi*

What is the locative ending of the following names: feminine singular? neuter singular? masculine or feminine plural?

The locative case of **rus** (*country*) is **rūrī;** the locative of **domus** (*home*) is **domī.**

B. The following names belong to several towns located along the Appian Way between Rome (in Latium) and Capua (in Campania). They are listed in the order you would visit them if you were traveling south. Write (1) the locative-case form and (2) the English meaning of each name:

1. Bovill*ae* –*ārum f pl*
2. Alb*a* Long*a* –*ae f*
3. Arīci*a* –*ae f*
4. Lānuvi*um* –*ī n*
5. For*um* –*ī* Appī *n*
6. Fērōni*a* –*ae f*
7. Terracīn*a* –*ae f*
8. Fund*ī* –*ōrum m pl*
9. Itr*ī* –*ōrum m pl*
10. Formi*ae* –*ārum f pl*
11. Minturn*ae* –*ārum f pl*
12. Capu*a* –*ae f*

4 Let's read about a trip that Marcus, Cornelia, and their parents took along the Appian Way to Capua. Pay particular attention to place name accusative cases (*to* a place), ablative cases (*from* a place), and locative cases, which appear in bold type:

Marcus et soror sua, Cornēlia, et parentēs iter per Viam Appiam facĕre cōnstituērunt; nam **Capuam** in Campāniam īre volēbant. Marcus et Cornēlia erant excitātī, quia numquam anteā iter per Campāniam fēcerant. "Capua," inquit pater, "est noster locus dēstinātus. Capua centum trīgintā mīlia passuum **Rōmā** abest. Crās māne prīmā hōrā **Rōmā** discēdēmus, nam iter erit longissimum."

Postrīdiē frāter et soror prīma lūce ex cubiculīs in viam festīnāvērunt, ubi servī raedam iam parābant. Post ientāculum, Cornēlia et Marcus in raedam ascendērunt; deinde parentēs in raedam ascendērunt. Denique raedārius in raedam ascendit et equōs incitāvit. Raeda per urbis viās festīnāvit, et mox per Portam Capēnam* in Viam Appiam pervēnit.

Via Appia erat plēna vehiculōrum omnis generis. Marcus et Cornēlia tot vehicula numquam anteā vīderant: currūs, carrōs, lectīcās, plaustra,

iter facĕre *to take a trip, travel*
cōnstituō –ĕre –ī –tum *to decide (to)*
nam *conj for*
excitātus –a –um *excited*
locus dēstinātus –ī m *destination*
 centum trīgintā mīlia passuum *130 miles (literally: 130 thousands of paces)*
 absum abesse āfuī *to be distant*
 crās māne *tomorrow morning*
discēdō –ĕre discessī *to depart*
postrīdiē *(on) the next day*
 lux lūcis f *light;*
 prīmā lūce *at dawn*
ascendō –ĕre –ī *to climb*
raedārius –ī m *driver, coachman*
incitō –āre –āvī –ātus *to urge on*
perveniō –īre pervēnī *(in or ad + acc) to arrive at, reach*
genus –eris *n kind, type*

carpenta. Sed vehiculum vēlōcissimum erat cisium, in quō puer sē amīcae suae iactābat. Illud cisium omnia alia vehicula facile praeterībat. Vehicula tardissima erant plaustra et carrī, quōs bovēs trahēbant. Ā sinistrā et ā dextrā, Marcus et Cornēlia multās villās pulchrās vīdērunt. Vīdērunt etiam multōs servōs in agrīs et in olīvētīs labōrantēs. Circā hōram diēī tertiam, Montem Albānum subiērunt, ubi Alba Longa est. "Rōmulus et Remus," inquit māter, "**Albae Longae** ōlim nātī sunt." "Id sciō. Et Rhea Silvia erat māter eōrum," respondit Cornēlia.

sē iactāre (+ *dat*) *to show off to*
praetereō –īre –īvī –iī *to pass*
trahō –ĕre trāxī tractus *to pull*
olivētum –ī *n olive grove*
  circā hōram diēī tertiam *around 9:00 a.m.*
subeō –īre –īvī *or* **–iī** *to go up, climb*
ōlim *once upon a time*

Deinde **Arīciam** pervēnērunt. Familia prandium **Arīciae** sūmpsit. "Festīnāte," clāmāvit pater, "sī **Terracīnam** sub nocte pervenīre volumus."

sūmō –ĕre –psī –ptus *to eat, have (lunch)*
sub nocte *before nightfall*

Post prandium, in raedam ascendērunt, et raedārius equōs incitāvit. Circā decimam diēī hōram **Fōrum Appī** pervēnērunt, ubi erat statua Appī Claudī Caecī, quī Viam Appiam mūnīverat. "Ecce statuam!" exclāmāvit māter; Marcus autem et Cornēlia dormiēbant, nam fessī erant.

circā decimam diēī hōram *around 4:00 p.m.*
mūniō –īre –īvī –ītas *to build (a road)*
fessus –a –um *tired*

Post aliquot hōrās **Terracīnam** pervēnērunt. Hōc oppidum in ōrā maritimā situm est. Raedārius rotam sufflāmināvit et raeda prō caupōnā cōnstitit. Dum raedārius equōs pascit et eīs aquam dat, Marcus et Cornēlia cum parentibus caupōnam intrāvērunt. Caupōna erat plēna viātōrum. Aliī ad mēnsās cēnābant, aliī vīnum pōtābant et cantābant; aliī ante focum sedēbant et āleā lūdēbant.

rotam sufflāmināre *to put on the brake*
caupōna –ae *f inn*
  cōnsistō –ĕre cōnstitī *to stop*
  dum *while*
  pascō –ĕre pāvī pastus *to feed*
viātor –ōris *m traveler*
  cēnō –āre –āvī –ātus *to eat supper*
focus – ī *m fireplace*
āleā lūdĕre *to play dice; to gamble*
caupō –ōnis *m innkeeper*
adpōnō –ĕre adposuī adpositus *to serve*
  assum –ī *n roast*

Caupō Marcum et Cornēliam et parentēs ad mēnsam vocāvit et cibum eīs adposuit: assum, lactūcam, cāseum, pānem, fructum, et vīnum. Post cēnam familia dē itinere diū disputāvit. "Crās in marī natāre volam," dīxit Cornēlia. "Ōra maritima nōn procul abest."

disputō –āre –āvī –ātus dē (+ *abl*) *to discuss*
mare –is *n (Mediterranean) sea*
ōra maritima –ae *f seashore*
paulisper *for a little while*
dūrus –a –um *rough, hard*
temptō –āre –āvī –ātus *to try*

"Ego quoque," respondit Marcus. "Forsitan crās," dīxit pater, "paulisper natāre poteritis. Sed deinde iter **Capuam** continuābimus. Crēdite mihi, iter inter **Terracīnam** et **Capuam** longa et dūra erit. Nunc dormīre temptāte, sī potestis."

natātiō –ōnis *f swim*

Postrīdiē post natātiōnem in marī, familia **Terracīnā** discessērunt et sub nocte **Capuam** pervēnērunt.

*****Porta Capēna** gate in the Roman wall at which the Via Appia began.

C. Respondē ad hās quaestiōnēs:

1. Ubi Marcus et Cornēlia habitābant?

2. Ad quam urbem familia iter facĕre cōnstituērunt?

3. Cūr Marcus et Cornēlia erant excitātī?

4. Quot mīlia passuum Capua Rōmā abest?

5. Quod nōmen est portae in mūrō Rōmānō?

6. Quae animālia plaustra et carrōs trahēbant?

7. In quō oppidō familia prandium sūmpsit? (*Use locative*)

8. In quō oppidō statua Appī Claudī Caecī stābat? (*Use locative*)

9. In quō oppidō familia cēnāvit? (*Use locative*)

10. Quid Cornēlia et Marcus Terracīnae facĕre volēbant?

5 In the account of the Capua trip, distances were expressed in miles. A Roman mile was measured in paces. A pace was a large step (**passus –ūs m**). One thousand paces (**mille passūs**) constituted one mile. Notice that the adjective **mille,** modifying the plural noun **passūs,** is indeclinable. For the number 2000 and greater, however, the word for thousand(s) (**mīlia –ium n pl**) becomes a neuter plural noun, and **passus** is put into the genitive plural:

duo mīlia *passuum* two miles (literally: two thousands of paces)
decem mīlia *passuum* ten miles (literally: ten thousands of paces)

D. Complete the sentences below by using Latin to express the miles in parentheses:

1. (12 miles) Bovillae _____ Rōmā absunt.

2. (4 miles) Alba Longa _____ Bovillīs abest.

3. (45 miles) Terracīna _____ Rōmā abest.

4. (55 miles) Terracīna _____ Capuā abest.

5. (20 miles) Terracīna _____ Formiīs abest.

E. Write the proper case (accusative, ablative, or locative) of each town name in parentheses. Remember, no prepositions!

1. (at Lānuvium) Avus meus _____ habitat.

2. (from Lānuvium) Avus meus _____ ad Campāniam migrāvit (*moved*).

3. (from Arīcia) Marcus prīmā lūce _____ discessit.

4. (in Terracīna) Cornēlia prandium _____ sūmpsit.

5. (to Fundī) Familia mea iter _____ fēcit.

6. (in Alba Longa) Caupōnae _____ vīnum malum habent.

7. (at Forum Appī) Appius Claudius Caecus numquam _____ habitāvit.

8. (to Capua) Via Appia ab urbe Rōmā _____ dūcit.

9. (at Arīcia) Diāna templum clārissimum _____ habet.

10. (from Rome) Quandō Marcus _____ discessit, ad Campāniam īvit.

6 You already know the simple pronouns **is, ea,** and **id** (*he, she, it*). If we add the suffix *–dem* to these words, they mean *the same:*

Eīdem servī hanc lectīcam herī gestābant.

The same slaves carried this (the same) litter yesterday.

Eōdem diē Marcus ab Latiō ad Campāniam discessit.

On the same day, Marcus departed from Latium for Campania.

Here is the entire declension:

	SINGULAR			PLURAL		
NOM.	īdem	eadem	idem	eīdem	eaedem	eadem
GEN.	ēiusdem	ēiusdem	ēiusdem	eōrundem	eārundem	eōrundem
DAT.	eīdem	eīdem	eīdem	eīsdem	eīsdem	eīsdem
ACC.	eundem	eandem	idem	eōsdem	eāsdem	eadem
ABL.	eōdem	eādem	eōdem	eīsdem	eīsdem	eīsdem

Which letter disappeared from the masculine nominative singular? From the neuter nominative singular?

One more point! Apparently the Romans didn't like the sound of the letter **m** before the letter **d** (eu**m**dem, ea**m**dem), so they changed **m** to **n** (eu**n**dem, ea**n**dem). Look again at the plural forms. In what case does **m** change to **n?**

F. Complete the sentences by writing the correct forms of **īdem, eadem, idem:**

1. Illae trēs tabernae sunt in ＿＿＿＿＿＿ oppidō.

2. ＿＿＿＿＿＿ raedārius raedam per Portam Capēnam herī ēgit (*drove*).

3. Marcus semper cum ＿＿＿＿＿＿ amīcīs lūdit.

4. ＿＿＿＿＿＿ mūlī raedam nostram trāxērunt.

5. Omnēs viātōrēs per ＿＿＿＿＿＿ viam ad caupōnam pervēnērunt.

6. Senātōrēs in ＿＿＿＿＿＿ sellīs gestātōrīs iter Ardeam fēcērunt.

7. ＿＿＿＿＿＿ rota iterum est fracta.

8. ＿＿＿＿＿＿ pīlentum per urbis viās festīnāvit.

9. Mīlitēs mūrōs ＿＿＿＿＿＿ oppidōrum oppugnābat.

10. Hīc caupō ＿＿＿＿＿＿ cibum cōtīdiē adpōnit.

11. Ego ＿＿＿＿＿＿ tabernam praetereō cum (*when*) ad scholam eō.

12. Habitāsne in ＿＿＿＿＿＿ īnsulā Rōmae?

Compositiō

You sell used vehicles in a lot near the Appian Way. A customer stops to chat. Describe two or three vehicles to the customer, and explain how they can be used. Tell the customer the price of each vehicle. Don't hesitate to exaggerate in your descriptions. You might make a sale!

Dialogus

Buying from a used-wagon dealer? **Caveat emptor!** (*Let the buyer beware!*)

VOCĀBULA

habit*us* –*ūs* *m condition*
cār*us* –*a* –*um* *expensive*
anicul*a* –*ae* *f little old lady*
possideō –ēre possēdī possessus *to own*

dīvitēs *the rich*
tantummodo *only*
cōnstat (+ *abl*) *it costs*
pedibus īre *to go on foot*

Colloquium

Complete the dialog with expressions borrowed from the conversation or expressions of your own:

Salvē, mī amīce. Vīsne _____ _____? Multa vehicula excellentia habeō. Omnia vehicula mea sunt _____ _____.

Salvē. Vehiculum bonum emĕre volō, sed _____ _____ nōn habeō.

Hīc est _____ excellens et nōn cārum est.

Plaustrum? Ego agricola nōn sum, et neque _____ habeō.

Hīc est lectīca pulchra. Paene _____ Anicula eam possēdit.

Mē paenitet, sed ego neque _____ _____ neque _____ sum.

Hīc est cisium splendidum. Erit vehiculum velōcissimum in Viā Appiā. _____ _____ tē amābunt. Tantummodo mille dēnāriīs constat.

Mille dēnāriīs? Nesciō cūr, sed subitō _____ praeferō.

1. Fēcistīne umquam iter longum?

2. Quae urbs erat locus dēstinātus itineris tuī longissimī?

3. Quibuscum iter longissimum fēcistī?

4. Praefersne itinera longa an brevia?

5. Praefersne itinera in montēs an ad ōram maritimam?

6. Quot vehicula familiae tuae sunt?

7. Quandō sperās vehiculum tibi emĕre?

8. Praefersne vehiculum magnum et cārum an vehiculum parvum et vēlōx?

↻ THE LATIN CONNECTION

A. The word *mile* comes from the Latin **mīlle,** which means "one thousand." Can you explain how *mile* came from **mīlle?**

B. Perhaps you've heard someone say: "He went via the expressway to save time." What does *via* mean in this situation?

C. From which Latin word does the English word *itinerary* come?

D. The verb **trahō trahĕre trāxī trāctus** means *to pull* or *to draw*. It can be combined with several prefixes. Read the following sentences and decide which compound form best fits each sentence:

abstract	extract	retract
contract	distract	subtract
detract	protract	attract

1. A dentist sometimes will _____ an aching tooth.

2. If you're not careful, you can _____ a disease.

3. The airplane will _____ its landing gear after takeoff.

4. Will you _____ the discount from the list price?

5. With his long-winded speech, the chairman _____ the meeting.

6. Your mother probably has used vanilla _____ when cooking.

7. This unfortunate action will _____ from his good name.

8. A drop of honey will _____ more flies than a barrel of vinegar.

9. Don't let outside noises _____ you.

E. The Latin word **genus generis** *n* is the root for many English words. Write a definition for each of these English words, which are based on **genus.**

   1. genocide
   2. gender
   3. general
   4. genesis
   5. genetics
   6. genealogy
   7. genre

X | Amor et mātrimōnium

Irregular Adjectives

1 Modicum cultūrae

Much of Latin romantic literature is in the form of myths. Later in this lesson, we will get an idea of such myths by reading the love story of a young couple, Pyramus and Thisbe. The storyteller is the poet Ovid, who also wrote (what was at that time) a daring book called *The Art of Love* and a series of love letters supposedly from women of mythology to their lovers.

You may be surprised to learn the age at which ancient Romans became engaged to be married. Cicero, the famous Roman lawyer, public speaker, and politician, arranged for his daughter's engagement when she was ten years old! She married at age thirteen. This arrangement, probably common, ensured that property stayed in the right hands. If, however, the boy and girl strongly disliked each other, the engagement could be broken. Romans celebrated engagements with parties or banquets.

In the early days of Rome (until 445 B.C.), marriage between members of the wealthy patrician class and the poor plebeian class was forbidden by law. Marriages between Roman citizens and foreigners were legal, but the children of such marriages were not Roman citizens unless the father was the Roman citizen. If a Roman girl married a non-Roman, the children were not considered Romans unless Rome had a special treaty conferring the right of intermarriage on the husband's town.

When the day of the wedding (**nūptiae –ārum f pl**) arrived, the girl dedicated her dolls (**pūpa –ae f**) to the household gods (**Larēs –ium m pl**), symbolizing that the carefree days of her childhood were over. The bride wore a flame-colored veil and a white floor-length dress. A spear-shaped comb divided the bride's hair into six strands; for the first time in her life, the girl wore ribbons in her hair. On her head, the bride wore a crown of flowers (**corōna –ae f flōrida**).

Did you know that the Latin verb for a boy's marrying is different from that for the girl? The verb for the girl to marry is **nūbō –ĕre nūpsī nūpta** (+ *dat*). **Nūbĕre** means *to wear a veil*. The expression for the boy is **in mātrimōnium dūcĕre** or **uxōrem dūcĕre** (*to lead into matrimony* or *to lead a bride home*). "Taking home the bride" was one of the official acts of marriage.

According to custom, the bride waited at her father's house for the bridegroom to come to lead her to his home. (To welcome her, he had adorned the door with wreathes **serta –ae f**.) Before he took his bride home, the auspices were taken. (May was a particularly ill-omened month. The most propitious time for marriage was the second half of June.) If the omens were good, the bridal pair declared their consent by joining right hands at the direction of the matron of honor (**prōnuba –ae f**), who acted as a representative of the goddess Juno, the patroness of marriage. Regardless of the names of the bride and groom, all bridal couples then spoke the following words: **"Ubi Gaius, ego Gaia."** (*Where Gaius is, there I, Gaia, will be.*)

A wedding reception, held at the home of the bride, ended with a banquet (**cena –ae f nūptiālis**). Toward evening, the bridegroom conducted his bride to his home accompanied by a procession (**dēductiō –ōnis f**) of relatives and friends. At the head of the procession were three boys, one carrying the lighted wedding torch (**taeda –ae f nūptiālis**) the bride would use to light the fireplace in the groom's home. The other boys led the bride by the hand. The rest of the procession, including flute players, followed behind as they sang wedding songs. Upon arrival, the bride anointed the doorposts with fat and olive oil and wrapped strands of wool around the doorposts. She was then carried across the threshold to make sure she wouldn't stumble as she entered, since that would have been regarded as a very bad omen.

At last inside the groom's home, the bride lit the fire in the hearth. Then, having extinguished the torch, she threw it to the guests for good luck (just as a bride today throws her bouquet to members of her bridal group or all single women in attendance). The couple then exchanged gifts. The groom then gave his new wife fire and water as a sign of their future life together. The bride gave her husband a dowry from her father. This ended the wedding ceremony.

serta -ae f

nupta -ae f
corōna -ae f
vēlum -ī n

aedēs -is f

osculum -ī n

ānulus -ī m

nuptiae -ārum f pl

taeda -ae f nuptiālis

tībia -ae f

tībīcen -inis m

dēductiō -ōnis f
pompa -ae f nuptiālis

ĀCTIVITĀS

A. Match the sentences with the pictures they describe:

Puer taedam nūptiālem tenet.
Puer ānulum puellae dat.
Nūpta sē ad nūptiās parat.
Tībīcen tībiā cantat (*plays the flute*).
Puer amōrem puellae mōnstrat.

Nūpta corōnam flōridam gestat.
Marītus iānuam domūs sertīs decorat.
Nūpta pūpam Laribus dēdicat.
Duo puerī nūptam dūcunt.
Puer ōsculum puellae dat.

1.

2.

3.

4.

5.

6.

7.

8.

9.

10.

3 At last! Ovid's tragic story of the lovers Pyramus and Thisbe:

Pȳramus et Thisbē domōs adiacentēs tenēbant. Alter erat iuvenis pulcherrimus in urbe; altera erat virgō bellissima et tenera et amābilis. Tempore amor inter iuvenem et virginem magis et magis crēvit. Pȳramus vērō Thisbēn in mātrimōnium dūcěre volēbat et Thisbē Pȳramō nūběre volēbat. Patrēs autem mātrimōnium prohibuērunt. Sed quod parentēs prohibēre nōn poterant, erat amor mūtuus inter amantēs, nam amor vincit omnia.

Rīma in pariete inter domōs erat. Nēmō autem anteā rīmam illam notāvit. Amantēs ipsī rīmam invēnērunt, nam amor viam semper inveniet. Postquam parentēs dormītum ībant, Pȳramus et Thisbē amōrem mūtuum per rīmam exprimēbant. Utrimque ōscula dabant et verba blanda inter sē fēcērunt. Quō magis parentēs Pȳramum et Thisbēn sēgregāre temptābant, eō magis amor inter eōs crēvit.

Quōdam diē duo amantēs cōnsilium sēcrētum iniērunt: fūrtim ē domō posterā nocte rēpěre et convenīre extrā urbem sub quādam mōrō. Illa mōrus erat proxima gelidō fontī.

adiacēns –entis *adjacent*
    teneō –ēre –uī –tus *to occupy, live in*
alter ... altera *the one . . . the other*
    iuvenis –is *m young man*
    pulcher –ra –rum *handsome*
virgō –inis *f young girl*
    tempore *in time*
amor, amōris *m love*
    magis et magis *more and more*
crēscō –ěre crēvī *to grow*
    vērō *in fact*
autem *however*
    prohibeō –ēre –uī –itus *to prohibit, prevent*
quod *what*
mūtuus –a –um *mutual*
    amāns amantis *m/f lover*
rīma –ae *f crack*
    pariēs –etis *m (inner) wall*
notō –āre –āvī –ātus *to notice*
    ipse, ipsa, ipsum *self (myself, yourself, etc.)*
dormītum –īre *to go to sleep*
exprimō –ěre expressī
    expressus *to express*
    utrimque *on both sides (of the wall)*
    verba facěre *to speak words*
inter sē *to each other*
    blandus –a –um *endearing*
    quō magis ... eō magis *the more . . . the more*
sēgregō –āre –āvī –ātus *to keep apart*
cōnsilium inīre *to form a plan*
fūrtim repěre *to sneak*
    posterus –a –um *the following*
convenīre *to meet*
mōrus –ī *f mulberry tree*
    gelidus –a –um *cold*
    fōns, fontis *m spring*

Thisbē prīma ad mōrum pervēnit et sub arbore cōnsēdit. Ecce leō ōre cruentō ā recente caede ad fontem vēnit. Thisbē procul lūnae lūce leōnem vīdit et in spēluncam fūgit. Ut fūgit, vēlāmen dēmīsit. Leō vēlāmen ōre cruentō laniāvit. Postquam aquam ex fonte pōtāvit, leō in silvam rediit.

Paulō post, Pȳramus ad mōrum pervēnit. Vestīgia leōnis et vēlāmen cruentum vīdit. "Ūna nox," ait, "duōs amantēs perdet. Tū, mea Thisbē, fuistī dignissima longā vītā. Ego ipse sum causa mortis tuae. Ego iussī tē noctū venīre in tam perīculōsum locum. Sine tē vīvĕre nōlō." Vēlāmen Thisbēs ad mōrum tulit; ōscula lacrimāsque vēlāminī dedit. Deinde pectus sīcā perfōdit.

Thisbē ē spēluncā vēnit et corpus cruentum Pȳramī vīdit. Thisbē caput pallidum eius sustulit et multa ōscula dedit. "Pȳrame!" clāmāvit, "cūr hōc fēcistī? Pȳrame, tua cārissima Thisbē tē nōminat. Audī vōcem meam!" Ut autem vēlāmen cruentum suum vīdit, tandem causam vēram mortis intellēxit.

Ad nōmen Thisbēs, Pȳramus oculōs, ā morte iam gravātōs, aperuit, sed nihil dīcĕre poterat. "Manus tua et amor noster mortem tuam effēcērunt," clāmāvit Thisbē. "O parentēs miserrimī, quī nōs vīventēs sēgregāvistis, nunc ultima hōra vītae nōs iunget."

Haec verba dīcēns, pectus sīcā perfōdit et ē vītā discessit.

caedēs *–is f kill*   **procul** *from a distance*   **lux, lūcis** *f light*
spēlunca *–ae f cave*
vēlāmen *–inis n wrap*
   dēmittō *–ĕre* **dēmīsī**
   dēmissus *to drop*
laniō *–āre –āvī –ātus to tear up*
paulō post *a little later*
vestīgium *–ī n footprint*
perdō *–ĕre –idī –itus to destroy*
dignus *–a –um (+ abl) deserving of*
iubeō *–ēre* **iussī iussus** *to tell, order*
ferō ferre tulī lātus *to bring*
sīca *–ae f dagger*
perfodiō *–ĕre* **perfōdī perfossus** *to stab*

pallidus *–a –um pale*
tollō *–ĕre* **sustulī sublātus** *to raise*
cārus *–a –um dear*
nōminō *–āre –āvī –ātus to call by name*   **ut** *when, as*
tandem *finally*

gravātus *–a –um heavy*

efficiō *–ĕre* **effēcī effectus** *to bring about*

iungō *–ĕre* **iūnxī iūnctus** *to join*

discēdō *–ĕre* **discessī** *to depart*

ĀCTIVITĀS

B. Respondē Latīnē:

1. Quis erat virgō bellissima in urbe?

2. Quis erat iuvenis pulcherrimus in urbe?

3. Quis mātrimōnium inter amantēs prohibuit?

4. Quid amantēs in pariete invēnērunt?

5. Quid Pȳramus et Thisbē faciēbant postquam parentēs dormītum ībant?

6. Secundum cōnsilium, ubi convenīre cōnstituērunt (*they decided*)?

7. Quae fera ex silvā ad fontem vēnit?

8. Quō Thisbē fūgit?

9. Quid Thisbē casū (*accidentally*) dēmīsit?

10. Secundum Pȳramum, quae erat causa mortis Thisbēs?

 4 The suffix *–dam* added to the forms of the relative pronouns (**quī, quae, quod**) means "a certain":

Thisbē sub *quādam* arbore cōnsēdit.   *Thisbe sat down under a certain tree.*

In the declension of **īdem, eadem, idem**, we saw that the Romans did not like the sound of the letter **m** before the letter **d** (**eumdem** changed to **eundem**). What, then, would be the preferred form of **quemdam? Quamdam? Quōrumdam? Quārumdam?**

ĀCTIVITĀS

C. Write the correct form of **quīdam, quaedam, quoddam** for each of the following:

1. in (quōdam/quādam) urbe

2. ob (quōsdam/quāsdam) causās

3. in (quibusdam/quisdam) locīs

4. (quīdam/quaedam) iuvenēs

5. ad (quendam/quoddam) oppidum

6. vēlum (quārumden/quārundem) nūptārum

5 The story of Pyramus and Thisbe used the intensifying pronoun **ipse, ipsa, ipsum.** It is declined like **bonus –a –um** except in the nominative masculine and genitive and dative singular. Observe the declension below:

	SINGULAR			PLURAL		
NOM.	ipse	ipsa	ipsum	ipsī	ipsae	ipsa
GEN.	ipsīus	ipsīus	ipsīus	ipsōrum	ipsārum	ipsōrum
DAT.	ipsī	ipsī	ipsī	ipsīs	ipsīs	ipsīs
ACC.	ipsum	ipsam	ipsum	ipsōs	ipsās	ipsa
ABL.	ipsō	ipsā	ipsō	ipsīs	ipsīs	ipsīs

When a form of **ipse** *follows* the word it modifies, it means *self.* The forms of **ipse** mean *myself, yourself, himself, itself* (singular) or *ourselves, yourselves, themselves* (plural):

ego ipse *I myself*   **amantēs ipsī** *the lovers themselves*

In English, the word *myself* may be reflexive or intensive depending on its use in the sentence. Latin, however, has one form for the reflexive and another for the intensive. Study these examples:

INTENSIVE: **Virgō *ipsa* tabulātum lāvit.**   *The girl washed the floor herself.*
REFLEXIVE: **Virgō *sē* lāvit.**   *The girl washed herself.*

If the word *self* is intensive, the word *personally* can substitute for it in the sentence. An intensive simply adds emphasis:

Pater *ipse* in nūptiīs interfuit.   *The father himself (or personally) attended the wedding.*

When **ipse** *precedes* the word it modifies, it is still intensive but means *very* or *selfsame*:

Marītus vēnit *ipsō* diē quō nūpta sua eum exspectāvit.   *The bridegroom came on the very day on which his bride expected him.*

ĀCTIVITĀS

D. Complete these sentences by writing the correct form of **ipse, ipsa, ipsum**:

1. Marītus _____ nūptam domum dēduxit.

2. Parentēs _____ erant causa mortis amantium.

3. Thisbē dīxit: "Ego _____ nunc ē vītā discēdam."

4. Pȳramus dīxit: "Ego _____ nunc ē vītā discēdam."

5. Nūpta _____ gratiās mihi ob donum ēgit.

6 Several Latin adjectives have the same genitive and dative endings as **ipse**: *–īus* in the genitive and *–ī* in the dative. (You may remember that the demonstrative pronouns **ille** and **iste** have the same genitive and dative singular endings.) The most common of these adjectives are:

ali*us –a –ud*	*another*
alter, altera, alterum	*the other*
ūll*us –a –um*	*any*
nūll*us –a –um*	*no*
ūn*us –a –um*	*one, alone*
tōt*us –a –um*	*whole*
sōl*us –a –um*	*only, alone*

E. Complete the following sentences by writing the correct form of the adjective in parentheses. The nouns they modify are in bold type. (Remember that verbs such as **confīdĕre** *to trust*, **crēdĕre** *to believe*, **placēre** *to please*, and **servīre** *to serve* take the dative case.)

1. (tōtus) Nūpta per _____ **nūptiās** subrīdēbat (*smiled*).

2. (ūllus) Habēsne _____ **dōnum** nūptiāle prō nūptā?

3. (sōlus) _____ **amīcī** meī ad nūptiās meās nōn vēnērunt.

4. (tōtus) Populus _____ **oppidī** pompae aderant.

5. (nūllus) _____ **puellae** in nūptae domō erant.

6. (alter) Ego huic medicō sed nōn _____ **medicō** cōnfīdō.

7. (ūnus) Ego tantummodo _____ **dominō** servīre possum.

8. (nūllus) Ego ipse _____ **astrologō** crēdō.

9. (ūnus) Hae nūptiae _____ **patrī** sed nōn alterī placent.

10. (alius) Ego dōnum nōn huic sed _____ **nūptae** dedī.

7 Still more information on **alius, alia, aliud** and **alter, altera, alterum!** First, did you notice that the neuter of **alius** is *not* **alium** as you might expect, but **aliud** (just as the neuter form of **ille** is **illud**)? Furthermore, the genitive singular of **alius, alia, aliud** is **alterīus** for all three genders. Last, **alius** and **alter** can be used in pairs with the following meanings:

alius ... alius	*one ... another*
aliī ... aliī	*some ... others*
alter ... alter	*the one ... the other*
alterī ... alterī	*some ... the others*
Alius **Capuam amat;** *alius* **Rōmam praefert.**	*One likes Capua; another prefers Rome.*
Aliī **bene cantāre possunt;** *aliī* **bene saltāre possunt.**	*Some can sing well; others can dance well*

F. Complete the sentences by writing the correct forms of **alius** and **alter.** When pairs are requested, the word in parentheses appears twice. The word to be modified is in bold type:

1. (alius) **Nihil** _____ ā tē volō.

2. (alter . . . alter) Marītus in _____ **parte** urbis habitat, nūpta in

   _____ **parte.**

3. (alter . . . alter) Pater _____ **filiō** cisium dedit, _____ **filiō** raedam.

4. (alter . . . alter) Vīta _____ **marītī** fēlīx est, sed vīta _____ **marītī** īnfēlīx est.

5. (alius . . . alius) _____ **servī** in culīnā labōrant, _____ **servī** in olivētīs.

8 Let's peek in on a Roman wedding:

Herī nūptiīs apud amīcam meam Tulliam adfuī. Parentēs Tulliae laetissimī erant, quia Tullia Caeciliō, filiō senātōris, nūbēbat. Pater ipse iānuam et postēs sertīs laureīs decorāverat. Amīcī ex omnibus partibus urbis ad nūptiās vēnērunt: aliī a Monte Palatīnō, aliī ā Monte Aventīnō, et aliī a Campō Martiō.

Nūpta erat bellissima. Vēlum flammeum et vestem albam et longam gestābat. Ānulum aureum nūptiālem in digitō sinistrae manūs habēbat, quem Caecilius eī dederat. Suprā caput corōnam flōridam gestābat.

Tullia prīmō ante aedem in ātriō stetit, et pūpam suam Laribus dēdicāvit. Deinde Caecilius et nūpta manūs dextrās coniūnxērunt. Nūpta cōram prōnubā dīxit: "Ubi Gāius, ego Gāia." Ad haec verba, omnēs in ātriō applaudēbant et clāmābant "Talassiō! Talassiō!" Deinde omnēs cēnam nūptiālem sumpsērunt. Post cēnam, pompa nūptiālis ā Tulliae domō ad Caeciliī domum prōcessit. Trēs puerī nūptam in pompā dūxērunt. Alius taedam nūptiālem portāvit, alius nūptam manū dextrā dūxit, et alius nūptam manū sinistrā dūxit. Tībīcinēs tībiīs cantābant et

nūptiae -ārum *f pl wedding*
   apud (+ *acc*) *at the house of*
   adsum -esse -fuī (+ *dat*) *to be present at*
laetus -a -um *happy*
postis -is *m doorpost*
laureus -a -um *of laurel*
   decorō -āre -āvī -ātus *to decorate*
vēlum -ī *n veil*
   flammeus -a -um *flame-colored*
vestis -is *f gown*
suprā (+ *acc*) *on, on top of*
flōridus -a -um *of flowers*
aedes -is *f shrine*

coniungō -iungĕre -iunxī -iunctus *to join*
cōram (+ *abl*) *in the presence of*

Talassiō! *traditional wedding cry*

prōcēdō -ĕre prōcessī prōcessum *to proceed*

tībiīs cantābant *were playing their flutes*

omnēs in pompā carmina cantābant. Interdum "Talassiō!" clāmābant.

carmen *–inis* n song

Quandō pompa ad Caeciliī domum pervēnit, Caecilius ante iānuam cōnstitit et nūptam trāns līmen in ātrium portāvit. Omnēs amīcī et cognātī in ātriō convēnērunt, ubi Caecilius et Tullia ante aedem lībum nūptiāle ēdērunt. Deinde marītus ignem et aquam nūptae dedit. Nūpta ignem in focō taedā nūptiālī accendit. Deinde omnēs amīcī et cognāti domum rediērunt. Caecilius et Tullia fēlīciter in perpetuum exinde vīxērunt.

cōnsistō *–ĕre* **cōnstitī** *to take up position*
līmen *–inis* n *threshold*
   cognātus *–ī* m *relative*
lībum *–ī* n *cake*

focus *–ī* m *fireplace, hearth*
   taeda *–ae* f *torch*
   accendō *–ĕre* **accendī accensus** *to light*
in perpetuum exinde *ever after*

ĀCTIVITĀS

G. Respondē ad hās quaestiōnēs:

1. Quamobrem parentēs Tulliae laetissimī erant?
2. Quis iānuam et postēs sertīs laureīs decorāvit?
3. Quid nūpta suprā caput gestābat?
4. Quō colōre erat vēlum?
5. Quid nūpta in digitō habuit?
6. Quot puerī nūptam in pompā dūxērunt?
7. Quid puer prīmus manū tenēbat?
8. Quī tībiīs cantābant?
9. Quid omnēs in pompā interdum clāmābant?
10. Quid marītus nūptae in ātriō suō dedit?

VOCĀBULA

ratiō *–ōnis f reason*	**purgō** *–āre –āvī –ātus to clean*
rārō *rarely*	**obsōnō–āre –āvī –ātus to do the shopping*
Quid aliud? *What else?*	**Itane?** *Is that so?*
prorsum *absolutely*	**igitur** *then*
adōrō *–āre –āvī –ātus to adore*	**omnīnō nōn** *not . . . at all*
Ita est *That's right*	**facerem** *would I do*

Colloquium

Pretend you are Claudius. Complete the dialog with expressions from the previous conversation and from the chapter as a whole:

Claudī, mī amīce, ubi est uxor tua? Estne domī an in forō?	Marce, _____ _____ (Say that your wife is rarely at home.)
Cūr tam tristis es hodiē? Nōnne uxor tua domum cōtīdiē purgat?	_____ _____ (Say that she never cleans the house.)
Vultne uxor tua semper vestēs novās emēre, sicut omnēs uxōrēs?	_____ _____ (Say that clothes cost a lot of money.)
Misere Claudī! Coquitne uxor tua cibōs bonōs tibi. Estne uxor tua coqua bona?	_____ _____ (Say that she never cooks.)
Itane? Cūr igitur istam fēminam in mātrimōnium duxistī?	_____ _____ (Say that he doesn't understand. You love your wife.)

1. Amāsne nūptiīs adesse?

2. Habēbisne nūptiās magnās an parvās et prīvātās?

3. Praefersne marītum dīvitem an pulchrum an amābilem (nūptam dīvitem an pulchram an amābilem)?

4. Praefersne vēlum album an flammeum?

5. Quō annō aetātis tuae nūbēs (uxōrem dūcēs)?

6. Dēbetne pater an fīlia marītum sēligĕre (*select*)?

7. Labōrābisne forīs (*outside the home*) post mātrimōnium tuum?

8. Quot līberōs spērās habēre in familiā futūrā tuā?

Compositiō

Someday you may marry. In Latin, describe the physical and personal characteristics of your ideal spouse.

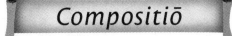 THE LATIN CONNECTION

A. Write the Latin sources for each of the following words. Then write the definitions of the English words.

EXAMPLE: marital   **marītus;** of or pertaining to a husband or marriage

1. revive

2. vestige

3. secretive

4. juvenile

5. adjacent

6. osculate

7. prenuptial

8. segregate

9. posterity

10. amateur

11. vivid

12. furtive

13. nullify
14. Florida
15. temporary
16. perdition
17. dormant
18. pale
19. nominate
20. spelunker

Recognitiō II

(Lēctiōnēs VI–X)

LĒCTIŌ VI

a. Relative pronoun meaning *who, which, that*. Although the genitive and dative were not used, they are given here for completeness:

	MASCULINE	FEMININE	NEUTER
	SINGULAR		
NOMINATIVE	**quī**	**quae**	**quod**
GENITIVE	**cūius**	**cūius**	**cūius**
DATIVE	**cui**	**cui**	**cui**
ACCUSATIVE	**quem**	**quam**	**quod**
ABLATIVE	**quō**	**quā**	**quō**
	PLURAL		
NOMINATIVE	**quī**	**quae**	**quae**
GENITIVE	**quōrum**	**quārum**	**quōtum**
DATIVE	**quibus**	**quibus**	**quibus**
ACCUSATIVE	**quōs**	**quās**	**quae**
ABLATIVE	**quibus**	**quibus**	**quibus**

b. The relative pronoun agrees in number and gender with its antecedent; however, its case is determined by its use in the relative clause.

c. Unlike English, the relative pronoun in Latin is never omitted from a sentence.

LĒCTIŌ VII

The pluperfect, or past perfect, tense refers to a past action that happened prior to another past action. The pluperfect combines the stem of the perfect tense (third principal part) and the imperfect tense of **sum**:

pugnāveram *I had fought*   **pugnāverāmus** *we had fought*
pugnāverās *you had fought*   **pugnāverātis** *you had fought*
pugnāverat *he/she/it had fought*   **pugnāverant** *they had fought*

LĒCTIŌ VIII

a. To form the present participles of the *–āre* conjugation of verbs, add *–āns* to the present stem: **port** + *–āns* (*carrying*). The complete declension is as follows.

	SINGULAR		PLURAL	
	M/F	N	M/F	N
NOM.	portāns	portāns	portantēs	portantia
GEN.	portantis	portantis	portantium	portantium
DAT.	portantī	portantī	portantibus	portantibus
ACC.	portantem	portāns	portantēs	portantia
ABL.	portantī(–*e*)*	portantī(–*e*)*	portantibus	portantibus

b. To form the present participles of the *–ēre* and *–ĕre* conjugations, add *–ēns* to the present stem: **mov** + *–ēns* (*moving*); **dīc** + *–ēns* (*saying*). The complete declension is as follows:

	SINGULAR		PLURAL	
	M/F	N	M/F	N
NOM.	movēns	movēns	moventēs	moventia
GEN.	moventis	moventis	moventium	moventium
DAT.	moventī	moventī	moventibus	moventibus
ACC.	moventem	movēns	moventēs	moventia
ABL.	moventī(–*e*)*	moventī(–*e*)*	moventibus	moventibus

* In the ablative singular for present active participles of all conjugations, an alternative ending *–e* is used in the ablative absolute (see Lēctiō XX) and in certain other circumstances.

c. To form the present participles of the *–iō* and *–īre* conjugations, add *–ēns* to the present stem, which ends in **i: accipi** + *–ēns* (*receiving*) and **audi** + *–ēns* (*hearing*). The complete declension is as follows:

	SINGULAR		PLURAL	
	M/F	N	M/F	N
NOM.	accipiēns	accipiēns	accipientēs	accipientia
GEN.	accipientis	accipientis	accipientium	accipientium
DAT.	accipientī	accipientī	accipientibus	accipientibus
ACC.	accipientem	accipiēns	accipientēs	accipientia
ABL.	accipientī(–e)*	accipientī(–e)*	accipientibus	accipientibus

* In the ablative singular for present active participles of all conjugations, an alternative ending *–e* is used in the ablative absolute (see Lēctiō XX) and in certain other circumstances.

LĒCTIŌ IX

a. Do not use the prepositions **ab** and **ad** with the names of towns and small islands. Thus, **Rōmā** means *from Rome* and **Rōmam** means *to Rome*. Most Latin town names are feminine or neuter singular. Less common are feminine and masculine plural names.

b. The LOCATIVE CASE indicates *in* or *at* a town or *in* or *on* a small island. The locative ending of a feminine singular name is *–ae.* The locative ending of a neuter singular name is *–ī.* The ending of masculine or feminine plural names of the second and first declensions is *–īs.* Examples of such names, as well as the special words **rūs** (*country*) and **domus** (*home*), are as follows:

NOMINATIVE/ GENITIVE	ACCUSATIVE	ABLATIVE	LOCATIVE
Rōma *–ae f*	**Rōmam** *to Rome*	**Rōmā** *from Rome*	**Rōmae** *in/at Rome*
Lānuvium *–ī n*	**Lānuvium** *to Lanuvium*	**Lānuviō** *from Lanuvium*	**Lānuviī** *in/at Lānuvium*
Formiae *–ārum f pl*	**Formiās** *to Formiae*	**Formiīs** *from Formiae*	**Formiīs** *in/at Formiae*
Fundī *–ōrum m pl*	**Fundōs** *to Fundi*	**Fundīs** *from Fundi*	**Fundīs** *in/at Fundi*
domus *–ūs f*	**domum** *home*	**domō** *from home*	**domī** *at home*
rūs, rūris *n*	**rūs** *to the country*	**rūre** *from the country*	**rūrī** *in the country*

c. When the suffix **–dem** is added to the simple pronouns **is, ea, id** (*he, she, it*), the words mean *the same*. The complete declension is:

	SINGULAR			PLURAL		
NOM.	īdem	eadem	idem	eīdem	eaedem	eadem
GEN.	eiusdem	eiusdem	eiusdem	eōrundem	eārundem	eōrundem
DAT.	eīdem	eīdem	eīdem	eīsdem	eīsdem	eīsdem
ACC.	eundem	eandem	idem	eōsdem	eāsdem	eadem
ABL.	eōdem	eādem	eōdem	eīsdem	eīsdem	eīsdem

LĒCTIŌ X

a. If the suffix **–dam** is added to the forms of the relative pronoun (**quī, quae, quod**), the combined words mean *a certain:*

quīdam vir	*a certain man*
quaedam urbs	*a certain city*
quoddam tempus	*a certain time*

b. One group of adjectives has irregular genitive and dative endings: **–īus** in the genitive and **–ī** in the dative. The following adjectives belong to this group:

alius *–a –ud*	*another*	**ūn**us *–a –um*	*one, alone*
alter, altera, alterum	*the other*	**tōt**us *–a –um*	*whole, entire*
ūllus *–a –um*	*any*	**sōl**us *–a –um*	*only, alone*
nūllus *–a –um*	*no*	**ipse** *–a –um*	*self*

c. The intensifying pronoun/adjective **ipse, ipsa, ipsum** adds emphasis and must be distinguished from the reflexive pronoun:

> INTENSIVE: **Servus *ipse* pecuniam cēlāvit.**
>
> *The servant himself hid the money.*
>
> REFLEXIVE: **Servus *sē* cēlāvit.**
>
> *The servant hid himself.*

The complete declension of **ipse, ipsa, ipsum** serves as a model for all the pronoun/adjectives of this group:

	SINGULAR			PLURAL		
NOM.	ipse	ipsa	ipsum	ipsī	ipsae	ipsa
GEN.	ipsīus	ipsīus	ipsīus	ipsōrum	ipsārum	ipsōrum
DAT.	ipsī	ipsī	ipsī	ipsīs	ipsīs	ipsīs
ACC.	ipsum	ipsam	ipsum	ipsōs	ipsās	ipsa
ABL.	ipsō	ipsā	ipsō	ipsīs	ipsīs	ipsīs

ĀCTIVITĀS

A. Look at each picture. Unscramble the letters and write the Latin name of each object:

1.
2.
3.
4.
5.
6.
7.
8.

B. Scrambled Sentences. Correctly order the words, and write the English translation of each sentence:

1. miserōs mangō servōs dūcit Rōmānum in malus Forum

2. nūptam mātrimōnium marītus suam dūcit in bellam

3. sub Rōmulum lupa Monte invenit Pālatīnō et Remum

4. grave gladiātor suum mōnstrāvit medicō vulnus

5. īvit Appiam in familia raedā tōta Viam novā per

6. senātōrem sex in portābunt gestātōriā servī sellā

RECOGNITIŌ II **165**

C. With the exception of one word, all words in each group belong to the same category (for example, verbs, ablatives, nouns). For each group, write the word that doesn't belong. Then, write the category to which the other words belong.

1. īnsecta, scūta, terra, animālia, cubita
2. bene, deinde, ipse, saepe, rapidē
3. quī, quod, quae, quibus, quia
4. pīstor, miser, mōns, homō, augur
5. ille, haec, istud, hōc, autem
6. dīcit, movēbit, dūcet, accipiet, ambulābit
7. velle, nōlle, ferre, fonte, īre
8. condō, conīciō, subitō, nōminō, veniō
9. puellam, dīcam, nūptam, arēnam, amphoram
10. propter, quamquam, antequam, sī, dōnec
11. cum, prope, inter, propter, sed
12. fortiter, acriter, iter, celeriter, fidēliter
13. bonum, parvum, tergum, tumidum, frīgidum
14. aut, et, sed, -que, est
15. nunc, mox, hōrā, herī, hodiē

D. Word Search. Review the list of words below, which are all things and places a Roman would see or use when traveling on the Appian Way. The puzzle contains the Latin equivalents of these words. First, give the Latin equivalent of each word. Then, locate each word in the puzzle. Words may read from left to right, right to left, up or down, or diagonally.

1.	carriage	12.	sea
2.	cart	13.	spoke
3.	chariot	14.	town on Appian Way
4.	coachman	15.	town on Appian Way
5.	horse	16.	town on Appian Way
6.	inn	17.	traveler
7.	innkeeper	18.	trip
8.	litter	19.	two-wheeled carriage
9.	mule	20.	wagon
10.	ox	21.	wheel
11.	road	22.	women's carriage

```
M  A  C  I  T  C  E  L  C  K  R
U  S  A  S  A  S  A  S  A  S  A
I  B  O  U  U  S  U  A  R  P  E
S  B  P  L  U  R  F  R  P  L  D
I  A  U  I  R  E  U  I  E  A  A
C  M  D  U  C  Q  N  C  N  U  R
V  A  C  S  A  U  D  I  T  S  I
R  I  U  L  U  U  I  A  U  T  U
R  A  A  P  P  S  X  X  M  R  S
V  O  E  T  O  C  A  R  R  U  S
H  I  T  D  O  N  E  R  A  M  U
S  S  A  A  A  R  A  I  T  E  R
```

E. Using the list below, write the letter of the word that belongs to each numbered group:

a.	Rōmulus	d.	grabātus	g.	bōs	j.	Fundī
b.	frōns	e.	pānis	h.	genū		
c.	taeda	f.	plaustrum	i.	servus		

1.	nūpta	pompa	marītus	prōnuba
2.	raeda	cisium	carpentum	lectīca
3.	unguis	calx	umerus	spīna
4.	Arīcia	Bovillae	Formiae	Terracīna
5.	mangō	catasta	manicae	titulus
6.	tempus	planta	femur	articulus
7.	mola	frūmentum	farīna	furnus
8.	Laurentia	Palātīnus	Faustulus	lupa
9.	armārium	mēnsa	candēlābrum	sella
10.	mulus	mannus	equus	asinus

F. Cruciverbilūsus:

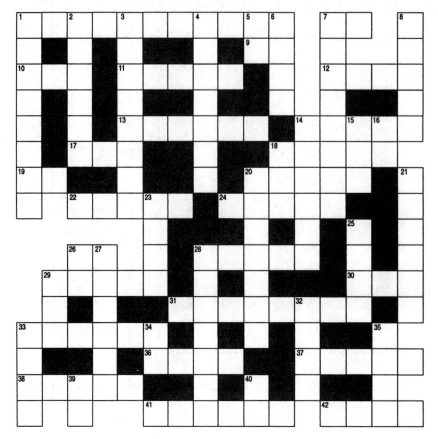

HORIZONTĀLE

1. marriage
7. from, by
9. you (*acc sing*)
10. for (*conj*)
11. often
12. he was going
13. elbows
14. father
17. or
18. alone
19. and
20. senate building
22. thigh

24. spear
26. you are
28. heavy (*n*)
29. daggers (*acc*)
30. they (*f pl*)
31. shepherds
33. happy
36. it will be
37. mule
38. round shield
41. beaver
42. roads

1. slave dealers
2. temples
3. insect
4. wedding
5. as, when
6. my (*m*)
7. animals
8. mother
14. gates
15. your (*f sing*)
16. you are
20. revolving auction block
21. spider
23. city
25. three
26. they (*m*)
27. oblong shield
28. sword
29. her own (*f sing*)
32. Rome
33. wolf (*f*)
34. himself
35. because
39. back, again (*prefix*)
40. I give

G. The Latin Connection. You may be unfamiliar with some of these words but, if you know their Latin origins, you should have a pretty good idea of their meanings. For each English derivative, write the Latin word from which it comes. Sometimes an English word comes from two Latin words. If you can, write both words:

1. pacify
2. unify
3. solitaire
4. unanimous
5. unison
6. unicycle
7. unilingual
8. education
9. nutrition
10. nominal
11. valediction
12. digital
13. cubit
14. genuflect
15. total
16. sole
17. cell
18. dolorous
19. sinister
20. partial
21. pastoral
22. vocal
23. title
24. dominate
25. molar
26. valve
27. circumstantial
28. lacrimose
29. servile
30. cook
31. repugnant
32. convention
33. deterrent
34. timorous
35. rotation
36. radiate
37. amorous
38. Montana
39. unique
40. nuptials

H. Below are nine definitions. Write the word that is missing from each definition. If the word is a noun, be sure to use the correct case. Then match each definition to the proper picture:

1. Quī _____ coquit est pīstor.

2. Quī _____ agitat (*drives*) est raedārius.

3. Quī _____ agitat est aurīga.

4. Quī _____ pāscit est pāstor.

5. Quī _____ cūrat est medicus.

6. Quī _____ adpōnit est caupō.

7. Quī _____ vēnditat est mangō.

8. Quī _____ in mātrimōnium dūcit est marītus.

9. Quī _____ cantat est tībīcen.

A.

B.

C.

D.

E.

F.

G.

H.

I.

I. Antonyms. Show your understanding of Latin vocabulary by writing the opposite of each Latin word. (Of course, each antonym should be in Latin!)

1.	ad	16.	vetus
2.	aestās	17.	calidus
3.	inimīcus	18.	ille
4.	anteā	19.	minimus
5.	malus	20.	optimus
6.	sine	21.	postquam
7.	nox	22.	salvē!
8.	accipĕre	23.	marītus
9.	ex	24.	vir
10.	mītis	25.	audāx
11.	grandis	26.	difficilis
12.	lentus	27.	sinister
13.	longus	28.	laetus
14.	pāx	29.	vērus
15.	magnus	30.	claudĕre

J. Synonyms. Do you know enough Latin to think of a word that means the same as each of the following? Give it a try by writing Latin synonyms for these vocabulary words:

1. lentus
2. vēlōx
3. validus
4. fortasse
5. propter
6. frequenter
7. atque
8. laetus
9. grandis
10. pariēs

PARS TERTIA

XI | Perseus

Passive Voice; Present, Imperfect, Future

1 Modicum cultūrae

Like people today, Romans were fascinated with stories about bigger-than-life heroes who perform fantastic feats no ordinary person can accomplish. Superman is simply one in a long line of fictional heroes that date even further back than the ancient Greeks and Romans. In fact, the lively imaginations of the Greeks were responsible for most of the hero stories the Romans later adopted.

Hercules was a kind of Superman, although he never flew through the air. Instead, he accomplished twelve seemingly impossible missions that required him to regularly risk his life for the sake of others. His only weapon—a big club! On one mission, he had to kill a lion; on another, he had to tame man-eating horses.

His toughest mission, however, was to descend to the realm of the dead and bring back alive Cerberus, the three-headed hound of the Underworld. The multitude of ancient Hercules statues scattered throughout the Mediterranean world is proof of this hero's immense popularity. The Roman emperor Commodus, who believed he was a reincarnation of the mythical hero, even commissioned statues of himself as Hercules!

Bearing an even greater resemblance to Superman, though, was another hero—Perseus. Thanks to winged sandals from Mercury, the winged messenger of the gods, Perseus could soar through the air. Pluto, the god of the dead, gave him a winged helmet that made him invisible whenever he chose. Mercury gave him a curved magical sword, with which he always succeeded in killing his foes. Like most heroes of the ancient Romans, Perseus was the son of a god (in this case, Jupiter) and a human mother (the Greek princess Danaë). Perseus was famous for performing two incredible feats: cutting off the head of the gorgon Medusa (a snake-haired woman who turned all who saw her into stone) and rescuing Princess Andromeda (who was chained to a cliff overlooking the sea) from a sea monster.

The ancients found it hard to imagine that the lives of such supermen would end in death like those of ordinary mortals; consequently, their tales had these heroes taken up to heaven to become constellations. You will need a good deal of imagination, however, to identify them in the sky, since only a few stars make up each constellation.

Perseus -ī m

parma -ae f

galea -ae f

solea -ae f

Gorgones -um fpl

Medūsa -ae f

Perseus -ī m

Cētus -ī m

Andromeda -ae f

Rēx Cepheus -ī m

Rēgīna Cassiopēa -ae f

ĀCTIVITĀS

A. Match the descriptions with the pictures:

Perseus in speculum spectat.
Solea ālās habet.
Perseus per āërem volat.
Galea ālās habet.

Perseus galeam induit.
Cētus est mōnstrum marīnum.
Gladius est curvus.
Perseus soleās induit.

1.

2.

3.

4.

5.

6.

7.

8.

3 To this point, all verbs in *Latin Is Fun* have been in the active voice. A verb is in the active voice when the subject is the person or thing that performs the action. If the subject *receives* the action of the verb, however, the verb is PASSIVE or in the passive voice. By studying the following pictures, you will see the difference between active and passive voice. Note the changes in the Latin verb:

1. Manūs meās *lavō*.   Ego ā mātre meā *lavor*.

2. Āthlētam *salūtāmus*.   Ab āthlētā *salūtāmur*.

3. Vulpēs cunīculum *petit*.   Vulpēs ā leopardō *petitur*.

4. Puerī canem *petunt*.   Puerī ā cane *petuntur*.

Look again at the first sentence. Which letter was added to **lavō** to form the passive? Now look at the second sentence; it has a plural verb. Which letter did the **s** in the ending become to form the passive? In the third sentence the active verb (third person singular) is **petit** (*chases*). Which letters were added to form the passive voice? The active verb (third person plural) of the fourth sentence is **petunt** (*they are chasing*). Which letters were added to form the passive voice?

The verbs in the first two sentences belong to the *–āre* conjugation; the verbs in the last two sentences belong to the *–ěre* conjugation. Yet, the letters added to form the passive voice were the same. In fact, the method of changing verbs from the present active to the present passive is *always* the same, regardless of the conjugation to which a verb belongs:

–ō changes to *–or* (amō, am***or***)   *–mus* changes to *–mur* (amā***mus***, amā***mur***)
–t changes to *–tur* (ama***t***, amā***tur***)   *–nt* changes to *–ntur* (ama***nt***, ama***ntur***)

Review the above sentences that contain passive verbs. Which preposition does each sentence contain? What case does this preposition always take? This preposition tells "by whom" the action was performed. This case is called *the ablative of personal agency*. It is also often used with animals: *ā cane* (*by a dog*).

4 Here's a story of superhero Perseus in action. Note in particular the passive verbs in bold type:

Perseus erat fīlius Iovis; ēius māter erat Danaē. Māter et fīlius in īnsulā Serīphō habitābant, in quā Polydectēs erat rēx. Danaē ā Polydectē **adamābātur,** sed Danaē rēgem nōn amābat. Rēx vērō eam in mātrimōnium dūcěre cupiēbat. Hōc cōnsilium autem neque mātrī neque fīliō placuit. Quamquam māter ā rēge **adamābātur,** fīlius ā rēge **timēbātur.**

Rēx autem Perseum dīmittěre cupiēbat. Itaque rēx cōnstituit mittěre eum in iter longinquum et perīculōsum. Rēx Perseum ad sē vocāvit et dīxit: "Abī hinc ad terram longinquam, in quā Medūsa habitat. Necā Medūsam et caput ēius ad mē reportā."

Medūsa autem, sīcut suae duae sorōrēs, erat mōnstrum horribile, et eae Gorgōnēs **vocābantur.** Serpentēs in locō comae habēbant. Quīcumque faciem Medūsae aspiciēbat, statim in saxum **mūtābātur.**

Antequam Perseus discessit, Plūtō, deus īnferōrum, galeam magicam eī dedit. Per hanc galeam magicam Perseus **reddēbātur** invīsibilis. Mercurius eī soleās ālātās dedit, quibus per aërem volāre poterat. Etiam magicum gladium curvum eī dedit, quō Medūsam necāre poterat. Minerva parmam speculārem eī dedit et dīxit: "Nōlī aspicěre Medūsam nisi per hanc speculārem

Danaē *–ēs f Greek female name* (*acc:* **Danaēn**)

Polydectēs *–ae m Greek male name* (*acc:* **Polydectēn**)
adamō *–āre –āvī –ātus to love deeply*
vērō *in fact* **cupiō** *–ěre –īvī* (*or –iī*) *to wish*
cōnsilium *–ī n idea, plan*

dīmittō *–ěre dīmīsī dīmissus to get rid of*
longinqu*us* *–a –um faraway, distant*
abī hinc! *go* (*from here*)!
reportō *–āre –āvī –ātus to bring back*
sīcut *just as, like*
Gorgō *–ōnis f Gorgon*
in locō (*+ gen*) *in place of, instead of*
quīcumque quaecumque *whoever;* **quodcumque** *whatever*
   aspiciō *–ěre aspexī aspectus to look at*
discēdō *–ěre discessī discessus to leave, depart*
īnferī *–ōrum m pl the dead, the underworld*
reddō *–ěre –idī –itus to render, make*
ālātus *–a –um winged*
speculāris *–is –e mirror-like, shiny*
nisi *except*

parmam. In memoriā tenē: quīcumque faciem Medūsae aspiciet, in saxum **mūtābitur.**"

Perseus deinde soleās ālātās pedibus nexit et in āërem ascendit. Diū per caelum volāvit, dōnec ad eum locum pervēnit, in quō Medūsa cum cēterīs Gorgōnibus dormiēbat.

Perseus, in parmam speculārem īnspiciēns, Medūsae caput gladiō curvō magicō dētruncāvit. Cēterae Gorgōnēs statim ē somnō **excitābantur** et Perseum oppugnābant.

Perseus autem galeam magicam citō induit et in caelum ascendit, et caput Medūsae ad aulam Polydectae reportāvit. Rēx malus id avidē aspexit et statim in saxum **mūtābātur.** Māter ēius, ex aulā currēns, Perseum magnō cum gaudiō excēpit. "Mī fīlī," inquit māter lacrimāns, "ego ā rēge malō diū **terrēbar.** Nunc ā tē **servor.** Dēnique fēlīciter vīvere poterimus."

in memoriā tenēre *to remember, keep in mind*

nectō *–ere* **nexī** *to tie*
dōnec *until*

cēterī *–ae –a the remaining, the rest of*
īnspiciō *–ere* **īnspexī īnspectus** *to look into*
dētruncō *–āre –āvī –ātus to cut off*
somnus *–ī m sleep*   **excitō** *–āre –āvī –ātus to awaken*
oppugnō *–āre –āvī –ātus to attack*
aula *–ae f palace*
avidē *eagerly*

gaudium *–ī n joy*   **excipiō** *–ere* **excēpī exceptus** *to welcome*
dēnique *at last*

ĀCTIVITĀS

B. Respondē ad quaestiōnēs:

1. Quis erat pater Perseī?

2. Quod nōmen erat mātrī?

3. Ubi habitābant māter et fīlius?

4. Quot sorōrēs habuit Medūsa?

5. Quid est Gorgō?

6. Quid Gorgōnēs in locō comae habēbant?

7. Quid Perseum invīsibilem reddidit?

8. Quī deus soleās ālātās Perseō dedit?

9. Quid praeterea Perseum dedit?

10. Quis dedit Perseō parmam speculārem?

5 Let's look at the active and passive forms of an *–āre* verb in the present, imperfect, and future tenses. To keep things simple, we won't list the second person because the first and third persons of the verb occur much more frequently and should be learned first:

		ACTIVE		PASSIVE
PRESENT:	**vocō**	*I am calling, I call*	**vocor**	*I am called*
	vocat	*he/she/it is calling*	**vocātur**	*he/she/it is called*
	vocāmus	*we are calling*	**vocāmur**	*we are called*
	vocant	*they are calling*	**vocantur**	*they are called*
IMPERFECT:	**vocābam**	*I was calling, I called*	**vocābar**	*I was called*
	vocābat	*he/she/it was calling*	**vocābātur**	*he/she/it was called*
	vocābāmus	*we were calling*	**vocābāmur**	*we were called*
	vocābant	*they were calling*	**vocābāntur**	*they were called*
FUTURE:	**vocābō**	*I will call*	**vocābor**	*I will be called*
	vocābit	*he/she/it will call*	**vocābitur**	*he/she/it will be called*
	vocābimus	*we will call*	**vocābimur**	*we will be called*
	vocābunt	*they will call*	**vocābuntur**	*they will be called*

ĀCTIVITĀTĒS

C. Below are the active forms of **mittĕre** (*to send*). Write the corresponding passive forms. (Remember what happens to the endings of the verb **vocāre**: **–ō** changes to **–or**, **–mus** changes to **–mur**, **–t** changes to **–tur**, and **–nt** changes to **–ntur**.)

PRESENT: mittō
                mittit
                mittimus
                mittunt
IMPERFECT: mittēbam
                mittēbat
                mittēbāmus
                mittēbant
FUTURE: mittam
                mittet
                mittēmus
                mittent

6 As you learned earlier, when a sentence has a passive verb, you can expect to find that the person (or animal) by whom the action is performed is in the ablative case with the prepositions **ā** or **ab**:

Medūsa *ā Perseō* necābitur.   *Medusa will be killed by Perseus.*

But if the action is performed *by means of something*, no preposition is used:

Medūsa *gladiō curvō* necābitur.   *Medusa will be killed with a curved sword.*

ĀCTIVITĀTĒS

D. In the following sentences, distinguish between the ablative of personal agency (which requires the prepositions **ā** or **ab**) and the ablative of means or instrument. Write the phrase in parentheses that is correct for each sentence:

1. Perseus (galeā magicā / ā galeā magicā) invīsibilis redditur.

2. Danaē (rēge malō / ā rēge malō) adamābātur.

3. Multī (ā Medūsae capite / Medūsae capite) in saxum mūtābantur.

4. Galea magica (Perseō / ā Perseō) gestātur.

5. Ego (ā Gorgōnibus / Gorgōnibus) facile terreor.

6. Perseus (ā rēge Polydectē / rēge Polydectē) magnopere timēbātur.

7. Medūsa et sorōrēs (multīs / ā multīs) Gorgōnēs vocantur.

8. Nōs omnēs (parentibus nostrīs / ā parentibus nostrīs) amāmur.

E. Rewrite the following sentences, changing them from the passive to the active. (The object of the preposition will become the subject of the active sentence.)

> EXAMPLE: Galea magica ā **Perseō** gestābātur.
>
> **Perseus** galeam magicam gestābat.

1. Perseus ā rēge in terram longinquam mittēbātur.

2. Caput Medūsae ā Perseō dētruncābātur.

3. Medūsa propter superbiam suam ā Minervā in puellam dēformem (*ugly*) mūtābātur.

4. Perseus et Danaē ab Acrisiō in īnsulam Serīphum mittēbantur.

5. Caput Medūsae ā Perseō ad aulam Polydectae reportābātur.

6. "Cūr tantum ā rēge Polydectē timeor?" rogāvit Perseus.

7. Raeda nostra ā raedāriō optimō agitātur.

8. Cibus bonus nōbīs ab illō caupōne adpōnitur.

F. Rewrite the following sentences, changing them from the active to the passive. (The direct object of the active sentence will become the subject of the passive sentence. The subject of the active sentence will become the object of the prepositions ā or **ab** or the instrumental ablative.)

> EXAMPLE: Spectātōrēs **gladiātōrem** victōrem laudant.
>
> **Gladiātor** victor ā spectātōribus laudātur.

1. Perseus mātrem maximē amat.
2. Perseus Medūsam dormientem necābit.
3. Gorgōnēs Perseum oppugnābant.
4. Māter nōs ē somnō māne excitābit.
5. Serpentēs suprā Medūsae caput Perseum nōn terrent.
6. Quis Perseum in terram longinquam mittet?
7. Perseus speculum ante sē tenēbat.
8. Fābulae dē Perseō mē semper dēlectant.

G. Below are descriptions of things happening now. Rewrite the sentences so that these things happened in the past by changing the sentences to the imperfect tense:

1. Aqua ab Aquāriō portātur.
2. Aegrī ā medicō cūrantur.
3. Vulnera rētiāriī ā medicō sānantur.
4. Oculī meī fūmō īnflammantur.
5. Ego et Claudius ab avō et aviā ēducāmur.
6. Haec medīcīna ab aegrīs nōn sūmitur.
7. Ego ā magistrīs meīs semper attentē (*closely*) observor.
8. Futūra ab auguribus Rōmānīs praedīcuntur.

H. You are reminiscing with a friend about your childhood. Complete the following sentences by writing the correct passive imperfect form of the verb in parentheses:

1. (amāre) Ego ā parentibus semper _____.
2. (dēfendĕre) Ego ā frātre maiōre nātū interdum _____.
3. (verberāre) Ego et frātrēs meī ā parentibus numquam _____.
4. (addūcĕre) Ego et soror mea ad thermās ā mātre _____.
5. (docēre) Ego ā magistrīs optimīs Latīnē _____.

6. (vīsitāre) Multa oppida inter Rōmam et Capuam ā familiā meā _____.

7. (nārrāre) Multae fābulae dē Perseō ā patre mihi _____.

8. (lavāre) Quandō īnfāns eram, ego ā mātre cōtīdiē _____.

I. These events happened in the past. Here's your chance to become a great astrologer! Predict that these events will happen in the future by rewriting the imperfect-tense verb in each statement in the future tense. Be careful! The future tense of the last four verbs is formed differently from that of the first four:

1. Duodecim vulturēs ā Rōmulō observābantur.

2. Urbs nova ā Rōmulō aedificābātur.

3. Urbs Rōma ā multīs aliēnīs vīsitābātur.

4. Ego prīmā lūce ē somnō excitābar.

5. Multa verba ā senātōribus in cūriā dīcēbantur.

6. Vōx āctōris per theātrum audiēbātur.

7. Medūsa et sorōrēs ā Perseō vincēbantur.

8. Ego et frāter meus ab aviā magnō cum gaudiō excipiēbāmur.

7 Learning the passive infinitive form is easy! All you have to do is change the final –*e* to –*ī*:

ACTIVE		PASSIVE	
portāre	*to carry*	**portārī**	*to be carried*
movēre	*to move*	**movērī**	*to be moved*
dūcĕre	*to lead*	**dūcī**	*to be led*
accipĕre	*to receive*	**accipī**	*to be received*
audīre	*to hear*	**audīrī**	*to be heard*

Did you notice that the passive infinitive of the –*ĕre* and –*iō* conjugations omits two letters? Which two letters were omitted in **dūcī** and **accipī**?

ĀCTIVITĀTĒS

J. Write the active and passive infinitives of the following verbs:

1. amō

2. adiuvō

3. terreō

4. respondeō

5. scrībō

6. gerō

7. aspiciō

8. incipiō

9. mūniō

10. fīniō

K. Read the following sentences. Sentence sense will suggest which infinitive (enclosed in parentheses) is appropriate in each sentence. Write the correct infinitive. Note that **videor** may mean *I am seen* but much more frequently means *I seem*:

1. Danaē ā rēge Polydectē (amāre/amārī) vidēbātur.

2. Caput Medūsae hominēs in saxum (mūtāre/mūtārī) poterat.

3. Gorgōnēs serpentēs in locō comae (habēre/habērī) dīcuntur.

4. Rēx Polydectēs Perseum (dīmittĕre/dīmittī) cupīvit.

5. Gorgōnēs ā Perseō ē somnō (excitāre/excitārī) vidēbantur.

6. Perseus ā Gorgōnibus (oppugnāre/oppugnārī) dīcēbātur.

7. Perseus Medūsam (aspicĕre/aspicī) nōn poterat nisi per speculum.

8. Via Appia ab Appiō Claudiō Caecō (mūnīre/mūnīrī) dīcitur.

8 Let's read more about the adventures of Perseus! Passive verbs are in bold type:

Perseus, postquam Medūsam dētruncāvit et mātrem suam servāvit, per āērem volāns, ad Aethiopiam vēnit ubi Cēpheus erat rēx. Hīc rēx fīliam bellissimam habēbat, quae Andromeda **vocābātur.** Rēgīna, quae Cassiopēa **vocābātur,** ōlim dē pulchritūdine fīliae suae sē iactāverat. Quōdam diē, dum rēgīna Cassiopēa et fīlia sua in ōrā maritimā stābant, māter dīxit: "In aquā, mea fīlia, multae nymphae pulchrae habitant, sed tū es multō pulchrior quam omnēs istae nymphae."

Aethiopia *–ae f Ethiopia*

ōlim *once*
  pulchritūdō *–inis f beauty*
  sē iactāre dē *(+ abl) to boast about*
dum *while*

Subitō Neptūnus, hīs verbīs īrātus, ex aquā surrēxit et magnā vōce clāmāvit: "Ob hanc superbiam, sacrificium postulō. Necte fīliam tuam scopulō prope mare. Cētum, mōnstrum marīnum, mittam. Hōc mōnstrum fīliam tuam dēvorābit. Fīlia ā tē nōn **servābitur.** Neque ā patre suō **servābitur.**"

surgō *–ĕre* **surrēxī** *to rise*
  magnus *–a –um loud*
postulō *–āre –āvī –ātus to demand*
nectō *–āre –āvī –ātus to tie up*
scopulus *–ī m cliff*   **cētus** *–ī m shark, whale, sea monster*
marīnus *–a –um (of the) sea*
dēvorō *–āre –āvī –ātus to devour*

Itaque Andromeda ā servīs rēgis scopulō prope mare **nectēbātur,** dum Cēpheus et Cassiopēa et populus inopēs circumstābant. Cētus iam ōrae maritimae appropinquābat, cum subitō Perseus, per āērem volāns, puellam

inopēs *helplessly*
appropinquō *–āre –āvī –ātus (+ dat) to approach*

trementem cōnspicuit. Omnēs in ōrā maritimā oculōs in puerum volantem convertērunt. Tamquam fulmen, Perseus dē caelō dēscendit et cētum gladiō magicō oppugnāvit. Ter Perseus corpus mōnstrī gladiō suō perfōdit. Ter cētus magnā vōce fremuit. Omnēs circumstantēs tremuērunt. Sed Perseus sōlus ā mōnstrō nōn **terrēbātur.** Iterum atque iterum Perseus cētum gladiō suō perfōdit. Dēnique Perseus mōnstrum necāvit et Andromedam līberāvit. Rēx Perseō dīxit: "Quia tū sōlus fīliam bellissimam servāvit, ego eam tibi in mātrimōnium dabō." Omnēs deinde ad aulam īvērunt, ubi Perseus Andromedam in mātrimōnium dūxit.

Post multōs annōs, rēx Cēpheus et rēgīna Cassiopēa et Andromeda et Perseus et cētus in cōnstellātiōnēs **convertēbantur.** Etiam nunc eōs in caelō vidēre possumus.

tremō *–ĕre –uī to tremble*
 cōnspiciō *–ĕre cōnspexī*
 cōnspectus *to spot*
oculōs convertĕre in (+ *acc*) *to turn* (*the eyes on*)
tamquam *like*   **fulmen** *–inis* n *lightning*
ter *three times*
fremō *–ĕre –uī to roar*
iterum *again*

līberō *–āre –āvī –ātus to free*

L. Respondē ad quaestiōnēs:

1. Quōmodo Perseus ad Aethiopiam vēnit?

2. Quis erat rēx Aethiopiae?

3. Quis erat rēgīna Aethiopiae?

4. Dē quō Cassiopēa sē iactāverat?

5. Quem deum Cassiopēa hīs verbīs offendit?

6. Quid Neptūnus ob Cassiopēae superbiam postulāvit?

7. Quid mīsit Neptūnus ex marī?

8. Ubi Andromeda nectēbātur?

9. Quis Andromedam Perseō in mātrimōnium dedit?

10. Ubi Cēpheum et Cassiopēam et Andromedam et Perseum et cētum vidēre possumus?

VOCĀBULA

avē *hello*
quamobrem *why*
gerō *–ĕre* **gessī gestus** *to wear*
fīō *I become*
nūgās! *nonsense!*
plānē *clearly, plainly*
forte *by chance*

sī forte vidēbō *if I happen to see*
certē *without fail*
blatta *–ae* f *cockroach*
nequīrēs *you couldn't*
continuō *continuously*
continuō īnspicĕre *to keep looking into*
dīrectē *directly*

Rēs Persōnālēs

A. Using the Latin passive voice, list four things that happened to you in the past.

EXAMPLE: Ego ab amīcīs adiuvābar. (*I was helped by my friends.*)

B. Name three persons you consider to be heroes. Explain why you chose each person.

Compositiō

As you read the adventures of Perseus, you saw the kind of Superman (**Supervir** *–virī m*) he was and what he could do. Describe the physical appearance of the modern-day Superman and explain what he is able to do.

Complete this dialog with expressions from the previous conversation, substituting your own expressions whenever you can:

⟲ THE LATIN CONNECTION

A. What does the expression **et cētera** mean?

B. How is **et cētera** commonly abbreviated?

C. **Somnus** means *sleep.* What problem does someone with insomnia have?

D. The Latin suffix *–ficāre* means *to make, to cause* and is used in combinations such as **aedificāre** (*to make a building*) and **sacrificāre** (*to make sacred*). The suffix *–ficāre* appears in English as the suffix *–fy* as in *sanctify* (to make holy) [from **sanctus** (*holy*) and *–ficāre* (*to make*)]. Copy the chart below. For each English derivative listed in Column 1, write the Latin word from which it comes in Column 2. Then, in Column 3, write the meaning of each derivative:

EXAMPLE: sanctify   **sanctus** (*holy*) + *–ficāre* (*to make*)   *to make holy*

1. deify
2. diversify
3. falsify
4. fortify
5. justify
6. magnify
7. nullify
8. pacify
9. personify
10. simplify
11. unify
12. verify

Your teacher will ask you to use each verb in a sentence to make sure you know how to use it correctly.

XII | Tempestās

Perfect and Pluperfect Passive; Deponent Verbs

1 Modicum cultūrae

Today, we rely on television, the radio, and the newspaper for weather forecasts so we can plan activities. The Romans, however, did not have these resources. Instead, they had to observe nature closely for clues about the weather (**tempestās –atis** *f*). Since farming and sailing were important occupations in ancient Rome and since success in both depended on knowledge of the weather, the Romans eagerly established a body of weather lore, which they passed from generation to generation. Sailors determined the beginning and end of the sailing season as well as the approach of storms at sea from the rising and setting of various stars and constellations. Farmers used this information to figure out when to plow, sow, and harvest crops. The everyday Roman farmer and sailor probably knew more about astronomy than most people know today.

As you might expect, the Romans attributed changes in the weather to the gods. Jupiter was the god of thunder, lightning, and rain. Iris was the goddess of the rainbow, and Aeolus was the god of the winds. In fact, the Romans did not regard the stars as inanimate objects; instead, they believed the skies were populated with mythological persons and animals. In the last chapter you read how Perseus, Andromeda, Cepheus, Cassiopea, Cetus, and even Medusa's head wound up as constellations. As you know, the planets were identified with Roman gods. (How many do you remember?) In addition, you read in Lesson III that the twelve signs of the zodiac have Latin names. In fact, all 88 constellations in the Northern Hemisphere have Latin names!

Did you know that, some 1500 years before Columbus, Greeks and Romans knew that the earth was round and that it revolved around its own axis in twenty-four hours? One astronomer even figured out the circumference of the earth and divided the earth into torrid, temperate, and frigid zones.

2 Vocābula

ventus -ī m

fulmen -inis n

nix, nivis f

grandō -inis m

imber -bris m

pluvius arcus -us m

glaciēs -ēī f

pila nivea -ae f

stiria -ae f

ĀCTIVITĀTĒS

A. Match the descriptions with the pictures:

Stīriae dē tēctō dēpendent.
Pluvius arcus multōs colōrēs habet.
Ventus vehementer flat.
Puer in glaciē cadit.
Puerī virum ex nive faciunt.

Grandō in puerī caput cadit.
Puellae pilās niveās conīciunt.
Fulmen inter nūbēs corūscat (*flashes*).
Imber dē caelō cadit.

1.

2.

3.

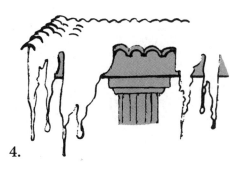

4.

5.

6.

7.

8.

9.

B. We use certain impersonal verbs to describe the weather. Figure out the meanings of the Latin verbs by looking at the pictures they describe:

1. Pluit.

2. Ningit.

3. Grandinat.

4. Fulminat.

3 Since you are now familiar with the passive voice of verbs in the present, imperfect, and future tenses, let's learn the passive forms of the other two tenses: the perfect and the pluperfect.

Before we begin, though, we must first look at the principal parts of verbs. You have already learned about the first three principal parts of verbs: present tense, infinitive, and perfect tense:

portō   *I carry, am carrying*
portāre   *to carry*
portāvī   *I carried, have carried*

There is a fourth principal part, called the PERFECT PASSIVE PARTICIPLE: **portātus –a –um,** which means *carried* or *having been carried.*

ĀCTIVITĀS

C. Write the four principal parts of each of the following verbs. Use **portō** as a model:

EXAMPLE: **portō   portāre   portāvī   portātus**

1. amō

2. optō

3. vocō

4. salūtō

4 Very good! With only a few exceptions (**dare,** for example), the formation of the principal parts of the **–āre** conjugation is regular. Unfortunately, the principal parts of other verbs are not quite so regular, so from now on you will learn the principal parts of all verbs. Learning the four principal parts helps you recognize and translate verbs. All good Latin dictionaries list each verb's four principal parts.

Now we can form the perfect passive tense. It consists of the perfect passive participle plus the present tense forms of **sum:**

portātus sum	*I was carried*	**portātī sumus**	*we were carried*
portātus es	*you were carried*	**portātī estis**	*you were carried*
portātus est	*he was carried*	**portātī sunt**	*they were carried*

> **CAUTION:** Don't confuse the auxiliary verb **sum** with the word **sum** when it serves as the main verb of a sentence:
>
> **Ego bonus *sum*.**   *I am good.*   (**Sum** is the main verb.)
> **Ego vocātus *sum*.**   *I was summoned.*   (**Sum** is the auxiliary verb.)

The pluperfect passive tense consists of the perfect participle plus the imperfect tense of **sum:**

portātus eram	*I had been carried*	**portātī erāmus**	*we had been carried*
portātus erās	*you had been carried*	**portātī erātis**	*you had been carried*
portātus erat	*he had been carried*	**portātī erānt**	*they had been carried*

Actually, the participle has three endings just like the adjective **bonus -a -um**: **portā*tus* -*a* -*um*.** The subject of the sentence will determine which ending is to be used in the participle:

Andromeda ā Perseō līberā*ta* est.	*Andromeda was freed by Perseus.*
Mōnstrum marīnum ā Perseō necā*tum* erat.	*A sea monster had been killed by Perseus.*
Hae trēs sorōrēs vocā*tae* sunt Gorgōnēs.	*These three sisters were called Gorgons.*
Eīdem virī in lectīcā portā*tī* erant.	*The same men had been carried in the litter.*

ĀCTIVITĀS

D. Write the following perfect-passive verbs in the pluperfect passive:

1. Speculum ā Perseō manū sinistrā portātum est.

2. Medūsa ā Perseō truncāta est.

3. Ubi vulnerātī estis?

4. Ego et soror in lectīcā portātī sumus.

5. Ego ā patrē vocātus sum.

6. Quamobrem tū ab omnibus amāta es?

5 As you read this story of a treasure hunt, you will notice several verbs in the perfect passive tense. These verbs are in bold type:

Erat diēs serēnus ultimā parte autumnī. Tempestās erat clāra. Sōl lūcēbat. Ego et amīcus Flaccus in ōrā maritimā ambulābāmus, cum Flaccus dīxit: "Vidēsne illam īnsulam? Abhinc multōs annōs, thēsaurus vastus ā pīrātīs ibi **occultātus est** in cavernā sub scopulō. Vīsne ad īnsulam nāvigāre et thēsaurum quaerěre? Sī illum thēsaurum inveniēmus, dīvitissimī erimus."

"Ita," ego respondī. Nāviculam Flaccī avidē cōnscendimus et vēla dedimus. Sed mox tempestās **mūtāta est.** Sōl nōn iam lūcēbat. Caelum nōn iam clārum sed nūbilum erat. Deinde imber caděre incēpit. Nōn sōlum pluit sed tonuit et fulmināvit. Ventī frīgidī ex septentriōnibus flābant. Propter imbrem et nebulam, neque ōra neque īnsula cōnspicī poterat. Tonitrus ā nōbīs **audītus est** et fulmen **vīsum est.** Nāvicula fluctibus altīs **pulsāta est.**

serēn*us* -*a* -*um* *calm, clear*
   ultim*us* -*a* -*um* *last*
lūceō -ēre luxī *to shine*

abhinc *ago*

thēsaur*us* -*ī* *m treasure*
   occultō -āre *to hide*
sub (+ *abl*) *at the foot of*
   scopul*us* -*ī* *m cliff*
quaerō -ěre quaesīvī quaesītus *to look for*
nāvicula -ae *f boat*
cōnscendō -ěre -ī *to climb aboard*
   vēla dare *to set sail*
mūtāta est *changed*
nūbil*us* -*a* -*um* *cloudy, overcast*
cadō -ěre cecidī casus *to fall*
   incipiō -ěre incēpī inceptus *to begin*
tonō -āre -uī *to thunder*
   fulminō -āre -āvī *to lighten*
septentriōnēs -um *m pl the north*
   flō -āre -āvī *to blow*
nebula -ae *f fog, mist*
tonitr*us* -*ūs* *m thunder*
pulsō -āre -āvī -ātus *to batter, pound*

"Dī superī," exclāmāvit Flaccus, "servāte nōs ā naufragiō."

Tunc maximē nāvis magna forte praeternāvigābat. Nāvicula nostra ā nāvis magistrō **cōnspecta est.** Ego et Flaccus dēnique **servātī sumus.**

"Cūr nāvigātis," interrogāvit nāvis magister, "cum pluit et tonat et fulminat? Haec tempestās est perīculōsa etiam nautīs."

"Nāvis magister," ego respondī, "quandō vēla dedimus, tempestās erat clāra. Neque pluēbat eō tempore neque tonābat neque fulminābat. Tantum posteā tempestās **mutāta est.**"

"Quō nāvigābātis?" interrogāvit nāvis magister.

"Ad īnsulam nōn procul abhinc, in quā ōlim thēsaurus vastus ā pīrātīs **occultātus erat.** Spēs nōbīs erat illum thēsaurum invenīre."

"Ille thēsaurus," rīdēbat nāvis magister, "iamprīdem **inventus est.** Ego ipse thēsaurum in cavernā sub scopulō invēnī, et nunc ego divitissimus sum!"

---

dī superī *gods above*
naufragium –ī *n shipwreck*

tunc maximē *just then*
  praeternāvigō –āre –āvī –ātus
    to sail by

(nāvis) magister –trī *m captain*
cum *when*
etiam *even*

tantum *only*

quō *where (to)*

nōn procul abhinc *not far from here*
spēs –ēī *f hope*

iamprīdem *long ago*

ĀCTIVITĀS

E. Respondē ad quaestiōnēs:

1. Ubi Flaccus et amīcus ambulābant?

2. Quid erat eōrum locus dēstinātus?

3. Quōmodo ad locum dēstinātum pervenīre (*arrive*) cupiēbant?

4. Quid in īnsulā occultātum erat?

5. Ā quō occultātum erat?

6. Quō tempore annī puerī nāvigāvērunt?

7. Quālis (*what kind of*) tempestās erat quandō puerī vēla dedērunt?

8. Cūr posteā neque ōra neque insula cōnspicī poterat?

9. Quid nāviculam pulsāvit?

10. Ā quō puerī dēnique servātī sunt?

6 When you make a Latin transitive verb (that is, it takes a direct object) passive, it then can have an intransitive sense. For example, **lavāre** means *to wash* someone or something. If the Romans wanted to use this word in an intransitive sense, they made the verb passive. You'll get the idea if you look at these pairs of sentences:

TRANSITIVE:	**Manūs meās lavō.**	*I am washing my hands.*
INTRANSITIVE:	**Nōn cōtīdīe lavor.**	*I don't wash every day.*
TRANSITIVE:	**Nāvis magister mentem mūtāvit.**	*The captain changed his mind.*
INTRANSITIVE:	**Tempestās repentē mutāta est.**	*The weather suddenly changed.*

ĀCTIVITĀS

F. Do you think you can tell the difference between a true passive verb and a passive verb that serves in an intransitive sense? Let's see! Write whether the verbs in the following sentences are TRUE PASSIVE or INTRANSITIVE:

1. Īnfāns ā mātre lavātur.

2. Āthlēta in tepidāriō lavātur.

3. Sella ā servō mōta est.

4. Canis numquam mōtus est.

5. Nix in imbrem mūtāta est.

6. Omnia in nātūrā mūtantur.

7 Certain Latin verbs, called DEPONENT VERBS, have *passive* forms but *active* meanings. Since even the Roman grammarians did not agree on why these verbs were called "deponent," it makes more sense to think of them as "fake passive verbs." For example, **admīror** does NOT mean *I am admired*; instead, it means *I admire*. Following are the principal parts of some very useful "fake passives":

admīror	**admīrārī**	**admīrātus sum**	*to admire*
cōnor	**cōnārī**	**cōnātus sum**	*to try*
videor	**vidērī**	**vīsus sum**	*to seem*
medeor (+ *dat*)	**medērī**	– – –	*to heal*
loquor	**loquī**	**locūtus sum**	*to speak*
nāscor	**nāscī**	**nātus sum**	*to be born*
sequor	**sequī**	**secūtus sum**	*to follow*
ūtor (+ *abl*)	**ūtī**	**ūsus sum**	*to use*
morior	**morī**	**mortuus sum**	*to die*
orior	**orīrī**	**ortus sum**	*to rise*

Notice that these verbs belong to various conjugations. As usual, those in the *-ĕre* family (**loquor, nāscor, sequor, ūtor**) drop the letters **e** and **r** in the infinitive. **Morior** (*to die*) belongs to the *-iō* conjugation and, therefore, also drops the **e** and **r** in the infinitive.

G. To practice seeing passive forms of verbs but understanding them in an active sense, write the English meanings of the following sentences:

1. Omnēs Perseum admīrantur.

2. Īnfāns loquī cōnātur.

3. Hiems autumnum sequitur.

4. Rōmānī Latīnē locūtī sunt.

5. Senātor iūstus esse vidētur.

6. Sōl in oriente oritur.

7. Nōn cupiō morī.

8. Quot īnfantēs cōtīdiē nāscuntur?

9. Pecūniā meā bene ūtor.

10. Medicī aegrīs medentur.

11. Quis tē secūtus est?

12. Quī Rōmae nāscuntur, sunt Rōmānī.

H. Read the following sentences carefully. Then write each present-tense verb in the pluperfect tense:

1. Omnēs Rōmānī Rōmulum admīrantur.

2. Omnēs līberī nivem cadentem admīrārī videntur.

3. Ego tē adiuvāre cōnor.

4. Gladiātōrēs gladiīs et ocreīs et scūtīs ūtuntur.

5. Sōl māne prīmā horā oritur.

6. Flōrēs hieme moriuntur.

7. Omnēs dē nive et glaciē loquuntur.

8. Frāterculus meus mē ubīque sequitur.

I. You are feeling contrary today. Answer the following questions in the negative:

1. Dē tempestāte locūtus(–a) es?

2. Amīcum tuum ad scholam herī secūtus(–a) es?

3. Hodiēne magistram tuam admīrātus(–a) es?

4. Cōnātus(–a) es cum amīcīs tuīs Latīnē loquī?

5. Admīrātus(–a) es pluvium arcum post imbrem?

J. Write each singular subject and verb in the plural:

1. Vēnātor bestiās sequitur.
2. Discipulus magistrō placēre cōnātur.
3. Ego fulmina in caelō vidēre videor.
4. Augur dē avibus loquitur.
5. Augur lituō ūtitur.
6. Nox diem sequitur.

K. Your friend doesn't know Latin but has to write a report on constellations. The friend has no idea of what the constellation names mean. Can you help your friend by writing the English meaning of each Latin name?

1. Aquila
2. Cētus
3. Columba
4. Lupus
5. Mēnsa
6. Plaustrum
7. Serpēns
8. Pāvō
9. Pictor
10. Sagitta
11. Sculptor
12. Canis Māior
13. Canis Minor
14. Musca
15. Caput Medūsae
16. Ursa Māior
17. Ursa Minor
18. Via Lactea

L. Rewrite the following sentences with the verb in the perfect tense:

1. Pluvius arcus imbrem saepe sequitur.
2. Glaciēs in viā esse vidēbātur.
3. Nix in montibus altissima esse vidētur.
4. Multī mīlitēs in proeliō moriēbantur.
5. Hieme omnēs dē grandine et glaciē et nive loquuntur.
6. Hī ventī ex septentriōnibus oriuntur.
7. Puerī mē pilīs niveīs icĕre (*hit*) cōnantur.
8. Thēsaurus in cavernā sub scopulō occultārī vidēbātur.

Compositiō

The weather influences all of us. It often restricts activities, but it also gives us many occasions for fun. Explain in Latin how the weather influences what you do.

VOCĀBULA

forīs *outside, outdoors*
nimis *too*
fīunt *get, become*
dēpendeō –ēre –ī *to hang down*

dētrahō –ĕre dētraxī dētractus *to pull off*
gustō –āre –āvī –ātus *to taste, eat*
exspectō –āre –āvī –ātus *to wait for*
libenter *gladly*

Quaestiōnēs Persōnālēs

1. Praefersne hiemem aestāti? Cūr?

2. Praefersne imbrem nivī? Cūr?

3. Lūdisne domī an forīs cum pluit?

4. Observāsne fulmen cum fulminat?

5. Cōnsīderāsne fulmen in caelō esse pulchrum?

6. Manēsne domī an forīs cum tonat et fulminat?

7. Quid magis timēs, fulmen an tonitrum?

8. Exspectāsne pluvium arcum post imbrem?

9. Fēcistīne umquam virum ex nive?

10. Placetne tibi in nive lūděre?

11. Gustāvistīne umquam stīriam?

12. Īcistīne (*hit*) umquam quemquam (*anyone*) pilā niveā? Quem?

Colloquium

You are the second person in this dialog. Complete it based on the model of the previous conversation:

Cupisne mēcum forīs lūděre?	_____ _____ (Say that it's cold outside today.)
Timēsne nivem et grandinem et glaciem?	_____ _____ (Say that you are not afraid of anything.)
Timēsne pilās niveās mēcum conjicěre?	_____ _____ (Say that you don't throw snowballs at girls.)
Timēsne ventōs frīgīdos ex septentriōnibus flantēs?	_____ _____ (Say that you prefer warm winds from the south.)
Cūr igitur mēcum forīs lūděre nōn vīs?	_____ _____ (Give your own response.)

⟳ THE LATIN CONNECTION

A. The fourth principal part of Latin verbs is often the source of other Latin words as well as English words. If you drop the *–us* ending of the past passive participle and add *–or,* you form the doer of the verb's action. If you drop the *–us* and add *–iō,* the result is a noun that describes that action:

respirō *–āre –āvī* **respirātus**   (*to breathe*):   **respirātor** *–ōris*   *m breather, respirator*

   respirātiō *–ōnis*   *f breathing, respiration*

Now write the Latin and English derivatives of these verbs in the same way:

1. **celebrō** *–āre –āvī* **celebrātus** (*to celebrate*)
2. **cōnsultō** *–āre –āvī* **cōnsultātus** (*to consult*)
3. **decorō** *–āre –āvī* **decorātus** (*to decorate*)
4. **līberō** *–āre –āvī* **līberātus** (*to free*)
5. **exhibeō** *–ēre –uī* **exhibitus** (*to exhibit*)
6. **moveō** *–ēre –ī* **mōtus** (*to move*)
7. **prohibeō** *–ēre –uī* **prohibitus** (*to prohibit*)
8. **agō** *–ĕre* **ēgī āctus** (*to do*)
9. **colligō** *–ĕre* **collēgī collēctus** (*to gather*)
10. **prōtegō** *–ĕre* **prōtēxī prōtēctus** (*to protect*)
11. **trahō** *–ĕre* **trāxī trāctus** (*to pull*)
12. **faciō** *–ĕre* **fēcī factus** (*to do*)
13. **inspiciō** *–ĕre* **īnspexī īnspectus** (*to look into*)
14. **audiō** *–īre –īvī* **audītus** (*to hear*)
15. **inveniō** *–īre* **invēnī inventus** (*to find*)

> **NOTE:** Some verbs don't give us two derivatives from the past participle. For example, the past participle of **doceō** is **doctus**. From **doctus** we derive **doctor** *–ōris m* (*teacher*). (Physicians took over this word in the 19th century.) But **doctiō** *–ōnis f*, which would mean *teaching*, does not exist. Instead, the Romans used the word **doctrīna** *–ae f* for *teaching*. Sometimes a simple verb, such as **dūcō**, does not give us two derivatives in exactly the same way, but it gives us our word *duct*. Its compound **prōdūcō** *–dūcĕre –dūxī –ductus* does provide two derivatives: *producer* and *production*.

B. Write the Latin source of each of the following English derivatives. If the source is a verb, write the infinitive:

1. tempest, tempestuous
2. glacier, glacial
3. translucent
4. ultimate
5. amble, ambulator
6. inflate, deflate
7. pulsate, pulsation, pulsator
8. occult
9. sequel, sequential, consequence
10. mortuary, mortician, mortify
11. orient, oriental, orientate, orientation
12. utility, utilize
13. cadence
14. expectation
15. serene
16. incipient
17. fulminate
18. thesaurus

XIII | Agricultūra

Fīō; Perfect Passive Participle

1 Modicum cultūrae

Because we live in an age of diverse professions, it's difficult to imagine what Roman life was like when practically every male worker was a farmer. Colonial life in America probably came closest to ancient Roman life, particularly in the first five or six hundred years of Roman history. In the early days of Rome, people regarded farming as the most respectable occupation in which a Roman citizen could engage. Its manual labor was highly esteemed. Even senators and high government officials owned farms and country estates. Cato the Censor, widely respected in his own day and equally regarded by later generations as an ideal role model, worked in his fields side-by-side with his slaves. He even wrote a book on how to be a successful farmer. Business and commerce, even the practice of medicine, were beneath the dignity of a true Roman. In those early centuries, Romans took pride in the simple life. People had what they needed to live by diligently working their small plots of land. Luxuries were few. One family had little reason to be jealous of another's wealth because everyone had nearly the same standard of living.

Of course, life does not stay the same. Gradually, many Romans began raising herds of sheep and cattle because it was more profitable than raising wheat, barley, and vegetables on a small plot. As centuries passed, large farms worked by crews of slaves supervised by foremen replaced the traditional small farms.

In many districts of Italy, people found it more and more profitable to cultivate grapevines and olive and fruit trees rather than grain. They realized they could import cheap grain from Sicily and North Africa to pay the tributes Rome required of its provinces, (People living in areas conquered by the Roman armies were called *provincials.*) Rome required grain tributes so it could feed its growing population, since many small farmers had moved to the city. Cheap imported grain—sold at low and sometimes below-market prices or even given away by scheming politicians—robbed small farmers of profits and, eventually, survival. Without the ability to sell their crops, small farmers fell into debt and, eventually, had to sell their farms to large landowners. Especially in Rome, people later looked back on their world of small farms and hearty farmers as the most glorious time in Roman history.

2 Pictured below are some typical Roman farm activities. Understandably, farmers needed tools to perform their chores. Can you identify the activities and the tools?

segetēs metĕre

furca -ae f

falx -cis f

arāre

serĕre

sārīre

arātrum -ī n

sarculum -ī n

arborēs amputāre

irrigāre

falcula -ae f

stabulum purgāre

vaccās mulgēre

secūris -is f

rutrum -ī n

pala -ae f

pābulum vaccīs dare

rastellus -ī m

ACTIVITĀTĒS

A. In each of the following activities, the farmer uses an implement. From the choices enclosed in parentheses, write the correct implement for each activity:

1. Agricola terram (arātrō/falce) arat.
2. Agricola plantās (situlā aquāriā/sarculō) irrigat.
3. Agricola arborēs (falculā/pālā) amputat.
4. Agricola stabulum (furcā/arātrō) purgat (*cleans*).
5. Agricola segetēs (rutrō/falce) metit (*harvest*).
6. Agricola agrum herbīs malīs (*weeds*) (sarculō/furcā) purgat.
7. Agricola terram (palā/rastellō) vertit (*turns under*).
8. Agricola arborem (secūrī/sarculō) dēcīdit (*cuts down*).
9. Agricola hortum (rastellō/rutrō) ērādit (*rakes*).
10. Agricola faenum (*hay*) (rastellō/falce) secat (*cuts*).

B. Can you identify these implements by sight? Match the following names with the pictures:

arātrum	furca	rutrum
falcula	pāla	sarculum
falx	rastellus	secūris

1.

2.

3.

4.

5.

6.

7.    8.   9.

3 Read the following account of life on the farm:

Agricola est semper occupātus, etiam hieme. Hieme īnstrūmentum reparat et arborēs amputat. Māne prīmā lūce vaccās mulget et eīs pābulum dat. Nōn sōlum stabulum sed etiam cohortem cōtīdiē purgat.

Prīmō vēre agrōs arat. Duo bovēs arātrum trahunt. Bovēs sunt lentī sed validī. Agricola, postquam agrōs arāvit, sēmen in terrā serit. In aliō agrō trīticum serit, aliō in agrō hordeum serit. Sī tempestās sicca est, plantās frequenter irrigat.

Per vēr et aestātem, trīticum et hordeum crēscunt. Sed etiam herbae malae in agrīs crēscunt.

Autumnō agricola trīticum et hordeum metit. Trīticum et hordeum plaustrō impōnit. Duo bovēs plaustrum ad āream prope vīllam trahunt, ubi frūmentum dēteritur. Postquam frūmentum dētrītum est, agricola trīticum et hordeum in horreō condit.

occupātus –a –um *busy*
īnstrūmentum –ī *n equipment*
  reparō –āre –āvī –ātus *to repair*   amputō –āre –āvī –ātus *to prune*
mulgeō –ēre mulsī mulsus *to milk*
  pābulum, –ī *n feed, fodder*
cohors –tis *f barnyard*
prīmō vēre *in early spring*
sēmen –inis *n seed*
trīticum –ī *n wheat*
  hordeum –ī *n barley*
serō –ĕre sēvī sātus *to sow*
  siccus –a –um *dry*

crēscō –ĕre crēvī crētus *to grow*
  herba mala –ae *f weed*

metō –ĕre messuī messus *to harvest, reap*
impōnō –ĕre imposuī impositus *to put on*
ārea –ae *f threshing floor*
  vīlla –ae *f farmhouse*
dēterō –ĕre dētrīvī dētrītus *to thresh*
horreum –ī *n barn*
condō –ĕre condidī conditus *to store*

ĀCTIVITĀS

C. Respondē Latīnē:

1. Quid facit agricola hieme?

2. Quō tempore annī agricola agrōs arat?

3. Quās segetēs agricola in agrīs serit?

4. Quid facit agricola postquam vaccās mulsit?

5. Quō tempore annī trīticum et hordeum crescunt?

6. Quid crescit inter plantās?

7. Sī caelum siccum est, quid facit agricola?

8. Quō tempore annī agricola segetēs metit?

9. Ubi frūmentum dēteritur?

10. Ubi agricola frūmentum condit?

4 Do you recognize this nursery rhyme?

Puelle caeruleë, age,
flā tuō cornū;
ovēs in prātō,
vaccae in segete;
hōc modō custōdīs ovēs tuās,
sub faenī metā
artē dormiēns?

puellus –ī in *little boy* **age** *come*
cornū –ūs n *horn*

seges –etis m *corn* (= *grain field*)

faenum –ī n *hay;* **faenī meta
–ae** f *haystack*
artē *fast, soundly, firmly*

5 The passive forms of **facĕre** are irregular in the present, imperfect, and future tenses:

PRESENT		IMPERFECT		FUTURE	
fīō	fīmus	fīēbam	fīēbāmus	fīam	fīēmus
fīs	fītis	fīēbās	fīēbātis	fīēs	fīētis
fit	fīunt	fīēbat	fīēbant	fīet	fīent

The perfect and pluperfect tenses are regular: **factus sum,** etc.; **factus eram,** etc. The passive infinitive is **fierī.** The passive forms have two basic meanings: *to be made* and *to become, get, turn:*

Inaurēs ex aurō *fīunt.*
Māla *fīunt* rubra autumnō.

The earrings are made of gold.
Apples turn red in the fall.

ĀCTIVITĀTĒS

D. Write the correct forms of **fierī** in the present tense for each sentence below:

1. Agricola _____ trīstis sī imber diū nōn cadit.

2. Ego ipse facile fatīgātus _____ sī celeriter currō.

3. Ego et frāter laetī _____ simul atque ad fundum avī pervēnimus.

4. Cūr tam īrātus _____ quandō ego tēcum nōn lūdō?

5. Autumnō diēs _____ frīgidī.

E. Change the imperfect verbs in the following sentences to perfect tense:

1. Horreum ex lignō (*wood*) fīēbat.

2. Pōmerīdiē nubēs ātrae fīēbant.

3. Haec arbor ēnormis fīēbat.

4. Ego propter cibum malum aeger fīēbam.

5. Nōs mox impatientēs tēcum fīēbāmus.

F. Convert the following verbs from perfect to pluperfect tense:

1. Labor paulātim (*little by little*) facilior factus est.

2. Post tempestātem caelum iterum clārum factum est.

3. Propter glaciem, viae perīculōsae factae sunt.

4. Post multōs mēnsēs sine imbre, agrī siccī factī sunt.

5. Pānis bonus ex hāc farīnā factus est.

6 Let's read the story of Cincinnatus, a man who lived in the early days of Rome. In later centuries, Romans admired this famous farmer for preferring the simple, rural life to that of an important political office in the city:

Lūcius Quīnctius Cincinnātus erat honestus patricius Rōmānus. Quamquam cōnsul factus erat, tamen vītam simplicem rūsticam amāvit. Fundus ēius trāns Tiberim erat parvus sed prōsperus quia in agrīs dīligentissimē labōrābat. Vītam rūsticam vītae urbānae praeferēbat.

> **honestus –a –um** *respectable*
> **patricius –ī** *m patrician*
> **tamen** *still, nevertheless*

Ubi autem hostēs exercitum Rōmānum circumclūserant, magnus timor senātum populumque Rōmānum occupāvit. "Sōlus Cincinnātus," omnēs aiēbant, "nōs tantā calamitāte cōnservāre potest." Senātus enim populusque Rōmānus Cincinnātō omnīnō cōnfīdēbant.

> **circumclūdō –clūdĕre –clūsī –clūsus** *to surround*
> **timor –ōris** *m fear*
> **occupō –āre –āvī –ātus** *to grip*
> **aiēbant** (*they*) *said*
>   **tantus –a –um** *such a great*
>   **cōnservō –āre –āvī –ātus** *to save*
> **enim** *for*
> **lēgātus –ī** *m envoy*

Statim lēgātī missī sunt ad Cincinnātum, quī tum agrum arābat. "Hostēs," aiēbant, "exercitum nostrum circumclūsērunt. Rōma ipsa magnō in perīculō est. Senātus populusque Rōmānus cupiunt tē exercituī praeficĕre."

> **praeficiō –ficĕre –fēcī –fectus** *to put in command of*

Haec verba audiēns, Cincinnātus arātrum statim relīquit, sūdōrem dētersit, togam induit, et ad cūriam festīnāvit, ubi dictātor factus est. Brevī tempore exercitum ex urbe ēdūxit et mediā nocte ad castra hostium pervēnit. Postrīdiē prīmā lūce exercitum Rōmānum contrā hostēs dūxit et magnā victōriā hostēs superāvit. Cincinnātus Rōmam exercitum et multōs captīvōs redūxit.

> **relinquō –ĕre relīquī relictus** *to leave*
>   **sūdor –ōris** *m sweat*
>   **dētergeō –ēre dētersī dētersus** *to wipe off*
> **castra –ōrum** *n pl camp*
>   **postrīdiē** *next day*
> **superō –āre –āvī –ātus** *to defeat*

Senātus populusque Cincinnātum dictātōrem diūtius esse cupīvērunt. Cincinnātus autem hunc honōrem recūsāvit. Post victōriam ad fundum trāns Tiberim cupidē sē recēpit et vītam prīvātī ēgit.

diūtius *for a longer time*
recūsō *–āre –āvī –ātus to turn down*
cupidē *eagerly*   **sē recipĕre** *to retire*   **vītam agĕre** *to lead a life*

ĀCTIVITĀS

G. Vērum aut falsum? For the following, write **Vērum** if a statement is true. If it is false, write **Falsum** and rewrite the statement to make it true:

1. Cincinnātus erat homo superbus et arrogāns.

2. Cincinnātus vītam urbānam nōn amāvit.

3. Fundus ēius trāns Tiberim erat situs.

4. Hostēs fundum ēius circumclūserant.

5. Senātus populusque Rōmānus Cincinnātum omnīnō timēbant.

6. Ubi lēgātī ad Cincinnātī fundum pervēnērunt, Cincinnātus trīticum metēbat.

7. Prīmō Cincinnātus Rōmam īre recūsāvit.

8. Ubi ad cūriam pervēnit, Cincinnātus cōnsul factus est.

9. Cincinnātus hostēs celeriter superāvit.

10. Post victōriam Cincinnātus Rōmae diū habitāvit.

 7 As you learned earlier, the perfect passive participle is the fourth principal part of active verbs. This participle, combined with the *present* forms of **sum,** forms the perfect passive tense; combined with the *imperfect* forms of **sum,** this participle forms the pluperfect passive tense:

Segetēs *messae sunt.*   *The crops were harvested.*   (Perfect tense)
Segetēs *messae erant.*   *The crops had been harvested.*   (Pluperfect tense)

The fourth principal part also functions as a participle that modifies a noun. (In other words, it functions as an adjective.)

Segetēs *messae* **in horreō conditae sunt.**
The harvested crops were stored in the barn.

Segetēs, ab agricolā *messae,* **in horreō conditae sunt.**
The crops, harvested by the farmer, were stored in the barn.

Segetēs, ab agricolā exeunte Septembrī *messae,* **in horreō Octōbrī conditae sunt.**
The crops, harvested by the farmer at the end of September, were stored in the barn in October.

Note the position of the participle in each sentence. The participle in Latin, unlike its English counterpart, does NOT appear right before or after the noun it modifies. It is positioned at *the end of the participial phrase.* The noun (**segetēs**) and the participle (**messae**) sandwich modifiers between them. The first example has no modifiers so the participle appears directly after the noun. If you remember this principle of Latin word order, you will more easily recognize word groups—words that belong together.

The participle, like any adjective, agrees with the noun it modifies in number, gender, and case. In the sentence above, is **segetēs** singular or plural? What is its gender? Its case?

ĀCTIVITĀS

H. Read the following sentences carefully, noting the noun modified by the missing participle. Using the principal parts of the verb listed in parentheses before each sentence, write the correct form of the participle. Then reread the sentence aloud, appropriately pausing between word groupings:

1. (metō –ĕre messuī messus) Trīticum, abhinc duōs diēs _____,
   ad āream portātum est.

2. (dēterō –ĕre dētrīvī dētrītus) Farīna facta est ex frūmentō, in āreā anteā

   _____.

3. (irrigō –āre irrigāvī irrigātus) Plantae, ā servīs nostrīs cōtīdiē

   _____, nunc vigent (*are thriving*).

4. (relinquō –ĕre relīquī relictus) Vaccae, in cohorte _____,
   nullam aquam habent.

5. (arō –āre arāvī arātus) Agrī fertilēs, a Cincinnātō _____,
   trāns Tiberim sitī erant.

6. (amputō –āre amputāvī amputātus) Arborēs, prīmō vēre

   _____, multum fructum autumnō ferunt (*bear*).

7. (serō –ĕre sēvī satus) Sēmen, prīmō vēre in agrīs _____,
   duodecim diēbus germinat.

8. (frangō –ĕre frēgī frāctus) Rāmus arboris, ventō validō _____,
   trāns viam cecidit.

9. (circum*clūdō –clūděre –clūsī –clūsus*) Exercitus Rōmānus, ab hostibus

_____, ā Cincinnātō līberātus est.

10. (cap*iō –ěre* cēpī captus) Cincinnātus Rōmam redūxit multōs hostēs, bellō

recente _____.

 As you discovered in the last chapter, the fourth principal part also gives us words for the doer of the action and a noun describing that action. For example, the fourth principal part **respirātus** (from **respirāre** *to breathe*) gives us **respirātor –ōris** m (*breather, respirator*) and **respirātiō –ōnis** f (*the act of breathing, breath, respiration*). In addition, most nouns of the fourth declension come from the fourth principal part of verbs. For example, **exerceō –ēre** means *to exercise* or *to train*. The fourth principal part is **exercitus,** which means *trained, exercised*. From it we get the noun **exercitus –ūs** m (*trained unit, army*). Below are a few other examples:

vīsus (from **videō**):	**vīsus –ūs** m *sight, sense of sight*
audītus (from **audiō**):	**audītus –ūs** m *hearing; sense of hearing; audit*
cursus (from **currō**):	**cursus –ūs** m *a run; course*
status (from **stō**):	**status –ūs** m *standing; status*

Do you get the idea? Here's a chance to prove it.

ĀCTIVITĀTĒS

I. For each participle, give the nominative of the fourth-declension noun, the genitive ending, the gender, and an English word derived from that Latin noun for each of the following:

EXAMPLE: **āctus** (from **agō** *to do*) 　　**āct*us* –ūs** m 　　*doing, action* 　　*act*

	PARTICIPLE	NOUN	MEANING	DERIVATIVE
1.	exitus (from **exeō** to go out)	_____	*going out*	_____
2.	aspectus (from **aspiciō** to view)	_____	*a look, view*	_____
3.	dēfectus (from **dēficiō** to fail)	_____	*a failing*	_____
4.	ēventus (from **ēveniō** to occur)	_____	*occurrence*	_____
5.	intellēctus (from **intellegō** to understand)	_____	*understanding*	_____

J. Let's review the entire fourth declension by declining the noun **exercitus**. Copy the columns below and write the correct declensions:

	SINGULAR	PLURAL
NOM.		
GEN.		
DAT.		
ACC.		
ABL.		

Quaestiōnēs Persōnālēs

1. Pecūniamne umquam ab amīcīs mūtuātus(–a) es (*have you borrowed*)?

2. Sī quid mūtuātus(–a) es, statim id reddistī?

3. Vestēsne an ōrnāmenta ā frātre aut sorōre mūtuātus(–a) es?

4. Esne tu avidus(–a) amīcōs aiuvāre?

5. Vīsne in fundō habitāre an fundum vīsitāre?

Compositiō

You are a famous artist! The President of the United States has commissioned you to paint a beautiful country scene. Before you begin painting, you need to plan what you will include in the scene. The following expressions may be helpful as you make your list. When you have finished your list, you might want to write down your descriptions in your notebook.

in abscēdentibus	*in the background*
in priōre parte	*in the foreground*
in mediā parte	*in the middle*
ā dextrā	*on the right*
ā sinistrā	*on the left*

Dialogus

VOCĀBULA

vicīnus –ī *m neighbor*
modo *just, just now*
immigrō –āre –āvī –ātus (in + *acc*)
  to move into
prōdest *it is good (to)*
quid *anything*
dēsīderō –āre –āvī –ātus *to need*
licetne mihi *may I*
mūtuor –ārī ātus *to borrow*

avidus –a –um *willing, eager*
herbae malae *f pl weeds*
vigeō –ēre –uī *to thrive*
quidnī? *why not?*
admodum *very*
obiter *by the way*
dēsiste! *hold it!*
satis *enough*
nebulō –ōnis *m airhead*

Complete the dialog between this farmer and his new neighbor Turnus based on the model of the previous conversation:

THE LATIN CONNECTION

A. The Latin verb **ferō** means *to bear, to produce*. Name an English adjective meaning *fruitful* that derives from this Latin verb. Then think of another English adjective meaning *fruitful* that comes from the verb's second meaning—*to produce*. The Romans might have used a form of the verb **ferō** as follows: **solum fertile** (*fertile soil*), **arborēs fertilēs** (*productive trees*), and **montēs aurō fertilēs** (*mountains productive of gold*).

B. The Romans had a god named **Sāturnus;** his function is suggested by the verb **serō serĕre sēvī satus**. With what activity was he associated? To be able to identify gods and goddesses in art, the ancient artists always represented each deity with a symbol. Do you remember Saturn's symbol? On our calendars, what day of the week is Saturn's day?

The **Sāturnālia** was a major holiday among the Romans, coming at the end of the year and lasting five days. On this holiday, people exchanged gifts and busied themselves with parties and merrymaking.

C. The English word *status* comes from the verb **stō stāre stetī status**. As we learned earlier, **status** (a fourth-declension noun) means *standing, position*. What is a *status symbol*? Can you give an example of a status symbol in your world? What is a *status report*? A *status seeker*?

The Latin phrase **status quō** has become a regular English noun. It means "the position, or condition, in which (we find ourselves)." Who prefers the **status quō**: a person who is content or a person who wants change?

D. Can you write the Latin source of each English derivative listed below?

1. arable	4. cornucopia	7. relinquish	10. hostile
2. fork	5. detergent	8. satiate	11. seminary
3. vaccine	6. purge	9. timorous	12. crescent

XIV | Lūsūs

Defective Verbs; Infinitives

1 Modicum cultūrae

Roman children did not have access to huge toy stores offering a wide variety of toys, so they were satisfied with simple toys and relied on their imaginations to entertain themselves. The Roman writer Horace recalled the first games (**lūsus** *–ūs m*) of his childhood: "building toy houses, harnessing mice to a little cart, playing 'odd and even,' and riding a long stick as a hobbyhorse." Children played leapfrog, jumped rope, spun tops, played jacks, rode on swings, played catch, played with dolls, and rolled hoops. The best hoops had little bells that jingled as they rolled!

Boys used sticks curved at one end (similar to hockey sticks) to play a game that resembled field hockey. They played various games of ball, but none (as far as we know) involved the use of a bat or racket. A very popular ballgame was trigon, played by three players standing to form a triangle. Each player had a leather-covered ball stuffed with hair. Players threw the balls to each other in quick succession. If you were one of these players, you definitely didn't want two balls coming at you while you still held your own ball in your hand! The winner was the one who dropped the ball least often. A referee judged if a ball was catchable; the official also counted the number of times each player dropped a ball.

Many of the games children played imitated adult life. They played school, used toy wooden swords as soldiers and gladiators, and raced "chariots." (Children harnessed goats, sheep, or dogs to pull their carts or little chariots, which were just big enough to hold one child.)

We also know that ancient Romans played games of skill in which pieces were moved on a game board according to rules similar to those of chess or checkers.

2   Vocābula

calamus -ī m   linea -ae f   hāmus -ī m

piscārī

natāre

rēmus -ī m

rēmigāre

eculeus -ī m

equitāre

pūpā lūdĕre

pilā lūdĕre

oscillum -ī n

ad fūnem salīre

oscillāre

arcus -ūs m   sagitta -ae f

culter -trī m vēnāticus

vēnābulum -ī n

canis -is m vēnāticus

vēnārī

ĀCTIVITĀS

A. Match the sentences with the pictures they describe.

Piscātor in flūmine piscātur.
Trēs puerī pilā lūdunt.
Puella ad fūnem salit.
Puer oscillat.

Vēnātor cum cane vēnāticō vēnātur.
Puer eculeō equitat.
Puellae cum pūpīs lūdunt.
Puer duōs rēmōs habet.

1.

2.

3.

4.

5.

6.

7.

8.

B. Write the plural forms of the singular subjects and verbs in the following:

1. Piscātor multōs piscēs captat.
2. Puella in oscillō sedēbat.
3. Puer pilā lūsit.
4. Vēnātor vēnābulum ad vulpem coniēcit.
5. Puer parvulus eculeō equitābat.
6. Frāter meus arcū et sagittā vēnātur.

C. Often, you need the right equipment to enjoy an activity. Can you identify the following pieces of equipment?

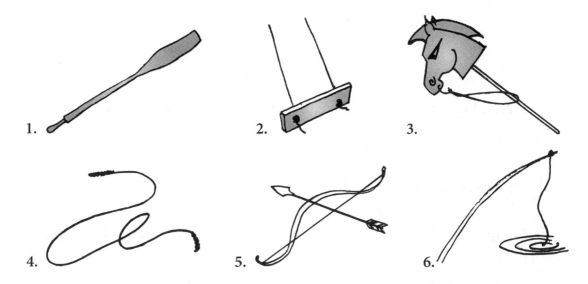

1. 2. 3.

4. 5. 6.

D. For each set of words or phrases below, write a sentence declaring that you use the item in the indicated activity. Study the following example. (Remember that the verb **ūtor ūtī ūsus sum** takes the ablative case.)

> EXAMPLE: (vēnābulum/vēnārī) Ego vēnābulō ūtor cum vēnor. *I use a hunting spear when I hunt.*

1. (calamus et līnea/piscārī)
2. (rēmus/rēmigāre)
3. (oscillum/oscillāre)
4. (fūnis/ad fūnem salīre)
5. (eculeus/equitāre)
6. (arcus et sagitta/vēnārī)

3 Some Latin verbs are called DEFECTIVE VERBS because they lack certain forms. The following verbs have a perfect tense with a present-tense meaning and a pluperfect tense with an imperfect-tense meaning:

meminī	*I remember*	**memin**eram	*I remembered*
nōvī	*I know*	**nōv**eram	*I knew*
ōdī	*I hate*	**ōd**eram	*I hated*

The perfect infinitive, which all verbs form with the perfect stem plus *–isse,* has a *present-tense* meaning in these defective verbs:

meminisse	*to remember*
nōvisse	*to know, be familiar with*
ōdisse	*to hate*

In all other verbs, the perfect infinitive (perfect stem plus *–isse*), has a *past-tense* meaning:

portāvisse	*to have carried*
mōvisse	*to have moved*
audīvisse	*to have heard*

NOTE: **Sciō** means *I know a fact;* **nōvī** means *I am familiar with* a person or place.

ĀCTIVITĀTĒS

E. Complete these sentences by writing the correct forms of **meminisse** in the perfect tense:

EXAMPLE: Vēnātor mē meminit.   *The hunter remembers me.*

1. Vēnātōrēs hunc locum nōn _____.

2. Vōsne illum piscātōrem _____?

3. Ego et Claudius hunc lūsum bene _____.

4. Ego ipse illum vēnātōrem _____.

5. Piscātor illud flūmen adhūc _____.

F. Write the missing correct forms of **nōvisse** in the pluperfect tense for the following sentences:

EXAMPLE: Ego puellam cum pūpā nōveram.   *I knew the girl with the doll.*

1. Vēnātōrēs hanc silvam bene _____.

2. Num tū illum piscātōrem _____.

3. Nōs illōs piscātōrēs adhūc _____.

4. Canis vēnāticus dominum suum statim _____.

5. Ego puellam oscillantem _____.

G. Write the correct forms of **ōdisse** in the perfect tense to complete these sentences:

1. Ego hunc labōrem neque amō neque _____.

2. Nōs nātūrāliter hostēs patriae _____.

3. Servī dominum crūdēlem _____.

4. Cūr tū istum mangōnem _____.

5. Frāter meus piscārī _____.

4 Let's read this account of a boy's first hunting and fishing trip:

Herī prīmum ego cum patre meō vēnātus sum. Canis vēnāticus noster, Dorceus, nōbīscum vēnit. Dorceus est canis vēnāticus perītus. Sēmitās per campōs optimē nōvit, quia cum patre frequenter vēnātus est.

Pater vēnābulum et cultrum vēnāticum sēcum ferēbat. Ego autem arcum et sagittam mēcum ferēbam. Dorceus avidē praecucurrit, nam sēmitās omnēs nōverat. Repentē cunīculus ex frutectō exsiluit. Ego ipse cunīculum nōn statim cōnspexī, sed Dorceus cunīculum statim vīderat et eum persecūtus est. Pater vēnābulum coniēcit sed frustrā. Ego arcum intendī sed frustrā. Cunīculus nōn sōlum celer sed etiam astūtus erat. Numquam rēctā cucurrit per dēnsum frutectum, sed trānsversē cucurrit. Dorceus quam celerimē cucurrit sed cunīculus etiam celerius cucurrit. Hōc modō cunīculus in dēnsō frutectō facilē effūgit.

Postrīdiē ego et pater piscātī sumus. Tiberis flūmen nōn procul ā domō nostrā abest. Pater meus est piscātor excellēns. Ego calamum longum mēcum ferēbam sed pater calamum multō longiōrem sēcum ferēbat. In rīpā flūminis sedēbāmus et escam hāmō impōnēbāmus. Simul atque hāmum in aquam iniciēbāmus, piscēs ad escam natāvērunt. Ego excitātus fīēbam et citō hāmum ex aquā extrāxī, sed piscem captāvī nullum. "Patientiam, patientiam, mī fīliolē," exclāmāvit pater rīdēns. "Nōlī extrahĕre līneam tuam tam citō. Exspectā dōnec piscēs escam sūmunt; tum hāmum ex aquā extrahe."

heri *adv yesterday* prīmum *for the first time*
vēnor *–ārī* vēnātus sum *to go hunting*
perītus *–a –um experienced*
sēmita *–ae f track, path*
campus *–ī m (untilled) field*
sēcum *with him*
praecurrō *–currĕre –cucurrī –cursum to run out ahead*
repentē *suddenly*
frutectum *–ī n underbrush*
exsiliō *–īre –uī to jump up, jump out*
persequor *–sequī –secūtus est to chase, pursue*
frustrā *in vain*
intendō *–ĕre* intendī intentus *to draw*
celer celeris celere *fast*
rēctā *in a straight line*
trānsversē *zig-zag*
quam celerrimē *as fast as possible*
effugiō *–ĕre* effūgī *to get away, escape*

rīpa *–ae f bank*
esca *–ae f bait*
impōnō *–pōnĕre –posuī –positus (+ dat) to put on*
extrahō *–ĕre* extraxī extractus *to pull out*
fīliolus *–ī m dear son*
exspectō *–āre –āvī –ātus to wait*
dōnec *until*

Ego escam rūrsus hāmō imposuī et hāmum in aquam iniēcī et expectābam. Piscēs rūrsus ad escam natābant. "Patientiam, patientiam!" mēcum cogitābam. Pater mē attentē observāvit sed nihil dīxit. Ut piscis escam sūmpsit, ego hāmum lentē ex aquā extrāxī. Ego meum piscem prīmum captāveram! Hōc modō ego alium piscem ex aliō captāvī.

rūrsus *again*

mēcum *to myself*
cogitō –āre –āvī –ātus *to think*
lentē *slowly*

alium ex aliō *one after another*

ĀCTIVITĀTĒS

H. Respondē ad quaestiōnēs:

1. Quis est Dorceus?
2. Cūr Dorceus sēmitās per campōs optimē nōvit?
3. Quid pater sēcum ferēbat?
4. Quid fīlius sēcum ferēbat?
5. Quid repente ē dēnsō frutectō exsiluit?
6. Quōmodō cunīculus per frutectum dēnsum cucurrit?
7. Quis celerius cucurrit, Dorceus an cunīculus?
8. Ubi pater fīliusque piscātī sunt?
9. Quid pater fīliusque hāmō impōnēbant?
10. Cūr fīlius prīmum piscem nōn captāvit?

I. We learned earlier that the perfect active infinitive is formed by adding *–isse* to the perfect stem. Write the perfect active infinitive of the following verbs used in the account of the boy's hunting and fishing trips. Then give their English meanings:

EXAMPLE: **natāre** *to swim*   **natāvisse**   *to have swum*

1. captāre *to catch*
2. rēmigāre *to row*
3. equitāre *to ride*
4. oscillāre *to swing*
5. intendĕre *to draw*
6. cōnspicĕre *to spot*
7. effugĕre *to escape*
8. impōnĕre *to put on*
9. praecurrĕre *to run ahead*
10. extrahĕre *to pull out*

5 To form the perfect passive infinitive, add **esse** to the fourth principal part of active verbs (the perfect passive participle):

> EXAMPLES: **portātus (–a –um) esse**   *to have been carried*
>
> **audītus (–a –um) esse**   *to have been heard*

Only transitive verbs (verbs that take a direct object) can form the perfect passive infinitive.

ĀCTIVITĀTĒS

J. Write the present passive infinitive and the perfect passive infinitive forms of the following verbs from this lesson. (To review the present passive infinitive, review Lesson XI.) Then write the English meaning of each form:

> EXAMPLE: **lūdō –ĕre lūsī lūsus** *to play:*   **lūdī** *to be played*
>
> **lūsus esse** *to have been played*

1. captō captāre captāvī captātus *to catch*
2. conīciō conīcĕre coniēcī coniectus *to throw*
3. cōnspiciō cōnspicĕre cōnspexī cōnspectus *to spot*
4. extrahō extrahĕre extrāxī extrāctus *to pull out*
5. impōnō impōnĕre imposuī impositus *to put on*

K. Next, write the perfect infinitive form of each deponent verb below. Remember that these verbs are passive in form but active in meaning:

> EXAMPLE: **vēnor vēnārī vēnātus sum** *to hunt:*   **vēnātus esse** *to have hunted*

1. admīror admīrārī admīrātus sum *to admire*
2. cōnor cōnārī cōnātus sum *to try*
3. videor vidērī vīsus sum *to seem*
4. loquor loquī locutus sum *to speak*
5. nāscor nāscī nātus sum *to be born*
6. sequor sequī secūtus sum *to follow*
7. ūtor ūtī ūsus sum (+ abl) *to use*
8. morior morī mortuus sum *to die*
9. orior orīrī ortus sum *to rise*

VOCĀBULA

alterī *the other*
trūdō –ĕre trūsī trūsus *to push*

ferae –ārum *f pl wild animals*

Assume the first part in the dialog with little Marcus. Ask questions that correspond to the answers:

Marce, _____

Nōlō lūděre cum pūpīs. Ego sum puer magnus, et magnī puerī cum pūpīs nōn lūdunt.

_____ ?

Minimē, nōlō trūděre tē in oscillō tuō.

_____ ?

Minimē, nōlō salīre ad fūnem. Quid alterī puerī dicent?

_____ ?

Nōlō lūděre tēcum aut cum aliīs puellīs. Cum puerīs magnīs lūděre vōlō.

Using complete Latin sentences, describe five games or activities in which you have participated, either with your sisters and brothers or with your friends. Use the imperfect tense.

Compositiō

You are responsible for designing a summer program for young children. Write a letter to their parents, describing activities and games the children will enjoy at the summer camp.

THE LATIN CONNECTION

A. At the end of Lesson XII, we learned that the last principal part of Latin verbs is often the source of other Latin words. If you drop the *–us* and add *–iō* to the last principal part, you have the Latin noun that describes the action of the verb:

EXAMPLE: **oscillātus** (*swung*) gives **oscillātiō** *–ōnis f swinging*

Write the action noun and its meaning for each of the following verbs. For verbs numbered 5, 6, 8, 9, and 10, write the English noun derived from the verb.

1. equitāre
2. piscārī
3. vēnārī
4. rēmigāre
5. extrahĕre
6. exspectāre
7. cōgitāre
8. impōnĕre
9. vidēre
10. persequī

B. Can you name the Latin source of each of the following derivatives?

1. feral
2. primary
3. frustration
4. accelerate
5. arc

C. The pendulum of a clock is said to *oscillate*. What does it do? People who cannot make up their minds *oscillate* between two or more choices. An *oscillator* is a device that produces alternating current.

D. **Praecurrō** means *I run ahead.* Use the past participle to form the Latin doer of the action. What is this word's English derivative?

E. **Lūdō** means *I play.* **Collūdō** (from **cum-lūdō**) means *I play with* (someone). As you did in Exercise A, write the Latin action noun of this verb. What is its English derivative?

F. **Trūdō** means *I push.* What English derivatives come from the principal parts of **intrūdō? Prōtrūdō?**

XV Māne et noctū

Indirect Statements

1 Modicum cultūrae

In the earliest period of their history, the Romans allowed their hair, beards, and mustaches to grow freely. Cicero speaks of "the shaggy beard that we see on ancient statues and busts." A logical reason for this practice was the absence of any sharp razors to make shaving comfortable! Only in the second century B.C. did it become common to cut hair and shave beards. According to the author Varro, who lived in the first century B.C., the first barber came to Italy from Sicily in 300 B.C. However, even if no public barbershops existed in Italy before this person's arrival, early archaeological finds attest to the Romans' use of scissors and razors. Scipio Africanus, a great Roman general, is said to have started the fashion of daily shaving (around 150 B.C.), which later became the common practice.

Young men did not shave their first facial fuzz, allowing it to darken their faces until it was almost a beard; then a solemn family affair witnessed its shaving and consecration. Growing beards became fashionable again in the second century A.D., when the emperor Hadrian grew a beard to hide his facial blemishes, thereby setting a new trend. Beginning with the time of Emperor Constantine in the fourth century A.D., men once more adopted the clean-shaven look.

Long hair was the custom for Roman women. Many of the hair styles in the early centuries A.D. were very elaborate and required the skilled hands of a beautician. Hairpieces, wigs, and dyes were in commonly use by both women and (frequently) men. (Men tried all sorts of remedies for baldness and, as a last resort, wore hairpieces.) Dark hair was typical of Mediterranean people. Some brunettes who wished to be blondes used a dye imported from northern Europe to bleach their hair or wore blond or red wigs made from the hair of slaves.

Like modern women, Roman ladies spent time and money on makeup, such as rouge (called *blush* today), lipstick, and eye shadow. They darkened their eyelashes and eyebrows with mascara made from the soot of oil lamps. Unwanted hair became the subject of attack, as women plucked their eyebrows with tweezers and rubbed off unwanted body hair with pumice. Face packs and perfumed olive oil kept their skin soft. Parasols protected their skin from the tanning, hot rays of the sun. Strangely, Romans didn't regard soap as a cleansing agent until the late fourth century A.D.! Even then it was used only to clean wounds. Instead, Romans used perfumes to give their bodies pleasant scents. The cosmetics industry did a booming business, flattering the vanity of both women and men.

2 Vocābula

expergīscor –ī
experrēctus sum

surgō –ĕre surrēxī
surrēctus

mē lavō –āre –āvī lautus

vestēs induō –ĕre –ī
indūtus

dentēs purgō –āre
–āvī –ātus

capillōs crīspō –āre
–āvī –ātus

capillōs pectō –ĕre pexī pexus

barbam rādō –ĕre rāsī rāsus

vestēs exuō –ĕre –ī exūtus

dormītum eō īre –ĭī/–īvī –ĭtus

dormiō –īre –īvī –ītus

somniō –āre –āvī –ātus

novācula –ae f

pecten –inis m

calamistrum –ī n

speculum –ī n

ĀCTIVITĀS

A. Match the descriptions with the pictures:

Melissa capillōs calamistrō crīspat.
Māter dentēs purgat.
Ego dē piscātiōne somniō.
Pater barbam novāculā rādit.

Claudius sē lavat.
Marcellus vestēs exuit.
Paula capillōs pectine pectit.
Terentia expergiscitur.

1.

2.

3.

4.

5.

6.

7.

8.

3 A direct quotation repeats the exact words of a speaker. Although the Romans did not use quotation marks to set off direct quotations, it is customary for us to add these marks in both Latin and English sentences:

Melissa dīcit, "Pater meus barbam rādit." *Melissa says, "My father is shaving."*

An indirect quotation repeats the thoughts but not the exact words of the speaker:

Melissa dīcit patrem suum barbam rādĕre. *Melissa says that her father is shaving.*

Look at the subject of the indirect quotation. In what case is the subject? Now look at the verb. What form does it have? In English the indirect statement is often introduced by the conjunction *that,* although sometimes the conjunction is omitted. Latin does NOT use a conjunction to introduce an indirect statement. The Romans had a different way of showing that a quotation was indirect. They put the subject in the accusative case and changed the verb to the infinitive.

Latin introduces indirect statements with verbs that mean *say* but also with verbs that mean *hear* (**audīre**), *believe* (**crēdĕre**), *know* (**scīre**), *think* (**putāre, consīderāre**), and the like. We have a similar construction in English:

Crēdō **eum esse bonum.** *I believe him to be good.*
Aestimō **eam esse amīcam bonam.** *I consider her to be a good friend.*

However, we don't say: *I say him to be generous.*

When the subject of the indirect quotation is the same as the subject of the main verb, the accusative of a reflexive pronoun becomes the subject of the indirect quote.

DIRECT: **Pater meus dīcit, "Ego dentēs purgo."** *My father says, "I am cleaning my teeth."*

INDIRECT: **Pater meus dīcit *sē* dentēs**   *My father says that he is cleaning*
            purgāre.   *his teeth.*

Of course, a predicate adjective in an indirect statement is also in the accusative case and agrees with the subject of the infinitive.

Crēdō hanc *viam* esse *perīculōsam*.   *I believe that this road is dangerous.*

Notice that the present infinitive in the indirect statement shows that an act is occurring at same time shown by the tense of the main verb:

Sentiō tempestātem *esse* adversam.   *I realize that the weather is bad.*
Sēnsī tempestātem *esse* adversam.   *I realized that the weather was bad.*

ACTIVITĀTĒS

B. Rewrite each sentence, changing the direct quotation to an indirect statement.

1. Pater dīcit, "Ego barbam novāculā rādō."

2. Melissa dīcit, "Soror mea capillōs pectine pectit."

3. Claudius dīxit, "Ego bene māne (*early in the morning*) surgō."

4. Marcella dīxit, "Frāter meus manūs et faciem lāvat."

5. Terentia dīcit, "Ego capillōs calamistrō crīspō."

C. Now do just the opposite! Rewrite each indirect statement as a direct quotation.

1. Marcella nūntiāvit sē bene māne semper surgěre.

2. Paula dīcit frātrem pectinem habēre.

3. Melissa dīcit sorōrem capillōs numquam crīspāre.

4. Terentia dīxit Marcum scholam ōdisse.

5. Māter putāvit Terentiam vestēs induěre.

4 Let's look in on a typical Roman family early morning scene. Mother is in the kitchen, and the children are in their bedrooms.

MĀTER: Melissa et Terentia, surgite! Iam hōra diēī tertia est. Melissa, excitā ē somnō frātellum tuum, Claudium.

> **excitō** *–āre –āvī –ātus to wake up*
> **somnus** *–ī m sleep*
> **frātellus** *–ī m little brother*

MELISSA: Māter, Claudius nōn vult expergīscī. Sub strāgulō iacet et nōn movētur. Dictitat: "Ōdī expergiscī. Ōdī oculōs aperīre bene māne."

> **strāgulum** *–ī n blanket*
> **dictitō** *–āre to keep saying*

MĀTER: Terentia, experrēcta es? Vōcem tuam nōn audiō. Age dum, surgě et ī in Claudī cubiculum et excitā eum ē somnō.

> **age dum** *come on*

TERENTIA: Māter, Claudius dīcit sē esse nimis somnolentum et ergō surgĕre nōn posse.

MĀTER: Terentia, extrahe istum pigrum Claudium ē lectulō suō!

TERENTIA: Māter, frātellus dēnique surrēxit, sed lavārī nōn vult. Dīcit aquam esse nimis frīgidam.

MĀTER: Claudī, vestēs indue et dentēs purgā. Illud dentifricium faciet dentēs tuōs candidōs et splendidōs.

CLAUDIUS: Mamma, tunicam meam et calceōs meōs invenīre nōn possum. Et dentifricium invenīre nōn possum. Quis habet dentrificium?

MĀTER: Melissa, ubi est dentifricium? Invenī id prō Claudiō.

TERENTIA: Mater, capillōs meōs pectĕre volō, sed Melissa pectinem meum et speculum meum rūrsus habet. Melissa rēbus meīs semper ūtitur.

MĀTER: Melissa, ubi est speculum tuum? Redde speculum et pectinem Terentiae. Audīsne mē? Nōlī ūtī rēbus Terentiae.

MELISSA: Māter, ego ipsa speculum dēsīderō. Capillōs meōs calamistrō crīspō. Quōmodō possum capillōs crīspāre sine speculō? Māter, Claudius rūrsus dormītum īvit.

MĀTER: Properāte, līberī! Ientāculum est parātum.

MELISSA: Veniō, māter.

TERENTIA: Ego quoque veniō.

MĀTER: Claudī, venī statim; aliōquīn ego ipsa veniam et tē ē lectulō tuō extraham! Audīsne me?

CLAUDIUS: Ita, Mamma!

somnolentus -a -um *sleepy*
  ergō *therefore*
piger pigra pigrum *lazy*
lectulus -ī *m (small) bed*

dēnique *finally, at last*

dentifricium -ī *n tooth powder*
  candidus -a -um *white*
splendidus -a -um *shiny*

rūrsus *again*

reddō -ĕre -idī -itus *to give back*

dēsīderō -āre -āvī -ātus *to need*

līberī -ōrum *m pl children*

aliōquīn *otherwise*

ĀCTIVITĀTĒS

D. Respondē ad quaestiōnēs:

1. Quota hōra est cum māter līberōs ē somnō excitat?

2. Quis expergīscī nōn vult?

3. Quamobrem Claudius sē lāvāre nōn vult?

4. Quid Claudius invenīre nōn potest?

5. Quō līberī dentēs purgant?

6. Quamobrem Terentia nōn potest capillōs pectĕre?

7. Quid facit Melissa calamistrō?

8. Quid māter prō līberīs parāvit?

E. Quid facis bene māne?

EXAMPLE:

Ego expergīscor.

1.

2.

3.

4.

5.

6.

F. Quid facis noctū?

1.

2.

3.

4.

5.

6.

5 The perfect infinitive in the indirect statement represents an action that occurred before the time shown by the tense of the main verb:

Helena *dīcit* sē capillōs crīspāvisse.

Helen SAYS that she CURLED her hair.

Helena *dīxit* sē capillōs crīspāvisse.

Helen SAID that she HAD CURLED her hair.

ĀCTIVITĀTĒS

G. Rewrite the sentences, changing each direct quotation to an indirect statement. (Remember that you form the perfect active infinitive by adding *–isse* to the perfect active stem.)

1. Claudius dīxit, "Vēnātor arcum et sagittam habuit."
2. Publius dīcit, "Piscātōrēs multōs piscēs captāvērunt."
3. Marcella dīxit, "Ego in merīdiem dormīvī."
4. Tullia dīxit, "Ego capillōs pexī."
5. Claudius dīxit, "Ego dē scholā somniāvī."

H. This time let's do the opposite. Write each indirect statement as a direct quotation:

1. Marcellus meminit sē dentēs nōn purgāvisse.
2. Gāius meminit pectinem suum suprā lectum fuisse.
3. Terentia audīvit Claudium expergīscī nōluisse.
4. Marcus dīxit sorōrēs suās capillōs cōtīdiē calamistrō crīspāvisse.
5. Pater dīcit sē bene māne barbam rāsisse.

6 You have mastered the art of forming the perfect *active* infinitive by adding *–isse* to the perfect active stem (**pexisse** *to have combed*), but do you remember how to form the perfect *passive* infinitive? What do you add to the fourth principal part (that is, the perfect passive participle)? If you said **esse,** you were correct (**pexus esse** *to have been combed*)! Remember that **pexus –a –um** must agree with the subject:

Capillī illīus puerī videntur numquam pexī esse.

The hair of that boy seems never to have been combed.

In this example, **pexī** agrees with **capillī.** Furthermore, remember that in "fake passive" (deponent) verbs, the form is passive but the meaning is active:

Sciō Mārcum templa Rōmae admīrātum esse.

I know that Marcus admired the temples of Rome.

In that sentence, **admīrātum esse** is passive in form but active in meaning.

I. Rewrite the following sentences, changing each direct quotation to an indirect statement:

EXAMPLE: Puella dīxit, "Capillī meī in tōnstrīnā crīspātī sunt."
Puella dīxit capillōs suōs in tōnstrīnā crīspātōs esse.

1. Piscātor dīxit, "Trēs piscēs ūnā hōrā captātī sunt."

2. Māter dīxit, "Ientāculum parātum est."

3. Marcus dīcit, "Capillī meī pexī sunt."

4. Melissa dīxit, "Ego ā mātre vocāta sum."

5. Vēnātor dīxit, "Vēnābulum in vulpem coniectum est."

J. Rewrite the following sentences, changing each direct quotation to an indirect statement. Notice that the verb in the direct quotation is a deponent verb, passive in form but active in meaning:

1. Pater dīxit, "Omnēs virum fortem admīrātī sunt."

2. Melissa dīcit, "Terentia speculō meō ūsa est."

3. Māter dīxit, "Sōl hōrā diēī prīmā ortus est."

4. Marcus dīxit, "Avia mea abhinc decem annōs mortua est."

5. Terentia dīxit, "Melissa mātrem in culīnam secūta est."

K. We have seen that a verb that is normally transitive (takes a direct object) can be used intransitively by using either the passive or the reflexive form of the verb:

EXAMPLE: Cum ego dormiō, mē nōn moveō   *When I sleep, I don't move.*
(nōn moveōr).

Rewrite the following sentences, substituting the reflexive verb for the passive verb. The meaning of the sentence, of course, will remain the same:

1. Mārcus cōtīdiē lavātur.

2. Mārcus et soror nunc lavantur.

3. Ego mox lavābor.

4. Ego et Paulus māne lavābāmur.

5. Mārcus lavārī nōn vult.

Dialogus

VOCĀBULA

tōnstrīna *–ae f barbershop; beauty salon*
tōnstrīx *–īcis f hairdresser*
tondeō *–ēre totondī tōnsus to cut*
tingō *–ĕre tinxī tinctus to dye, color*
flāvus *–a –um blond*
cōmō *–ĕre cōmpsī cōmptus to do, to set (hair)*
ita quidem *yes, indeed*

modus *–ī m style, fashion*
novissimus *–a –um latest*
supercilium *–ī n eyebrow*
ēvellō *–ĕre –ī evulsus to pluck*
aliquid amplius *anything else*
nempe *well*
palpebra *–ae f eyelash*

Quaestiōnēs Persōnālēs

1. Quotā hōrā expergīscitur māter tua?

2. Expergīscitur pater tuus antequam an postquam māter?

3. Quis excitat tē ē somnō?

4. Surgisne statim an iacēs paulisper sub strāgulō?

5. Quandō dentēs purgās, māne an noctū?

6. Crīspāsne capillōs tuōs?

7. Praefersne lavārī aquā frīgidā an tepidā an calidā?

8. Quis in familiā tuā barbam rādit?

9. Dē quō somniās?

10. Habuistīne umquam somnia tumultuōsa (*nightmares*) ?

Compositiō

In complete Latin sentences, list four or five things you do in the morning before you leave for school.

Colloquium

Silvia is a hairdresser at a beauty salon. Octavia has just arrived to have her hair done. As Silvia in this exchange, respond to your client's questions:

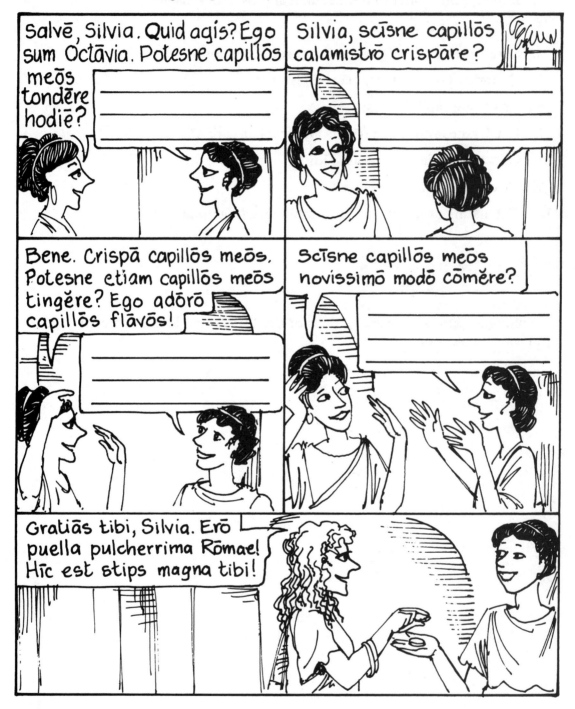

VOCĀBULA

scīsne *do you know how to*   **stips** *–is f tip*

THE LATIN CONNECTION

A. Supply the Latin origin of each word below. Then write a brief definition of each English word:

1. dormitory

2. dormant

3. lavatory

4. somnolent

5. insomnia

6. novice

7. candid

8. candidate

9. mode

10. to tinge

11. to purge

12. purgatory

13. modern

14. supercilious

B. 1. Roman politicians running for office wore a distinctive, shiny white toga. In Latin, *flat* white is **albus –a –um.** What Latin adjective best describes the shiny white toga candidates wore?

2. In which season are trees and plants dormant?

3. A capillary is a tiny blood vessel. From the Latin origin of this word, what does such a minute blood vessel resemble? What is a capillary's Latin name?

Recognitiō III

(Lēctiōnēs XI–XV)

 **LĒCTIŌ XI**

a. To form the passive voice of the first, second, and third persons, change

–am to *–ar*   *–mus* to *–mur*
–ō to *–or*   *–nt* to *–ntur*
–t to *–tur*

b. The passive forms of the first, second, and third persons of the *–āre* (first) conjugation are:

PRESENT:	**vocor**	*I am called*	**vocāmur**	*we are called*
	vocāris	*you are called*	**vocāminī**	*you are called*
	vocātur	*he/she/it is called*	**vocantur**	*they are called*
IMPERFECT:	**vocābar**	*I was called*	**vocābāmur**	*we were called*
	vocābāris	*you were called*	**vocābāminī**	*you were called*
	vocābātur	*he/she/it was called*	**vocābantur**	*they were called*
FUTURE:	**vocābor**	*I will be called*	**vocābimur**	*we will be called*
	vocāberis	*you will be called*	**vocābiminī**	*you will be called*
	vocābitur	*he/she/it will be called*	**vocābuntur**	*they will be called*
INFINITIVE:	**vocārī**	*to be called*		

c. The passive forms of the first, second, and third persons of the *–ēre* (second) conjugation are:

PRESENT:	**moveor**	*I am moved*	**movēmur**	*we are moved*
	movēris	*you are moved*	**movēminī**	*you are moved*
	movētur	*he/she/it is moved*	**moventur**	*they are moved*
IMPERFECT:	**movēbar**	*I was moved*	**movēbāmur**	*we were moved*
	movēbāris	*you were moved*	**movēbāminī**	*you were moved*

(continued)

	movēbātur	he/she/it was moved	movēbantur	they were moved
FUTURE:	movēbor	I will be moved	movēbimur	we will be moved
	movēberis	you will be moved	movēbiminī	you will be moved
	movēbitur	he/she/it will be moved	movēbuntur	they will be moved
INFINITIVE:	movērī	to be moved		

d. The passive forms of the first, second, and third persons of the *–ĕre* family of verbs are:

PRESENT:	mittor	I am sent	mittimur	we are sent
	mitteris	you are sent	mittiminī	you are sent
	mittitur	he/she/it is sent	mittuntur	they are sent
IMPERFECT:	mittēbar	I was sent	mittēbāmur	we were sent
	mittēbāris	you were sent	mittēbāminī	you were sent
	mittēbātur	he/she/it was sent	mittēbantur	they were sent
FUTURE:	mittar	I will be sent	mittēmur	we will be sent
	mittēris	you will be sent	mittēminī	you will be sent
	mittētur	he/she/it will be sent	mittentur	they will be sent
INFINITIVE:	mittī	to be sent		

e. The passive forms of the first, second, and third persons of the *–īre* verb family are:

PRESENT:	audior	I am heard	audīmur	we are heard
	audīris	you are heard	audīminī	you are heard
	audītur	he/she/it is heard	audiuntur	they are heard
IMPERFECT:	audiēbar	I was heard	audiēbāmur	we were heard
	audiēbāris	you were heard	audiēbāminī	you were heard
	audiēbātur	he/she/it was heard	audiēbantur	they were heard

(continued)

FUTURE:	audiar	*I will be heard*	audiēmur	*we will be heard*
	audiēris	*you will be heard*	audiēminī	*you will be heard*
	audiētur	*he/she/it will be heard*	audientur	*they will be heard*
INFINITIVE:	audīrī	*to be heard*		

f. The passive forms of the first, second, and third persons of the *–iō* family of verbs are:

PRESENT:	accipior	*I am received*	accipimur	*we are received*
	acciperis	*you are received*	accipiminī	*you are received*
	accipitur	*he/she/it is received*	accipiuntur	*they are received*
IMPERFECT:	accipiēbar	*I was received*	accipiēbāmur	*we were received*
	accipiēbāris	*you were received*	accipiēbāminī	*you were received*
	accipiēbātur	*he/she/it was received*	accipiēbantur	*they were received*
FUTURE:	accipiar	*I will be received*	accipiēmur	*we will be received*
	accipiēris	*you will be received*	accipiēminī	*you will be received*
	accipiētur	*he/she/it will be received*	accipientur	*they will be received*
INFINITIVE:	accipī	*to be received*		

LĒCTIŌ XII

a. The perfect tense of any verb in the passive voice consists of the perfect passive participle plus the present forms of **sum:**

portāt*us* (*–a –um*) sum	*I was carried*	**portātī (*–ae –a*) sumus**	*we were carried*
portāt*us* (*–a –um*) es	*you were carried*	**portātī (*–ae –a*) estis**	*you were carried*
portāt*us* (*–a –um*) est	*he/she/it was carried*	**portātī (*–ae –a*) sunt**	*they were carried*

PERFECT PASSIVE INFINITIVE: **portāt*us* (*–a –um*) esse**   *to have been carried*

b. The pluperfect tense of any verb in the passive voice consists of the perfect passive participle plus the imperfect forms of **sum:**

portāt*us* (*–a –um*) **eram**	*I had been carried*	**portāt***ī* (*–ae –a*) **erāmus**	*we had been carried*
portāt*us* (*–a –um*) **erās**	*you had been carried*	**portāt***ī* (*–ae –a*) **erātis**	*you had been carried*
portāt*us* (*–a –um*) **erat**	*he/she/it had been carried*	**portāt***ī* (*–ae –a*) **erant**	*they had been carried*

c. The perfect passive participle has three endings. The subject of the verb determines which ending should be used.

d. Certain Latin verbs are called DEPONENT VERBS ("fake passive verbs") because they are passive in form but active in meaning:

admīr*or* *–ārī* **admīrātus sum**	*to admire*
loquor loquī locūtus sum	*to speak*
ūtor ūtī ūsus sum (+ *abl*)	*to use*

LĒCTIŌ XIII

a. The passive forms of **facĕre** are irregular in the present, imperfect, and future:

PRESENT:		IMPERFECT:		FUTURE:	
fīō	**fīmus**	**fīēbam**	**fīēbāmus**	**fīam**	**fīēmus**
fīs	**fītis**	**fīēbās**	**fīēbātis**	**fīēs**	**fīētis**
fit	**fīunt**	**fīēbat**	**fīēbant**	**fīet**	**fīent**

INFINITIVE: **fīerī** *to be made; to become, get*

b. The perfect and pluperfect passive forms of **facĕre** are regular: **factus** sum, etc.

c. The perfect participle (fourth principal part of transitive verbs) combines with the present and imperfect tenses of **sum** to form the perfect and pluperfect passive tenses of any verb. The present participle may also function simply as a participle that modifies a noun or pronoun. In Latin, the participle does not appear immediately before or after the word it modifies as it does in English. Instead, a Latin present participle appears at the end of the participial phrase:

Segetēs, ab agricolā initiō Septembris messae, in horreō mox cōnditae sunt.	*The crops harvested by the farmer at the beginning of September were soon stored in the barn.*

LĒCTIŌ XIV

a. Some Latin verbs, because they lack certain forms, are called DEFECTIVE VERBS. The following verbs have a perfect tense with a present meaning and a pluperfect tense with an imperfect meaning:

meminī	*I remember*	**memineram**	*I remembered*	**meminisse**	*to remember*
nōvī	*I know*	**nōveram**	*I knew*	**nōvisse**	*to know*
ōdī	*I hate*	**ōderam**	*I hated*	**ōdisse**	*to hate*

b. The perfect passive infinitive consists of the perfect passive participle (fourth principal of transitive verbs) plus **esse:**

portāt*us* (–*a* –*um*) esse   *to have been carried*

c. The perfect infinitive of deponent verbs ("fake passive verbs") is passive in form but active in meaning:

cōnātus esse	*to have tried*
locūtus esse	*to have spoken*

LĒCTIŌ XV

a. In Latin, an indirect quotation is expressed by putting the subject of the direct quotation into the accusative case and changing the verb of the direct quotation to the infinitive. The present infinitive expresses action happening at the same time as that of the main verb; the perfect infinitive expresses action that occurred before that of the main verb:

Quis dīcit flūmen esse altum?	*Who says that the river is deep?*
Quis dīxit flūmen esse altum?	*Who said that the river was deep?*
Quis dīxit flūmen fuisse altum?	*Who said that the river had been deep?*

b. If the subject of the indirect quotation is the same as the subject of the main verb, the reflexive pronoun is used in the indirect statement:

DIRECT:	**Mārcus dīxit, "Ego sum cīvis Rōmānus."**	*Marcus said, "I am a Roman citizen."*
INDIRECT:	**Mārcus dīxit *sē* esse cīvem Rōmānum.**	*Marcus said that he was a Roman citizen.*

ĀCTIVITĀTĒS

A. In the pictures below, twelve people are engaged in various activities. Complete the description below each picture by writing the correct form of a verb chosen from the following list:

crīspāre	expergīscī	lūděre	purgāre
dormīre	induěre	oscillāre	somniāre
equitāre	lavārī	piscārī	vēnārī

1. Terentia capillōs calamistrō _____ . 2. Melissa dē amīcō suō _____ .

3. Claudius bene māne _____ . 4. Puerī aquā tepidā _____ .

5. Frātellus eculeō _____ . 6. Pater et fīlius hāmō _____ .

7. Sorōrēs vestēs _____ .

8. Claudia oscillō _____ .

9. Pūblius dentēs dentifriciō _____ .

10. Marius cum cane vēnāticō _____ .

11. Iūlia cum pūpā _____ .

12. Īnfāns artē _____ .

B. Only one of the hunters is fully equipped for the hunt. Pick out that hunter from the description.

Vēnātor canem vēnāticum sēcum habet.
Vēnātor arcum habet.
Vēnātor calceōs gestat.

Vēnātor vēnābulum habet.
Vēnātor cultrum vēnāticum habet.
Vēnātor sagittās habet.

C. How many of these words do you remember? Fill in the Latin words; then read down the boxed column to find the mystery word that ties together the other words:

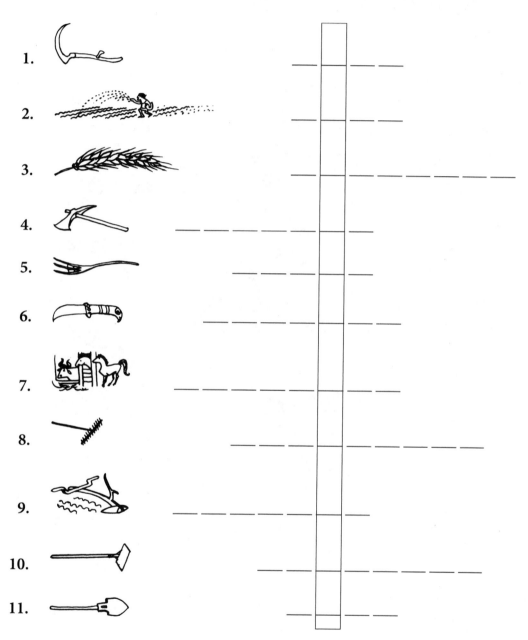

D. Look at this picture of stars and constellations. Find the six constellations that relate to the myth of Perseus. Write a simple statement in Latin identifying or saying something about each constellation:

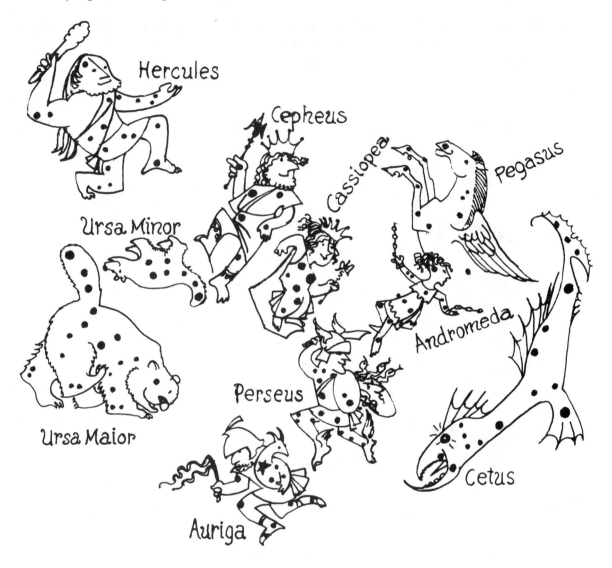

E. Cruciverbilūsus:

HORIZONTĀLE

1. blond
5. he loves
7. lightning
10. hope
13. chair
14. whole
16. with
17. you are
19. why
20. love
22. horn
23. thing
24. wind

26. quickly
28. where
31. yes
32. go away!
34. place
36. cockroach
40. cages
41. his own
43. or
44. bait
45. again
48. you
49. in the morning

52. ox
54. trip
55. on top of
57. use
58. unless
59. but
60. to use
61. tooth
65. or
67. to God
69. most eagerly
70. pride

1. underbrush	22. oar	41. under
2. to	23. icicle	42. if
3. one	25. as, when	46. last
4. himself	26. knife	47. sea monsters
6. three	27. then	50. art, skill
7. scythe	29. that	51. sailors
8. me	30. this	53. Gorgon
9. shipwreck	33. wing	56. I become
11. comb	35. bear	62. we
12. I am	36. well	63. through
13. slave	37. air	64. it
15. three times	38. player	66. you
18. rarely	39. boat	67. concerning
19. house	40. untilled field	68. on account of

F. Unscramble these mythological names. Then unscramble the circled letters to find out what the message is:

A S M D U E   ⬤ ☐ ☐ ☐ ☐ ☐

R S E S U P E   ☐ ☐ ⬤ ☐ ☐ ☐ ⬤

I O S S P E A C A   ☐ ☐ ☐ ☐ ☐ ⬤ ☐ ☐ ☐

R A N D O D M A E   ☐ ⬤ ☐ ☐ ☐ ⬤ ☐ ☐ ☐

E C U H E S P   ☐ ☐ ☐ ☐ ☐ ⬤ ☐

S T U E C   ☐ ☐ ⬤ ☐ ☐

Cētus est: ☐ ☐ ☐ ☐ ☐ ☐ ☐ ☐

G. Quid in hāc pictūrā vitiōsum est? What is wrong in this picture? Ten things are wrong with this picture. It's up to you to find and describe them—in Latin, of course!

H. Picture Story. Can you read this story? Whenever you come to a picture, read the Latin word it represents:

Claudius erat 🖼 Rōmānus annōrum tredecim.

Claudius cum 🖼 rurī habitābat. 🖼 sua, quae

Terentia vocāta est, undēcim annōs nāta erat. 🖼

suus, quī Gaius vocātus est, octō annōs nātus erat.

Quia aestās erat, Claudius 🖼 aut 🖼

volēbat. Novum 🖼 habēbat. Terentia autem

praeferēbat 🖼 aut 🖼 lūdĕre aut 🖼.

Frātellus 🖼 volēbat. Sed 🖼, quī agricola erat,

in agrīs occupātus erat. Quia diēs clārus erat, pater

faenum 🖼 secuit. Deinde pater faenum 🖼

collēgit et in 🖼 condidit. Deinde pater 🖼 ex

prātō in 🖼 ēgit (drove) et 🖼 eīs dedit. 🖼

autem in hortō laborābat. Māter hortum 🖼 sāruit et

plantās aquā 🖼. Pōmerīdiē incēpit 🖼 et tonāre

(to thunder). Mox 🖼 cadĕre incēpit. Tōta familia citō in

villam properāvit.

PARS QUĀRTA

XVI | Status fēminārum Rōmānārum

–ūrus Conjugation

 1 Modicum cultūrae

Roman history spanned more than 1000 years and is commonly divided into three periods: the Monarchy, or kings (approximately 750 to 500 B.C.); the Republic (roughly 500 to 1 B.C.); and the Empire, or emperors (from about A.D. 1 to 500). You can imagine the many changes that took place in Roman culture. You might be surprised to learn, however, that although the status of women improved over time, women continued to hold a position inferior to that of men. It was truly a man's world.

Women could not vote or hold political office. Rome had no female rulers, although women were often very influential behind the scenes. Courts permitted no female lawyers or jurors. A woman had no property rights. The father of an unmarried woman (**virgō –inis** f) owned everything and had absolute control over her. As a married woman (**mātrōna –ae** f), she surrendered total control to her husband. He owned his wife just as he owned their home and other property.

When he died, she inherited nothing; their entire estate passed to their sons. If they had no sons, the estate went to the most directly related male relatives. However, women could alter this arrangement if they entered into a marriage called **ūsus**. In this type of marriage, a wife was still a member of her father's family. When her father died, she had the right to her inheritance. To exercise this right, she had to spend three nights a year away from her husband's house. As time went on, this type of marriage became increasingly common and, in general, women's social lives became progressively less restrictive.

Even their names shortchanged women! Men customarily had three names: **praenōmen**, **nōmen**, and **cognōmen** (for example, Marcus Tullius Cicero). The **praenōmen** was his first name. The **nōmen**, a word that usually had an *–ius* ending, indicated the clan (or extended family) to which he belonged. The **cognōmen** was his family name. Very impressive! Each girl or woman, however, usually had simply one name, which was often the feminine form of her father's name. Marcus Tullius Cicero, for instance, might have named his daughter simply Tullia. Some female names indicated the girl's birth order, such as Maxima (*eldest*), Secunda, and Tertia. When a girl or woman needed two names for more precise identification, her second name was most likely the genitive-case name of her father or husband.

Evidence suggests that some girls attended school, but historians aren't certain if boys and girls attended the same classes. Whether a girl lived in the city or in the country, her education (under her mother's guidance) was directed toward marriage, which occurred as early as the thirteenth or fourteenth year. A young girl learned to spin wool into thread and weave that thread into garments. Her mother taught her how to shop for and prepare food and how to run the household, including the management of slaves. When she married, a woman brought her husband a dowry in the form of money or landed property. In case of divorce, the husband had to return the dowry to the woman's father. By the time of the Empire, divorce was very common.

In earlier times, dancing, singing, and playing musical instruments were considered improper for women. They could not become actresses until the time of the Empire, and even then actresses were scorned by most people. Women who really wanted to act on the stage became actresses anyway. Women were not allowed to drink wine unless it was mixed with water and honey. You might call this beverage the soft drink of antiquity!

Still, in comparison to women in Greece and the nations of the Near East, Roman women enjoyed a considerable amount of freedom. For example, Athenian women were confined to their home's women's room so male visitors would not see them. The married Roman lady, by contrast, carried out her daily work in the atrium, the main and also most public area of the home. In the dining room, the wife and children sat at the table while the husband generally reclined. Roman women moved freely in public. They could attend the theater, the amphitheater, the race track, and the public baths at certain hours. A wife went to dinner parties with her husband and attended religious services reserved only for women.

Even the Roman legislature had something to say about what women could and couldn't do! Legislators passed laws to limit the amount of jewelry women could wear. They passed laws that banned females from wearing flashy clothes. They even passed laws about women's use of carriages. Generally, these laws were ignored.

2 Vocābula

Can you identify these daily activities of Roman women?

suĕre

coquĕre

obsōnāre

ūtensilia culīnae lavāre

domum purgāre

nēre

vestēs texĕre

cibum adpōnĕre

aquam ē cisternā haurīre

3 You have learned the future tense of Latin verbs. In Latin, as in English, the future can be expressed in two ways: "I will clean the house" (**domum purgābō**) and "I am going to clean the house" (**domum purgātūrus(-a) sum**). There is no great difference in meaning between these two future forms in either language. To form this alternate Latin future, drop the ending of the fourth principal part of the verb and add **-ūrus, -ūra, -ūrum.** The auxiliary verb (a form of **sum**) can either precede or follow the main verb.

Below is a short story about women's activities in a Roman household. Pay attention to the alternate forms of the future, which are in bold type. Notice that the auxiliary verb **sum** can appear either before or after the verb that ends in **-ūrus:**

Pater meus, quī advocātus est, multōs clientēs habet. Hī clientēs sunt etiam ēius amīcī. Clientēs sunt plēbēī, sed pater est patricius. Quia pater aliquot amīcōs ad cēnam hodiē **vocātūrus est,** māter et mea maxima soror omnia **parātūrae sunt.** Prīmum, pater et clientēs in tablīnum **itūrī sunt,** ubi dē rēbus negōtiālibus **locūtūrī sunt.** Deinde ad mēnsam in trīclīniō **accubitūrī sunt.**

    Prīmum māter ad macellum **itūra est,** ubi pānem et holera et vīnum et carnem **obsōnātūra est.** Deinde māter et mea soror maxima, ūnā cum ancillā, tōtam domum **sunt purgātūrae.** Soror cubicula **ōrdinātūra est.** Māter autem tablīnum et trīclīnium **est purgātūra.** Ancilla aquam **haustūra est** ē cisternā, quae in ātriō sub pavīmentō est. Ancilla pavīmentum in ātriō **est lavātūra.** Quia ego parvulus puer sum, mihi licet tōtum diem lūděre, dum aliī tōtum diem labōrant.

    Māter sororque cēnam in culīnā **coctūrae sunt.** "Simul atque cēnam coxī," ait māter sorōrī, "ego cibum convīvīs **sum adpositūra** et tū **es adiūtūra** mē."

    Sic pater **est futūrus** laetus et contentus, et omnēs clientēs **futūrī sunt** grātī.

advocātus -ī *m lawyer*

plēbēius -a -um *plebeian, common people*
patricius -a -um *patrician*
vocō -āre -āvī -ātus *to invite*
eō īre īvī itus *to go*
negōtiālis -is -e *business*
accumbō -ěre accubuī accubitus *to recline*

obsōnō -āre -āvī -ātus *to shop (for)*

ancilla -ae *f maid*
ōrdinō -āre -āvī -ātus *to set in order, arrange*

pavīmentum -ī *n floor*
parvulus -a -um *small, young*
licet mihi *I am allowed*

convīva -ae *m guest* **adpōnō -ěre adposuī adpositus** *to serve (food)*

grātus -a -um *grateful*

ĀCTIVITĀS

A. Respondē Latīnē:

1. Quōs pater est vocātūrus ad cēnam?

2. Suntne clientēs plēbēī an patriciī?

3. Estne pater plēbēius an patricius?

4. Quis ad macellum ītūra est?

5. Quid ibī obsōnātūra est?

6. Quis cubicula ōrdinātūra est?

7. Quis tablīnum et trīclīnium purgātūra est?

8. Quis aquam ē cisternā est haustūra?

9. Ubi est cisterna?

10. Quid ancilla purgātūra est?

4 In the story you just read, verbs ending in **–ūrus** appeared in combination with only present-tense forms of **sum.** However, forms of **sum** in *other* tenses also can be used as the auxiliary or helping verb:

Māter trīclīnium *purgātūra erat.*	*Mother was going to clean the dining room.*
Pater aliquot clientēs ad cēnam *vocātūrus fuit.*	*Father was going to invite some clients to dinner.*

ĀCTIVITĀTĒS

B. Complete each sentence below with the correct imperfect–tense form of **sum:**

1. Soror mea vestēs lavātūra _____.

2. Ancillae ūtensilia culīnae lavātūrae _____.

3. Pater clientēs ad cēnam nōn vocātūrus _____.

4. Ego et soror domum purgātūrae _____.

5. Claudia, ubi fructūs et holera obsōnātūra _____?

6. Ancillae, quandō vōs cubiculum meum ōrdinātūrae _____?

C. Write the correct ending of the verb and the appropriate form of the auxiliary verb to complete each sentence below. The principal parts of unfamiliar verbs and meanings are provided:

1. **suō –ĕre suī sūtus** *to sew*

   Māter meam tunicam veterem sūt _____ _____.

2. **hauriō –īre hausī haustus** *to draw out*

   Terentia, quandō aquam ē cisternā haust _____ _____?

3. **neō nēre nēvī nētus** *to spin*

   Omnēs fīliae meae lānās nēt _____ _____.

4. **adpōnō –ĕre adposuī adpositus** *to serve*

   Servī nostrī vīnum convīvīs adposit _____ _____.

5. **obsōnō –āre –āvī –ātus** *to shop for*

   Māter, sī tū pomerīdiē ad macellum it _____ _____,

   obsōnāt _____ _____ holera?

6. **texō –ĕre texuī textus** *to weave*

   Quid ancillae crās text _____ _____, tunicās an stolās?

D. Each sentence below uses a regular future tense verb. Rewrite each verb in the complete alternate future form (ending with *–ūrus*):

1. Ancillae togās novās texent.

2. Quis aquam ē cisternā nunc hauriet?

3. Ego ipse aquam ē cisternā numquam hauriam.

4. Rōmulus et Remus aquam ē flūmine haurient.

5. Avia mea lānās nēbit.

6. Ego et amīcae ūtensilia culīnae lavābimus.

7. Terentia, num plūs pānis in pistrīnā obsōnābis?

8. Duo servulī cibum familiae meae adpōnent.

E. Finish each sentence below by supplying the correct forms of the *–ūrus* verb and **sum** in the perfect tense:

1. Hostēs Rōmae aquam ex aquaeductū publicō haust _____ _____.

2. Quattuor convīvae cum uxōribus ad mēnsam accubit _____ _____.

3. Puellae lānās nēt _____ _____.

4. Ego et ancillae togās et stolās sūt _____ _____.

5. Māter, ego ipsa stolam meam sūt _____ _____.

6. Servī ūtēnsilia culīnae ē trīclīniō in culīnam portāt _____ _____.

5 A *–ūrus* verb without an auxiliary verb can function as a future participle with several meanings:

Senātor ex sellā surrexit,   *The senator rose from his seat, about to*
    ōrātiōnem *habitūrus*.   *(intending to) give a speech.*

When the *–urus* verb functions in this way, it is called a *future participle*.

F. Supply the correct ending of the future participle in each sentence below:

1. Soror mea, comam crispātūr _____, calamistrum ubīque quaesīvit.

2. Convīvae trīclīnium intrāvērunt, prandium sumptūr _____.

3. Ancillae in culīnam ambulāvērunt, ūtensilia lautūr _____.

4. Pater aquam calidam rogāvit, barbam rāsūr _____.

5. Marcella balneum intrāvit, sē lautūr _____.

6. Servī bene māne experrectī sunt, parātūr _____ ientāculum.

6 In Lesson XV, you learned how to express an indirect statement with the present and perfect infinitives. Remember that the action expressed by the *present* infinitive takes place AT THE SAME TIME AS the action expressed by the main verb. The action described by the *perfect* infinitive takes place BEFORE the action of the main verb. The *future* infinitive expresses an action that occurs AFTER that of the main verb. The future infinitive consists of the future participle plus **esse:**

DIRECT QUOTATION:	**Helena dīcit: "Familia mea domī *cēnātūra est."***	*Helen says: "My family is going to eat dinner at home."*
INDIRECT STATEMENT:	**Helena dīcit familiam suam domī *cēnātūram esse.***	*Helen says that her family is going to eat dinner at home.*
DIRECT QUOTATION:	**Helena dīxit: "Familia mea domī *cēnātūra est."***	*Helen said: "My family IS going to eat dinner at home."*
INDIRECT STATEMENT:	**Helena dīxit familiam suam domī *cēnātūram esse.***	*Helen said that her family WAS going to eat dinner at home.*

G. Rewrite each direct quotation as an indirect statement:

1. Cornēlius dīcit: "Ancillae nostrae futūrae sunt fidēlēs."

2. Ancilla dīxit: "Dominus noster dōnum mihi datūrus est."

3. Clientēs dīxērunt: "Marcus Tullius est futūrus advocātus excellēns."

4. Claudia dīcit: "Soror mea capillōs pexūra est."

5. Frātellus dīxit: "Māter cēnam excellentem coctūra est."

6. Melissa dīxit: "Ancillae crās nōn labōrātūrae sunt."

7. Claudīus dīxit: "Ego aliquandō senātor futūrus sum."

8. Servī dīxērunt: "Nōs cēnam bonam hodiē adpositūrī sumus."

H. Change the indirect statements to direct quotations:

1. Crēdō mē bene dormītūrum esse.

2. Sciō ancillās futūrās esse industriōsās.

3. Pater dīxit mātrem lactūcam et carōtās et cucumerēs in macellō emptūram esse.

4. Vīcīnus meus dīxit sē iter per Campāniam factūrum esse.

5. Amīcus ad mē scrīpsit sē mox in Hispāniam ēmigrātūrum esse.

6. Omnēs dīcunt sē prō patriā moritūrōs esse.

I. Substitute the future infinitive for the present infinitive in these indirect statements. The principal parts of the verb are provided before each sentence:

1. **rādō rādĕre rāsī rāsus**

   Pater dīxit sē barbam novāculō novō rādĕre.

2. **surgō –ĕre surrēxī surrēctus**

   Māter dīcit sē bene māne surgĕre.

3. **suō –ĕre suī sūtus**

   Melissa dīxit ancillam tunicās veterēs nōn suĕre.

4. **induō –ĕre induī indūtus**

   Pater dīcit convīvās omnēs togam induĕre.

5. **purgō –āre –āvī –ātus**

   Māter dīcit frātellum dentēs nōn purgāre.

6. **sum esse fuī futūrus**

   Quī in urbe vīvunt dīcunt vītam rūrī multō meliōrem esse.

 7 Earlier, you learned about the place women held in Roman society. Learn more about relationships between Roman women and men by reading these letters between a boy and a girl:

Cornēlius Clārae salūtem dīcit.*

Ex quō diē ego tē cum mātre tuā in Fōrō Rōmānō vīdī et tēcum locūtus sum, tē ubīque quaesīvī. Quotiēns ego thermās frequentō, tē quaerō. Quotiēns forum aut macellum vīsō, tē quaerō. Crēde mihi, Clāra, erat amor prīmā speciē. Tē vehementer dēsīderō. Sine tē nōn possum vīvĕre. Putō quidem tē esse puellam pulcherrimam tōtīus Italiae. Crās ego cum amīcīs ad Circum Maximum itūrus sum, quia glādiātōrēs nōtissimī ibi pugnātūrī sunt. Spērō mē tē ibi

* Typical beginning of a Roman letter

salus –ūtis *f* greetings; **salūtem dīcere** *to greet*
ex quō diē *ever since the day*
quaerō –ĕre quaesīvī quaesītus *to look for*
quotiēns *whenever*
vīsō –ĕre vīsī vīsus *to visit*
prīmā speciē *at first sight*
vehementer *terribly*
dēsīderō –āre –āvī –ātus *to miss*
quidem *really*

nōtus –a –um *well-known, famous*

rūrsus cōnspectūrum esse. Ego et amīcī semper in ōrdine quārtō aut quīntō sedēmus. Quaere nōs ibi! Mūnusculum bellum tibi adferam. Sciō tē nōn Rōmae habitāre sed Arīciae; Arīcia autem nōn procul ab urbe abest. Amor viam semper invenīre potest. Venī, quaesō, sī mē amās. Cūrā ut valeās. Rōmae data.

rūrsus *again*

ordō *-inis m row*

mūnusculum *-ī n a little present*
    bellus *-a -um* **nice**   **adferō**
    -ferre -tūlī -lātum to bring

quaesō *please*   **cūrā ut valeās**
    take care of yourself
Rōmae data *mailed in Rome*

Tuus,

Cornēlius

Clāra Cornēliō salūtem dīcit.

Epistulam tuam magnō cum gaudiō accēpī. Verba tua mē valdē dēlectāvērunt. Ex quō diē ego tē in Fōrō Rōmānō vīdī et tēcum locūta sum, tē cōnstanter in animō habuī. Ubicumque ego sum, dē tē cōgitō, etiam tum cum domum purgō aut lānās neō aut vestēs texō aut in oppidō obsōnō. Ego quoque tē vehementer dēsīderō. Frequenter cum mātre meā dē tē loquor. Māter putat tē esse iuvenem excellentem et hūmānissimum. "Cornēlius," inquit māter, "habitum patricium habet. Oportet tē nūběre talī iuvenī! Crēde mihi, Clāra, inveniēs nēminem meliōrem." Cum mātre cōnsentiō ex tōtō.

gaudium *-ī n joy*
dēlectō *-āre -āvī -ātus to delight*

cōnstanter *constantly*
    animus *-ī m mind, heart*
    ubicumque *wherever*
etiam *even*   **tum cum** *then when*

iuvenis *-is m young man*
    hūmānus *-a -um kind*
habitus *-ūs m bearing, looks*
oportet tē *you ought*
    talis *-is -e such a*
cōnsentiō *-īre cōnsēnsī*
    cōnsensus *to agree*
    ex tōtō *completely*

Sciō Arīciam nōn procul ab urbe Rōmā distāre; sciō perinde multōs viātōrēs cōtīdiē ad urbem iter facěre. Iter ad urbem rārō fēcī, et numquam per mē. Ut scīs, puellae honestae numquam per sē iter faciunt. Praetereā, urbēs magnae mē terrificant.

distō *-āre -āvī to be distant*
    perinde *furthermore*
rārō *rarely*
per mē *by myself* **ut** *as*
    honestus *-a -um respectable*
praetereā *moreover*
terrificō *-āre -āvī -ātus to terrify*

Sī ego Rōmam veniam et tē in Circō Maximō propter turbās magnās nōn cōnspiciam, venī Arīciam. Domus mea est facilis inventū, quia Arīcia est oppidulum. Venī quam prīmum. Cūrā ut valeās. Arīciae data.

turba *-ae f crowd*
facilis inventū *easy to find*
oppidulum *-ī n little town*
    quam prīmum *as soon as*
    possible

Tua,

Clāra

Are you curious to find out what happened? Did Clara find Cornelius in the Circus Maximus? If you can't wait to find out, turn your book upside down. The answer is there!

Clāra Rōmam iter fēcit cum mātre. Circum Maximum intrāvit et Cornēlium ubique quaesīvit sed eum cōnspicěre nōn potuit. Oculī eius erant plēnī lacrimārum. Trīstissima erat. Dēnique Clāra audīvit vōcem dīcentem: "Clāra, Clāra, ego sum hīc! Est tuus Cornēlius!" Clāra cucurrit obvia eī (*to meet him*). Nunc oculī Clārae erant plēnī lacrimārum gaudiī.

Dialogus

VOCĀBULA

profundō –ĕre profūdī profūsus *to shed*
amāns amantis *m lover, boyfriend*
quondam *once*
accidō –ĕre –ī accīsus *to happen*
nebulō –ōnis *m airhead*
argentum –ī *n cash, dough*
iūrō –āre –āvī –ātus *to swear*

caudex –icis *m blockhead*
iamdūdum *long ago*
repudiō –āre –āvī –ātus *to jilt*
urbānus –a –um *sophisticated*
crūdus –a –um *crude*
mītis –is –e *gentle*
marsuppium –ī *n money bag*

Quaestiōnēs Persōnālēs

1. Adiuvāsne patrem aut mātrem domī?

2. Purgāsne et ōrdinās cubiculum tuum?

3. Lavāsne ūtensilia culīnae interdum?

4. Potesne cēnam coquĕre?

5. Obsōnāsne umquam in macellō cum mātre tuā?

6. Quis vestēs tuās suit, tū an māter?

7. Habēsne ancillam domī tuae?

8. Cōgitāsne fēminās Rōmānās vītam fēlīcem ēgisse (led)?

Compositiō

From what you know about Roman life, list three activities that Roman women did that women or girls do today. What are three ways in which Roman and American women differ?

Colloquium

Complete this dialog between Helena and Agrippina based on the previous conversation:

THE LATIN CONNECTION

A. As we have learned, the verb **vocāre** has several meanings, although its most common meaning is *to call.* Various English compounds result when **vocāre** combines with different prefixes. First, write the meanings of the following derivatives. Then use each derivative in an English sentence. Last, write an English noun that shares the same Latin root.

1. evoke

2. convoke

3. invoke

4. provoke

5. revoke

6. What is an *irrevocable* decision?

7. What is a vocation? An *avocation?*

B. From which Latin words did the following words come?

1. utensils

2. concoct

3. suture

4. exhausted

5. grateful

6. ingrate

7. clientele

8. Patrick

9. ancillary

10. repudiate

11. consensus

12. urbane

13. profuse

14. unanimous

15. convivial

16. delectable

17. visa

18. animated

XVII | In officīnā tignāriā

Present Subjunctive

1 Modicum cultūrae

If you were to travel through the narrow, winding streets of ancient Rome, you would see master craftsmen (**magister –trī** *m*) assisted by their young apprentices (**discēns –entis** *m*) and other workers in their little workshops (**officīna –ae** *f*). The craftsmen and their families lived in crowded, dingy apartments consisting of a room or two in the upper stories of ramshackle apartment buildings. The ground floors often housed workshops, retail stores, and small fast-food restaurants. Fires and collapsed buildings were very common in Rome. Craftsmen led a hard life. Work began at sunup and continued until sundown. Earnings were just enough to sustain day-to-day life.

The Romans had no labor unions to bargain for higher wages, shorter working hours, or better working conditions. The workshop owner set the wage; it was not negotiable. Of course, he had to compete with other shops for the best workers he could afford to hire. Members of the various trades formed guilds (**collēgium –ī** *n*), which might be called social clubs. For instance, Rome had **collēgia** of weavers, shoemakers, blacksmiths, silversmiths, goldsmiths, potters, leather workers, dyers, bakers, barbers, stonemasons, and carpenters. The patroness of many **collēgia** was Minerva, the goddess of handicrafts. (Do you remember the craft in which she competed with Arachne? If not, look back to Lesson V for the answer.) Minerva's temple was located on the Aventine Hill, which was heavily populated by the lower classes (the plebeians). Not all guilds chose Minerva, however. A wall painting from Pompeii shows that Daedalus, who was regarded as the first carpenter in history, was the patron of the carpenter's guild. It was natural for members of a trade to band together to form **collēgia** because of their common interests. The organizations gave members opportunities to "talk shop" with one another on holidays and to find out about new developments in their trades. Politicians gradually realized that they could bribe a **collēgium** to gain the votes of the members; in exchange for their votes, tradesmen had a little more money on which to live. The government later passed laws to end this arrangement between crooked politicians and impoverished craftsmen.

In contrast to modern-day factories with their hundreds and even thousands of workers, Roman workshops always remained small. With no electric power to drive machines, ancient tradesmen could not mass produce on assembly lines. They used only simple tools to craft their items, especially since the Romans were not great inventors. Consider their farming methods, for example. Cato, who wrote a book on farming around 200 B.C., describes all of the tools farmers of the time needed to run a farm. Writing on farming *250 years later,* Columella mentions the same tools! Evidence suggests that the same was true of all other trades and crafts. Let's consider the tasks of a carpenter (**tignārius** *–ī m*). He used an axe to chop down a tree. Then, since the Romans never realized they could harness the Tiber River to power sawmills, he used a handsaw to cut the log into boards (**tabul***a* *–ae f*). Next, the carpenter planed or filed the boards until they were smooth—slow, painstaking work. The Romans were, however, familiar with the lathe (**torn***us* *–ī m*) so they could produce decorative legs for tables, chairs, and other furniture. (Daedalus was believed to have invented the lathe, the saw, the carpenter's level, and other tools.) Wall paintings from Pompeii and elsewhere in the Roman world show that these carpenters produced beautiful work. Unfortunately, moisture caused many of their creations to decay over time.

2 Let's look at a typical carpenter shop in the bustling, noisy **Subūra** section of ancient Rome. Study the picture carefully to help you remember the names of the tools:

serra -ae f

malleus -ī m

securis -is f

tignārius -ī m

scalpellum -ī n

terebra -ae f

discens -entis m

tignum -ī n

tornus -ī m

scōpae -ārum f lp

tabula -ae f

magister -trī m

scobis -is f

runcīna -ae f

clāvus -ī m

3 Now let's read an interview that might have taken place between a master carpenter and his new apprentice:

DISCĒNS: Salvē, magister. Ut intellegō, obligātus sum laborāre in tuā officīnā tignāriā. Nōmen mihi est Mārcus Spurius, Mārcī filius.

MAGISTER: Salvē, Mārce. Nōnne cupis fierī tignārius? Immō, quid facĕre potes? Potesne ūtī runcīnā aut scalpellō?

DISCĒNS: Neque runcīnā neque scalpellō umquam usus sum. Ūsque adhūc scholam frequentābam.

MAGISTER: Potesne serram dūcĕre rēctā līneā?

DISCĒNS: Nōn omnīnō serram dūcĕre possum. Numquam tabulam serrā secuī. Pater meus numquam mē docuit serram dūcĕre.

MAGISTER: Potesne ūtī terēbrā?

DISCĒNS: Terēbra? Quid est terēbra?

MAGISTER: Hīc est terēbra. Terēbra est īnstrūmentum quō tignum aut tabulam perforāmus.

DISCĒNS: Numquam anteā terēbram vīdī, sed volō discĕre terēbrā ūtī.

MAGISTER: Potesne ūtī malleō?

DISCĒNS: Possum. Pater meus malleum domī habet. Ego clāvōs malleō saepe fīxī. Ōlim cistam pulchram fabricāvī.

MAGISTER: Potesne tornum tractāre? Potesne pedēs mēnsae aut sellae tornāre?

DISCĒNS: Quid est tornus? Numquam dē tornō audīvī. Explicā, quaesō, mihi tornum.

MAGISTER: Tornus est īnstrūmentum quō rotundāmus lignum, exemplī grātiā, cum pedēs mēnsae tornāmus. Comprehendisne?

DISCĒNS: Incertus sum.

MAGISTER: Nōlī timēre. Paulātim docēbō tē ūtī omnibus īnstrūmentīs in hāc officīnā. Sī dīligenter laborābis et praecepta mea audiēs, fiēs aliquandō tignārius excellēns. Hodiē autem officīnam purgābis. Scobis ubīque est. Age, cape scōpās et scobem verre!

---

ut *as*   obligātus sum *I am supposed*

immō *well*
runcīna –ae *f plane*
   scalpellum –ī *n chisel*

umquam *ever*
   usque adhūc *up till now*

serram dūcĕre rēctā līneā *to saw in a straight line*
nōn omnīnō *not at all*
   secō –āre –uī sectus *to cut*
serrā secāre *to saw (cut with a saw)*

terēbra –ae *f drill*

īnstrūmentum –ī *n tool*
perforō –āre –āvī –ātus *to drill a hole in*

discō –ĕre didicī (+ *inf*) *to learn how to*
malleus –ī *m hammer*
clāvus –ī *m nail*
   fīgō –ĕre fīxī fīxus *to drive in*
   ōlim *once*
   cista –ae *f box*
fabricō –āre –āvī –ātus *to make, put together*
tractō –āre –āvī –ātus *to handle*
pēs pedis *m leg (of chair, etc.)*
   sella –ae *f chair*
   tornō –āre –āvī –ātus *to turn out (on a lathe)*
explicō –āre –uī –itus *to explain*
rotundō –āre –āvī –ātus *to make round*
   lignum –ī *n wood*
comprehendō –ĕre –ī
   comprehensus *to understand*
incertus –a –um *uncertain, not sure*
paulātim *little by little*
praeceptum –ī *n instruction*
   audīre *to listen to*
aliquandō *someday*
scobis –is *f sawdust*
   age *come on*
scōpae –ārum *f pl broom*
   verrō –ĕre –ī versus *to sweep up*

ĀCTIVITĀTĒS

A. Imagine that your father sent you to a Roman hardware store (**taberna ferrāria**) to purchase the household tools in the following pictures. Write the Latin name of each tool you see:

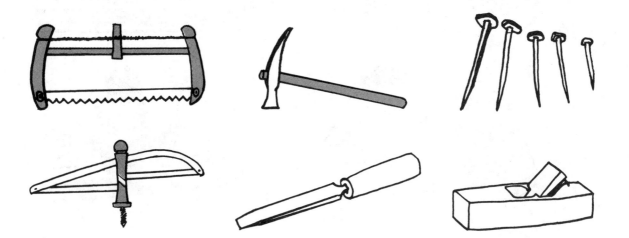

B. Quid faciunt discentēs in officīnā tignāriā? Match the phrases with the pictures:

Discentēs tignum serrā secant.
Discēns scobem scōpīs verrit.
Tignārius pedem mēnsae in tornō
   tornat.
Discēns tignum terēbrā perforat.
Discentēs tigna in officīnam portant.

Parvulus cum scobe lūdit.
Tignārius clāvum in tabulam
   malleō fīgit.
Discēns tignum runcīnat.
Discentēs cum magistrō loquuntur.
Discēns urnam clāvōrum tollit.

1.

2.

3.

4.

5.

6.

7.

8.

9.

10.

4 Every verb you have used so far has been in the indicative mood. "Mood" does not, in this case, refer to the way people feel. Instead, it means the "mode" or way in which speakers communicate information. The "indicative mood" of a verb states a fact. At times, though, you may want to express a wish, a possibility, or a deliberation. To express these secondary ideas, change the form of the verb. The sentence, then, is in the SUBJUNCTIVE MOOD.

First, let's review how we express these thoughts in English:

WISH:	God *be* with you.
POSSIBILITY:	You *may* always *be* happy.
DELIBERATION:	What am I to do? (What *should* I do?)

In the first sentence, notice how the form of the verb changed to express a wish. In the second sentence, the auxiliary (helping) verb *may* indicates possibility. In the third sentence, the word *should* shows the speaker's uncertainty. Modern English rarely uses the subjunctive mood (in which the verb's form changes). Instead, it normally uses auxiliary verbs, such as *may, should, would,* to express shades of meaning other than fact. However, if you read a page by a Roman writer, you will find subjunctive forms everywhere!

Simply stated, to form the present subjunctive Latin changes the *typical* vowel of the indicative. Look at these two columns:

INDICATIVE	SUBJUNCTIVE
port*ō*	port*em*
port*ās*	port*ēs*
port*at*	port*et*
port*āmus*	port*ēmus*
port*ātis*	port*ētis*
port*ant*	port*ent*

What is the typical vowel of the indicative endings? Which vowel substitution made the word *sound* different from the indicative? When the Romans heard **portet** instead of **portat**, they immediately realized that **portet** did not mean *he carries* but, rather, *he may carry* or *he should carry* or *let him carry*.

Now let's learn how Latin uses the subjunctive. The Romans used the subjunctive to express purpose. In English we express purpose in several ways:

The carpenter works
> *to support* his family.
> *in order to support* his family.
> *so that he may support* his family.

Each version of the sentence above has exactly the same meaning. Most often, English sentences express purpose by using an infinitive ("to support" in the first sentence).

Latin, however, *never* uses an infinitive to express purpose. The Latin construction is similar to the third version. It uses the conjunction **ut** (*so that*) followed by a verb in the *subjunctive mood* to express "may support." Latin also does not need an auxiliary verb; it simply changes the vowel in the verb to express purpose. For example, the Latin verb **sustentō –āre –āvī –ātus** means *to support*. Study these sentences:

Tignārius familiam suam *sustentat*.   *The carpenter supports his family.*
Tignārius labōrat ut familiam suam *sustentet*.   *The carpenter works to support his family.*

Because the first sentence states a fact, the verb in both English and Latin is in the *indicative* mood. The second sentence, though, states why the carpenter works (his purpose for working). To express purpose, Latin uses the purpose clause (the conjunction **ut** followed by the verb in the *subjunctive* mood). Did you notice that the final vowel of **sustentat** changed to **sustentet** in the second sentence?

Identifying word groupings, such as purpose clauses, helps you understand Latin sentences. Latin also has a *negative* purpose clause, which is introduced by the conjunction **nē**. Read the following sentences:

Fīlius patrem suum nōn *suscitat*.   *The son does not wake up his father.*
Fīlius tacitē ambulat nē patrem suum *suscitet*.   *The son walks quietly in order not to wake up his father.*

Again, the first sentence simply *indicates* a fact so the verb is in the *indicative* mood. The second sentence contains a clause that begins with the conjunction **nē** and ends with the verb **suscitet** in the *subjunctive* mood.

> **CAUTION:** Don't confuse **ut** (meaning *as* or *when* if used with the indicative) with **ut** (meaning *in order that* or *so that* if used with the subjunctive).

ĀCTIVITĀS

C. Combine the following sentences, changing the second sentence to a purpose clause:

> EXAMPLE: Tignārius labōrat. Familiam sustentat.
>
> Tignārius labōrat **ut familiam sustentet.**

1. Discentēs veniunt. Officīnam tignāriam purgant.

2. Tignārius serram capit. Tabulam longam serrā secat.

3. Discentēs runcīnā ūtuntur. Tignum grave runcīnant.

4. Ego et discēns terēbrā ūtimur. Tabulās perforāmus.

5. Tignārius officīnam bene māne (*early in the morning*) intrat. Multās hōrās ibi labōrat.

6. Discentēs extrā officīnam circumstant. Tornum novum nōn tractant (*handle*).

7. Discēns ē cubiculō suō venit. Amīcum suum nōn ē somnō excitat.

8. Collēgium tignāriōrum in prīmō ōrdine sedet. Gladiātōrēs optimōs spectat.

5 To form the subjunctive of the *–āre* (first) conjugation, you changed the typical vowel **a** to **e**. Notice what happens in the other conjugations:

INDICATIVE	SUBJUNCTIVE	INDICATIVE	SUBJUNCTIVE
mov*eō*	mov*eam*	dūc*ō*	dūc*am*
mov*ēs*	mov*eās*	dūc*is*	dūc*ās*
mov*et*	mov*eat*	dūc*it*	dūc*at*
mov*ēmus*	mov*eāmus*	dūc*imus*	dūc*āmus*
mov*ētis*	mov*eātis*	dūc*itis*	dūc*ātis*
mov*ent*	mov*eant*	dūc*unt*	dūc*ant*

(continued)

INDICATIVE	SUBJUNCTIVE	INDICATIVE	SUBJUNCTIVE
capiō	capiam	audiō	audiam
capis	capiās	audīs	audiās
capit	capiat	audit	audiat
capimus	capiāmus	audīmus	audiāmus
capitis	capiātis	audītis	audiātis
capiunt	capiant	audiunt	audiant

Notice that all verbs in the first-person singular of the present subjunctive end in –*m*. What vowel of the subjunctive endings is typical of all conjugations except the first? Why couldn't this typical vowel be used for the first conjugation?

ĀCTIVITĀS

D. Complete the sentences below by writing the correct form of the subjunctive of each verb in parentheses:

1. Discēns officīnam intrat ut tornum novum (vidēre).
2. Puellae comam calamistrō crīspant ut amantibus suīs (placēre).
3. Discentēs dīligenter labōrant ut plūs pecūniae (facĕre).
4. Ego et discentēs interdum latēmus nē magister nōs (invenīre).
5. Multī officīnam nostram intrant ut sellās et mēnsās (emĕre).
6. Ancilla aquam ē cisternā haurit ut ātrium (lavāre).
7. Māter et soror, ītisne nunc in forum ut holera (obsōnāre)?
8. Ancillae in culīnam eunt ut cēnam prō convīvīs (coquĕre).
9. Discentēs in officīnā conveniunt ut praecepta magistrī (audīre).
10. Māter in ātriō cōnsīdit ut lānās (nēre [*to spin*]).

6 The subjunctive forms of the verbs **esse** and **posse** are irregular; that is, they don't fall into the pattern we just observed for other verbs:

sim	possim
sīs	possīs
sit	possit
sīmus	possīmus
sītis	possītis
sint	possint

ĀCTIVITĀS

E. For each sentence below, write the correct present-subjunctive form of the verb in parentheses:

1. Parentēs meī Rōmam iter faciunt ut cum avō et aviā (esse).

2. Ego in prīmō ōrdine theātrī semper sedeō ut melius vidēre (posse).

3. Frāter meus prope illam puellam sedet ut cum eā loquī (posse).

4. Ego et Fabius nunc ex urbe exīmus nē noctū in mediā urbe (esse).

5. Frātellus aquam ē cisternā haurit ut sē lavāre (posse).

6. Melissa, manēsne domī ut cum parentibus tuīs (esse).

7 In English, we change word order to indicate an indirect question. The Romans used the subjunctive mood in indirect questions:

DIRECT: **Ubi est pecten meus?**   *Where is my comb?*
INDIRECT: **Caecilia quaerit *ubi pecten suus sit.*** *Caecilia asks where her comb is.*

Many Latin verbs can introduce an indirect question, such as:

rogāre, interrogāre, quaerĕre, inquīrĕre (*to ask*)
scīre (*to know*) **and nĕscīre** (*not to know*)
expōnĕre, explicāre (*to explain*)
intellegĕre, vidēre (*to understand*)
ambigĕre (*to be unsure, to wonder*)

The word order of Latin indirect questions has one peculiarity, however. The Romans often placed the indirect question *first* in the sentence. Note the word order of this sentence:

***Ubi discentēs sint* nĕsciō.**   *I don't know where the apprentices are.*

In effect, the ancients said, "Where the apprentices are I do not know."

ĀCTIVITĀS

F. Each sentence below contains an indirect question. Identify each question and rewrite it as a direct question:

EXAMPLE: <u>Ubi sim</u> nĕsciō.   Ubi sum?

1. Magister vult scīre quid nōs faciāmus.

2. Scīsne quid faciās?

3. Quid senātor dīcat nōn intellegō.

4. Cūr tignārius illum malleum habeat nĕsciō.

5. Magister quaerit quid discēns facĕre possit.

6. Nōn possum expōnĕre cūr Rōmam sīc amem.

7. Cūr tignārius īrātus sit nunc videō.

8. Ambigō num (*whether*) ille Rōmae habitet.

9. Magister quaerit quandō discentēs labōrātūrī sint.

10. Qualis persōna tū sīs nēsciō.

8 Although Daedalus is credited with having been the world's first carpenter and the inventor of several important tools, these accomplishments were not the main reason for his fame. Daedalus and his son Icarus were the ancient counterparts of the Wright brothers! According to legend, they were the first humans to fly. Let's read how that happened:

Daedalus cum fīliō Īcarō in īnsulā Crētā vīxit. Tignārius perītissimus erat. Dīcitur invēnisse serram et tornum et multa alia īnstrūmenta tignāria. Itaque Mīnōs, rēx Crētae, Daedalum ad aulam suam vocāvit et dīxit: "Mōnstrum ferōcissimum in aulā habēmus. Hōc mōnstrum puerōs puellāsque dēvōrat. Vocātur Mīnōtaurus, id est, 'Mīnōis taurus.' Est sēmihomō et sēmitaurus. Iubeō tē labyrinthum aedificāre ut istud mōnstrum ibi inclūdāmus."

Postquam Daedulus labyrinthum aedificāvit, Mīnōs Daedalum ipsum, ūnā cum fīliō Īcarō, in labyrinthō inclūsit quia rēx nōluit Daedalum sēcrētum labyrinthī revēlāre cuiquam. Sed Daedalus iānuam sēcrētam labyrinthī facile aperuit et cum fīliō ad montem altum fūgit.

Quōdam diē pater fīliō dīxit: "Exulēs in hāc īnsulā sumus. Neque terra neque mare viam salūtis dat. Sed via per caelum nōbīs patet. Ālās ex avium pennīs faciam ut hōc modō ad salūtem volāre possīmus." Pater fīliusque pennās aquilārum colligunt ut ex hīs pennīs magnās ālās faciant. Dum pater dīligenter labōrat, fīlius cum pennīs lūdit. Pater pennās in ōrdine pōnit et eās līnō et cērā ligāvit. Dēnique alae erant parātae. Daedalus ālās umerīs fīliī adaptāvit, deinde ipse ālās induit. Mandāta stricta fīliō dedit: "Īcare, mī fīliole, nōlī celsius volāre, nē radiī sōlis cēram ālārum tuārum liquefaciant. Nōlī dēmissius volāre, nē alae tuae flūctūs maris tangant." Ut fīliō mandāta dedit, genae patris maduērunt, et manūs tremuērunt. Ōscula fīliō dat, et ante volat. Fīlius sequitur.

vīvō –ĕre vīxī vīctus *to live*
perītus –a –um *skillful*

Mīnōs –ōis *m Minos, king of Crete*

sēmihomō –inis *m half-man*
  sēmitaurus –ī *m half-bull*
  iubeō –ēre iussī iussus *to order*
labyrinthus –ī *m labyrinth, maze*
  aedificō –āre –āvi –ātus *to build*
inclūdō –ĕre inclūsī inclūsus *to lock up*
sēcrētum –ī *n secret*
  revēlō –āre –āvi –ātus *to reveal*
  cuiquam *to anyone*

quōdam diē *one day*
  exul –īs *m exiled person*

via salūtis *road to safety*
  pateō –ēre –uī *to lie open*
āla –ae *f wing*
  penna –ae *f feather*
colligō –ĕre collēgī collēctus *to gather*

līnum –ī *n twine*   **cēra –ae** *f wax*
  ligō –āre –āvi –ātus *to tie*
adaptō –āre –āvi –ātus *to adapt*
mandātum –ī *n instruction*
celsius *too high*
  radius –ī *m ray*
liquefaciō –facĕre –fēcī –factus *to melt*   **dēmissius** *too low*
tangō –ĕre tetigī tactus *touch*
gena –ae *f cheek*

Prīmō Īcarus mandāta patris in memoriā tenēbat. Mox celsius et celsius volāre temptāvit puer et incēpit gaudēre audācī volātū. Radiī sōlis autem cēram ālārum liquefaciēbant. "Pater!" Īcarus clāmāvit, "pater, adiuvā mē, servā mē!" ut in mare cecidit. "Īcare!" clāmāvit anxius pater, "ubi es?" "Īcare" rūrsus dīxit et pennās in flūctibus cōnspexit. Etiamnunc mare, in quō Īcarus periit, Mare Īcarium vocātur. Postquam pater maestus corpus fīliī sepelīvit, in Ītaliam volāvit.

madeō –ēre –uī *to be wet with tears*
tremō –ēre –uī *to tremble*
  ante *out ahead*
  celsius *higher*
gaudeō –ēre (+ abl) *to enjoy*
  volātus –ūs *m flight*
anxius –a –um *anxious, worried*
rūrsus *again*
etiamnunc *even now, still today*
  pereō –īre –iī *to perish*
maestus –a –um *grieving*
sepeliō –īre –īvī **sepultus** *to bury*

ĀCTIVITĀS

G. Respondē Latīnē:

1. Ubi Daedalus habitāvit?

2. Quis erat fīlius Daedalī?

3. Quis erat rēx īnsulae?

4. Quāle mōnstrum rēx in aulā habēbat?

5. Quid rēx iussit Daedalum aedificāre?

6. Quod nōmen erat mōnstrō?

7. Cūr Daedalus ex labyrinthō effugĕre potuit?

8. Ex quō Daedalus ālās fēcit?

9. Quid cēram ālārum Īcarī liquefēcit?

10. Quō volāvit pater post mortem fīliī?

VOCĀBULA

intentē *intently*
sustineō –ēre –uī sustentus *to hold up*
aug̱ur –uris *m augur, seer*
Inaugurāsne? *Are you taking the auspices?*
captō –āre –āvī –ātus *to catch*

plaudō –ĕre plausī plausus *to flap*
tamquam *like*
cauda –ae *f tail*
mementō *remember!*
repente *all of a sudden*

1. Scīsne ūtī malleō?

2. Potesne serram rēctā līneā dūcĕre?

3. Potesne clāvōs fīgĕre?

4. Fabricāvistīne aliquid īnstrūmentīs tignāriīs?

5. Vidistīne umquam tignārium, tornum tractantem?

6. Purgāsne cubiculum tuum scōpīs?

7. Habetne pater tuus multa īnstrūmenta tignāria?

8. Ūtitur frequenter pater īnstrūmentīs tignāriīs?

Compositiō

Nearly every homeowner has a number of tools for making household repairs. Suppose a small child looked into a tool chest and asked you to explain the functions of various tools. In Latin, explain how the following tools are used. Use this example to help you begin each explanation: *A file is a tool that people use to . . .*

serra **malleus** **secūris** **runcīna** **terēbra**

Colloquium

In this dialog between Tullia and Claudius (her little brother), Claudius sometimes has a problem finding the right words. Help him by writing the words he needs based on the previous conversation:

Salvē, frātelle. Quamobrem ad caelum tam intentē spectās?

Salvē, Tullia. Ego _____ in caelō observō.

Vīsne avēs captāre? Aut factus es augur? Inaugurāsne?

Ego _____ nōn captō. Quōmodō avēs per aërem _____ possint, nōn intellegō. Quid eās in _____ sustineat nesciō.

O Claudī, est simplex. Avēs alās habent. Quandō avēs alās plaudunt, volāre possunt.

Ego alās ex _____ _____ faciam et eās umerīs meīs adaptābō ut volāre tamquam _____ possim.

Avēs autem pennās in caudā habent, sed tū nullam caudam habēs, frātelle.

Sī alās et caudam ex _____ faciam, nōnne volāre poterō?

Sed mementō, avēs pennās etiam in capite et per totum corpus habent.

Nesciō cūr, sed repente ego praeferō _____.

⟲ THE LATIN CONNECTION

A. What is the Latin origin of *serrated?*

What is a *serrated* blade?

B. What are the Latin origins and definitions of the following words?

1. radius
2. ligature
3. humerus
4. aviary
5. caudal
6. sustain
7. precept
8. crucifixion
9. scalpel
10. college
11. to turn
12. mandate
13. liquefy
14. tremulous
15. tangible
16. malleable
17. revelation

C. What comes to mind when you picture a factory that *manufactures* products? Most of us picture machines producing objects, right? According to its Latin roots, what does the word *manufacture* actually mean?

D. The verb **secō secāre secuī sectus** means *to cut.* Listed below are ten English derivatives of this verb. How is each defined?

1. vivisection
2. intersection
3. to dissect
4. to bisect
5. a sect
6. section
7. cross-section
8. sectional furniture
9. secant
10. insect

XVIII | Mōns Vesuvius

Imperfect Subjunctive

1 Modicum cultūrae

Of all the natural catastrophes that occurred in the Roman world, by far the most famous was the eruption of the volcano on Mount Vesuvius, which is located about seven miles inland from the Bay of Naples. The eruption occurred on August 24 in the year A.D. 79. It was the height of the vacation season, when hordes of vacationers from Rome and elsewhere crowded the resort towns and beaches of the Bay of Naples. A severe earthquake in A.D. 63 had caused heavy damage in the towns of Campania, the district in which Mount Vesuvius lies. Public buildings toppled. Many people were left homeless. A flock of 600 sheep disappeared in a huge crack in the earth's surface. Residents felt earth tremors before Mount Vesuvius erupted, but no one paid much attention to them because tremors were common throughout Campania.

The great eruption lasted three days. When it ended, the towns of Pompeii and Herculaneum were totally destroyed. A teenager, Gaius Plinius Secundus (or Pliny), lived at Misenum on the northern shore of the Bay of Naples. He left a short but vivid eyewitness account of what happened during those dreadful days of August 24 through August 26.

A tremendous mushroom cloud, rising high into the sky above Vesuvius, appeared across the Bay of Naples. At times the cloud was white; other times it was murky with dust (**pulvis** *–eris m*) and ashes (**cinis** *–eris m*). The volcano spewed spectacular sheets of flame at night. Soon, thick ash and small, hot stones (**lapillī** *–ōrum m pl*) began to fall across a wide area, eventually covering everything like snow. The thick odor of sulfur was everywhere, making breathing difficult. The next day, a cloud of dust and ashes blocked out the sun. Houses shook and threatened to collapse. Those inside houses ran outdoors; those who were outdoors ran into houses and public buildings. Children screamed for parents as day turned to night; parents called to their children, and husbands for their wives. Many of those who tried to leave the town of Misenum lost their way in the pitch darkness. Earth tremors tossed their vehicles from one side of the road to the other. Many thought it was the end of the world. Pliny himself believed he and those around him would die. Tugging his mother by the hand, he forced her to escape with him. When the sun reappeared, people discovered an entirely changed landscape. Misenum was covered with a deep layer of ash and pumice, lava that had cooled and solidified. All of this destruction in a town about 15 miles northwest of the crater!

In Pompeii, just south of Vesuvius, the situation was far worse. The eruption occurred as the townspeople were seated in a theater watching a performance. Fortunately, many of Pompeii's 22,000 people had time to gather whatever valuables they could carry and were able to leave early morning on August 24. Some two thousand people died of suffocation. Twenty to twenty-five feet of ash and pumice covered the city, leaving only the tops of public and private buildings visible. Survivors used these protruding ruins to locate and dig out at least some of what they had left behind. Later eruptions and the work of nature and man eventually erased all traces of the city until it was excavated in modern times. Excavations have continued for well over 100 years; at present, about eighty-five percent of Pompeii has been excavated.

The volcano's other target, the city of Herculaneum, lay on the shore of the Bay of Naples. It, too, was buried but by a river of volcanic mud—in some places to a depth of some 50 feet. All buildings in its wake vanished. Only a small section of Herculaneum has been excavated because the modern town was built over the ancient ruins.

Mōns Vesuvius

vapor -ōris m

fumus -ī m

pulvis -eris m

flamma -ae f

Neāpolis

Mīsēnum

lapillī -ōrum mpl

Herculāneum
sulfur -uris n

Sinus Neāpolitānus

Pompeiī

Surrentum

cinis -eris m

pūmex -icis m

Capreae I.

3 Read this eyewitness account of the eruption of Vesuvius:

Ego sum Gāius Plīnius, duodēvīgintī annōs nātus. Apud avunculum habitō, cūius vīlla est suprā collem nōn procul ab ōrā maritimā. Oppidum Mīsēnum vocātur. Vīlla sita est in septentriōnālī parte sinūs Neāpolitānī. Quōdam diē mēnsis Augustī ego in āreā domūs legēbam et studēbam. Hōrā ferē septimā, māter mea indicāvit nūbem inūsitātam appārēre trāns sinum. Māter clāmāvit: "Spectā nūbem mīram, ex Monte Vesuviō orientem. Quid significat haec nūbēs mīra?"

apud (+ *acc*) *at the house of, with*

septentriōnālis *-is -e northern*
sinus *-ūs m bay*
   Neāpolitānus *-a -um of Naples*
ārea *-ae f* **domūs** *yard*
ferē *about, around*
inūsitātus *-a -um unusual*
   appāreō *-ēre -uī to appear*
mīrus *-a -um strange*
oriēns *-entis rising*
   significō *-āre -āvī -ātus to mean*

Tremor terrae per multōs diēs praecesserat. Ille tremor terrae erat minus formīdābilis quia tremōrēs terrae in Campāniā erant solitī. Ego ipse volēbam continuāre legēre et studēre, sed māter mea hōc perīculō novō territa erat. Ego librum meum dēposuī et cum tōtā familiā ascendī locum, ex quō illud mīrāculum maximē cōnspicī poterat. Nūbēs, ex crātēre oriēns, erat candida interdum, interdum erat obscūra et maculōsa. Iam Mōns Vesuvius cinerem et fūmum et vapōrem et pūmicem ēiciēbat. Tālem ēruptiōnem numquam anteā vīdimus.

Mox dē caelō cadēbat cinis, quī paulātim calidior et dēnsior fīēbat. Iam familia et omnēs oppidānī erant trepidissimī. Aliī intrā tēcta manēre cupiēbant, aliī in apertō deambulāre praeferēbant, nam frequentibus vastīsque tremōribus tēcta nūtāre incipiēbant.

In apertō autem ob lapillōs cadentēs, multī cervīcālia capitibus imposuērunt. Praetereā, gravis odor sulfuris erat ubīque et movēbat lacrimās et tussim. Diēs fīēbat nox. Audīvimus ululātūs fēminārum, vagītūs īnfantium, clāmōrēs virōrum. Aliī requīrēbant vōcibus parentēs; aliī requīrēbant līberōs; aliī requīrēbant coniugēs; aliī requīrēbant amīcōs. Omnēs crēdidērunt illam futūram esse noctem novissimam in mundō.

Dēnique tertiō diē lūx rediit et sōl refulsit, sed aër erat lūridus. Omnia erant mūtāta. Omnia altō cinere erant obducta tamquam altā nive.

Postrīdiē nūntius pervēnit, quī dīxit Vesuvium duo oppida dēlēvisse, Pompēiōs et Herculāneum. Ego ipse ēruptiōnem Vesuviī semper in memoriā retinēbō.

praecēdō –ĕre praecessī to precede
formīdābilis –is –e frightening
solitus –a –um usual, customary

dēpōnō –ĕre dēposuī dēpositus to put down
mīrāculum –ī n strange sight
  maximē best
crātēr –ēris m crater
interdum sometimes
  obscūrus –a –um murky
maculōsus –a –um spotty
pumex –icis m lava

oppidānī –ōrum m pl townspeople
  cines –erum m pl ashes
  trepidus –a –um alarmed
in apertō in the open
  deambulō –āre –āvī to walk around
vastus –a –um enormous
nūtō –āre to totter
cervīcal –ālis n pillow
moveō –ēre mōvī mōtus to cause
tussis –is f cough, coughing
ululātus –ūs m wail **vagītus –ūs** m cry
requīro –ĕre requisīvī requisītus to look for
  vōcibus requīrĕre to yell for
coniūnx coniugis m/f spouse
novissimus –a –um last
lūx lūcis f daylight
refulgeō –ēre refulsī to shine again
lūridus –a um smoky
altus –a –um deep
obductus –a –um covered
  tamquam as if
postrīdiē on the following day

ĀCTIVITĀS

A. Respondē Latīnē:

1. Apud quem habitāvit Gāius Plīnius?

2. Ubi erat ēius vīlla?

3. Quis indicāvit Plīniō nūbem inūsitātam?

4. Quid tum Plīnius faciēbat?

5. Ex quō monte nūbēs mīra orta est?

6. Quid per multōs diēs ēruptiōnem praecesserat?

7. Quae Mōns Vesuvius ēiciēbat?

8. Quid multī oppidānī capitī imposuērunt?

9. Quid omnēs crēdidērunt?

10. Quae oppida Vesuviō dēlēta sunt?

 You have learned how to form indirect questions in the present tense. If the verb that introduces the indirect question is in the past tense, the verb in the indirect question also must be in the past tense:

Ubi *essem* nēscīvī.   *I didn't know where I was.*

Discēns exposuit cūr tam sērō   *The apprentice explained why he*
  labōrāret.   *was working so late.*

In both examples, the verb of the indirect question is in the *imperfect* subjunctive. Forming the imperfect subjunctive is simple. Add the personal endings **–m, –s, –t, –mus, –tis, –nt** to the present infinitive of any verb, including **esse** and **posse**:

portāre + *–m* = portāre*m*   portāre + *–mus* = portārē*mus*
portāre + *–s* = portārē*s*   portāre + *–tis* = portārē*tis*
portāre + *–t* = portāre*t*   portāre + *–nt* = portāre*nt*

ĀCTIVITĀS

B. Identify the indirect question. Then rewrite it as a direct question:

EXAMPLE: Amita quaesīvit <u>ubi incendium esset.</u> **"Ubi incendium est?"**

1. Avunculus quaesīvit cūr in āreā domūs sedērem.

2. Cūr tam mīra nūbēs suprā Vesuvium esset nēsciēbam.

3. Cūr lapillī dē caelō caderent diū nōn intellēxī.

4. Ego ambigēbam quōmodo mē servātūrus essem.

5. Vīcīnus meus ā mē quaesīvit cūr omnēs fūgerent.

6. Oppidānī ā mē rogāvērunt in quā tabernā cervīcālia emĕre possint.

7. Quid in apertō facerētis nēsciēbātis.

8. Quid senātor dē causīs ēruptiōnis Montis Vesuviī dīceret nōn intellegēbam.

9. Amita ā mē quaesīvit num familia salva in apertō esset.

10. Ego ab avunculō quaesīvī quid ēruptiōnem Montis Vesuviī movēret (*caused*).

5 The purpose clause, both positive (with **ut**) and negative (with **nē**), requires the imperfect subjunctive if the main verb is in the past tense:

Multī ex oppidō Mīsēnō fūgērunt
    ut mortem certam *ēvītārent*.

Many fled from the town of Misenum
to avoid (or, in order that they
might avoid) certain death.

Here, the main verb (**fūgērunt**) is in the past tense, so the verb in the purpose clause (**ēvītārent**) is in the imperfect subjunctive.

ĀCTIVITĀTĒS

C. Combine the two sentences by making the second sentence a purpose clause:

1. Avunculus meus ad Montem Vesuvium īvit. Nūbem inūsitātam observābat.

2. Multī cervīcālia in capite gestābant. Caput contrā lapillōs prōtegēbant.

3. Līberī ad sinum Neāpolītānum īvērunt. In sinū natābant.

4. Famila mea in apertō dormīvit. Ruīnam (*collapse*) vīllae ēvītābat.

5. Oppidānī Mīsēnum relīquērunt. In aliō oppidō salūtem inveniēbant.

6. Ego et Fabius in āreā domūs sedēbāmus. Librōs cōmicōs ibi legēbāmus.

D. Rewrite the following sentences from past to present tense:

1. Ego et amīcus trāns sinum Neāpolītānum nāvigāvimus ut Pompēiōs vīsitārēmus.

2. Ascendistisne Montem Vesuvium ut crātērem vidērētis?

3. Ante ēruptiōnem amita in forum īvit ut obsōnāret.

4. Avus et avia post ēruptiōnem Mīsēnum vēnērunt ut mē vīsitārent.

5. Haec nōn dīxī ut tē terrērem.

6. Parentēs per Mīsēnum cucurrērunt ut līberōs requīrerent.

6 Contrary to what you might expect, if a verb of fearing (**timeō**, for example) is part of the main clause, the conjunction **nē** is used to introduce a *positive* idea while **ut** introduces a *negative* idea:

Timeō *ut* pater veniat.   *I am afraid that my father is NOT coming.*
Timeō *nē* pater veniat.   *I am afraid that my father IS coming.*

E. Read the following sentences carefully, remembering that with verbs of fearing, **ut** means *that . . . not* and **nē** means *that*. The most common verbs of fearing are **timeō** *–ēre –uī* and **metuō** *–ĕre –ī*. Of these, **metuō** expresses a stronger fear. Convert the following sentences from present to past by changing the tenses of both verbs:

1. Timeō nē tremor terrae Mīsēnum dēleat.

2. Timēmus ut vīllam nostram servēmus.

3. Metuisne nē pater tē cum amante videat?

4. Omnēs timent nē haec nox sit novissima in mundō.

5. Metuimus ut amīcōs nostrōs ob pulverem et fūmum inveniāmus.

6. Ille metuit nē pūmex et lapillī arborēs ac plantās ac flōrēs dēleant.

7 As you know, the conjunctions **sī** (*if*) and **nisi** (*unless, if . . . not*) introduce CONDITIONAL clauses in Latin. Look at these *simple* conditions:

Sī hoc *crēdis,* errās.	*If you believe this, you are wrong.*
Sī Romae *manēbis,* Caesarem vidēbis.	*If you stay in Rome, you will see Caesar.*
Nisi dīligenter labōrābis, pecūniam nōn habēbis.	*If you don't work hard, you won't have (any) money.*

In the first sentence, the **sī** clause simply states *if you believe this.* It does not imply that you believe or do not believe. Therefore, this is a *simple* condition. The second **sī** clause is also a simple condition. Notice that the verb of the **sī** clause is in the future tense. (In English we use the present tense—*if you stay*—even though it has a future sense—*if you will stay in Rome.*) Don't you agree that the Latin is more precise with its use of the future tense in the **sī** clause (**manēbis**)? Now read this sentence:

Sī pecūniam *habērem,* fēlīx essem.	*If I had money, I would be happy.*

This **sī** clause implies that I do not have money; therefore, we call it a contrary-to-fact condition. In this situation, Latin puts the verb into the imperfect subjunctive. In English, we use what looks like the *past* tense of the verb (if I *had*) to express a *present* contrary-to-fact condition. (We mean to say "if I had money right now.") The Romans, too, used the imperfect tense of the subjunctive.

ĀCTIVITĀTĒS

F. Complete the following contrary-to-fact conditions referring to the present time by writing the correct forms of the imperfect subjective of **habēre** and **esse**:

1. Sī pater pecūniam (habēre), ille fēlīx (esse).

2. Sī amīcī meī pecūniam (habēre), illī fēlīcēs (esse).

3. Sī ego et pater pecūniam (habēre), nōs fēlīcēs (esse).

4. Sī tū pecūniam (habēre), tū fēlīx (esse).

5. Sī omnēs pecūniam (habēre), omnēs fēlīcēs (esse).

6. Sī tū et frāter pecūniam (habēre), vōs fēlīcēs (esse).

G. Write the correct forms of the verbs in parentheses to complete the following contrary-to-fact conditions. The first verb is part of the **sī** clause:

1. (sedēre/posse)   Sī Plīnius in āreā domūs _____,
   sinum vidēre _____.

2. (stāre/cadēre)   Sī ego in apertō _____, lapillī in
   caput meum _____.

3. (habēre/manēre)   Sī oppidānī cervīcālia _____,
   illī in apertō _____.

4. (habēre/fugĕre)   Sī familia cisium _____, ex
   oppidō ad collēs _____.

5. (habēre/volāre)   Sī ego ālās _____, per aërem
   _____.

6. (metuĕre/manēre)   Sī ego ēruptiōnem _____, ego
   domī _____.

7. (amāre/relinquĕre)   Sī tū mē vērō _____, tū mē nōn
   nunc _____.

8. (habēre/dare)   Sī ego anulum aureum _____,
   ego eum tibi _____.

9. (habēre/nēre)   Sī ancillae plūs temporis _____,
   eae lānās _____.

10. (esurīre/ēsse)   Sī tu vērō _____, tū cibum
    simplicem _____.

11. (habēre/rādĕre)   Sī ego novāculam _____, ego
    barbam iam _____.

12. (pluĕre/manēre)   Sī _____, ego et amīcus in vīllā
    _____.

Dialogus

VOCĀBULA

adhūc *still*
rēs reī *f situation*
nūper *recently*
omittō –ĕre omīsī omissus to *lose*
dēspērō –āre –āvī –ātus to *despair*
Quid est? *What's the trouble?*
iam pluit *it has been raining*

urceātim pluĕre to *rain buckets*
iocus –ī *m joke;* **iocum facis!** *you're kidding!*
metō –ĕre messuī messus to *harvest*
abhinc *from here*
salvus –a –um *safe*

Rēs Persōnālēs

Suppose you are part of the theater audience in Pompeii, enjoying the show until you are interrupted by the loud roar of Mount Vesuvius' eruption. Like others, you see the huge cloud of ash rise high into the air. (One can easily see the top of Vesuvius from the theater of Pompeii.) Read the following list of actions you could take, but be careful! You must remain calm and do things in their proper order. Write the numbers 1–12 in a column on a separate sheet of paper. Then order the steps listed below with 1 being the first action you would take and 12, the last:

Ex urbe statim fugerem.
Cibum et potiōnem prō fugā colligerem.
Parentēs meōs requīrerem.
Domum dīrēctō īrem.
Pecūniam meam caperem.
Ex theātrō currerem.
Amīcōs meōs adiuvārem.
Canem (aut fēlem) meum servārem.
Cīvēs veterēs adiuvārem.
Raedam aut cisium requīrerem.
Magistrum meum servārem.
Amīcīs valē dīcerem.

Compositiō

You are the mayor of Pompeii. Mount Vesuvius has just erupted. People are panicking. Should they stay in their houses and wait out the eruption, gather their belongings before leaving, locate a carriage so they can ride out, take time to locate family members, or simply run for their lives? Someone notices you. Soon everyone is begging for your advice. You must take charge. Use the imperative form, positive or negative, to tell people what to do. Address your orders to men, women, children, or slaves.

How good is your memory? See how many of the missing words you can supply in this dialog between a farmer and his sympathetic friend.

THE LATIN CONNECTION

For each of the following words, write its Latin source:

1. eruption
2. miracle
3. intrepid
4. desperate
5. sulfur
6. joke
7. appear
8. formidable
9. inevitable
10. incinerate
11. pulverize
12. perfume
13. vapor
14. significant
15. deposit
16. vast
17. conjugal
18. mundane
19. lurid
20. crater
21. pumice
22. sinuses
23. apparent
24. indication
25. inflammation
26. trepidation
27. mirage
28. deposition

XIX | Iūstitia

Pluperfect Subjunctive

 ## Modicum cultūrae

The profession of law in ancient Rome was both honorable and useful, especially if you wanted to become an important politician. True, some Roman army generals became important political leaders, but the vast majority of statesmen were lawyers. A father who wanted his sons to succeed took them to the Roman Forum to learn public speaking and study law. Later, the father placed his sons under the care of a famous statesman or teacher. In this way, Cicero's father introduced his son to famous legal experts in Rome. Cicero went on to become the most famous lawyer in the Roman world.

There are, of course, some important differences between a Roman advocate and a modern lawyer. Most lawyers today make a living exclusively by practicing law. In Rome, however, the practice of law was only one of the many activities of a politician. Income from a legal practice was of minor importance; a Roman politician practiced law only for the authority and political prestige it would bring him. In fact, a law passed in 204 B.C. forbade lawyers to accept money or gifts for pleading cases in court. The ancients felt that the practice of demanding a fee in advance, as many lawyers do today, was particularly dishonorable. They even assigned different titles to lawyers. An advocate (**advocātus –ī m**) gave legal help to clients to advance his political career. A lawyer who represented the lower classes (**causidicus –ī m**) regularly accepted fees to defend people in court. The **advocātus** felt superior to the **causidicus**. Over time, clients paid advocates who defended them when their trials ended successfully; however, payment was never compulsory.

If a Roman wanted to bring a civil suit (a case that asked for money damages from the defendant) against another, he personally had to arrest the person and bring him to court. So that the defendant could not complain he had not been summoned to court, the accuser brought witnesses with him to issue the summons. The accuser and the defendant then went before the chief justice (**praetor –ōris m**) for a hearing (**praeiūdicium –ī n**). The **praetor** decided if the accuser had sufficient reason for a lawsuit. He then set the fine or other punishment to be applied if the defendant were found guilty in the trial.

In court during a civil case, the **advocātus** helped his client in very limited ways. He stood near him, made suggestions, and spoke on his behalf, as a character witness would today. The client had to speak for himself. Today's lawyer handles every aspect of the civil case.

In a criminal case, both the accused and the accuser had to act as their own lawyers. No public prosecutor or district attorney prosecuted the criminal. Trials were citizens prosecuting citizens. The defendant (the accused) had the right to a public trial, in which he or she could cross-examine his accuser. Much-publicized criminal trials and famous lawyers attracted huge crowds in the Roman Forum. Both parties in the criminal case surrounded themselves in court with influential friends, whose very presence might influence jurors. A panel of up to 60 jurors (**iūdex –icis m**) chosen from a list of about 4,000 men of the upper classes heard the case in the presiding presence of a **praetor.**

Roman trials were brief, generally completed in a day or less. Complicated or important cases could last several days but, unlike some modern trials, they did not continue for weeks, months, or (sometimes) years. In a case of capital punishment, the convicted criminal could appeal only once—to the assembly of citizens.

When a person was found guilty, he was fined or deprived of some of his civil rights, such as the right to vote or to run for office. In more serious cases, the guilty person was exiled (banished from the country) or executed. No Roman citizen could be crucified (executed on a cross) or scourged (flogged, whipped); however, there remained many other methods of punishment. The convicted citizen could be thrown off the Tarpeian Cliff on the Capitoline Hill; the guilty Roman could be strangled or starved to death in prison. He could be sentenced to work in the mines, never again to see the light of day. He could be sentenced to fight wild beasts in the arena or to fight to death as a gladiator. Beheading was common. Death by fire was sometimes the punishment for committing arson.

The Romans did not sentence people to long prison terms because they had no huge penitentiaries as we have today. In fact, Rome had only one small prison, at the foot of the Capitoline Hill. It actually had been a cave! A prisoner had to stay in this prison before trial if he could not afford bail. Convicted prisoners who were sentenced to death returned to the prison to be executed. Cicero actually ordered some political prisoners in this prison to be executed before they even had trials. For this, Cicero himself was sent into exile. Visitors today can still see this cave-turned-prison, although it has been converted into a Christian chapel.

In the early days of Rome, what we today would consider minor offenses often warranted the death penalty. In later centuries, the court permitted the defendant to go into voluntary exile, even before the trial was over.

Did you know that Rome got along for 700 years without a police force to maintain order? Magistrates, such as the **aedilēs** (aedīl*is* –*is m*), had certain police powers and must have employed a group of men to maintain order and make arrests. It was the Emperor Augustus who, near the end of his reign in A.D. 14, created a new force, organized in a semi-military fashion. The force consisted of seven cohorts (divisions), each consisting of a thousand men known as **vigilēs** (**vigil** –*is m*). These men, former slaves, served as both firemen and policemen. Their commander, a member of the middle class, had the title of prefect. Such was the arrangement in the city of Rome. Other cities and towns generally copied the Roman model when they created their fire brigades and police forces.

A. Study the courtroom (**iūdicium** *–ī n*) in the courthouse (**basilica** *–ae f*) and see if you can answer these questions in Latin:

1. Quis in tribunālī sedet?

2. Quī in subselliīs sedent?

3. Quot iūdicēs in hōc iūdiciō sunt?

4. Quis accūsat reum?

5. Quis dēfendit reum?

6. Statne an sedet reus?

7. Quis adiuvat accūsātōrem?

8. Quem indicat accūsātor?

3 Let's eavesdrop on this conversation between two robbers as they sit in their small apartment to discuss the robbery they just committed. Pay special attention to the verbs in bold type. Each is in the pluperfect subjunctive to indicate a past contrary-to-fact condition:

LONGĪNUS: Dēnique salvī sumus in hōc stabulō. Ego autem exanimātus sum.

SABĪNUS: Dīc mihi, quantum argentum in saccō est? Sumusne nunc dīvitēs?

LONGĪNUS: Quantum argentum in saccō sit nēsciō. Poterimus argentum ēnumerāre sērius. Prīmum animam recipiāmus! Numquam anteā tam rapidē cucurrī.

SABĪNUS: Cōgitāsne argentārium in tabernā argentāriā nōs recognōvisse?

LONGĪNUS: Nēsciō. Vīdistīne ēius vultum? Ego vīdī nōnnūllōs testēs, extrā argentāriam tabernam stantēs. Cōgitāsne aliquem ex testibus nōs recognōvisse? Vīdistīne vigilem in angulō stantem? In quam partem vigil spectābat? Meā opīniōne, sī iste nōs **vīdisset,** nōs certē **apprehendisset.**

SABĪNUS: Etiamsī vigil nōs **vīdisset,** numquam nōs **captāvisset.** Cucurrimus tamquam cervī. Praetereā, iste est nimis crassus ut nōs captet.

LONGĪNUS: Sī argentārius aut ūnus ex testibus nōs **captāvisset,** nōs in iūdicium **rapuisset.** Sī vigil ipse nōs **apprehendisset,** in carcere nunc sederēmus.

SABĪNUS: Nōlī mentiōnem facěre dē iūdiciō aut dē carcere. Mentiō dē carcere praecipuē mē trepidissimum semper facit.

LONGĪNUS: Immō, aperiāmus saccum et videāmus quid intus sit. Nunc tempus est praedam dīviděre. Ēnumerābō dēnāriōs: ūnus, duo, trēs, quattuor, quīnque . . .

Tunc maximē vigil iānuam pulsāvit et in eōrum cellam inruit. "Vōs lātrōnēs, nōlīte movērī! Vīdistisne meam clāvam? Mēherculē, ego eā ūtar sī necesse est. Trādite mihi illum saccum pecūniae. Venīte mēcum!" Vigil deinde manicās (*handcuffs, manacles*) eīs induit.

LONGĪNUS: Domine, quōmodo scīvistī ubi cella mea sit?

VIGIL: Est simplex. Ecce, est forāmen in īmō saccō. Ut vōs lātrōnēs cucurristis, nummī per hōc forāmen in crepīdinem dēcidēbant. Illī nummī mē dīrectō ad cellam vestram duxērunt. Ego vōs accūsō lātrōciniī.

stabul*um* –ī *n* —dwelling, abode
exanimāt*us* –a –um out of breath

argent*um* –ī *n* cash, dough
  sacc*us* –ī *m* bag

ēnumerō –āre –avī –ātus *to count up*
  sērius *later*
animam recipěre *to catch (one's) breath*

argentāri*us* –ī *m* banker
  taberna argentāria *f* bank
recognōscō –ěre recognōvī recognitus *to recognize*
vult*us* –ūs *m* expression
nōnnūll*ī* –ae –a *some*
  test*is* –is *m/f* witness
aliquis *someone*
angul*us* –ī *m* corner
pars partis *f* direction

apprehendō –ěre –ī apprehēnsus *to arrest*
etiamsī *even if*
tamquam *like*   **cervus –ī** *m* deer
nimis crassus ut *too fat to*

in iūdicium *to court*   **rapiō –ěre –uī –tus** *to haul off*
carcer –eris *m* jail

praecipuē *in particular*
trepid*us* –a –um *nervous*

immō *well*
intus *inside*
praed*a* –ae *f* loot

tunc maximē *just then*
  pulsō –āre –āvī –ātus *to knock at*
cell*a* –ae *f* (little) room
inruō –ěre –ī *to rush in*
  lātrō –ōnis *m* robber
clāv*a* –ae *f* billy club
  mēherculē! *so help me!*
trādō –ěre trādidī trāditus *to hand over*
Domine Sir

forāme*n* –inis *n* hole
  in īmō saccō *in the bottom of the bag*
numm*us* –ī *m* coin
crepīdō –inis *f* sidewalk
  dēcidō –ěre –ī *to fall (down)*
lātrōcini*um* –ī *n* robbery

B. Respondē Latīnē:

1. Quis lātrōcinium committēbant?
2. Quis erat illō tempore in tabernā argentāriā?
3. Quid lātrōnēs ex tabernā cēpērunt?
4. Quō lātrōnēs post lātrōcinium fūgērunt?
5. Ut fugēbant, nōnne lātrōnēs cōnspexērunt vigilem?
6. Cūr vigil nōn posset captāre lātrōnēs, etiamsī vigil lātrōnēs vīdīsset?
7. Cūr lātrōnēs pecūniam nōn statim ēnumerāvērunt?
8. Habitābantne lātrōnēs in domō aut in īnsulā?
9. Quis iānuam lātrōnum pulsāvit?
10. Quid vigil manibus lātrōnum induit?

C. Are you a good **vigil?** Try to answer these questions without looking back at the scene of the robbery. Give yourself one demerit each time you have to look again before answering:

1. Quota hōra erat quandō lātrōnēs ex tabernā exībant?
2. Quot virī in crepīdine erant?
3. Quot fēminae in crepīdine stābant?
4. Quot testēs vīdērunt lātrōnēs ex tabernā currentēs?
5. Quot persōnae in raedā sedēbant?
6. Ante quam tabernam stetit vigil?
7. Quid vigil manū dextrā tenēbat?
8. Gerēbantne lātrōnēs barbās?
9. Quae tabernae erant proximae tabernae argentāriae?
10. Ubi erat canis?

4 To express a contrary-to-fact condition referring to the past, use the PLUPER-FECT SUBJUNCTIVE:

Sī tē *vīdissem*, tē *salūtāvissem*.   *If I had seen you, I would have greeted you.*

In this sentence, the speaker implies that he had not seen you. The pluperfect sub-junctive, like the imperfect subjunctive, is easy to form. Just as the endings *–m, –s, –t, –mus, –tis, –nt* added to the *present* infinitive form the imperfect subjunctive, so the same endings added to the *perfect* infinitive form the *pluperfect subjunctive*.

Do you remember how to form the perfect infinitive? Add *–isse* to the perfect stem, which is found in the third principal part of the verb minus the personal ending:

portāv– + *–isse* + *–m* = portāvisse*m* portāv– + *–isse* + *–mus* = portāvissē*mus*
portāv– + *–isse* + *–s* = portāvissē*s* portāv– + *–isse* + *–tis* = portāvissē*tis*
portāv– + *–isse* + *–t* = portāvisse*t* portāv– + *–isse* + *–nt* = portāvisse*nt*

ĀCTIVITĀTĒS

D. Rewrite the following sentences from present to past contrary-to-fact conditions:

> EXAMPLE: Sī pecūniam *habērem,* fēlīx *essem.*
>
> Sī pecūniam *habuissem,* fēlīx *fuissem.*

1. Sī ego cervīcal capitī impōnerem, salvus essem.
2. Sī ego et dominus cervīcālia capitī impōnerēmus, salvī essēmus.
3. Nisi collem ascenderem, ēruptiōnem Vesuviī vidēre nōn possem.
4. Sī in āreā domūs manērem, māter mē nōn invenīret.
5. Sī nōs prope Montem Vesuvium vīverēmus, magnō in perīculō essēmus.
6. Amīcī, sī cervīcālia capitī impōnerētis, salvī essētis.

E. Convert the following past contrary-to-fact to present contrary-to-fact conditions:

1. Sī tū in crepīdine stetissēs, lātrōcinium vīdissēs?
2. Sī multam pecūniam habuissēs, eam in tabernā argentāriā dēposuissēs?
3. Sī lātrōnēs raedam habuissent, eī salvī effūgissent.
4. Sī vigil nōn tam crassus fuisset, lātrōnēs facile apprehendisset.
5. Sī ego vigilem in angulō stantem vīdissem, eum salūtāvissem.
6. Sī plūs temporis habuissēmus, prius (*sooner*) ad tē litterās scripsissēmus.

5 Longinus and Sabinus were taken to court. To imagine the trial scene, look at this picture. Then read the record of their trial, which took place in the Roman Forum's Basilica Iūlia, just across from the **cūria.**

Iūdicium Longīnī atque Sabīnī in Basilicā Iūliā

PRAETOR: Petītor, quis es tū et quem accūsās?

ACCUSĀTOR: Vir illūstris, ego sum argentārius. Nōmen mihi est Lūcius Laelius Lepidus, Lepidī fīlius.* Tabernam argentāriam in Subūrā exerceō. Taberna mea est optima taberna argentāria tōtīus Romae et . . . .

PRAETOR: Satis, satis! Quid reī fēcērunt? Quid est crīmen?

ACCUSĀTOR: Ego sum victima lātrōciniī. Hunc crīminālem et ēius socium accūsō lātrōciniī. Ego iūstitiam crīminālem flāgitō. Herī post merīdiēm grassātor iste cum sociō suō argentāriam tabernam meam intrāvit et saccum pecūniae clepsit. Nisi magnā cum vōce exclāmāvissem, hīc

petītor *–ōris m plaintiff*

accusātor *–ōris m prosecutor*
　vir illūstris *Your Honor*

exerceō *–ēre –uī –itus to manage,*
　run

satis *enough*
　reus *–ī m defendant*
crīmen *–inis n charge*

socius *–ī m accomplice*
iūstitia *–ae f justice*
　flāgitō *–āre –āvī –ātus to demand*
grassātor *–ōris m hoodlum*
clepō *–ere clepsī cleptus to steal,*
　swipe
nisi *unless*

*Very formal, proud response

grassātor tōtam pecūniam meam clepsisset. Ubi sunt iūs et ōrdō in hāc urbe? Istī grassātōrēs poenam dare dēbent. Rogō ut tū hōs reōs sevērē pūniās.

PRAETOR: Reë, estne hōc vērum? Intrāvistīne tabernam argentāriam et pecūniam clepsistī? Quod nōmen est tibi?

LONGĪNUS: Sum Longīnus. Numquam anteā pecūniam umquam clepsī. Vir illūstris, ego sum innocēns; nōn sum lātrō; nēmō in totā urbe est honestior quam ego. Iūdicēs, vidētis quam pauper ego sim. Ecce meam tunicam sordidam! Ecce calceōs meōs! Sunt plēnī forāminum. Sī ego et socius pecūniam clepsissēmus, nunc vestēs novās gestārēmus. Negō mē lātrōcinium commīsisse.

ADVOCĀTUS: Cliēns meus, iūdicēs, est homō honestus. Familiam suam amat, uxōrem amat, līberōs suōs amat; ille etiam canēs vīcīnitātis amat. Spectāte lacrimās ēius! Nē condemnētis hunc miserum hominem. Absolvite eum.

PRAETOR: Vigil, habēsne testimōnium in hunc reum?

VIGIL: Vir illūstris, nisi ego ipse Longīnum ex tabernā argentāriā currentem vīdissem, eum nōn accūsārem. Habēbat saccum pecūniae in manū. Socius ēius etiam intererat. Ambō in culpā sunt. Longīnum et Sabīnum ūsque ad eōrum cellam secūtus sum. Quandō cellam intrāvī, ego invēnī hōs duōs grassātōrēs, rīdentēs et praedam ēnumerāntēs. Sint iūs et ōrdō in viīs urbis nostrae! Flāgitō iūstitiam crīminālem.

PRAETOR: Iūdicēs, absolvētisne reōs an condemnābitis? Prōnuntiāte sententiam vestram.

IŪDICĒS: Vir illūstris, hōs lātrōnēs condemnāmus. Eōs nōn ad bestiās damus neque ad mūnus glādiātōrium condemnāmus. Neque dē Rūpe Tarpeiā eōs praecipitābimus. Purgantō viās urbis per trēs annōs.

PRAETOR: Sīc fīat.

---

iūs iūris *n law* **ōrdō −inis** *m order*
poena −ae *f penalty*; **poenam dare** *to pay the penalty*
pūniō −īre −īvī −ītus *to punish*

quam *than*
 iūdex −icis *m juror*
 quam *how*
sordidus −a −um *dirty*

negō −āre −āvī −ātus *to deny*
 committō −ĕre commīsī commissus *to commit*
advocātus −ī *m defense lawyer*
 cliēns −entis *m client*
vīcīnitās −ātis *f neighborhood*
condemnō −āre −āvī −ātus *to condemn*
absolvō −ĕre −ī absolūtus *to acquit*
testimōnium −ī *n evidence*
 in (+ *acc*) *against*

intersum −esse −fuī *to be involved*
 ambō −ae −ō *both*
 in culpā esse *to be guilty*

prōnuntiō −āre *to pronounce*
 sententia −ae *f verdict*

ad bestiās dare *to make (them) fight wild beasts*
 mūnus −eris *n show, contest;*
 ad mūnus gladiātōrium *to fight as gladiators*
Rūpēs −is *f Cliff*
praecipitō −āre −āvī −ātus *to throw down* **purgantō** *they shall clean*
sīc fīat *so be it*

ĀCTIVITĀS

F. Respondē Latīnē:

1. In quā parte urbis erat taberna argentāria?
2. Quis erat accūsātor?
3. Quī erant reī?
4. Quis dīxit sē esse victimam lātrōciniī?
5. Quis iūstitiam crīminālem flāgitāvit?
6. Quī grassātor saccum argentī manū tenēbat?
7. Quis dīxit sē numquam anteā pecūniam clepsisse?
8. Num vērum est Longīnum fuisse honestissimum hominem in urbe Rōmā?
9. Quis testimōnium dedit Longīnum uxōrem et līberōs et canēs vīcīnitātis amāre?
10. Quam poenam grassātōrēs dabunt?

VOCĀBULA

festīnō –āre –āvī –ātus to rush
celeber –bris –bre famous
fīō fierī factus sum to take place;
   to become
dēfēnsor –ōris m defense lawyer
spērō –āre –āvī –ātus to hope

aliquandō someday
potestās –ātis f power
auctōritās –ātis f authority, prestige
prōsum prōdesse prōfuī (+ dat) to
   be good for

Quaestiōnēs Persōnālēs

1. Nōvistīne (*do you know*) advocātum clārum?

2. Estne advocātus in familiā tuā?

3. Cupisne esse advocātus/advocāta aliquandō?

4. Estne vigil in familiā tuā?

5. Praefersne esse advocātus/advocāta an vigil an medicus/medica?

6. Quis est ūtilior (*more useful*), advocātus an vigil?

7. Sī nūllam pecūniam habērēs, cibumne cleperēs?

8. Sī lātrōnem ex tabernā currentem vidērēs, apprehenderēsne eum aut vocārēs vigilem?

9. Sī amīcus aut amīca in carcere esset, eum aut eam vīsitārēs?

10. Praefersne potestātem auctōritātemque an iūstitiam lībertātemque?

Compositiō

You are a police officer in your hometown. Someone has just attempted to hold up the bank. As you come around the corner on your beat, a suspicious-looking character runs from the scene of the crime. Since yours is a small town, you know everyone in town; this fellow is an outsider. You grab him. List the questions you will ask him to determine if he is the culprit.

Colloquium

Complete the dialog based on the model of the previous conversation:

THE LATIN CONNECTION

What are the Latin origins of the following English words?

1. accusation
2. judicial
3. sack
4. testimony
5. angle
6. incarcerate
7. intrepid
8. victim
9. kleptomaniac
10. penal
11. justice
12. jury
13. order
14. culpable
15. subpoena
16. prejudice
17. comprehend
18. mention
19. cell
20. innocent
21. negate
22. absolve
23. ambidextrous
24. criminal
25. commit
26. tribunal
27. pronounce
28. sentence
29. celebrity
30. vigilant
31. precipitation
32. punitive

XX | Rēs pūblica

Ablative Absolute

1 Modicum cultūrae

Who ruled Rome? What kind of government did Rome have? During the first 250 years of its existence (753 to 500 B.C.), seven kings ruled Rome, one after the other, beginning with Romulus. The king consulted the senate, which in Romulus's time is said to have consisted of 100 elder citizens, who met in the senate building (**cūria –ae** *f*) in the Roman Forum. Eventually the senate numbered 300 senators, who were former elected officials. A senator was easy to recognize with his white toga with a broad crimson border and his special gold ring. Senators also wore special shoes, tied with red laces around the ankle and just below the knee.

When the last Roman king, Tarquin the Proud, was overthrown, the Romans decided to elect two men called consuls (**cōnsul –is** *m*) to head the new government, which the Romans called **rēs pūblica** (the Republic). Each consul had equal power and the right to veto the acts of the other. If war broke out, the consuls also served as the battlefield commanders. Consuls held office for only one year; Romans identified each year by the names of the ruling consuls: "the year when so-and-so and so-and-so were consuls." (Obviously, they couldn't use the abbreviations B.C. and A.D. as we do today.)

Each consul had a bodyguard unit of twelve men called **lictors** (**lictor** *–ōris m*). Every lictor carried a bundle (**fascēs** *–ium m pl*) of rods (**virga** *–ae f*) and an axe (**secūris** *–is f*), which symbolized the consul's power to inflict corporal (bodily), and even capital (life-depriving), punishment on evildoers. Lictors daily walked ahead of the consuls to clear the way through the crowds. For centuries, only men of the Roman nobility (patricians) could become consuls. Consuls had the power to call a meeting of the senate and preside over it. At the end of their terms, they spent another year governing one of the Roman provinces. Can you imagine if our country had two presidents, each able to veto the decisions of the other? Worse yet, can you imagine conducting presidential elections every year? Yet, the Romans made this system work for almost 500 years.

The consuls couldn't do every task governing Rome required so, eventually, the Assembly of the People elected two praetors (**praetor** *–ōris m*) to serve as judges. Praetors were similar to the justices of our Supreme Court. As Rome grew bigger and more complicated, the number of praetors increased. For a long time, only a patrician could be elected praetor. As the representative of the consul, the praetor had the right to preside over the Assembly of the People and to conduct military affairs under the direction of a consul. Although the praetor had great power, his was inferior to that of the consuls. (The public had no doubt of the consul's superiority over a praetor, since twelve lectors escorted a consul while only six accompanied a praetor!) During his year in office, the praetor was in charge of the judicial system; in the following year he, like the consuls, governed one of the provinces.

As the city grew, the Assembly of the People elected another pair of men called aediles (**aedīlis** *–is m*), whose job was to supervise the construction of public buildings. These men also had charge of the temples, baths, marketplaces, and streets. It was their duty to ensure that law and order were maintained in public places. For that reason, the aediles had certain police powers. They also oversaw public events, such as gladiatorial shows, chariot and horse races, and theater performances.

Ranking below the praetors were the quaestors (**quaestor** *–ōris m*), who were in charge of the public treasury. They collected money for the state and made payments from the treasury as the law or a magistrate required. They were also in charge of all public records. A large number of clerks worked under their direction. Quaestors, like consuls, praetors, and aediles, held office for one year. After his one-year term in Rome, a quaestor served as second in command to a provincial governor. To become a life member of the senate, a man had to have held at least the office of quaestor.

Usually, a man of ambition moved up the political ladder from quaestor to consul. This sequence was called the **cursus honōrum,** or career of public offices. The Latin word **honor** *–ōris m* was used to refer to a political office because that's what it was: simply an honor. Since magistrates received no salary, only the rich could afford to run for office. The struggle of the lower classes for the right to hold high office continued for centuries until they finally succeeded.

In times of national emergency, a dictator was appointed; all other office-holders temporarily resigned. Twenty-four lictors accompanied the dictator, indicating that his power was equal to the combined powers of the two consuls. A dictator could hold office for the duration of the emergency or for six months, whichever ended first. His powers were so great that everyone feared that a dictator might become dictator for life if he were left in office more than six months. Julius Caesar became dictator for life, which is why many Roman senators feared him and ultimately assassinated him on the Ides of March (March 15), 44 B.C.

Rome never had a democracy. In fact, the word *democracy* did not exist in Latin! Cicero said that government by the people was anarchy (*a state of lawlessness and disorder*). After the early kings ceased to rule, certain families of the upper class—the patricians—held the high offices of government, while the people of the lower classes—the plebeians—fought to gain civil rights. Just as the plebeians were finally enjoying full civil rights, the Republic ended and the Empire began under Augustus. Emperors ruled the Roman world in one form or another for the next 500 years.

fascēs -ium mpl
virga -ae f secūris -is f
sceptrum -ī n

consul -is m
toga -ae (f) praetexta

corrigia -ae f

calceus -ī (m) consulāris

lictor -ōris m

praetor -ōris m

sella -ae (f) curūlis

quaestor -ōris m

aedīlis -is m

A. Match the descriptions with the pictures:

Cōnsul togam praetexta induit.
Lictor fascēs suprā umerum sinistrum portat.
Cōnsul calceum corrigiā rubrā ligat.
Sex lictōrēs praetōrem prōsequuntur (*escort*).
Quaestor pecūniam numerat.
Aedīlis cōnstrūctiōnem templī cūrat (*supervises*).
Duodecim lictōrēs cōnsulem prōsequuntur.
Cōnsul scēptrum manū dextrā tenet.

1.

2.

3.

4.

5.

6.

7.   8.

3 Would you have liked being the child of a famous politician and lawyer in ancient Rome? This is how Cicero's son saw his life:

Nōmen mihi est Mārcus Tullius Cicerō. Pater meus idem nōmen habet. Pater est ambitiōsissimus senātor. Vult esse cīvis prīmus Rōmae. Abhinc quattuor annōs, pater meus erat candidātus, nam volēbat fierī cōnsul. Erant multī competītōrēs. Nōn omnēs competītōrēs erant amīcī patris. Exemplī grātiā, Clōdius et Catilīna erant inimīcī. Petītiō duōs mēnsēs dūrāvit.

competītor *–ōris m opponent*

petītiō *–ōnis f campaign*
 dūrō *–āre –āvī –ātus to last*

Ego puer quattuordecim annōrum eram, sed ego omnia bene in memōriā teneō. Cōtīdiē clientēs, officiī grātiā, ad domum nostram vēnērunt. In ātriō congregātī sunt. Bene māne pervēnērunt. Interdum collēgium tignāriōrum, interdum collēgium pistōrum aut tōnsōrum patrem meum vīsitāvit. Ātrium nostrum paene semper plēnum clientium erat. Nūllum locum habēbam ubi ego lūderem.

officiī grātiā *to pay their respects*
congregor *–ari –atus sum to congregate*
perveniō *–īre pervēnī to arrive*

paene *almost*

Māter cum sorōre meā, Tulliā, et cum ancillīs, sportulam clientibus parābat, nam sīc mōs erat. Clientēs semper sportulās exspectābant. Deinde pater iūs et rem pūblicam cum clientibus disputāvit, quia pater meus advocātus perītissimus est. Posteā clientēs patrem ad forum prōsecutī sunt. In forō pater ōrātiōnēs longās habēbat, et populō multā prōmīsit. Deinde pater per omnēs vīcōs urbis in togā candidā ambiit, nam sīc mōs est. Postrēmō, diēs suffrāgiī aderat.

sportula *–ae f lunch basket*
 mōs mōris *m custom*
rēs pūblica *f politics*
disputō *–āre –āvī –ātus to discuss*

prōsequor *–ī prōsecūtus sum to escort*
 ōrātiōnem habēre *to give a speech*
vīcus *–ī m ward*   **ambiō** *–īre –iī –ītus to campaign*
suffrāgium *–ī n vote;* **diēs suffrāgiī** *election day*
 adsum adesse adfuī *to be at hand*
suffrāgium ferre *to cast a ballot*
ēligō *–ěre ēlēgī ēlēctus to elect, choose*

Cīvēs Rōmānī omnēs in Campum Mārtium īvērunt ut suffrāgium ferrent et duōs cōnsulēs ex tam multīs competītōribus ēligerent. Pater meus et socius ēius, Gāius Antōnius, cōnsulēs ēlēctī sunt. Mīlia cīvium patrī "tibi fēlīciter!" acclāmāvērunt.

tibi fēlīciter! *congratulations!, bravo!*
acclāmō *–āre –āvī –ātus to shout*

Quandō pater ē Campō Mārtiō discessit, ut in forō apud populum appārēret, duodecim lictōrēs, fascēs in umerō sinistrō portantēs, eum prōsecūtī sunt. Post eum multī senātōrēs et clientēs et amīcī et familia secūtī sunt. In cūriā pater togam candidam exuit et togam praetextam cum lātō clāvō induit. Porrō, calceōs cōnsulārēs cum corrigiīs rubrīs induit. Mox pater ē cūriā exiit et rōstra ante cūriam ascendit. Ut pater in sellā curūlī sedēbat, omnēs in forō "tibi fēlīciter!" acclāmāvērunt. Pater deinde ōrātiōnem habuit ut omnibus suffrāgātōribus gratiās ageret.

Quam superbus patre meō eram! Exemplum mīrābile mihi praebuit.

apud (+ *acc*) *before*
 appāreō *–ēre –uī to appear*

praetexta *crimson-bordered*
lātus –a –um *broad*
 clāvus –ī *m* (*crimson*) *stripe*
 porrō *besides, furthermore*
corrigia –ae *f shoelace*
rōstra –ōrum *n pl rostrum,*
 (*speaker's*) *platform*
sella curūlis *official chair*
suffrāgātor –ōris *m voter*
superbus –a –um (+ *abl*) *proud of*
 exemplum praebēre *to set an*
  example
mīrābilis –is –e *wonderful*

ĀCTIVITĀS

B. Respondē Latīnē:

1. Quot annōs abhinc erat Mārcus Tullius candidātus?

2. Quot mēnsēs dūrāvit petītiō?

3. Quī erant competītōrēs inimīcī?

4. Quae collēgia domum Cicerōnis vīsitābant?

5. Quid pater in ātriō disputāvit?

6. Quō cīvēs Rōmānī īvērunt ut suffrāgia ferrent?

7. Quot lictōrēs Mārcum Tullium in forum prōsecūtī sunt?

8. Quid lictōrēs suprā umerum sinistrum portābant?

9. Ubī pater in sellā curūlī sedēbat et ōrātiōnem habēbat.

10. Quamobrem Mārcus Tullius hanc ōrātiōnem habuit?

4 The Latin verb systems did not have past active participles except in "fake passive" (deponent) verbs. The Romans could not say "having seen" or "having heard," for example. They were able to say **secūtus** *having followed* and **locūtus** *having spoken* because **sequor sequī secūtus sum** and **loquor loquī locūtus sum** are "fake passives":

Haec *locūtus*, rōstra ascendit. *Having said this, he went up to the rostrum.*

If they wanted to use the verb **dīcō,** however, they could NOT say **Haec *dictus*, rōstra ascendit.**

Why not? Because **dictus** means *having been said.* What then did the Romans do? They put the noun or pronoun—in this instance, a pronoun—and the past passive participle into the ABLATIVE CASE:

Hīs *dictīs*, cōnsul rōstra per gradūs ascendit.

Having said this (literally, *these things having been said), the consul climbed the steps to the rostrum.*

The literal translation above is awkward, don't you think? More natural-sounding translations include: *Having said this,* or *After he had said this,* or *When he had said this,* or *As soon as he had said this.* When translating this kind of construction, use any conjunction that fits the situation.

This construction is called ABLATIVE ABSOLUTE because (1) the noun/pronoun and the participle are in the ABLATIVE CASE and (2) the construction is grammatically independent of the main clause. (No conjunction connects this clause to the rest of the sentence.) "Absolute" comes from the verb **absolvō absolvĕre absolvī absolūtus.** This verb has several meanings: *to release, to acquit, to free,* and *to complete.* An ABLATIVE ABSOLUTE, therefore, is a phrase that is "complete by itself" and "freed" from the main clause without using a conjunction. The noun or pronoun may remain in the ablative absolute only when it refers to a person or thing different from the main clause.

ĀCTIVITĀTĒS

C. Convert the subordinate clause to an ablative absolute:

> EXAMPLE: **Cicerō, postquam ōrātiōnem *habuit,* domum rediit.**
>
> *After giving his speech, Cicero returned home.*
>
> *Ōrātiōne habitā,* **Cicerō domum rediit.**

NOTE: Because the name **Cicerō** begins the sentence and appears before **postquam** in the dependent clause, you can expect **Cicerō** to be the subject of both the dependent and the main clause.

> EXAMPLE: **Postquam Cicerō ōrātiōnem *habuit,* turba "tibi fēlīciter" acclāmāvit.**
>
> *After Cicero had given his speech, the crowd cried "Bravo!"*
>
> *Ōrātiōne ā Cicerōne habitā,* **turba "tibi fēlīciter" acclāmāvit.**

NOTE: Because the word **Cicerō** in this second example follows the conjunction **postquam,** we know that **Cicerō** is the subject of only the dependent clause and that the main clause will have a different subject (**turba**).

1. Praetor, postquam iūs disputāvit, basilicam intrāvit.

2. Mārcus, ubi competītōrēs cōnspexit, nihil dixit.

3. Aedīlis, simul atque forum intrāvit, rōstra per gradūs ascendit.

4. Clientēs, postquam sportulam accēpērunt, abīvērunt.

5. Cōnsul, postquam scēptrum accēpit, in sellā curūlī cōnsēdit.

6. Postquam cīvēs suffrāgia tulērunt, Cicerō in forō appāruit.

D. Change each ablative absolute to a dependent clause. Use the conjunction that best suits the sentence: **ubi** (*when*), **cum prīmum** (*as soon as possible*), **simul atque** (*as soon as*), **postquam** (*after*).

1. Cōnsulibus novīs ēlectīs, populus deīs grātiās ēgit.

2. Cērā pennārum liquefactā, Īcarus dē caelō in mare cecidit.

3. Rēgibus expūlsīs, populus Rōmānus duōs cōnsules ēlēgit.

4. Lātrōnibus comprehēnsīs, testēs nōn iam erant territī.

5. Saccō argentī cleptō, grassātōres ex tabernā argentāriā ruērunt.

6. Lātrōciniō commissō, grassātōrēs poenam dedērunt.

E. Identify the dependent clause. Then rewrite it as an ablative absolute:

1. Cum prīmum advocātus reum accūsāvit, praetor in tribūnālī cōnsēdit.

2. Ubī populus Cicerōnem ēlēgērunt, Catilīna ex urbe fūgit.

3. Postquam Mārcus Tullius ōrātiōnem habuit, populus applausit.

4. Cum prīmum tignārius officīnam aperuit, turba introībat (*entered*).

5. Postquam ancillae cēnam parāvērunt, convīvae trīclīnium intrāvērunt.

6. Simul atque ego vigilem vocāvī, grassātōrēs tabernam meam relīquērunt.

5 Although Latin has no past active participle, it does have a present active participle that can be used in the ablative absolute:

Populō *audiente*, praetor ōrātiōnem habuit.   *As the people were listening, the praetor gave a speech.*

Did you notice the ending of **audiente**? In Lesson VIII, you learned that the ablative singular ending for present participles is usually –*ī* but sometimes –*e*. In ablative absolute constructions, the Romans used the –*e* ending.

F. Convert the ablative absolute to a dependent clause, using the conjunctions **ubi** (*when*), **ut** (*as*), or **dum** (*while*). Always use the present tense (called historical present) with the conjunction **dum:**

1. Daedalō dīligenter labōrante, Īcarus cum pennīs lūdēbat.

2. Omnibus clientibus tacentibus, advocātus loquī incēpit.

3. Familiā dormiente, lātrō vīllam intrāvit.

4. Cōnsule in sellā curūlī sedente, praetor suprā rōstra stābat.

5. Competītōribus domī manentibus, Mārcus Tullius per urbem ambiit.

6. Candidātō togam candidam gestante, cōnsul togam praetextam gestābat.

G. Write the dependent clause as an ablative absolute:

1. Dum populus cōnsulem exspectat, competītōrēs suprā rōstra appāruērunt.

2. Ut praetor per Sūbūram ambulābat, sex lictōrēs prope forum stābant.

3. Ut populus suffrāgia ferēbat, turba in Campō Mārtiō dē lībertāte clāmabat.

4. Dum māter in macellō obsōnat, īnfāns cōnstanter vagiēbat.

5. Dum clientēs in ātriō stant, ego et pater sportulās suprā mēnsam pōnēbāmus.

6. Dum pater dīcit, omnēs in ātriō silēbant.

6 The verb **sum** has no present participle. It would be **ēns entis,** which is used with a few verbs, such as **absum** (*I am absent*); the participle is **absēns** (abs + ēns entis). Since the participle does not exist on its own, the ablative absolute that would normally contain the participle usually consists of two nouns in the ablative:

Marcellō dūce, **exercitus Rōmānus Germānōs vīcit.**

Under the leadership of Marcellus (literally, Marcellus [being] the leader), the Roman army defeated the Germans.

The dating of Roman years is a common use of this type of ablative absolute:

Mārcō Tulliō Gāiō Antōniō cōnsulibus, **rēs pūblica erat salva.**

In the consulship of Marcus Tullius and Gaius Antonius (literally, Marcus Tullius [and] Gaius Antonius [being] consuls), the government was safe.

H. Transform each ablative absolute into a dependent clause introduced by **ubi**:

1. Rōmulō rēge, vīta erat simplex.

2. Antōniō praetōrē, iūdicia erant iūsta.

3. Tarquiniō Superbō rēge, populus Rōmānus rebellāvit (*rebelled*).

4. Appiō Claudiō cōnsule, mīlitēs Rōmānī prīmam viam longam mūnīvērunt (*built*).

5. Serviō Tulliō rēge, mūrus prīmus Rōmae aedificātus est.

6. Lūciō Domitiō aedīle, templum novum in Aventīnō colle aedificātum est.

I. In the following sentences, the noun or pronoun and the participle are provided in the nominative case. Change them to the ablative case to form an ablative absolute:

1. (Cōnsul ēlectus), omnēs cīvēs deīs grātiās ēgērunt.

2. (Praetor praesēns), reus sē dēfendet.

3. (Urbs relicta), iter per Campāniam fēcimus.

4. (Haec verba dicta), cōnsul dē rōstrīs dēscendit.

5. (Ōrātiō audīta), cōnsul īrātus fīēbat.

6. (Dominus absēns), servī laetissimī erant.

7. (Mīra nūbēs vīsa), oppidānī Mīsēnī erant trepidī.

8. (Lātrōnēs apprehēnsī), argentārius in tabernam suam rediit.

J. At the beginning of each sentence below is a noun in the nominative case and an infinitive. Construct an ablative absolute by changing the noun to the ablative case and the infinitive to a present participle in the ablative case. Note that the "fake passive" (deponent) verbs have *active* forms and *active* meanings in the present participles (**loquēns –entis** *speaking*, **admīrāns –antis** *admiring*, **moriēns –entis** *dying*, **oriēns –entis** *rising*):

EXAMPLE: (Mīlitēs audīre), dux ōrātiōnem habuit.
Mīlitibus audientibus, dux ōrātiōnem habuit.
As the soldiers listened, the general made a speech.

1. (Cōnsul iubēre), lictōrēs fascēs virgārum et secūrim portant.

2. (Cōnsulēs iubēre), lictor secūrim ē fascibus remōvit.

3. (Cōnsulēs praeesse), populus "vōbīs fēlīciter" acclāmāvit.

4. (Populus admīrārī), cōnsul rōstra ascendit.

5. (Advocātus dēfendere), reus ā iūdicibus absolūtus est.

6. (Cōnsul loquī), omnēs senātōrēs in cūriā sīlēbant.

7. (Sōl orīrī), populus in Campum Mārtium inīvērunt.

8. (Sōl caděre), populus domum rediit.

9. (Cōnsul morī), lictōrēs fascēs dēmittēbant (*lowered*).

10. (Cōnsul praesidēre), senātus legem novam tulit (*passed*).

Quaestiōnēs Persōnālēs

1. Praefersne rēgem et rēgīnam praesidentī in patriā nostrā?

2. Vīdistīne umquam candidātum?

3. Praefersne vītam pūblicam an prīvātam quandō adultus (-a) eris?

4. Spērāsne aliquandō collēgium frequentāre?

5. Praefersne collēgium prope domum tuam an collēgium procul ā domō?

6. Paterne tuus collēgium frequentāvit?

7. Māterne tua collēgium frequentāvit?

8. Habēsne sorōrem an frātrem quī nunc collēgium frequentat?

Compositiō

Walking in the crowded Roman Forum, you see a consul making his way through the crowd. What clues helped you identify the man as a consul?

VOCĀBULA

comitia *–ōrum n pl* elections
victus *–ī m* loser
mihi nōn cūrae sunt *(they) are of no concern to me*
cūr tandem *just why*

immō *well, . . .*
amāns *–antis f* girlfriend
margō *–inis m* edge, fringe
quotiēns *whenever*

Colloquium

In this dialog Marcellus wants to know why his friend went to the Campus Martius. Complete this conversation as Marcellus' friend, explaining your own reasons for going to the Campus Martius.

Unde venīs, amīce(-a)?	Salvē, Marcelle. Ego _____ _____ Veniō.
Cūr tam laetus(-a) es? Numquam tē tam laetum(-am) vīdī. Quid ibi vīdistī et fēcistī? Nōnne comitia erant hodiē in Campō Martiō?	_____ _____ _____ _____.
Tū suffragium ferre nōndum potes. Tū nimis parvus(-a) es. Quī candidātī vīcērunt?	_____ _____ _____ _____.
Cūr tandem in Campum Martium īvistī, sī candidātī tibi nōn cūrae sunt?	_____ _____ _____ _____.

↺ THE LATIN CONNECTION

A. 1. What is the Latin origin of the English word *status?* What are the principal parts of this Latin root?

2. The following words come from the same Latin verb. Explain their meanings by relating them to their Latin root:

    a. stable

    b. stability

    c. instability

    d. constant

    e. stature

B. What are the Latin origins of the following words?

1.	rostrum	8.	to rebel
2.	mores	9.	apprehend
3.	acclaim	10.	honest
4.	absent	11.	congregation
5.	scepter	12.	office
6.	victum	13.	margin
7.	latitude	14.	endure

C. Roman political campaigns used language that has given us several familiar English words. What are the Latin sources of the following words? Explain what the English words mean by connecting them to their root words.

1.	elect	6.	suffrage
2.	election	7.	ambition
3.	eligible	8.	competitor
4.	electoral college	9.	petition
5.	candidate	10.	honor

Recognitiō IV

(Lēctiōnēs XVI–XX)

LĒCTIŌ XVI

a. To form the ALTERNATE FUTURE, add the ending *–ūrus* (*–ūra –ūrum*) to the stem of the perfect participle (the fourth principal part) of a verb. Then combine this form with the forms of **sum:**

vocātūr*us* (*–a*) sum	*I'm going to call*	**vocātūr*ī* (*–ae*) sumus**	*we're going to call*
vocātūr*us* (*–a*) es	*you're going to call*	**vocātūr*ī* (*–ae*) estis**	*you're going to call*
vocātūr*us* (*–a*) est	*he/she is going to call*	**vocātūr*ī* (*–ae*) sunt**	*they're going to call.*

This alternate future may also mean *I am about to call* or *I intend to call.*

b. In the same way, a past tense of **sum** (**eram** or **fuī**) can be added:

vocātūr*us* (*–a*) eram/fuī	*I was going to call, I was about to call, I intended to call*

c. The verb with the *–ūrus* ending, but without a form of **sum**, may be used as a future participle, with several meanings:

Senātor ex sellā surrēxit, ōrātiōnem *habitūrus*.	*The senator rose from his seat, about to give a speech/intending to give a speech.*

d. The future infinitive consists of the future participle plus **esse**. In an indirect statement, the future infinitive represents an action occurring after the action of the main verb:

Helena dīxit sē domī *cēnātūram esse*.	*Helen said that she would dine at home/was going to dine at home.*

LĒCTIŌ XVII

a. A verb in the SUBJUNCTIVE MOOD expresses something other than simple fact. The present subjunctive expresses a wish, possibility, doubt, or polite command. The present subjunctive is formed by changing the *typical* vowel in the ending of a verb:

voc*em*	**mov***eam*	**dūc***am*	**cap***iam*	**aud***iam*
voc*ēs*	mov*eās*	dūc*as*	cap*iās*	aud*iās*
voc*et*	mov*eat*	dūc*at*	cap*iat*	aud*iat*
voc*ēmus*	mov*eāmus*	dūc*āmus*	cap*iāmus*	aud*iāmus*
voc*ētis*	mov*eātis*	dūc*ātis*	cap*iātis*	aud*iātis*
voc*ent*	mov*eant*	dūc*ant*	cap*iant*	aud*iant*

Notice that the first person subjunctive ends in *–m* in all conjugations.

b. The subjunctive forms of **esse** and **posse** are irregular:

sim	possim
sīs	possīs
sit	possit
sīmus	possīmus
sītis	possītis
sint	possint

c. Certain Latin conjunctions require the subjunctive. The conjunction **ut** with the verb in the subjunctive gives us a purpose clause:

Labōrāmus ut edāmus.   *We work in order to eat.*

The conjunction **nē** with the verb in the subjunctive gives us a negative purpose clause:

Labōrāmus nē famem habeāmus.   *We work in order not to go hungry.*

LĒCTIŌ XVIII

a. The imperfect subjunctive is formed by adding the endings *–m, –s, –t, –mus, –tis, –nt* to the present infinitive of any verb:

vocāre– + *–m* = vocāre*m*   vocāre– + *–mus* = vocārē*mus*
vocāre– + *–s* = vocārē*s*   vocāre + *–tis* = vocārē*tis*
vocāre– + *–t* = vocāre*t*   vocāre– + *–nt* = vocāre*nt*

b. If the verb that introduces an indirect question is in the past tense, the verb in the indirect question is in the imperfect subjunctive:

Ubi *essem* nēscīvī.   *I didn't know where I was.*

c. A purpose clause, whether positive (with **ut**) or negative (with **nē**), requires a verb in the imperfect subjunctive if the main verb of the sentence is in the past tense:

Multī Mīsēnō fūgērunt ut mortem   *Many fled from Misenum to avoid*
certam *ēvītārent.*   *certain death.*

d. After a verb of fearing (such as **timeō, metuō**), the conjunction **nē** is used to introduce a *positive* idea and **ut** is used to introduce a *negative* idea:

Timeō *nē* pater veniat.   *I am afraid that my father is coming.*
Timeō *ut* pater veniat.   *I am afraid that my father is not coming.*

If the verb in the main clause is in the past tense, the verb in the subordinate clause is also in the past tense:

Metuī nē amita sērius *pervenīret.*   *I was afraid that my aunt would arrive late.*
Metuī ut amita mea hodiē   *I was afraid that my aunt would*
pervenīret.   *not arrive today.*

e. In simple conditions, the verb of the **sī** clause as well as the verb of the conclusion is in the indicative mood. Contrary-to-fact conditions referring to the present tense, however, require a verb in the **sī** clause in the imperfect subjunctive:

Sī amīcōs *habērem*, fēlīx *essem*.   *If I had friends, I'd be happy.*

LĒCTIŌ XIX

a. To form the pluperfect subjunctive, add the endings *–m, –s, –t, –mus, –tis, –nt* to the perfect active infinitive of any verb:

vocāv– + –isse + –m = vocāvissem   vocāv– + –isse + –mus = vocāvissēmus
vocāv– + –isse + –s = vocāvissēs   vocāv– + –isse + –tis = vocāvissētis
vocāv– + –isse + –t = vocāvisset   vocāv– + –isse + –nt = vocāvissent

b. To form a contrary-to-fact condition referring to the past, use the pluperfect subjunctive:

Sī tē *vīdissem*, tē *salūtāvissem*.   *If I had seen you, I would have greeted you.*

c. It is possible to have the verb of the **sī** clause in the pluperfect subjunctive and the verb of the conclusion in the imperfect subjunctive:

Sī dīligentius *labōrāvissem*, dīves   *If I had worked harder, I'd be rich now.*
nunc *essem*.

a. An ABLATIVE ABSOLUTE usually consists of a noun and a participle in the ablative case. The noun cannot be related to any word in the main clause:

> **Hīs dictīs, senātor rōstra ascendit.** *Having said this* (literally, *these words having been said*), *the senator climbed the rostrum.*

b. The ablative absolute may consist of a noun and a present active participle in the ablative case. The present participle of deponent verbs is active in form and meaning:

> **Deīs adiuvantibus, ego cōnsul fīam.** *With the help of the gods, I shall become consul.*

> **Senātōre loquente, cōnsul abiit.** *While the senator was talking, the consul left.*

c. The verb **sum** has no present participle. An ablative absolute that would normally contain that participle usually consists of two nouns in the ablative case:

> **Marcellō dūce, vincēmus.** *Under the leadership of Marcellus* (literally, *Marcellus being the leader*), *we shall win.*

d. The ablative absolute is equivalent to various adverbial clauses introduced by the conjunctions (*when, while, because, although, if*) depending on the context:

> **Discipulīs loquentibus, magistra erat īrāta.** *Because the students were talking, the teacher was angry.*

ĀCTIVITĀTĒS

A. Use the following phrases to complete the descriptions under the pictures:

lānās net	reum indicat	manicās induit
saccum pecūniae clepit	suffrāgium fert	cibum convīvīs adpōnit
capitī impōnit	pūmicem et fūmum ēicit	latrōnēs persequitur
holera obsōnat	serrā secat	per gradūs ascendit

1. Cīvis Rōmānus

2. Tignārius tabulam

3. Vigil lātrōnī

4. Plīnius cervīcal

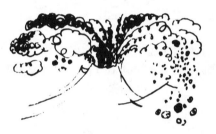

5. Ancilla

6. Amita

7. Mōns

8. Senātor rōstra

9. Vigil duōs

10. Accūsātor

11. Lātrō

12. Servus

B. Word search. Fifteen words related to Roman law are hidden in this puzzle. Words can read from left to right, right to left, up or down, or diagonally. Locate each word; then write it in your notebook.

```
L  A  M  U  I  C  I  D  U  I
A  D  V  X  L  S  X  R  U  U
N  V  M  I  U  A  E  S  S  D
U  O  A  I  G  C  T  U  Z  I
B  C  N  Q  R  I  E  R  Q  C
I  A  I  A  T  R  L  X  O  E
R  T  C  I  S  O  C  I  U  S
T  U  A  P  R  A  E  T  O  R
A  S  A  C  I  L  I  S  A  B
A  C  C  U  S  A  T  O  R  Q
```

C. Below are 10 pictures showing activities in which Romans participated. Complete the description below each picture by writing the correct perfect-tense form of the appropriate verb. Select the verbs from the following list:

| gerĕre | texĕre | haurīre | volāre | clepĕre |
| loquī | verrĕre | habēre | ūtī | accumbĕre |

1. Ancilla aquam ē cisternā

2. Māter atque fīlia tunicās

3. Senātor ōrātiōnem

4. Daedalus per āĕrem

5. Convīvae ad mēnsam

6. Serva cubiculum scōpīs

7. Advocātus cum reō

8. Lātrō ānulum aureum

9. Tignārius terēbrā

10. Senātōrēs togās praetextās

D. Cruciverbilūsus:

HORIZONTĀLE

1. to avoid
6. so
9. such a
13. you are
14. to harvest
15. or
16. he/she/it goes
17. immediately
18. they were
20. take (imperative)

21. whole
23. so
25. again, back (*prefix*)
27. to tie
29. cause (*acc*)
30. previously, before
31. on
32. if
33. urn
34. so great (*f pl*)

35. at that time, then
37. on account of
39. apartment building
41. to be
45. or
46. not
47. cistern
49. then
51. well known, noted
52. it

54. rostrum	61. she	67. royal (court)
57. I will go	63. rose	68. courthouse
58. heart	64. I wear	69. speech
59. you loved (*sing*)	65. Roman male dress	

PERPENDICULĀRE

2. old	26. and	48. so many
3. shop, inn	27. broad	50. one (*m abl*)
4. thing	28. cheek	52. there
5. it is	29. citizen	53. I give
7. aunt	30. mind	55. his own
8. memory	33. to use	56. I shave
9. three	35. you	57. trip
10. air	36. handcuff	58. camp
11. enough	38. well	60. policeman
12. also	40. they are	61. I go
19. wing	42. saw	62. robber
22. I hold	43. out of breath	63. rarely
23. he	44. corners	66. from
24. board	47. shoelace	

E. Here's a word-chain activity that will test your command of Latin vocabulary. For each of the following, form a new Latin word from the one above it by changing one letter at a time:

EXEMPLUM: C O M A
  R O M A
  R O S A
  R O T A

U N U S   R U R S U S   N O V U S   F E R O

_ _ _ _   _ _ _ _ _ _   _ _ _ _ _   _ _ _ _

_ _ _ _   _ _ _ _ _ _   _ _ _ _ _   _ _ _ _

A V I S   C U R V U S   M O D U S   T E R O

F. The consul in the **cūria** has asked you to fetch one of his lictors. You find five of them standing just outside the senate building. Choose the right lictor from the consul's description below:

Capillōs dēnsōs habet.
Calceōs gestat.
Barbam curtam gerit.
Semper subrīdet.

Fascēs ēius secūrim nōn habent.
Fascēs suprā umerum sinistrum portat.
Tenet sagulum (*his cape*) manū dextrā.
Tunicam suprā genū gerit.

G. Unscramble these words. Then reorder the circled letters to learn where these things originate:

```
P O R A V

U M F U S

L U S U F R

L A M M F A

E X M U P

N I C I S
```

H. All but one word in each of the following groups represent the same part of speech, such as verbs, adjectives, adverbs, ablative nouns, and conjunctions. For each group, write the grammatical word that doesn't belong. Then write the part of speech the group (minus the misfit!) represents:

1. posteā ut postquam simul atque dum

2. macellum tablīnum forum pavīmentum iterum

3. quaerĕre fugĕre induĕre suēre mare

4. ibi mox suprā etiam deinde

5. humānus rūrsus honestus sōlus novus

6. argentō malleō clāvō populō plaudō

7. inter tandem per ob propter

8. dum id ista eadem ille

I. How many of these words do you remember? Write the Latin word for each illustration. Then read down the boxed column to find out who owns these objects.

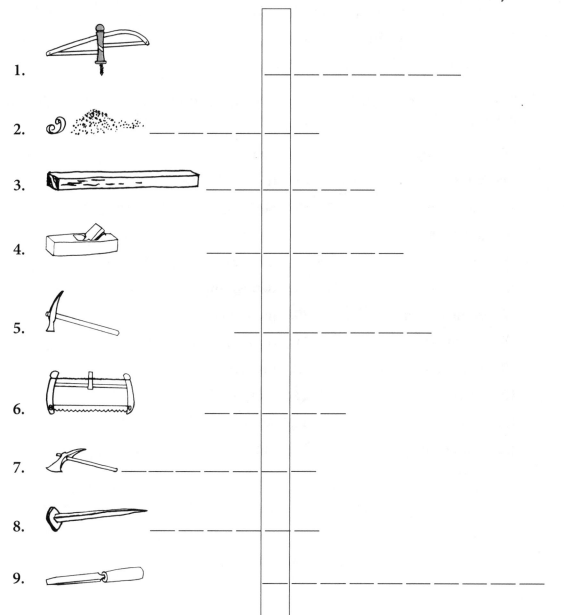

1. _____ _____ _____ _____ _____

1. _____

2. _____

3. _____

4. _____

5. _____

6. _____

7. _____

8. _____

9. _____

J. The words of each group in the left column belong to the same category or topic (right column). Number a paper from 1–8. Write the letter of the correct category for each group:

1.	pūmex, cinis, vapor, fūmus	a.	quaestor
2.	malleus, clāvus, serra, secūris	b.	Arīcia
3.	praetor, iūdex, iūdicium, basilica	c.	tablīnum
4.	suffrāgium, competitor, candidātus, suffrāgātor	d.	tornus
5.	aedīlis, cōnsul, dictātor, praetor	e.	crātēr
6.	Mīsēnum, Rōma, Pompēiī, Herculāneum	i.	texēre
7.	obsōnāre, coquĕre, nēre, suĕre	g.	petītiō
8.	trīclīnium, cubiculum, ātrium, peristȳlium	h.	reus

K. The Latin Connection. Write the Latin word from which each English word comes:

1.	matron	14.	tabulate
2.	virgin	15.	turn
3.	patrician	16.	perforate
4.	apposition	17.	evident
5.	context	18.	insular
6.	oration	19.	deposition
7.	resurrection	20.	judicious
8.	noted	21.	durable
9.	humane	22.	prosecute
10.	distant	23.	margin
11.	profuse	24.	servile
12.	repudiate	25.	amicable
13.	mitigate		

Vocābula Latīna–Anglica

The masculine, feminine, and neuter forms are given for adjectives: **clārus** *-a -um;* **facilis** *-is -e.* Adjectives of the third declension with a single ending are followed by a semicolon and the genitive singular: **vetus; veteris.** Endings are italicized to distinguish them clearly from the stems of words. The following abbreviations occur:

abl	=	ablative	*interj*	=	interjection
acc	=	accusative	*m*	=	masculine
adj	=	adjective	*n*	=	neuter
adv	=	adverb	*pl*	=	plural
conj	=	conjunction	*pref*	=	prefix
dat	=	dative	*prep*	=	preposition
f	=	feminine	*pron*	=	pronoun
indecl	=	indeclinable	*rel*	=	relative

ā, ab *prep* (+ *abl*) from, by, after;
 nōmināre ā sē to name after oneself
ā–, ab– *pref* from, away
abeō *-īre -iī or -īvī -itum* to go away, leave
abhinc *adv* from here, ago; **abī abhinc!** go!, leave!
absolvō *-ĕre -ī* **absolūtus** to acquit
absum abesse āfuī to be distant
accendō *-ĕre* **accendī accēnsus** to light
accidō *-ĕre -ī* to happen
accipiō *-ĕre* **accēpī acceptus** to accept, receive
acclāmō *-āre -āvī -ātus* to shout (*in approval*)
accumbō *-ĕre* **accubuī accubitus** to recline (*at the table*)
accūsātor *-ōris m* plaintiff, prosecutor
accūsō *-āre -āvī -ātus* to accuse, charge
ācer ācris ācre sharp, keen
acētum *-ī n* vinegar

aciēs *-ēī f* battle line
āctivitās *-ātis f* activity
āctor *-ōris m* actor
āctrīx *-īcis f* actress
acūleus *-ī m* sting
acūtus *-a -um* sharp
ad *prep* (+ *acc*) to, for (the purpose of)
ad– *pref* to, toward, intensely
adamō *-āre -āvī -ātus* to love deeply
adaptō *-āre -āvī -ātus* to adapt, fit
addūcō *-ĕre* **addūxī adductus** to take to
adeō *-īre -iī -itus* to go to, approach
adferō *-ferre -tulī -lātus* to bring to, to bring along
adhibeō *-ēre -uī -itus* to show
adhūc *adv* till now, still
adiacēns *-entis* adjacent
adiaceō *-ēre -uī* to lie next to
adiuvō *-āre* **adiūvī adiūtus** to help
admīrābilis *-is -e* wonderful
admīror *-ārī -ātus sum* to admire

admodum *adv* very

adōrō *–āre –āvī –ātus* to adore, worship

adpōnō *–ĕre* **adposuī adpositus** to serve (*food*)

adsum adesse adfuī to be present, to be at hand

adversārius *–ī m* opponent

adversus *–a –um* bad

advocātus *–ī m* advocate, lawyer

aedēs *–is f* shrine; **aedēs** *–ium f pl* home

aedificō *–āre –āvī –ātus* to build

aedīlis *–is m* aedile (*an official*)

aeger *–gra –grum* sick

āër āëris *m* air

aestās *–ātis f* summer

aestimō *–āre –āvī –ātus* to consider, think

aestus *–ūs m* tide

aetās *–ātis f* age

Aethiopia *–ae f* Ethiopia

afferō afferre attulī allātus to bring to

afficiō *–ĕre* **affēcī affectus** to influence

Āfrica *–ae f* Africa

ager agrī *m* field; **agrī** *–ōrum m pl* countryside

agitō *–āre –āvī –ātus* to drive

agō *–ĕre* **ēgī actus** to drive, to lead (*a life*); **age!** *interj* come!, come on!

agricola *–ae m* farmer

aiēbant they said

Āiāx *–ācis m* Ajax

āla *–ae f* wing; **ālās plaudĕre** to flap the wings

ālātus *–a –um* winged

Alba Longa *–ae f* town in Latium, located 15 miles southeast of Rome

alea *–ae f* die; **aleā lūdĕre** to play dice, to gamble

aliēnus *–ī m* stranger, foreigner

aliōquīn *adv* otherwise

aliquandō *adv* someday

aliquid amplius anything else

aliquis alicūius *pron* someone

aliquot *indecl adj* some

alius *–a –ud* other, another; **alius ex aliō** one after another

alter altera alterum the other

altus *–a –um* high, tall, deep

amābilis *–is –e* lovable

amāns *–antis m/f* lover; *m* boyfriend; *f* girlfriend

amārus *–a –um* bitter

ambigō *–ĕre* to wonder, be uncertain

ambiō *–īre –iī –ītum* to campaign

ambitiōsus *–a –um* ambitious

ambō *–ae –ō* both

amīca *–ae f* (girl)friend

amīcus *–a –um* friendly

amīcus *–ī m* (boy)friend

amita *–ae f* aunt

āmittō *–ĕre* **āmīsī āmissus** to lose

amō *–āre –āvī –ātus* to love

amor *–ōris m* love

amphitheātrum *–ī n* amphitheater

amphora *–ae f* amphora (*large storage jar*)

amputō *–āre –āvi –ātus* to prune

Amūlius *–ī m* brother of King Numitor and uncle of Rhea Silvia

an *conj* or

ancilla *–ae f* maid

Andromeda *–ae f* daughter of King Cepheus and Queen Cassiopeia

angulus *–ī m* corner

angustus *–a –um* narrow

anicula *–ae f* little old lady

anima *–ae f* breath; **animam recipĕre** to catch one's breath

animal *–ālis n* animal

animus *–ī m* mind, heart

annus *–ī m* year

ante *prep* (+ *acc*) in front of, before; *adv* out ahead, previously

anteā *adv* previously, before

antecēdō *–cēdĕre –cessī* to go before, precede

antequam *conj* before

antīquus *–a –um* ancient

ānulus *–ī m* ring

anus *–ūs f* old lady

anxius *–a –um* anxious, worried

aperiō *–īre* **aperuī apertus** to open

apertus *-a -um* open; **in apertō** in the open

apis *-is f* bee

apodȳtērium *-ī n* dressing room

appareō *-ēre -uī -itum* to make one's appearance, show up, appear

applaudō *-ĕre* **applausī applausus** to applaud

apprehendō *-ĕre -ī* to arrest

appropinquō *-āre -āvī -ātus* (+ *dat*) to approach

Aprīlis *-is m*: **mēnsis Aprīlis** April

apud *prep* (+ *acc*) among, at the house of, with, before, in the presence of

aqua *-ae f* water

Aquārius *-ī* constellation Aquarius (*water carrier*)

aquila *-ae f* eagle

ara *-ae f* altar

Arachnē *-ēs f* Arachne (*Lydian girl, changed into a spider*)

arānea *-ae f* spider

arātrum *-ī n* plough

arbor *-oris f* tree

arca *-ae f* chest

arcus *-ūs m* bow

Ardea *-ae f* town in Latium

ardeō *-ēre* **arsī arsum** to burn, glow

ārea *-ae f* open space, threshing floor; **ārea domūs** yard

arēna *-ae f* sand, arena

argentārius *-a -um* banker's, of a bank; *m* banker; **taberna argentāria** bank

argentum *-ī n* cash, dough

Arīcia *-ae f* town in Latium, located about 18 miles south of Rome

Ariēs *-etis m* constellation Aries (*ram*)

armārium *-ī n* cupboard, closet, cabinet

arō *-āre -āvī -ātus* to plough

arrogāns; arrogantis arrogant

ars artis *f* skill

artē *adv* fast, sound (*asleep*)

articulus *-ī m* joint; **dolor articulōrum** arthritis

artifex; artificis artistic, skillful

arx arcis *f* citadel

ascendō *-ĕre -ī* **ascēnsum** to climb, rise

Asia *-ae f* Asia

aspectus *-ūs m* look, view

aspiciō *-ĕre* **aspexī aspectus** to watch, look at

assum *-ī n* roast

assūmō *-ĕre -psī -ptus* to assume

astrologia *-ae f* astrology

astrologus *-ī m* astrologer

astrum *-ī n* star

astūtus *-a -um* clever, astute

asȳlum *-ī n* asylum, refuge

āter *-ra -rum* dark, black

āthlēta *-ae m* athlete

āthlēticus *-a -um* athletic

atque *conj* and

ātrium *-ī n* entrance room

attentē *adv* carefully, attentively, closely

auctōritās *-ātis f* authority, prestige

audāx; audācis bold

audiō *-īre -īvī -ītum* to hear, to listen to

audītōrium *-ī n* lecture hall

audītus *-ūs m* hearing

augur *-uris m* augur, seer

augurāculum *-ī n* place of augury

Augustus *-ī m* Augustus (*first Roman emperor*); **mēnsis Augustus** August

aula *-ae f* palace

aurātus *-a -um* gold-plated

aureus *-a -um* gold(en)

aurīga *-ae m* charioteer

auris *-is f* ear

autem *adv* now, however

autumnus *-ī m* autumn

avārus *-a -um* greedy

avē *interj* hello!

Aventīnus *-a -um* Aventine (Hill)

avia *-ae f* grandmother

avidē *adv* eagerly

avidus *-a -um* eager, willing

avis *-is f* bird

avus *-ī m* grandfather

balneolum *-ī n* little bath

balneum *-ī n* bath; **balnea** *-ōrum n pl* public bath

barba *-ae f* beard; **barbam rādĕre** to shave off the beard

basilica *-ae f* courthouse

bellum *-ī n* war

bellus *-a -um* nice, pretty

bene *adv* well, fine; **bene māne** early in the morning

beneficium *-ī n* kindness, good deed

benignē *adv* warmly, kindly

benignus *-a -um* kind

bēstia *-ae f* wild beast; **ad bēstiās dare** to condemn to fight wild beasts

bēstiārius *-ī m* fighter of wild animals

bibliothēca *-ae f* library

bibō *-ĕre bibī bibitus* to drink

bis *adv* twice

blandus *-a -um* endearing

blatta *-ae f* cockroach

bonus *-a -um* good

bōs bovis *m* ox

Bovillae *-ārum f pl* town in Latium, located about 10 miles south of Rome

bracchium *-ī n* arm, claw

brevis *-is -e* short, brief

Britannia *-ae f* Britain, England

cadō *-ĕre cecidī cāsum* to fall

caedēs *-is f* murder; kill

caelum *-ī n* sky, heaven, climate

Caesar *-aris m* Caesar

caestus *-ūs m* boxing glove

calamistrum *-ī n* curling iron

calamitās *-ātis f* calamity

calamus *-ī m* fishing pole

calceus *-ī m* shoe

caldārium *-ī n* hot room, hot bath

calidus *-a -um* hot

calx calcis *f* heel

Campānia *-ae f* district in central Italy, south of Latium

campus *-ī m* (untilled) field; **Campus Mārtius** Field of Mars

Cancer *-rī m* constellation Cancer (*crab*)

candēlābrum *-ī n* candlestick, candelabrum

candidātus *-a -um* whitened; *m* candidate

candidus *-a -um* white

canis *-is m* dog; **Canis Māior** *m* constellation Canis Major (*great dog*); **Canis Minor** constellation Canis Minor (*little dog*); **canis vēnāticus** hunting dog

cantō *-āre -āvī -ātus* to sing; **tibiā cantāre** to play the flute

cantor *-ōris m* singer; flutist

caper *-rī m* goat

capillī *-ōrum m pl* hair; **capillōs crispāre** to curl the hair; **capillōs pectĕre** to comb the hair

capiō *-ĕre cēpī captus* to take, capture

Capitōlīnus *-a -um* Capitoline; *m* Capitoline (Hill)

Capricornus *-ī m* constellation Capricorn (*sea-goat*)

captīvus *-ī m* captive, prisoner

captō *-āre -āvī -ātus* to catch

Capuā *-ae f* city in Campania, south of Rome

caput *-itis n* head; **Caput Medūsae** constellation Caput Medusa (*head of Medusa*)

carcer *-eris m* jail

carmen *-inis n* song

carōta *-ae f* carrot

carpentum *-ī n* two-wheeled buggy

carpō *-ĕre -sī -tus* to find fault with, carp at

carrūca *-ae f* traveling carriage; **currūca dormītōria** sleeping carriage

carrus *-ī m* two-wheeled cart

cārus *-a -um* dear, expensive

casa *-ae f* hut, house

Cassiopēa *-ae f* Cassiopea, wife of Cepheus, king of Ethiopia

castor *-oris m* beaver

castra *-ōrum n pl* camp

cāsus *-ūs m* case; **eō cāsū** in that case

catasta *-ae f* slave block

catulus *-ī m* cub

cauda *-ae f* tail

caudex –icis m blockhead
caupō –ōnis m innkeeper
caupōna –ae f inn
causa –ae f cause; causā (+ gen) for the sake of
causidicus –ī m lawyer
cautus –a –um cautious
cavea –ae f cage
caverna –ae f hole, cavern
celeber –ris –re famous
celebrō –āre –āvī –ātus to celebrate
celer celeris celere fast
cella –ae f (little) room, storeroom
celsus –a –um high; celsius too high
cēna –ae f dinner, supper
cēnō –āre –āvī –ātus to eat supper, dine
Cēpheus –ī m Cepheus, king of Ethiopia, father of Andromeda
cēra –ae f wax
cerebrōsus –a –um hot-headed
certāmen –inis n contest
certē adv certainly, surely, without fail
certō –āre –āvī –ātus to compete
certus –a –um certain, sure
cervīcal –ālis n pillow
cervix –īcis f neck
cervus –ī m deer
cēterī –ae –a remaining, rest of; et cētera and so forth
cētus –ī m sea monster
cibus –ī m food, meal
cicōnia –ae f stork
cinis –eris m ashes
circum prep (+ acc) around
circumambulō –āre –āvī to walk around
circumclūdō –clūděre –clūsī –clūsus to surround
circumstō –stāre –stetī to stand around
circus –ī m racetrack
cisium –ī n two-wheeled carriage
cista –ae f box
cisterna –ae f cistern
citō adv quickly
cīvis –is m/f citizen
cīvitās –ātis f state
clāmō –āre –āvī –ātus to shout

clārus –a –um clear, bright, famous
claudō –ěre clausī clausus to close
clāva –ae f billy club
clāvus –ī m (crimson) border, nail
clepō –ěre –sī –tus to steal
cliēns –entis m client
cōgitō –āre –āvi –ātus to think; cōgitāre sēcum to think to oneself
cōgō –ěre coēgī coāctus to force
cohors –tis f barnyard
collēgium –ī n guild, college
colligō –ěre collēgī collēctus to gather, collect
collis –is m hill
color –ōris m color
Columba –ae f constellation Columba (dove)
columna –ae f column
coma –ae f hair
cōmicus –a –um comic, funny
comitia –ōrum n pl elections
comittō –ěre commīsī commissus to commit
commūnis –is –e common
cōmō –ěre compsī comptus to do, set (hair)
compeditī –ōrum m pl members of a chain gang
competītor –ōris m opponent
comprehendō –ěre –ī comprehensus to arrest; to understand
condemnō –āre –āvī –ātus to condemn
condiscipulus –ī m classmate
condō –děre –didī –ditus to store up; to found (a city)
confīdō –ěre confīdī confīsus sum (+ dat) to trust
congregō –āre –āvī –ātus to congregate
conīciō –ěre coniēcī coniectus to hurl; to guess
coniungō –ěre coniūnxī coniūnctus to join
coniūnx –iugis m/f spouse
cōnor –ārī –ātus sum to try
cōnscendō –ěre –ī to climb aboard

cōnsentiō _–īre_ **cōnsensī cōnsensus** to agree

cōnservō _–āre –āvī –ātus_ to save

cōnsiderō _–āre –āvī –ātus_ to consider

cōnsīdō _–sīděre –sēdī –sessum_ to sit down

cōnsilium _–ī n_ idea; plan; advice; **cōnsilium inīre** to form a plan

cōnsistō _–ěre_ **cōnstitī** to stop, take up position

cōnsobrīnus _–ī m_ cousin

cōnspiciō _–ěre_ **cōnspexī cōnspectus** to spot

cōnstanter _adv_ constantly

cōnstellātiō _–ōnis f_ constellation

cōnstituō _–ěre –ī –tus_ to decide

cōnstō _–stāre –stetī_ (+ _abl_ of cost) to cost

cōnstructiō _–ōnis f_ construction

cōnsul _–is m_ consul

cōnsulāris _–is –e_ consular, of a consul

cōnsultō _–āre –āvī –ātus_ to consult

cōnsūmō _–sūměre –sumpsī –sumptus_ to consume, eat

contendō _–ěre –ī_ **contentus** to fight, contend

contineō _–ěre –uī_ to hold together, contain

contingit _–ěre_ **contigit contactus** to happen; **contingit** it happens; **sīc contingit** (+ _dat_) that's what happens to

continuō _adv_ continuously; **continuō inspicěre** to keep on looking

continuō _–āre –āvī –ātus_ to continue

continuus _–a –um_ continuous

contrā _adv_ on the other hand; _prep_ (+ _acc_) against

contrōversia _–ae f_ controversy, argument

conveniō _–īre_ **convēnī conventum** to come together, gather, agree

convertō _–ěre –ī_ **conversus** to turn; **oculōs convertěre in** (+ _acc_) to turn to look at

convīva _–ae m/f_ (dinner) guest

convīvium _–ī n_ banquet, party, dinner party

convocō _–āre –āvī –ātus_ to call together

coquō _–ěre_ **coxī coctus** to cook, bake

cor cordis _n_ heart

coram _prep_ (+ _abl_) in the presence of

corbis _–is f_ basket

corōna _–ae f_ crown

cornū _–ūs n_ horn

corpus _–oris n_ body

corrigia _–ae f_ shoelace

corūscō _–āre –āvī_ to flash

cōtīdiē _adv_ daily

crās _adv_ tomorrow; **crās mane** tomorrow morning

crassus _–a –um_ fat

crātēr _–ēris m_ crater

crēdō _–děre –didī –ditus_ (+ _dat_) to believe

crepīdō _–inis f_ sidewalk

creō _–āre –āvī –ātus_ to create

crēscō _–ěre_ **crēvī crētus** to grow

crīmen _–inis n_ charge, crime

crīminālis _–is –e_ criminal; **crīminālis** _–is m_ criminal

crīspō _–āre –āvī –ātus_ to curl

crocodīlus _–ī m_ crocodile

crūdēlis _–is –e_ cruel

crūdus _–a –um_ crude

cruentus _–a –um_ bloody

crūs crūris _n_ leg

cubiculum _–ī n_ bedroom

cubitum _–ī n_ elbow

cucumis _–eris m_ cucumber

cūius whose

culpa _–ae f_ fault, guilt; **in culpā esse** to be guilty

culter _–trī m_ knife; **culter vēnāticus** hunting knife

cultūra _–ae f_ culture

cum _prep_ (+ _abl_) with; against (_an opponent_)

cum _conj_ when; **cum subitō** when suddenly

cum prīmum _adv_ as soon as possible

cuniculus _–ī_ rabbit

cupidē _adv_ eagerly

cupiō *–ĕre –īvī or –iī –ītus* to wish, want

cūr *adv* why; **cūr tandem** just why

cūra *–ae f* care, worry, concern; **cūrae esse** to be of concern

cūria *–ae f* senate building

cūrō *–āre –āvī –ātus* to take care, see to it, supervise, treat, cure

curriculum *–ī n* chariot, racetrack

currō *–ĕre* cucurrī cursum to run

currus *–ūs m* chariot

cursor *–ōris m* **runner**

cursus *–ūs m* course; **cursus honōrum** career of public offices

curtus *–a –um* short

curvus *–a –um* curved

Danaē *–ēs f (acc:* **Danaen**) Danae, mother of Perseus

datus *–a –um* mailed; **Rōmae data (epistula)** mailed in Rome

dē *prep* about, concerning

dē– *pref* down, thoroughly

deambulō *–āre –āvī* to stroll, walk around

dēbēō *–ēre –uī –itum* to owe

decem *indecl* ten

December *–bris m:* **mēnsis December** December

dēcernō *–cernĕre –crēvī –crētus* to decide

dēcidō *–ĕre* dēcidī to fall down

dēcīdō *–ĕre* dēcīsī dēcīsus to cut down

decōrō *–āre –āvī –ātus* to decorate

dēdicō *–āre –āvī –ātus* to dedicate

dēductiō *–ōnis f* bridal procession

dēfectus *–ūs m* defect, failing

dēfendō *–dĕre –dī –sus* to defend

dēfēnsor *–ōris m* defense lawyer

dēficiō *–ficĕre –fēcī –fectum* to run low

deinde *adv* then, next, after that

delectāmentum *–ī n* entertainment

dēlectō *–āre –āvī –ātus* to delight

dēleō *–ēre –ēvī –ētus* to destroy

dēmissus *–a –um* low; **demissior** too low

dēmittō *–ĕre* dēmīsī dēmissus to drop; to get rid of

dēnārius *–ī m* "dollar"; a common, small silver Roman coin about the size of a penny

dēnique *adv* finally, at last

dēnotō *–āre –āvī –ātus* to mark down

dēns dentis m tooth

dēnsus *–a –um* dense, thick

dentifricium *–ī m* tooth powder

dēpendeō *–ēre –ī* to hang down

dēpōnō *–ĕre* dēposuī dēpositus to put down

dēserta *–ōrum n pl* desert

dēsīderō *–āre –āvī –ātus* to need, miss, desire

dēsistō *–ĕre* dēstitī to stop; **dēsiste!** hold it!

dēspērātus *–a –um* desperate

dēspērō *–āre –āvī –ātus* to despair

dētergeō *–ēre* dētersī dētersus to wipe off

dēterō *–ĕre* dētrīvī dētrītus to thresh

dēterreō *–ēre –uī –itus* to frighten away, prevent, deter

dētrahō *–ĕre* dētrāxī dētrāctus to pull off

dētruncō *–āre –āvī –ātus* to cut off, behead

dēveniō *–īre* dēvēnī dēventum to come down

dēvorō *–āre –āvī –ātus* to devour

dexter *–tra –trum* right

dialogus *–ī m* conversation, dialog

dictātor *–ōris m* dictator

dīcō *–ĕre* dīxī dictus to say

dictitō *–āre –āvī –ātus* to keep saying

diēs *–ēī m* day

difficilis *–is –e* difficult

diffīdō *–ĕre –ī (+ dat)* to distrust

digitus *–ī m* finger

dignus *–a –um (+ dat)* deserving of

dīligenter *adv* carefully, diligently, hard

dīmittō –ĕre dīmīsi dīmissus to get rid of

dīrectē adv directly

dīrectō adv directly

discēdō –ĕre discessī discessum to depart, leave

discēns –entis m apprentice

discipulus –ī m pupil, student

discō –ĕre didicī to learn

disputō –āre –āvī –ātus to discuss

distō –āre to be distant

discobolus –ī m discus thrower

discus –ī m discus

diū adv long, for a long time; diū et ācriter long and hard; diūtius for a longer time

dīves; dīvitis rich; dīvitēs –um m pl the rich

dō dare dedī datus to give

doceō –ēre –uī –tus to teach, tell, explain

doleō –ēre –uī to hurt

dolor –ōris m pain; dolor articulōrum arthritis; dolor capitis headache

domesticus –a –um domestic

domina –ae f lady of the house, mistress; domina! madam!

dominus –ī m master, owner; domine! sir!

domus –ūs f home; domī at home; domō from home; domum (to) home

dōnec conj until

dōnum –ī n gift

dormiō –īre –īvī –ītum to sleep; dormītum īre to go to sleep

dūcō –ĕre dūxī ductus to lead; in mātrimōnium dūcĕre to marry

dum conj while

duo duae duo two

duodēvīgintī indecl eighteen

duplex; duplicis double

dūrō –āre –āvī to last

dūrus –a –um rough, hard, tough

ē– pref out; thoroughly, up

e (ex) prep (+ abl) out of

ea f she; it (referring to feminine noun)

ecce! look!

eculeus –ī m hobbyhorse

edō ēsse ēdī ēsus to eat

ēdō –ĕre –idī –itus to provide

ēducō –āre –āvī –ātus to raise (children)

efficiō –ĕre effĕcī effectus to bring about, cause

effugiō –ĕre –ī to escape, run away, get away

ego pron I

ēiciō –ĕre ēiēcī ēiectus to throw out, eject

eius pron his, her, its

elephantus –ī m elephant

ēlegāns; ēlegantis elegant

elementum –ī n element

ēligō –ĕre ēlēgī ēlēctus to elect, choose

ēmigrō –āre –āvī –ātus to move, emigrate

emō –ĕre ēmī emptus to buy

enim conj for

ēnormis –is –e enormous

ēnumerō –āre –āvī –ātus to count up

eō īre īvī or iī itus to go; eāmus let's go!

epistula –ae f letter

equitō –āre –āvī to ride (a horse)

equus –ī m horse

ērādō –ĕre ērāsī ērāsus to rake

ergā prep (+ acc) toward

ergastulum –ī n prison farm

ergō adv therefore

errō –āre –āvī –ātus to be wrong, err, wander

ērūptiō –ōnis f eruption

esca –ae f bait

essedum –ī n (light, two-wheeled) carriage

ēsuriō –īre to be hungry, go hungry

etiam adv even, also

etiamnunc adv even now, still today

etiamsī conj even if

Eurōpa –ae f Europe

ēvellō –ĕre –ī ēvulsus to pluck

ēveniō –īre ēvēnī ēventus to occur

ēventus –ūs m occurrence, event

ēvitō –āre –āvī –ātus to avoid

ex– *pref* out, thoroughly, up

ex *prep* (+ *abl*) out of, from, of; **ex hōc** from now on

exanimātus –a –um out of breath

exardescō –ĕre exarsī to flare up

excellēns; excellentis excellent

excipiō –ĕre excēpī exceptus to welcome, catch

excitātus –a –um excited

excitō –āre –āvī –ātus to awaken

exemplum –ī *n* example; **exemplī grātiā** for example; **exemplum praebēre** to set an example

exeō –īre –īvī or **–iī –itum** to go out

exerceō –ēre –uī –itus to train, run (*a shop, company*); **sē exercēre** to train, practice, exercise

exercitātiō –ōnis *f* exercise

exercitus –ūs *m* army

exhauriō –īre exhausī exhaustus to draw out, drain

exhibeō –ēre –uī –itus to show

exinde *adv* thereafter

exitus –ūs *m* exit, going out

expellō –ĕre expulī expulsus to expel, drive out

expergīscor –ī experrēctus sum to wake up

explicō –āre –uī –itus to explain

expōnō –ĕre exposuī expositus to explain

exprimō –ĕre expressī expressus to express

exsiliō –īre –uī to jump up, jump out

exspectō –āre –āvī –ātus to wait (for)

extrā *prep* (+ *acc*) outside of

extrahō –ĕre extrāxī extrāctus to pull out

exul –is *m* exiled person, exile

exultō –āre –āvī to exult

exuō –ĕre exuī exūtus to take off

fabricō –āre –āvī –ātus to make, put together

facile *adv* easily

facilis –is –e easy; **facilis inventū** easy to find

faciō –ĕre fēcī factus to do, make, cause

faenum –ī *n* hay

falcula –ae *f* pruning knife

falx –cis *f* scythe

famēs –is *f* hunger

familia –ae *f* family, household; **familia rūstica** slaves on a country estate; **familia urbāna** slaves belonging to a city household

farīna –ae *f* flour

fascēs –ium *m pl* fasces (*rods and ax carried by the lictors*)

fascia –ae *f* bandage

fastīdiōsus –a –um picky

fatigātus –a –um exhausted

Februārius –ī *m*: **mēnsis Februārius** February

fēlīciter! congratulations (**tibi** to you)!, bravo!

fēlīx; fēlīcis happy, lucky

fēmina –ae *f* woman

femur –oris *n* thigh

fenestra –ae *f* window

ferae –ārum *f pl* wild animals

ferē *adv* about, around, approximately

ferō ferre tulī lātus to bring, carry, take

Fērōnia –ae *f* town south of Rome

ferōx; ferōcis *adj* ferocious

ferula –ae *f* whip

fessus –a –um tired

festīnō –āre –āvī to rush, hurry up

fēstus –a –um festive; **fēstus diēs** holiday, feast day

fidēlis –is –e faithful

fīgō –ĕre fixī fixus to drive in

fīliolus –ī *m* baby boy, dear son

fīō fierī factus sum to be made, become, get, turn, take place

fiat sīc so be it

flāgitō –āre –āvī –ātus to demand

flamma –ae *f* flame

flammeus –a –um orange, flame-colored

flāvus –a –um blond
fleō flēre flēvī flētum to cry
flō flāre flāvī flātum to blow
flōridus –a –um of flowers, flowery
flōs flōris m flower
flūctus –ūs m wave
fluitō –āre –āvī to float
flūmen –inis n river
fluō –ĕre fluxī fluxum to flow
flūvius –ī m stream
focus –ī m fireplace, hearth
fōns fontis m fountain, spring
forāmen –inis n hole
forīs adv outside, out of doors
forma –ae f shape
Formiae –ārum f pl town in Latium,
    south of Rome
formīca –ae f ant
formīdābilis –is –e frightening
forsitan adv perhaps, maybe
fortasse adv perhaps, maybe
forte adv by chance; sī forte tē vidēbō if
    I happen to see you
fortis –is –e brave
fortiter adv bravely
fortūna –ae f fortune
fortūnātus –a –um fortunate
forum –ī n marketplace; forum boārium
    cattle market
Forum Appiī n town in Latium, 43 miles
    southeast of Rome
frāctus –a –um broken
frangō –ĕre frēgī frāctus to break
frātellus –ī m little brother
frāter –tris m brother
frāterculus –ī m little brother
frātricīdium –ī n fratricide
fremō –ĕre –uī –itum to roar
frequēns; frequentis frequent
frequenter adv frequently
frequentō –āre –āvī –ātus to attend
frīgidārium –ī n cold bath, cold room
frīgidus –a –um cool
frōns frontis f forehead
frūctus –ūs m fruit
frūmentum –ī n grain, wheat

frūstrā adv in vain, to no purpose
frūtectum –ī n underbrush
fuga –ae f escape
fugiō –ĕre fūgī fūgitūrus to flee, run
    away
fugitīvus –ī m fugitive
fulmen –inis n lightning
fulminō –āre –āvī to lighten
fūmus –ī m smoke
Fundī –ōrum m pl town in Latium,
    southeast of Rome
fundō –ĕre fūdī fūsus to pour
fundus –ī m farm
fūnis –is m rope; ad fūnem salīre to
    jump rope
furca –ae f fork
furnus –ī m oven, furnace
furtim adv stealthily; furtim rēpĕre
    to sneak
futūra –ōrum n pl future

galea –ae f helmet
Gallia –ae f Gaul
gallīna –ae f hen, chicken
gaudeō –ēre (+ abl) to enjoy
gaudium –ī n joy
gelidus –a –um cold
Geminī –ōrum m pl constellation
    Gemini (twins)
gena –ae f cheek
gener –erī m son-in-law
genocīdium –ī n genocide
genū –ūs n knee
genus –eris n kind, type
Germānia –ae f Germany
Germānī –ōrum m pl Germans
germicīdium –ī n germicide
germinō –āre –āvī –ātus to germinate,
    sprout
gerō –ĕre gessī gestus to wear, to carry;
    bellum gerĕre to fight a war
gestō –āre –āvī –ātus to wear, carry
gladiātor –ōris m gladiator
gladiātōrius –a –um gladiatorial
gladius –ī m sword
glōria –ae f glory

Gorgō –ōnis f Gorgon (*female monster*)
grabātus –ī m cot
gradus –ūs m step, **per gradūs ascendĕre** to go up the steps
Graecia –ae f Greece
Graecus –a –um Greek
grandinat –āre –āvit to hail
grandis –is –e big, huge
grandō –inis m hail
grassātor –ōris m hoodlum
grātiā *prep* (+ *gen*) for the sake of; **exemplī grātiā** for example
grātus –a –um grateful
gravātus –a –um heavy
gravis –is –e heavy, serious
gustō –āre –āvī –ātus to taste, eat
gymnasium –ī n gymnasium

habeō –ēre –uī –itus to have
habitō –āre –āvī –ātus to live, dwell
habitus –ūs m bearing, looks, condition
haltēr –ēris m weight (*for exercise*)
hāmus –ī m hook
harēna –ae f sand
harūspex –icis m diviner, soothsayer
hasta –ae f spear
hauriō –īre hausī haustus to draw
herba –ae f grass, herb; **herba mala** weed
herbicīdium –ī n herbicide
Herculāneum –ī n town on the Bay of Naples
herī *adv* yesterday
hīc *adv* here
hīc haec hōc *pron* this
hinc *adv* from here; **hinc ... hinc** on one side ... on the other side
hippodromus –ī m racetrack, hippodrome
hodiē *adv* today
holus –eris n vegetable
homicīdium –ī n homicide
homō –inis m person; **hominēs** people
honestus –a –um honorable, respectable
honor –ōris m political office
hōra –ae f hour

hordeum –ī n barley
hōroscopium –ī n horoscope
horreum –ī n barn
horribilis –is –e horrible
hortus –ī m garden; **hortī publicī** park
hospitālitās –ātis f hospitality
hostis –is m enemy
hūc *adv* here, to this place
hūmidus –a –um humid

iaceō –ēre –uī to lie (down)
iactō –āre –āvī –ātus to toss; **sē iactāre dē** (+ *abl*) to boast about
iaculātor –ōris m hurler
iaculum –ī n javelin
iam *adv* already, by now, now; **iam trēs hōrās labōrō** I have been working for three hours
iamdūdum *adv* long ago
iamprīdem *adv* long ago
ianua –ae f door
Iānuārius –ī m: **mēnsis Iānuārius** January
ibi *adv* there
icō –ĕre īcī ictus to hit, sting
ictus –ūs m bite, sting
id n it
īdem eadem idem *pron, adj* the same
ientāculum –ī n breakfast
ignis –is m fire
ille illa illud *pron* that
imbecillus –a –um weak
imber –bris m rain
immigrō –āre –āvī (in + *acc*) to move into
immō *adv* well
impōnō –ĕre imposuī impositus (+ *dat*) to put on
īmus –a –um lowest; **in īmō saccō** at the bottom of the bag
in *prep* (+ *acc*) against, into, to; (*with abl*) in on
inaugurō –āre –āvī –ātum to look for an omen, take the auspices
inauris –is f earring

incendium –ī n fire
incendō –ĕre –ī incēnsus to light
incertus –a –um unsure, uncertain
incipiō –ĕre incēpi inceptus to begin
incitō –āre –āvī –ātus to urge on
inclūdō –ĕre inclūsī inclūsus to lock
    up, enclose
indicō –āre –āvī –ātus to point out
indicō –ĕre indīxī indictus to declare
induō –ĕre –ī indūtus to put on
industrius –a –um industrious
ineō inīre iniī or inīvi initus (in + acc)
    to go into
infāns –antis m/f baby
infanticīdium –ī n infanticide
īnfēlīx; īnfēlīcis unhappy; unlucky
īnferī –ōrum m pl the dead; underworld
īnfestus –a –um hostile
īnflammātus –a –um inflamed
īnfundō –ĕre īnfūdī īnfūsus to pour
    into
inhabitō –āre –āvī –ātus to inhabit
inimīcus –a –um unfriendly
inimīcus –ī m (personal) enemy
inīciō –ĕre iniēcī iniectus to throw
    into
innocēns; innocentis innocent
inops; inopis helpless
inquiētus –a –um restless
inquirō –ĕre inquisīvī inquisītus to
    ask, enquire; inquit he/she says
inruō –ĕre –ī to rush in
īnscrībō –ĕre īnscripsī īnscriptus to
    write on
īnsecticīdium –ī n insecticide
īnsectum –ī n insect
īnserō –ĕre –uī –tus to insert, put into
īnspiciō –ĕre īnspexī īnspectus to look
    into
īnstrūmentum –ī n tool, equipment
insula –ae f apartment building, island
intellectus –ūs m understanding,
    intellect
intellegēns; intellegentis intelligent
intellegō –ĕre intellēxī intellēctus to
    understand

intendō –ĕre –ī intentus to draw
intentē adv intently
inter prep (+ acc) between, during;
    inter sē with each other
interdum adv at times, sometimes
interrogātum –ī n question
interrogō –āre –āvī –ātus to ask
intersum –esse –fuī to be involved,
    participate; (with dat or in + abl)
    to be present at, participate in
intrō –āre –āvī to enter
intrōeō –īre –īvī to enter
intus adv inside
inūsitātus –a –um unusual
inveniō –īre invēnī inventus to find,
    come upon, invent
invideō –ĕre invīdi (+ dat) to envy
invīsibilis –is –e invisible
iocus –ī m joke; iocum facis! you're
    kidding!
ipse ipsa ipsum pron –self, himself,
    herself, itself
īra –ae f anger
īracundus –a –um quick-tempered
īrātus –a –um angry
īre see eō
is m he; it (referring to masculine noun)
irrigō –āre –āvī –ātus to water
irrītābilis –is –e irritable
iste ista istud pron that
ita adv so, thus, yes; ita est that's right;
    ita quidem yes indeed; itane? is
    that so?
Ītalia –ae f Italy
itaque conj and so
iter –ineris n trip; iter facĕre to take a
    trip, travel
iterum adv again
Itrī –ōrum m pl town south of Rome
    in Latium
iuba –ae f mane
iubeō –ēre iussī iussus to order
iūdex –icis m judge, juror
iūdicium –ī n trial, court, courtroom,
    verdict
Iūlius –ī m: mēnsis Iūlius July

iungō –ĕre iūnxī iūnctus to join
Iūnius –ī *m:* **mēnsis Iūnius** June
iūrō –āre –āvī –ātus to swear
iūs iūris *n* law
iūstitia –ae *f* justice
iūstus –a –um just, fair
iūvenis –is *m* young man
iuvō –āre iūvī iūtus to help

labor –ōris *m* work; **labōrēs** troubles
labōrō –āre –āvī –ātus to work
labyrinthus –ī *m* labyrinth, maze
lac lactis *n* milk
lacōnicum –ī *n* sauna
lacrima –ae *f* tear
lacrimō –āre –āvī to cry
lactūca –ae *f* lettuce
laetus –a –um happy
lāna –ae *f* wool; **lānās nēre** to spin
　　wool
laniō –āre –āvī –ātus to tear up, rip
　　to pieces
lanista –ae *m* trainer
Lānuvium –ī *n* town in Latium, south
　　of Rome
lapillus –ī *m* little stone
Larēs –ium *m pl* household gods
lateō –ĕre –uī to hide
Latīnē *adv* (in) Latin; **Latīnē docēre** to
　　teach Latin; **Latīnē loquī** to speak
　　Latin
Latium –ī *n* district in central Italy just
　　south of the Tiber River
latrīna –ae *f* toilet
latrō –ōnis *m* robber
lātus –a –um broad
laudō –āre –āvī –ātus to praise
laureus –a –um of laurel
lavō –āre lāvī lautus to wash; **sē lavāre**
　　to wash (oneself)
lectīca –ae *f* litter
lectulus –ī *m* (small) bed
legātus –ī *m* envoy, delegate
legiō –ōnis *f* legion
legō –ĕre lēgī lēctus to read
lentē slowly

lentus –a –um slow
leō –ōnis *m* lion; **Leō** constellation Leo
　　(*lion*)
leopardus –ī *m* leopard
levō –āre –āvī –ātus to lift
libenter *adv* gladly
liber –brī *m* book
līberālis –is –e generous
līberī –ōrum *m pl* children
liberō –āre –āvī –ātus to free, liberate
libertās –ātis *f* liberty
Lībra –ae *f* constellation Libra (*scales*)
lībum –ī *n* cake
licet –ĕre –uit it is allowed; **licet mihi** I
　　am allowed, I may; **licet** *interj* well!
lictor –ōris *m* lictor, bodyguard
lignum –ī *n* wood
līgō –āre –āvī –ātus to tie
līlium –ī *n* lily
līmen –īnis *n* threshold, doorstep
līnea –ae *f* line, string
līnum –ī *n* twine
liquefaciō –facĕre –fēci –factus to melt
litterae –ārum *f pl* letter
lituus –ī *m* augur's staff
locus –ī *m* place; **in locō** (+ *gen*) in place
　　of; **locus dēstinātus** destination
longē *adv* far
longinquus –a –um distant, far, far away
longus –a –um *adj* long
loquor loquī locūtus sum to speak
lūceō –ēre luxī to shine
luctātor –ōris *m* wrestler
lūdō –ĕre lūsī lūsus to play
lūdus –ī *m* game, school; **lūdī** public
　　games
lūna –ae *f* moon
lupa –ae *f* (female) wolf
lupus –ī *m* (male) wolf
lūridus –a –um smoky, yellowish
lūsor –ōris *m* player
lūstrō –āre –āvī –ātus to **look** over
lūsus –ūs *m* game
lūx lūcis *f* light, daylight; **prīmā lūce**
　　at dawn
Lȳdia –ae *f* country in Asia Minor

macellum *–ī n* produce market, grocery store

macula *–ae f* spot

maculōsus *–a –um* spotty

madeō *–ēre –uī* to be wet (*with tears*)

maestus *–a –um* grieving

magis *adv* more; **magis et magis** more and more

magister *–trī m* teacher, master craftsman

magistra *–ae f* teacher

magnificē *adv* magnificently

magnificus *–a –um* magnificent

magnopere *adv* greatly

magnus *–a –um* big, important, great, loud

Māius *–ī m:* **mēnsis Māius** May

māior māior māius bigger, older

maleficium *–ī n* evil deed

malleus *–ī m* hammer

mālum *–ī n* apple

malus *–a –um* bad

mamma *–ae f* mom, mommy

mandātum *–ī n* instruction

māne *adv* in the morning; **bene māne** early in the morning

maneō *–ēre* **mānsī mānsūrus** to stay

mangō *–ōnis m* slave dealer

manīcae *–ārum f pl* handcuffs

mannus *–ī m* pony

manus *–ūs f* hand

mare *–is n* sea

margō *–inis m* edge, fringe, border

marīnus *–a –um* sea–, of the sea

maritimus *–a –um* sea–, of the sea

marītus *–ī m* husband

marsuppium *–ī n* moneybag

Mārtius *–ī m:* **mēnsis Mārtius** March

matella *–ae f* chamberpot

māter *–tris f* mother

mathēmaticus *–ī m* astrologer, mathematician

mātrīcidium *–ī n* matricide

mātrimōnium *–ī n* marriage; **in mātrimōnium dūcěre** to marry

mātrōna *–ae f* married woman

maximus *–a –um* biggest, oldest

mē *pron* me; **mēcum** with me, to myself

medeor *–ērī* (+ *dat*) to heal

medica *–ae f* (female) doctor

medicus *–ī m* doctor

Medūsa *–ae f* one of the three Gorgons

mehercule *interj* by heaven!, so help me!

mel mellis *n* honey

melior melior melius better

melius *adv* better

meminī *–isse* to remember; **mementō!** remember!

memoria *–ae f* memory; **in memoriā tenēre** to remember, keep in mind

mēns *–tis f* mind

mēnsa *–ae f* table; **Mensa** constellation Mensa (*table mountain*)

mēnsis *–is m* month

mentiō *–ōnis f* mention

mereō *–ēre –uī –itus* to earn

merīdiēs *–ēī m* noon

meta *–ae f* stack; **faenī meta** haystack

metō *–ěre* **messuī messus** to reap, harvest

metuō *–ěre –ī* to fear

meus *–a –um* my

migrō *–āre –āvī* to move

mīles *–itis m* soldier

Minerva *–ae f* Minerva, goddess of handicrafts

minimē *adv* no; **minimē vērō** no, not at all

minimus *–a –um* smallest, youngest

Mīnōs *–ōis m* Minos (*king of Crete*)

minor minor minus smaller, younger

Mīnōtaurus *–ī m* Minotaur

Minturnae *–ārum f pl* town in Latium, south of Rome

mīrābilis *–is –e* wonderful

mīrāculum *–ī n* miracle, strange sight

mīrus *–a –um* strange

Mīsēnum *–ī n* town on the northern tip of the Bay of Naples

miser *–era –erum* poor, miserable, pitiful

mītis –is –e gentle, tame, mild

modicum –ī n a bit, modicum

modo adv just, just now; **modo ... modo** sometimes ... sometimes

modus –ī m way, method, style, fashion

mola –ae f millstone, flour mill

momentum –ī n importance; **momentum temporis** moment

moneō –ēre –uī –itus to warn

mōns montis m mount

mōnstrō –āre –āvī –ātus to show

mōnstrum –ī n monster

mora –ae f delay

morior morī mortuus sum to die

mors mortis f death

mortālitās –ātis f mortality

mōrus –ī f mulberry tree

mōs mōris m custom

mōtiō –ōnis f movement

moveō –ēre mōvī mōtus to move, cause

mox adv soon, then

mulgeō –ēre mulsī mulsus to milk

multī –ae –a many

multitūdō –inis f crowd

multō adv much, by much; **multō nimis lentus** much too slow; **multō plūra** many more

multum adv a lot

multus –a –um much

mūlus –ī m mule

mundus –ī m world; **in mundō** on earth

mūniō –īre –īvī or –iī –ītus to fortify, build (a road)

mūnus –eris n show, contest; **ad mūnus gladiātōrium condemnāre** to condemn to fight as a gladiator

mūnusculum –ī n (little) present

mūrus –ī m wall; **mūrum dūcěre** to build a wall

mūsculus –ī m muscle

mūtābilis –is –e fickle, changeable

mūtō –āre –āvī –ātus to change

mūtuor –ārī –ātus sum to borrow

mūtuus –a –um mutual

nam conj for, because

nārrō –āre –āvī –ātus to tell, narrate

nascor nascī nātus sum to be born

nātālicia –ae f birthday party

nātālis –is –e: **diēs nātālis** birthday

natātiō –ōnis f swim

natō –āre –āvī to swim

nātus –a –um born, (with number of years) old

naufrāgium –ī n shipwreck

nāvicula –ae f boat

nāvis –is f ship; **nāvis magister** captain

nē conj (with purpose clauses) that not; (after verbs of fearing) that

nē adv not; **nē ... quidem** not even

–nē adv interrogative particle expecting a yes or no answer

Neāpolītānus –a –um adj Neapolitan

nebula –ae f fog, mist

nebulō –ōnis m airhead

necō –āre –āvī –ātus to kill

nectō –ěre nexī nexus to tie

negō –āre –āvī –ātus to deny

negōtiālis –is –e business

negōtiātor –ōris m businessman

nēmō –inis m no one

nempe adv of course

neō nēre nēvī nētus to spin

neque ... neque conj neither ... nor

nesciō –īre –īvī or –iī –itum not to know

niger –gra –grum black

nihil indecl nothing

nīmīrum adv of course

nimis adv too (excessively)

nimium adv too (excessively)

ningit –ěre ninxit to snow

nisi conj unless; except

nix nivis f snow

nōbilitās –ātis f nobility

nōbilis –is –e noble

noceō –ēre –uī (+ dat) to harm

noctū adv at night

nōlō nōlle nōluī to not want, to be unwilling; **nōlī (nōlīte)** (+ inf) do not...!

nōmen –inis n name, clan name
nōminō –āre –āvī –ātus to name
nōn adv no, not; **nōn iam** no longer; **nōn modo ... sed etiam** not only ... but also; **nōn procul abhinc** not far from here
nōndum adv not yet
nōnne adv introduces a question expecting a yes answer
nōnnūllī –ae –a some
nōs pron we, us
noster –tra –trum our
notō –āre –āvī –ātus to notice
nōtus –a –um well-known, noted
novācula –ae f razor
nōvī nōvisse to know, be acquainted with
novissimus –a –um latest, last
novus –a –um new
nox noctis f night
nūbēs –is f cloud
nūbilus –a –um cloudy, overcast
nūbō –ĕre nupsī nupta (+ dat) to marry
nūgae –ārum f pl nonsense; **nūgās!** nonsense!
nullus –a –um no
num adv introduces a question expecting a negative answer
num conj whether
numerō –āre –āvī –ātus to count
Numitor –ōris m Numitor (king of Alba Longa, grandfather of Romulus and Remus)
nummus –ī m coin
numquam adv never
nunc adv now
nūntiō –āre –āvī –ātus to announce
nūntius –ī m messenger
nūper adv recently
nūpta –ae f bride
nuptiae –ārum f pl wedding
nuptiālis –is –e wedding, nuptial
nūtō –āre –āvī to totter
nūtriō –īre –īvī or –iī –ītus to nourish, nurse
nux nucis f nut

ob prep (+ acc) on account of, because of
obductus –a –um covered
obēdiēns; obēdientis obedient
obēdiō –īre –īvī or –iī (+ dat) to obey
obiter adv by the way
oblectāmentum –ī n delight
obligō –āre –āvī –ātus to bind, oblige; **obligātus sum** (+ inf) I am supposed to
oblongus –a –um oblong
obscūrus –a –um murky
observō –āre –āvī –ātus to observe
obsōnō –āre –āvī to shop (for groceries); to go shopping
obstinātus –a –um obstinate, stubborn
obvius –a –um: **īre obvius** (+dat) to go to meet
occīdēns –entis setting
occīdō –ĕre –ī occīsus to kill
occultō –āre –āvī –ātus to hide
occupātus –a –um busy
occupō –āre –āvī –ātus to seize, grip
occurrō –ĕre –ī occursus (+dat) to run into, meet
ōceanus –ī m ocean
ocīnum –ī n clover
ocrea –ae f shinguard
Octōber –bris m: **mēnsis Octōber** October
oculus –ī m eye
ōdī ōdisse to hate
odor –ōris m odor
offendō –ĕre –ī offēnsus to offend
officīna –ae f workshop
officium –ī n duty; **officiī grātiā** to pay one's respects
ōlim adv once
olīvētum –ī n olive grove
Olympia –ae f Olympia, site of ancient Olympic games in Greece
Olympicus –a –um Olympic
ōmen –inis n omen
omittō –ĕre omīsī omissus to skip, forget about, lose
omnīnō adv entirely, completely; **nōn omnīnō** not at all

omni*s* –*is* –*e* every, each; **omnēs** (omnia) all

onerō –*āre* –*āvī* –*ātus* to load

on*us* –*eris* n burden, weight

opiniō –*ōnis* f opinion

oportet –*ēre* –*uit* it befits; **oportet tē** you ought

oppidānī –*ōrum* m pl townspeople

oppidul*um* –*ī* n little town

oppid*um* –*ī* n town

oppugnō –*āre* –*āvī* –*ātus* to charge, attack

optim*us* –*a* –*um* best

op*us* –*eris* n work

ōr*a* –*ae* f shore; **ōra maritima** seashore

ōrātiō –*ōnis* f speech; **ōrātiōnem habēre** to give a speech

ōrb*is* –*is* m globe; **orbis terrārum** the world

ōrdinō –*āre* –*āvī* –*ātus* to arrange, set in order

ōrdō –*inis* m row, order; **iūs et ōrdō** law and order

oriēns; orientis rising

orior orīrī ortus sum to rise

orō –*āre* –*āvī* –*ātus* to beg

oscillō –*āre* –*āvī* to swing

oscill*um* –*ī* n swing

ōscul*um* –*ī* n kiss

ovīl*e* –*is* n sheep fold

ov*is* –*is* f sheep

pābul*um* –*ī* n fodder, feed

paenē adv almost

paenitet –*ēre* –*uit* to cause regret; **mē paenitet** I am sorry, I regret

pal*a* –*ae* f spade

palaestr*a* –*ae* f palaestra, wrestling place, exercise yard

palaestric*us* –*ī* m coach

pallid*us* –*a* –*um* pale

palm*a* –*ae* f palm

palpēbr*a* –*ae* f eyelash

pān*is* –*is* m bread; **pānēs** loaves of bread

panthēr*a* –*ae* f panther

pāpiliō –*ōnis* m butterfly

parēns –*entis* m/f parent

pariēs –*etis* m (inner) wall

parm*a* –*ae* f (small, round) shield

pars partis f part, direction

parvul*us* –*a* –*um* small, young

parvul*us* –*ī* m little boy, young boy

parv*us* –*a* –*um* small, young

pass*us* –*ūs* m pace; **mīlle passūs** a mile

past*or* –*ōris* m shepherd

pateō –*ēre* –*uī* to lie open

pat*er* –*tris* m father

patiēns; patientis patient, tolerant

patienti*a* –*ae* f patience

patri*a* –*ae* f country, native land, native city

patricīdi*um* –*ī* n patricide

patrici*us* –*a* –*um* patrician

paulātim adv little by little

paulisper adv for a little while

paulō adv a little; **paulō post** a little later

pauper pauperis paupere poor

pavīment*um* –*ī* n pavement, floor

pāvō –*ōnis* m peacock; **Pāvō** constellation Pavo (peacock)

pax pācis f peace

pect*en* –*inis* m comb

pectō –*ĕre* pexī pexus to comb

pect*us* –*oris* n breast, chest

pecūli*um* –*ī* n personal savings

pecūni*a* –*ae* f money

pēior pēior peius worse

pell*is* –*is* f hide, skin, pelt

penn*a* –*ae* f feather

pensitō –*āre* –*āvī* –*ātus* to pay

per prep (+ acc) through; **per mē** by myself

per– pref thoroughly, up (**perficiō** I finish up)

perdō –*dĕre* –*didī* –*ditus* to destroy

pereō –*īre* –*iī* to die, perish

perfodi*ō* –*īre* **perfōdī perfossus** to stab

perforō –*āre* –*āvī* –*ātus* to drill a hole in, pierce, perforate

perīculōs*us* –*a* –*um* dangerous

perīcul*um* –*ī* n danger

perinde *adv* furthermore; **perinde ac**
  just as
peristȳlium *-ī n* (colonnaded) garden,
  courtyard
perītus *-a -um* experienced, skilled
perpaucī *-ae -a* very few
perpetuus *-a -um* constant; **in
  perpetuum** forever; **in perpetuum
  exinde** ever after
persequor *-sequī -secūtus sum* to chase,
  pursue
persōna *-ae f* person
persōnālis *-is -e* personal
perterritus *-a -um* scared stiff
pertineō *-ēre -uī* to belong to, pertain to
perveniō *-venīre -vēnī -ventum* to
  arrive (**ad** *or* **in** + *acc* at); to reach
pēs pedis *m* foot, leg; **īre pedibus** to go
  on foot
pessimus *-a -um* worst
pesticīdium *-ī n* pesticide
petītiō *-ōnis f* campaign
petītor *-ōris m* plaintiff
petō *-ĕre -īvī -ītus* to chase (after)
pexus *-a -um* (*past participle of* **pectō**)
  combed
philosophus *-ī m* philosopher
Pictor *-ōris m* constellation Pictor (*the
  Painter*)
pictūra *-ae f* painting, picture
piger pigra pigrum lazy
pila *-ae f* ball; **pilā lūdĕre** to play ball;
  pila nivea snowball
pīlentum *-ī n* women's carriage
pingō *-ĕre pīnxī pictus* to embroider,
  paint
pinguis *-is -e* fat
pinna *-ae f* fin
pīrāta *-ae m* pirate
piscātiō *-ōnis f* fishing
piscīna *-ae f* swimming pool, fish pond
piscis *-is m* fish; **Piscēs** constellation
  Pisces (*fish*)
piscor *-ārī -ātus sum* to go fishing
pīstor *-ōris m* baker
pīstrīna *-ae f* bakery

placeō *-ĕre -uī -itum* (+ *dat*) to please;
  urbs mihi placet I like the city
plānē *adv* clearly, plainly
planēta *-ae f* planet
planta *-ae f* plant, sole
plaudō *-ĕre plausī plausum* to flap
plaustrum *-ī n* wagon
plēbēius *-a -um* plebian
plēnus *-a -um* (+ *gen*) full of
plerīque pleraeque pleraque most
pluit *-ĕre pluit* to rain
plūs *adv* more; **plūs temporis** more
  time
Plūtō *-ōnis m* Pluto (*king of the
  underworld*)
pluvia *-ae f* rain
pluvius *-a -um* rain-, of rain, rainy;
  pluvius arcus rainbow
polītus *-a -um* polite, refined
pollex *-icis m* thumb
Polydectēs *-ae m* (*acc:* **Polydectēn**)
  Polydectes (*king of the island of
  Seziphos*)
pōmerīdē *adv* in the afternoon
pompa *-ae f* procession
Pompēiī *-ōrum m pl* city in Campania,
  a few miles south of Mount Vesuvius
pōnō *-ĕre posuī positus* to put, ask
popīna *-ae f* snack shop, restaurant
populāris *-is -e* popular
populus *-ī m* people
porcus *-ī m* pig
porrō *adv* besides, furthermore
porta *-ae f* gate; **Porta Capēna** gate in
  the ancient Roman wall marking the
  beginning of the Via Appia
possideō *-ēre possēdī possessus* to own
possum posse potuī to be able
post *prep* (+ *acc*) behind, after
post- *pref* behind, after
post *adv* afterwards, later; **paulō post**
  a little later
posteā *adv* afterwards, later on
posterus *-a -um* following
postis *-is m* doorpost
postmerīdīe *adv* in the afternoon

postquam *conj* after

postrīdiē *adv* on the following day

postulō *–āre –āvi –ātum* to demand

potestās *–ātis f* power

potiō *–ōnis f* drink

pōtō *–āre –āvī* pōtus to drink

praecēdō *–ĕre* praecessī praecessus to go before, precede

praeceptum *–ī n* instruction

praecipitō *–āre –āvi –ātus* to throw down (headfirst)

praecipuē *adv* especially

praecurrō *–currĕre –cucurrī –cursus* to run out ahead

praeda *–ae f* loot

praedīcō *–ĕre –dīxī –dictus* to predict

praeferō *–ferre –tulī –lātus* to prefer

praeficiō *–ficĕre –fēcī –fectus* to put (someone) in command of

praeiūdicium *–ī n* pretrial hearing

praemium *–ī n* award

praenōmen *–inis n* first name

praesideō *–sidĕre –sēdī* to sit before, preside

praesum *–esse –fuī* to be in charge, preside

praetereā *adv* besides, moreover

praetereō *–īre –īvī or –iī –itus* to pass

praetenāvigō *–āre –āvi –ātus* to sail by

praetextus *–a –um* having a border; **toga praetexta** toga with a broad crimson border

praetor *–ōris m* praetor

prandium *–ī n* lunch

prātum *–ī n* meadow

prīmō *adv* first, at first

prīmum *adv* first (of all), for the first time

prīmus *–a –um* first; **prīmō vēre** in early spring

prius *adv* first, sooner, previously

prīvātus *–a –um* private; *m* private citizen

prō *prep* (+ *abl*) on behalf of, for, instead of

prō– *pref* forward, forth

probātiō *–ōnis f* test

prōcēdō *–cēdĕre –cessī* to proceed, go on

procul *adv* at a distance, far; **procul ab** (+ *abl*) far from

prōdeō *–īre –iī –itums* to step forward

prodest *see* prosum

prōfundō *–fundĕre –fūdī –fūsus* to shed

prōhibeō *–ēre –uī –itus* to prohibit, prevent

prōiciō *–ĕre* prōiēcī prōiectus to throw forward, project

prōmittō *–mittĕre –mīsī –missus* to promise; **multa prōmittĕre** to make many promises

prōnuba *–ae f* bridesmaid, matron of honor

prōnūntiō *–āre –āvi –ātus* to pronounce

prope *prep* (+ *acc*) near

properō *–āre –āvi* to rush, hurry

propter *prep* (+ *acc*) on account of

prōrsum *adv* absolutely

prosperus *–a –um* favorable

prōsequor *–sequī –secūtus sum* to escort

prōsum prōdesse prōfuī (+ *dat*) to be good for

prōtegō *–tegĕre –tēgī –tectus* to protect

prōvocō *–āre –āvi –ātus* to challenge

proximus *–a –um* next, nearby; (+ *dat*) next (to)

prūdēns; prūdentis prudent

pūblicus *–a –um* public

puella *–ae f* girl

puellus *–ī m* little boy

puer *–ī m* boy

pugil *–is m* boxer

pugnō *–āre –āvi –ātus* to fight

pulcher *–chra –chrum* handsome, beautiful

pulchritūdō *–inis f* beauty

pulsō *–āre –āvi –ātus* to batter, pound, knock at

pulvis *–eris m* dust

pumex *–icis m* lava

pūniō *–īre –īvī or –iī –ītus* to punish

pūpa –*ae* f doll
purgō –*āre* –*āvī* –*ātus* to clean, clear away
purpureus –*a* –*um* crimson

quaerō –*ĕre* **quaesīvī quaesītus** to look for
quaesō please
quaestiō –*ōnis* f question
quaestor –*ōris* m quaestor (*financial officer*)
quālis –*is* –*e* what kind of
quam *adv* how; **quam superbus** how proud
quam *conj* as, than; **quam celerrimē** as fast as possible; **quam prīmum** as soon as possible
quamdiū *adv* how long
quamobrem *adv* why, that's why
quamquam *conj* although
quandō *adv* when
quattuor *indecl* four
quārtus –*a* –*um* fourth
quī quae quod *rel pron* who, which, that
quī quae quod *interrogative adj* which, what
quia *conj* because
quīcumque quaecumque quodcumque *pron* whoever, whatever
quid *pron* what; (*after* **sī**) anything; **quid est?** what's the trouble?; **quid est tibi?** what's wrong with you?
quīdam quaedam quoddam *pron* a certain; **quōdam diē** one day
quidem *adv* really, in fact
quidnam? *pron* just what?
quidnī *adv* why not
quīnque *indecl* five
quis *pron* who?
quō *adv* where (to)
quō *adv*: **quō magis . . . eō magis** the more . . . the more
quōmodo *adv* how
quondam *adv* once
quoque *adv* too

quot *indecl* how many
quotiēns *adv* how often; *conj* whenever
quōusque *adv* how long

radius –*ī* m ray, spoke
raeda –*ae* f four-wheeled carriage; **raeda meritōria** rental carriage
raedārius –*ī* m driver, coachman
rapidē *adv* rapidly, fast
rapidus –*a* –*um* fast
rapiō –*ĕre* –*uī* –*tus* to seize, kidnap; **in iūdicium rapĕre** to haul off to court
rārō *adv* rarely
rastellus –*ī* m rake
ratiō –*ōnis* f reason
re–*pref* back, backward, again
rebellis –*is* –*e* rebellious
rebellō –*āre* –*āvī* –*ātus* to rebel
recēns; recentis recent
recipiō –*ĕre* **recēpī receptus** to take back; **sē recipĕre** to retire
recognitiō –*ōnis* f review
recognōscō –*ĕre* **recognōvī recognitus** to recognize
rēctus –*a* –*um* straight; **rēctā lineā** in a straight line
recūsō –*āre* –*āvī* –*ātus* to refuse
reddō –*ĕre* **redidī reditus** to return, give back
redeō –*īre* –*iī* –*itum* to return, go back
redūcō –*dūcĕre* –*duxī* –*ductus* to lead back
refugiō –*ĕre* –*ī* to fall back
refulgeō –*ĕre* **refulsī** to shine again
regiō –*ōnis* f region
rēgnō –*āre* –*āvī* –*ātum* (*+ dat*) to rule over
rēgnum –*ī* n kingdom
relinquō –*ĕre* **relīquī relictus** to leave
remigō –*āre* –*āvī* to row
rēmus –*ī* m oar
reparō –*āre* –*āvī* –*ātus* to repair
repente *adv* all of a sudden, suddenly
repentīnus –*a* –*um* sudden
rēpō –*ĕre* –*sī* –*tum* to crawl

reportō *–āre –āvī –ātus* to bring back

repudiō *–āre –āvī –ātus* to jilt

repugnō *–āre –āvī* to fight back

requīrō *–ĕre* **requisīvī requisītus** to look for; **vōcibus requīrĕre** to yell for

rēs reī *f* thing, situation, matter; **rēs pūblica** government, politics

respirātiō *–ōnis f* breathing, breath

respirātor *–ōris m* respirator

respirō *–āre –āvī –ātus* to breathe

respondeō *–ĕre –ī* **respōnsum** to answer

restō *–āre* **restitī** to remain, be left over

rētē *–is n* net

rētiārius *–ī m* netman

retineō *–ēre –uī* **retentus** to hold back, retain

reus *–ī m* defendant, guilty one

revēlō *–āre –āvi –ātus* to reveal

rēx rēgis *m* king

rīdeō *–ēre* **rīsī rīsus** to laugh

rīdiculus *–a –um* ridiculous

rīma *–ae f* crack

rīpa *–ae f* bank

rōbustus *–a –um* strong, robust

rogō *–āre –āvi –ātus* to ask

Rōmānus *–a –um* Roman

Rōmulus *–ī m* Romulus, first king of Rome

rōstra *–ōrum n pl* rostrum, speaker's platform

rota *–ae f* wheel

rotundō *–āre –āvi –ātus* to make round

ruber rubra rubrum red

rūgiō *–īre –iī* to roar

ruīna *–ae f* collapse

runcīna *–ae f* (carpenter's) plane

runcīnō *–āre –āvi –ātum* to plane

ruō *–ĕre –ī –itūrus* to rush

rūpēs *–is f* cliff

rursus *adv* again

rūs rūris *n* country; **rūre** from the country; **rūrī** in the country; **rūs** *(acc)* to the country

rutrum *–ī n* shovel

Sabīnus *–a –um* Sabine; **Sabīnī** Sabines *(ancient neighbors of Rome)*

saccus *–ī m* bag

saepe *adv* often

sagitta *–ae f* arrow

Sagittārius *–ī m* constellation Sagittarius *(archer)*

saliō *–īre –iī* to jump; **ad fūnem salīre** to jump rope

salūs *–ūtis f* greeting, safety; **salūtem dare** *or* **dicĕre** to send greetings

salvē! (**salvēte!**) hello!

salvus *–a –um* safe

sandalium *–ī n* sandal

sānē *adv* yes

sānitās *–ātis f* health, sanity

sānō *–āre –āvī –ātus* to heal

sānus *–a –um* sound, healthy

sarculum *–ī n* hoe

sāriō *–īre –uī* to hoe

satis *adv* enough, sufficiently

Sāturnalia *–ium n pl* feast in honor of Saturn

saxum *–ī n* rock

scaena *–ae f* scene

scalpellum *–ī n* chisel

scēptrum *–ī n* scepter

schola *–ae f* school

scientia *–ae f* science, knowledge

sciō scīre scīvī scītus to know

sciūrus *–ī m* squirrel

scobis *–is f* sawdust

scopae *–ārum f pl* broom

scopulus *–ī m* (projecting) cliff

Scorpiō *–ōnis m* constellation Scorpio *(scorpion)*

scrībō *–ĕre* **scripsī scriptum** to write

Sculptor *–ōris m* constellation Sculptor *(sculptor or sculptor's workshop)*

scūtum *–ī n* (oblong) shield

sē *reflexive pron (acc or abl)* himself, herself, itself, themselves

secō *–āre –uī –tus* to cut

secrētum *–ī n* secret

secrētus *–a –um* secret

secūris *–is f (acc:* **securim***)* axe

sēcūritās –ātis f security
sed conj but
sedeō –ēre sēdī sessus to sit
seges –etis f crop, corn
sēgregō –āre –āvi –ātus to keep apart
sēligō –ēre sēlēgī sēlēctus to choose
sella –ae f chair; **sella curūlis** official
    chair; **sella gestātōria** sedan chair
semel adv once
sēmen –inis n seed
sēmihomō –inis m half-man
sēmita –ae f track, path
sēmitaurus –ī m half-bull
semper adv always
senātor –ōris m senator
sēnsus –ūs m sense
sententia –ae f verdict
sentiō –īre sēnsī sēnsus to realize
sepeliō –īre –īvī sepultus to bury
septem indecl seven
September –bris m: **mēnsis September**
    September
septentriōnalis –is –e northern
septentriōnēs –um m pl the North; **ex**
    septentriōnibus flantēs blowing from
    the North
sequor –ī secūtus sum to follow
serēnus –a –um calm, clear
sērius adv later, (too) late
sērius –a –um serious
Seriphus –ī f Greek island
serō –ēre sēvī sātus to sow
serō adv late
serpēns –entis m serpent
serpō –ēre –sī to crawl
serra –ae f saw; **serram dūcěre** to saw;
    serrā secāre to saw
serta –ae f garland
sērus –a –um late
sērva –ae f (female) slave
serviō –īre –iī (+ dat) to serve, be a
    slave to
servō –āre –āvī –ātus to save
servulus –ī m young slave
servus –ī m slave
sī conj if

sibi reflexive pron to himself/herself/
    itself/themselves
sīc adv in this way, thus, so
sīca –ae f dagger
siccus –a –um dry
Sicilia –ae f Sicily
sīcut conj just as, like
significō –āre –āvī –ātus to mean
signum –ī n sign
silentium –ī n silence
sileō –ēre –uī to be silent
silva –ae f forest, woods
similis –is –e similar, alike
simplex; simplicis simple
simul atque conj as soon as
sincērus –a –um sincere
sine prep (+ abl) without
singula –ōrum n pl details
sinister –tra –trum left
sinus –ūs m bay
situla –ae f bucket
situs –a –um located
socius –ī m accomplice
sōl –is m sun
solea –ae f sandal
solitus –a –um usual, customary
sōlus –a –um alone, only
somniō –āre –āvī –ātus to dream
somnium –ī n dream; **somnium**
    tumultuōsum nightmare
somnolentus –a –um sleepy
somnus –ī m sleep
sordidus –a –um dirty
soror –ōris f sister
Spartacus –ī m gladiator who led a
    revolt
speciēs –ēī f sight, appearance; **prīma**
    speciē at first sight
spectāculum –ī n show
spectātor –ōris m spectator
spectō –āre –āvī –ātus to watch, look at
speculāris –is –e adj mirrorlike, shiny
speculum –ī n mirror
spēlunca –ae f cave
spērō –āre –āvī –ātus to hope (for)
spēs spēī f hope

spīna –ae f spine

splendidus –a –um splendid, shiny

sportula –ae food basket, lunch basket

stabulum –ī n stable; dingy room, hole-in-the-wall

stadium –ī n stadium

stagnum –ī n pond

statim adv immediately

statua –ae f statue

status –ūs m standing, status

stella –ae f star

stīria –ae f icicle

stō stāre stetī statum to stand

stragulum –ī n blanket

strictus –a –um strict

studeō –ēre –uī to study

studiōsus –a –um studious

sub prep (+ abl) under, at the foot of; sub nocte before nightfall

subeō –īre –īvī or –iī –itus to go up, climb

subigō –igĕre –ēgī –actus to knead

subitō adv suddenly

subrīdeō –rīdēre –rīsī –rīsus to smile

subsellium –ī n bench, juror's bench

Subūra –ae f noisy commercial center in Rome

successus –ūs m success

sūdō –āre –āvī –ātus to sweat

sūdor –ōris m sweat

sufflāmen –inis n brake

sufflaminō –āre –āvī –atus to brake; rotam sufflāmināre to put on the brake

suffrāgātor –oris m voter

suffrāgium –ī n vote; diēs suffrāgiī election day; suffrāgium ferre to cast a vote

suīcīdium –ī n suicide

sulfur –uris n sulfur

sum esse fuī futūrus to be

summus –a –um highest

sūmō –ĕre sūmpsī sūmptus to take; to eat (a meal)

suō –ĕre suī sūtus to sew

superbia –ae f pride

superbus –a –um (+ abl) proud of

supercilium –ī n eyebrow

superior –ior –ius higher

superō –āre –āvī –ātus to overcome, defeat, win

superstitiō –ōnis f superstition

superstitiōsus –a –um superstitious

suprā (+ acc) on, on top of

suprēmus –a –um highest

surgō –ĕre surrexī surrectum to rise, get up

sustentō –āre –āvī –ātus to support, sustain

sustineō –ēre –uī to hold up

suus –a –um his/her/its/their own

taberna –ae f shop, store, booth, tavern; taberna ferrāria hardware store; taberna vināria wine shop

tablīnum –ī n study, den

tabula –ae f board

taeda –ae f torch

Talassiō! interj traditional wedding cry

tālis –is –e such a

tam adv (before adjectives and adverbs) so; tam . . . quam as . . . as

tamen adv still, nevertheless

tamquam conj like, as if

tandem adv finally; cūr tandem just why

tangō –ĕre tetigī tactus to touch

tantum adv only

tantummodo adv only

tantus –a –um so much, such a great

tardus –a –um slow

Taurus –ī m constellation Taurus (bull)

tēctum –ī n roof, house

tēla –ae f cobweb

tempestās –ātis f weather, storm

templum –ī n temple, section of the sky marked for augury

temptō –āre –āvī –ātus to try

tempus –oris n time; tempus annī season

tempus –oris n temple

teneō –ēre –uī –tum to hold, occupy, live in
tener –eris –ere tender, soft
tepidārium –ī *n* warm room, warm bath
tepidus –a –um lukewarm
ter *adv* three times
terēbra –ae *f* drill
tergum –ī *n* back
terra –ae *f* earth
terreō –ēre –uī –itus to frighten
terrificō –āre –āvī –ātus to terrify
territus –a –um frightened, scared
tertius –a –um third
testimōnium –ī *n* evidence, testimony
testis –is *m* witness
texō –ēre –uī –tum to weave
theātrum –ī *n* theater
thermae –ārum *f pl* public baths
thēsaurus –ī *m* treasure
Thrācia –ae *f* Thrace (*country north of Greece*)
tibi *pron* to you
tibia –ae *f* flute; **tībiā cantāre** to play the flute
tībīcen –inis *m/f* flute player
tignārius –a –um of a carpenter; **tignārius** *m* carpenter
tignum –ī *n* beam
tigris –is *f* tiger
timeō –ēre –uī to fear, be afraid (of)
timidus –a –um timid, afraid
timor –ōris *m* fear
tingō –ēre tinxī tinctus to dye, color
titulus –ī *m* sign, label
toga –ae *f* toga
tollō –ēre sustulī sublātus to raise
tomāclum –ī *n* sausage
tondeō –ēre totondī tonsus to cut
tonitrus –ūs *m* thunder
tonō –āre –uī to thunder
tonsor –ōris *m* barber
tonstrīna –ae *f* beauty salon; barbershop
tonstrīx –īcis *f* hairdresser
tornō –āre –āvi –ātus to turn out (*on a lathe*)

tornus –ī *m* lathe
tot *indecl* so many
tōtus –a –um whole, entire; **ex tōtō** completely
tractō –āre –āvī –ātus to handle
trādō –ēre trādidī trāditus to hand over
trahō –ēre trāxī trāctus to pull, draw
trāns *prep* (+ *acc*) across
trānseō –īre –iī –itum to move
trānsversē *adv* zigzag
tremō –ēre –uī to tremble
tremor –ōris *m* tremor
trepidus –a –um alarmed, nervous
trēs trēs tria three
tribūnal –ālis *n* judge's bench
trīclīnium –ī *n* dining room
tridēns –entis *m* trident
trīstis –is –e sad
trīticum –ī *n* wheat
trochus –ī *m* hoop
tū *pron* you
tum *adv* then, at that time; **tum cum** then when
tumeō –ēre –uī to swell
tumēns –entis swollen
tumor –ōris *m* swelling, lump
tunc *adv* then; **tunc maximē** just then
tunica –ae *f* tunic
turba –ae *f* crowd, mob
tussis –is *m* (*acc:* **tussim**) cough, coughing
tuus –a –um your
tympanum –ī *n* (solid) wheel, drum
tyrannicīdium –ī *n* tyrannicide

ubī *adv* where; *conj* when
ubīcumque *adv* wherever
ubīque *adv* everywhere
ullus –a –um any
ultimus –a –um last, final
ultrā *adv* more; *prep* (+ *acc*) beyond
ululātus –ūs *m* wail, cry
umerus –ī *m* shoulder
umquam *adv* ever
ūnā *adv* together; **ūnā cum** together with

ūnctiō –ōnis f massage, rubdown
ūnctōrium –ī n massage room
unde adv where (from)
unguis –is m fingernail
undique adv everywhere
ūnitās –ātis f unity
ūnus –a –um one
urbānus –a –um sophisticated
urbs urbis f city
urceātim adv by the bucket; urceātim pluĕre to rain buckets
urna–ae f urn
ursa –ae f bear; Ursa Māior constellation Ursa Major (*Great Bear* or *Big Dipper*); Ursa Minor constellation Ursa Minor (*Little Bear* or *Little Dipper*)
ursus –ī m bear
ūsque adv right up to; ūsque adhūc up till now
ut conj (*with indicative mood*) as, when; (*with subjunctive mood*) to, in order to
ūtensilia –ium n pl utensils; ūtēnsilia culīnae dishes
utique adv at least
ūtor ūtī ūsus sum (+ *abl*) to use
utrimque adv from both sides
uxor –ōris f wife; uxōrem dūcĕre to get married (*said of a male*)

vacca –ae f cow
vāgiō –īre –iī or –īvī to cry
vāgītus –ūs m cry (*of a baby*)
valdē adv a lot, hard
valeō –ēre –uī to be fine, well; Vale! Goodbye!
valētūdō –inis f health
validus –a –um strong
vallēs –is f valley
valvae –ārum f pl folding doors
vastus –a –um enormous, vast
vehementer adv hard, terribly
vehiculum –ī n vehicle
vēlāmen –inis n wrap, shawl
vēlōciter adv fast, quickly
vēlōx; vēlōcis fast
vēlum –ī n curtain; vēla dare to set sail

vēnābulum –ī n hunting spear
vēnātiō –ōnis f wild-animal hunt
vēnātor –ōris m hunter
venēnātus –a –um poisonous
venditor –ōris m vendor
veniō –īre vēnī ventus to come
vēnor –ārī –ātus sum to hunt, go hunting
ventus –ī m wind
vēr vēris n spring
verberō –ārē –āvī –ātus to beat
vērō adv in fact
vērrō –ĕre –ī versus to sweep up
versō –ārē –āvī –ātus to turn
vertebra –ae f vertebra
vertō –ĕre –ī versus to turn
vērus –a –um true
vester –tra –trum your
vestīgium –ī n footprint
vestis –is f clothing; vestēs exuĕre to undress; vestēs induĕre to get dressed
Vesuvius –ī m volcanic mountain southeast of Naples
veterānus –ī m veteran
vetus; veteris old
vexillum –ī n flag
via –ae f road; via strāta paved road, highway; via salūtis road to safety
Via Appia –ae f Appian Way (*first Roman highway*)
Via Lactea –ae f Milky Way
viātor –ōris m traveler
vīcēsimus –a –um twentieth
vīcīnitās –ātis f neighborhood
vīcīnus –a –um neighboring
victima –ae f victim
victor –ōris m victor, winner
victōria –ae f victory
victus –ī m loser
vīcus –ī m ward, block
videō –ēre vīdī vīsus to see
videor vidērī visus sum to seem
vigeō –ere –uī to thrive
vigil –is m policeman, fireman
vīlla –ae f farm house, country house

vīnārius –a –um (of) wine
vincō –ĕre vīcī victus to win, conquer
vīnum –ī n wine
viola –ae f violet
violentus –a –um violent
vir –ī m man; vir illustris! your honor!
virga –ae f rod, stick
virgō –inis (single) girl; Virgō
    constellation Virgo (maiden); Virgō
    Vestālis Vestal Virgin
vīsitō –āre –āvi –ātus to visit
vīsne see volo
vīsō –ĕre –ī to look at, visit
vīsus –ūs m sight
vīta –ae f life; vītam agĕre to lead a life
vitiōsus –a –um faulty, wrong, defective
vivārium –ī n zoo
vīvō –ĕre vixī victum to live
vīvus –a –um alive

vocābulum –ī n word
vocō –āre –āvī –ātus to call, invite
volātus –ūs m flight
volō –āre –āvī –ātus to fly
volō velle voluī to want, wish; vīsne?
    do you want, wish?
volvō –ĕre –ī volūtum to roll
vōs pron you
vōx vōcis f voice; cry; magnā cum vōce
    in a loud voice
vulnerātus –a –um wounded
vulnerō –āre –āvī –ātus to wound
vulnus –eris n wound
vultur –is m vulture
vultus –ūs m looks, expression

zōdiacus –ī m zodiac; zōdiacus circulus
    zodiac
zōdiacus –a –um zodiacal

Vocābula Anglica–Latīna

able, be able possum posse potuī
about (*concerning*) dē (+ *abl*);
  (*approximately*) circā
absolutely prōrsum
accept accipiō –ĕre accēpī acceptus
accomplice socius –ī *m*
account: on account of ob (+ *acc*),
  propter (+ *acc*)
ache dolor –ōris *m*
acquit absolvō –ĕre –ī absolūtus
across trāns (+ *acc*)
activity āctivitās –ātis *f*
actor āctor –ōris *m*
actress āctrix –īcis *f*
adapt adaptō –āre –āvī –ātus
adjacent adiacēns; adiacentis
admire admīror –ārī –ātus sum
adore adōrō –āre –āvī –ātus
advocate advocātus –ī *m*
aedile aedīlis –is *m*
afraid: be afraid of timeō –ēre–uī
after *conj* postquam; *prep* post (+ *acc*)
afternoon: in the afternoon pōmerīdiē
afterwards posteā
again iterum, rursus
against in (+ *acc*); (*an opponent*) cum
  (+ *abl*), contrā (+ *acc*)
age aetās –ātis *f*
ago abhinc
agree conveniō –venīre –vēnī –ventus
air āēr āēris *m*
alarmed trepidus –a –um
alike similis –is –e
alive vīvus –a –um
all omnēs –ēs –ia; **not at all** nōn omnīnō

almost paene
already iam
also etiam
altar ara –ae *f*
although quamquam
always semper
ambitious ambitiōsus –a –um
among apud (+ *acc*)
amphitheater amphitheātrum –ī *n*
amphora amphora –ae *f*
ancient antīquus –a –um
and atque, et
anger īra –ae *f*
angry īrātus –a –um
animal animal –ālis *n*
announce nuntiō –āre –āvī –ātus
another alius –a –um
answer rēspondeō –ēre –ī rēspōnsus
ant formīca –ae *f*
anxious anxius –a –um
any ūllus –a –um
anything else aliquid amplius
apartment building īnsula –ae *f*
appear appareō –ēre –uī –itus
applaud applaudō –ĕre applausī applausus
apple mālum –ī *n*
apprentice discēns –entis *m*
approach appropinquō –āre –āvī –ātus
  (+ *dat*)
arena arēna –ae *f*
argument contrōversia –ae *f*
arm bracchium –ī *n*
army exercitus –ūs *m*
around (*approximately*) ferē, circā; *prep*
  (+ *acc*) circum

arrange ōrdinō –āre –āvī –ātus
arrest comprehendō –ĕre –ī
   comprehēnsus
arrogant arrogāns; arrogantis
arrow sagitta –ae f
arthritis dolor –ōris m articulōrum
artistic artifex –icis
as ut (*with indicative*); **as . . . as** tam . . .
   quam; **as if** tamquam; **as soon as**
   possible cum prīmum
ashes cinis –eris m
ask inquirō –ĕre inquisīvī inquisītus;
   rogō –āre –āvī –ātus; (*questions*) pōnō
   –ĕre posuī positus
assume assūmō –ĕre –psī –ptus
astrologer astrologus –ī m
astrology astrologia –ae f
athlete āthlēta –ae m
athletic āthlēticus –a –um
attack oppugnō –āre –āvī –ātus
attend frequentō –āre –āvī –ātus
attentively attentē
augur augur –uris m
augur's staff lituus –ī m
augury augurium –ī n; **place of augury**
   augurāculum –ī n
aunt amita –ae f
auspices: take the auspices inaugurō –āre
   –āvī –ātus
authority auctōritās –ātis f
autumn autumnus –ī m
avoid ēvitō –āre –āvī –ātus
awaken excitō –āre –āvī –ātus
award praemium –ī n
away ā, ab *prep* (+ abl)
axe secūris –is f (acc secūrim)

baby īnfāns –antis m/f
back tergum –ī n
bad malus –a –um; (*unfavorable*) adversus
   –a –um
bag saccus –ī m
bait esca –ae f
bake coquō –ĕre coxī coctus
baker pīstor –ōris m
bakery pīstrīna –ae f

ball pila –ae f; **play ball** pilā lūdĕre
bandage fascia –ae f
bank taberna (–ae f) argentāria; (*of
   river*) rīpa –ae f
banker argentārius –ī m
banquet convīvium –ī n
barber tōnsor –ōris m
barbershop tōnstrīna –ae f
barley hordeum –ī n
barnyard cohors –tis f
basket corbis –is m/f; **lunch basket**
   sportula –ae f
bath balneum –ī n; (*cold bath*)
   frīgidārium –ī n; (*hot bath*) caldārium
   –ī n; (*warm bath*) tepidārium –ī n;
   (*large public baths*) thermae –ārum
   f pl; (*small bath*) balneolum –ī n
batter pulsō –āre –āvī –ātus
battle line aciēs –ēī f
bay sinus –ūs m
be sum esse fuī futūrus
beam tignum –ī n
bear (*male*) ursus ī m; (*female*) ursa –ae f
beard barba –ae f
bearing habitus –ūs m
beast bestia –ae f
beat verberō –āre –āvī –ātus
beautiful pulcher –chra –chrum
beauty pulchritūdō –inis f
beauty salon tōnstrīna –ae f
beaver castor –ōris m
because quod, quia, quoniam; **because
   of** ob (+ acc), propter (+ acc)
become fīō fierī factus sum
bed lectus –ī m; (*small*) lectulus –ī m
bedroom cubiculum –ī n
bee apis –is f
before *prep* ante (+ acc); (*in the presence
   of*) apud (+ acc); *conj* antequam
beg orō –āre –āvī –ātus
begin incipiō –ĕre incēpī inceptus
behalf: on behalf of prō (+ abl)
behead dētruncō –āre –āvī –ātus
behind post (+ acc)
believe crēdō –dĕre –didī –ditus (+ dat)
belong (to) pertineō –ēre –uī

bench subselli*um* –ī *n*

besides praetereā; porrō

best *adj* optim*us* –a –um; *adv* maximē

better *adj* melior melior melius; *adv* melius

between inter (+ *acc*)

beyond ultrā (+ *acc*)

big magn*us* –a –um

bigger māior māior māius

biggest maxim*us* –a –um

billy club clāv*a* –ae *f*

bind obligō –āre –āvī –ātus

bird av*is* –is *f*

birth *adj* nātāl*is* –is –e

birthday di*ēs* (–ēī *m*) nātālis

birthday party nātālici*a* –ae *f*

bit modic*um* –ī *n*

bite ict*us* –ūs *m*

bitter amār*us* –a –um

black āt*er* –ra –rum, nig*er* –ra –um

blanket strāgul*um* –ī *n*

block vic*us* –ī *m*

blockhead caud*ex* –icis *m*

blond flāv*us* –a –um

bloody cruent*us* –a –um

board tabul*a* –ae *f*

boast (about) sē iactārē (dē + *abl*)

boat nāvicul*a* –ae *f*

body corp*us* –oris *n*

bold aud*āx* –ācis

book lib*er* –brī *m*

booth tabern*a* –ae *f*

border margō –inis *m*; (*crimson*) clāv*us* ī *m*

born nāt*us* –a –um; be born nascor nascī nātus sum

borrow mūtuo*r* –ārī –ātus sum

both ambō –ae –ō

bottom īm*us* –a –um; at the bottom of the bag in īmō saccō

bow arc*us* –ūs *m*

box cist*a* –ae *f*

boxer pugil –is *m*

boxing glove caest*us* –ūs *m*

boy puer –ī *m*

boyfriend am*āns* –antis *m*

brake sufflāminō –āre –āvī –ātus

brake *n* sufflām*en* –inis *n*; put on the brake rotam sufflāmināre

brave fort*is* –is –e

bravely fortiter

bravo! fēlīciter!

bread pān*is* –is *m*; loaves of bread pān*ēs m pl*

break frangō –*ĕ*re frēgī frāctus

breakfast ientācul*um* –ī *n*

breath anim*a* –ae *f*; catch one's breath animam recipĕre; out of breath exanimāt*us* –a –um

breathe respirō –āre –āvī –ātus

bride nūpt*a* –ae *f*

bridal procession dēductiō –ōnis *f*

brief brev*is* –is –e

bright clār*us* –a –um

bring ferō ferre tulī lātus; bring about efficiō –ĕre effēcī effectus; bring along ad*ferō* –ferre –tulī –lātus bring back reportō –āre –āvī –ātus; bring to afferō afferre attulī allātus

Britain Britanni*a* –ae *f*

broad lāt*us* –a –um

broken frāct*us* –a –um

broom scōp*ae* –ārum *f pl*

brother frāt*er* –tris *m*; little brother frātell*us* –ī *m*

buck dēnāri*us* –ī *m*

bucket situl*a* –ae *f*; to rain buckets urceātim pluĕre

buggy (*two-wheeled*) carpent*um* –ī *n*

build aedificō –āre –āvī –ātus; (*road*) mūniō –īre –īvī –ītus

bull taur*us* –ī *m*

burden on*us* –eris *n*

burn arde*ō* –ēre arsī arsus

bury sepeliō –īre –īvī sepultus

business negōti*um* –ī *n*; *adj negōtiālis –is*

businessman negōtiāt*or* –ōris *m*

busy occupāt*us* –a –um

but sed

butterfly pāpiliō –ōnis *m*

buy emō –*ĕ*re ēmī emptus

cabinet armārium –ī n
cage cavea –ae f
cake lībum –ī n
calamity calamitās –ātis f
call vocō –āre –āvī –ātus; **call together** convocō –āre –āvī –ātus
calm serēnus –a –um
camp castra –ōrum n pl
campaign petītiō –ōnis f
candelabrum candēlābrum –ī n
candidate candidātus –ī m
candlestick candēlābrum –ī n
captain nāvis magister –trī m
captive captīvus –i m
capture capiō –ĕre cēpī captus
care cūra –ae f
career (*political*) cursus (–ūs m) honōrum
carefully dīligenter
carp at carpō –ĕre –sī –tus
carpenter tignārius –ī m
carriage (*traveling*) carrūca –ae f; (*two-wheeled*) cisium –ī n; (*light two-wheeled*) essedum –ī n; (*four-wheeled*) raeda –ae f; (*women's*) carpentum –ī n, pilentum –ī n
carrot carōta –ae f
carry gerō –ĕre gessī gestus; ferō ferre tulī lātus
cart (*two-wheeled*) carrus –ī m
case cāsus –ūs m; **in that case** eō casū
cash argentum –ī n
catch captō –āre –āvī –ātus
cattle market forum (–ī n) boārium
cause n causa –ae f
cause efficiō –ĕre effēcī effectus
cautious cautus –a –um
cave spelunca –ae f
celebrate celebrō –āre –āvī –ātus
certain quīdam quaedam quoddam; (*sure*) certus –a –um
certainly certē
chain gang compeditī –ōrum m pl
chair sella –ae f
challenge prōvocō –āre –āvī –ātus
chamberpot matella –ae f

chance: **by chance** forte
change mūtō –āre –āvī –ātus
changeable mūtābilis –is –e
charge oppugnō –āre –āvī –ātus; crīmen –inis n
chariot curriculum –ī n
charioteer aurīga –ae m
chase persequor –sequī –secūtus sum
cheek gena –ae f
chest arca –ae f
chicken gallīna –ae f
children līberī –ōrum m pl
chisel scapellum –ī n
choose ēligō –ĕre ēlēgī ēlēctus
cistern cisterna –ae f
citadel arx arcis f
citizen cīvis –is m/f
city urbs urbis f
classmate condiscipulus –ī m
claw bracchium –ī n
clean purgō –āre –āvī –ātus
clear clārus –a –um
clearly plānē
clever astūtus –a –um
client cliēns –entis m
cliff scopulus –ī m
climb ascendō –ĕre –ī ascēnsum; **climb aboard** cōnscendō –ĕre –ī
close claudō –ĕre clausī clausus
closely attentē
closet armārium –ī n
clothing vestis –is f
cloud nūbēs –is f
cloudy nūbilus –a –um
clover ocinum –ī n
coach palaestricus –ī m
coachman raedārius –ī m
cobweb tēla –ae f
cockroach blatta –ae f
coin nummus –ī m
cold gelidus –a –um; frīgidus –a –um
collapse ruīna –ae f
college collēgium –ī n
color n color –ōris m
color tingō –ĕre tīnxī tīnctus
column columna –ae f

comb pectō –ĕre pexī pexus; pecten
 –inis *m*

come veniō –īre vēnī ventus; **come on!**
 age!; **come together** conveniō –venīre
 –vēnī –ventus; **come upon** inveniō
 –venīre –vēnī –ventus

comic cōmicus –a –um

commit committō –ĕre commīsī
 commissus

common commūnis –is –e

compete certō –āre –āvī –ātus

completely omnīnō

concern cūra –ae *f*; **be of concern to**
 cūrae esse (+ *dat*)

concerning dē (+ *abl*)

condemn condemnō –āre –āvī
 –ātus

condition habitus –ūs *m*

congratulations! fēlīciter!

congregate congregō –āre –āvī –ātus

consider consīderō –āre –āvī –ātus

constant perpetuus –a –um

constantly cōnstanter

constellation cōnstellātiō –ōnis *f*

construction cōnstructiō –ōnis *f*

consul cōnsul –is *m*

consular cōnsulāris –is –e

consult cōnsultō –āre –āvī –ātus

consume cōnsumō –sūmĕre –sūmpsī
 –sūmptus

contain contineō –ēre –uī contentus

contend contendō –ēre –ī –tum

contest certāmen –inis *n*

continue continuō –āre –āvī –ātus

continuous continuus –a –um

continuously continuō

controversy contrōversia –ae *f*

cook coquō –ĕre coxī coctus

cool frīgidus –a –um

corn seges –itis *f*

corner angulus –ī *m*

cost cōnstō –stāre –stetī (+ *abl*)

cot grabātus –ī *m*

cough tussis –is *m* (*acc*: tussim)

count numerō –āre –āvī –ātus; **count up**
 ēnumerō –āre –āvī –ātus

country (*native land*) patria –ae *f*;
 (*opposite of city*) rūs rūris *n*; **from the**
 country rūre; **in the country** rūrī; **to**
 the country rūs

course cursus –ūs *m*; **of course** nīmīrum

court iūdicium –ī *n*

courthouse basilica –ae *f*

courtroom iūdicium –ī *n*

courtyard peristȳlium –ī *n*

cousin cōnsōbrīnus –ī *m*

countryside agrī –ōrum *m pl*

covered obductus –a –um

cow vacca –ae *f*

crab cancer –crī *m*

crack rīma –ae *f*

crater crātēr –ēris *m*

crawl rēpō –ĕre –sī –tum

create creō –āre –āvī –ātus

crime crīmen –inis *n*

criminal crīminālis –is –e; crīminālis –is *m*

crimson purpureus –a –um

crocodile crocodīlus –ī *m*

crop seges –etis *f*

crowd multitūdō –inis *f*

crown corōna –ae *f*

crude crūdus –a –um

cruel crūdēlis –is –e

cry *intr* fleō flēre flēvī flētus; (*of a baby*)
 vāgiō –īre –iī *or* –īvī ītus; vagītus –ūs *m*

cub catulus –ī *m*

cucumber cucumis –eris *m*

culture cultūra –ae *f*

cupboard armārium –ī *n*

curl crispō –āre –āvī –ātus

curling iron calamistrum –ī *n*

curtain vēlum –ī *n*

curved curvus –a –um

custom mōs mōris *m*

cut secō –āre –uī –tus; (*hair*) tondeō
 –ēre totondī tonsus; **cut down** dēcīdō
 –cīdĕre –cīdī –cīsus

customary solitus –a –um

dagger sīca –ae *f*

daily cōtīdiē

danger perīculum –ī *n*

dangerous perīculōsus –a –um
dark āter –ra –rum
day diēs –ēī m; **one day** quōdam diē;
   on the following day postrīdiē
daylight lux lūcis f
dear cārus –a –um
death mors mortis f
decide dēcernō –cernĕre –crēvī –crētus
declare indīcō –ĕre indīxī indictus
decorate decorō –āre –āvī –ātus
deep altus –a –um
deer cervus –ī m
defeat superō –āre –āvī –ātus
defect defectus –ūs m
defend dēfendō –ĕre –ī dēfēnsus
defendant reus –ī m
defense lawyer dēfēnsor –ōris m
delay mora –ae f
delegate legātus –ī m
delight dēlectō –āre –āvī –ātus;
   oblectāmentum –ī n
demand postulō –āre –āvī –ātus
den tablīnum –ī n
dense dēnsus –a –um
deny negō –āre –āvī –ātus
depart discēdō –ĕre discessī discessus
desert dēserta –ōrum n pl
desire dēsīderō –āre –āvī –ātus
despair dēspērō –āre –āvī –ātus
desperate dēspērātus –a –um
destination locus (–ī m) dēstinātus
destroy deleō –ēre –ēvī –ētus
details singula –ōrum n pl
deter dēterreō –ēre –uī –itus
devour dēvorō –āre –āvī –ātus
dictator dictātor –ōris m
die alea –ae f; **play dice** aleā lūdĕre
die morior morī mortuus sum
difficult difficilis –is –e
diligent dīligēns; dīligentis
dine cēnō –āre –āvī –ātus
dining room trīclīnium –ī n
dinner cēna –ae f; **eat dinner** cēnō
   –āre –āvī –ātus
direction pars partis f
directly dīrēctō

dirty sordidus –a –um
discus discus –ī m
discus thrower discobolus –ī m
dishes ūtēnsilia (–ium n pl) culīnae
dispute disputō –āre –āvī –ātus
distance: at a distance procul
distant longinquus –a –um; **be distant**
   absum abesse āfuī
distrust diffidō –ĕre –ī (+ dat)
do faciō –ĕre fēcī factus; (hair) cōmō –ĕre
   compsī comptus
doctor medicus –ī m; medica –ae f
dog canis –is m
doll pūpa –ae f
dollar dēnārius –ī m
door: folding doors valvae –ārum f pl
doorpost postis –is m
doorstep līmen –inis n
double duplex; duplicis
dough (money) argentum –ī n
dove columba –ae f
drain exhauriō –īre exhausī exhaustus
draw trahō –ĕre trāxī trāctus; (water,
   etc.) hauriō –īre hausī haustus; (bow)
   intendō –ĕre –ī intentus
dream somniō –āre –āvī –ātus; somnium
   –ī n
dress: get dressed vestēs induō –ĕre –ī
dressing room apodȳtērium –ī n
drill perforō –āre –āvī –ātus; terēbra –ae f
drink potō –āre –āvī potus; potiō –ōnis f
drive agitō –āre –āvī –ātus; agō –ĕre ēgī
   āctus; **drive in** (nail) figō –ĕre fīxī fixus
driver raedārius –ī m
drop dēmittō –ĕre dēmīsī dēmissus
drum tympanum –ī n
dry siccus –a –um
during inter (+ acc)
dust pulvis –eris m
duty officium –ī n
dwell habitō –āre –āvī –ātus
dye tingō –ĕre tīnxī tīnctus

each omnis –is –e
eager avidus –a –um
eagerly avidē; cupidē

eagle aquil*a –ae f*
ear aur*is –is f*
early in the morning bene māne
earn mere*ō –ēre –uī –itus*
earring inaur*is –is f*
earth terr*a –ae f;* (*world*) mund*us –i m;*
   on earth in mundō
easy facil*is –is –e*
eat ēdō esse ēdī ēsum; (*a meal*) sūmō
   –ĕre sūmpsī sūmptus
edge margō *–inis m*
elbow cubit*um –ī n*
elect ēlig*ō –ĕre* ēlegī ēlēctus
election day di*ēs (–ēī m)* suffrāgiī
elections comiti*a –ōrum n pl*
elegant ēlegāns; ēlegantis
element element*um –ī n*
embroider pingō *–ĕre* pīnxī pictus
emigrate ēmigr*ō –āre –āvī –ātus*
enclose inclūd*ō –ĕre* inclūsī inclūsus
endearing bland*us –a –um*
enemy (*public*) host*is –is m;* (*personal*)
   inimīc*us –ī m*
England Britanni*a –ae f*
enjoy gaude*ō –ĕre* (+ *abl*)
enormous ēnorm*is –is –e*
enough satis
enter intr*ō –āre –āvī;* intrōe*ō –īre –īvī*
entertainment dēlectāment*um –ī n*
entire tōt*us –a –um*
entirely omnīnō, ex tōtō
envoy legāt*us –ī m*
envy invide*ō –ēre* invīdī (+ *dat*)
equipment īnstrūment*um –ī n*
err err*ō –āre –āvī –ātus*
eruption ēraptiō *–ōnis f*
escape *intr* effugi*ō –ĕre –ī*
escape *n* fūg*a –ae f*
escort prōsequor prōsequī prōsecūtus
   sum
especially praecipuē
even etiam; **even if** etiamsī; **even now**
   etiamnunc
event ēvent*us –ūs m*
ever umquam; **ever after** in perpetuum
   exinde

every omn*is –is –e*
everywhere ubīque; **from everywhere**
   undique
evidence testimōni*um –ī n*
example exempl*um –ī n;* **for example**
   exemplī grātiā
excellent excellēns; excellentis
except nisi
excited excitāt*us –a –um*
exercise exerce*ō –ēre –uī –itus; reflex* sē
   exercēre
exercise yard palaestr*a –ae f*
exhausted fatigāt*us –a –um*
exile exili*um –ī n;* (*person in exile*) exul
   –is m
exit exit*us –ūs m*
expel expell*ō –ĕre* expulī expulsus
expensive cār*us –a –um*
experienced perīt*us –a –um*
explain explic*ō –āre –uī –itus*
express exprim*ō –ĕre* expressī expressus
expression (on face) vult*us –ūs m*
exult exult*ō –āre –āvi*
eye ocul*us –ī m*
eyebrow supercili*um –ī n*
eyelash palpebr*a –ae f*

fact: in fact quidem, vērō
failing dēfect*us –ūs m*
fair iūst*us –a –um*
faithful fidēl*is –is –e*
fall cad*ō –ĕre* cecidī casus; **fall down**
   dēcid*ō –cidĕre –cidī*
family famili*a –ae f*
famous clār*us –a –um*
far *adj* longinqu*us –a –um; adv* longē; **by**
   far longē; **far away** longinqu*us –a –um;*
   far from procul ab (+ *abl*)
farm fund*us –ī m*
farmhouse vīll*a –ae f*
farmer agricol*a –ae m*
fasces fasc*ēs –ium m pl*
fashion mod*us –ī m*
fast celer celeris celere, rapid*us –a –um;*
   adv rapidē, vēlōciter; (*asleep*) artē; **as**
   fast as possible quam celerrimē

fat crass*us* *–a* *–um*

fault culp*a* *–ae f*; **find fault with** carpō *–ĕre* carpsī carptus

faulty vitiōs*us* *–a* *–um*

favorable prōsper*us* *–a* *–um*

fear time*ō* *–ēre* *–uī*; tim*or* *–ōris m*

feather penn*ā* *–ae f*

feed pabul*um* *–ī n*

ferocious fer*ōx*; ferōcis

festive fēst*us* *–a* *–um*

few pauc*ī* *–ae* *–a*; **very few** perpauc*ī* *–ae* *–a*

fickle mūtābil*is* *–is* *–e*

field (*untilled*) camp*us* *–ī m*; (*tilled*) ag*er* *–rī m*

fight pugn*ō* *–āre* *–āvī* *–ātus*

fin pinn*a* *–ae f*

final ultim*us* *–a* *–um*

finally dēnique

find inven*iō* *–īre* invēnī inventus

fine *adv* bene; **be fine** val*eō* *–ēre* *–uī*

finger digit*us* *–ī m*

fingernail ungu*is* *–is m*

fire ign*is* *–is m*; incendi*um* *–ī n*

fireman vigil *–is m*

fireplace foc*us* *–ī m*

first prīm*us* *–a* *–um*; **first name** praenōm*en* *–inis n*; **for the first time** prīmum; *adv* prīmō; **at first** prīmō; **first of all** prīmum

fish pisc*or* *–ārī* *–ātus sum*; pisc*is* *–is m*

fishing pole calam*us* *–ī m*

fish pond piscīn*a* *–ae f*

fit adapt*ō* *–āre* *–āvī* *–ātus*

flag vexill*um* *–ī n*

flame flamm*a* *–ae f*; **flame-colored** flamme*us* *–a* *–um*

flap plaud*ō* *–ĕre* plausī plausus (*+ abl*)

flare up exardēsc*ō* *–ĕre* exarsī

flash corusc*ō* *–āre* *–āvī*

flee fug*iō* *–ĕre* fūgī fūgitus

flight volāt*us* *–ūs m*

float fluit*ō* *–āre* *–āvī* *–ātus*

floor pavīment*um* *–ī n*

flour farīn*a* *–ae f*

flour mill mol*a* *–ae f*

flow flu*ō* *–ĕre* flūxī flūxus

flowery florid*us* *–a* *–um*

flute tībi*a* *–ae f*; **play the flute** tībiā cantāre

flute player tībīc*en* *–inis m*; cant*or* *–ōris m*

fly vol*ō* *–āre* *–āvī* *–ātus*

fodder pabul*um* *–ī n*

fog nebul*a* *–ae f*

follow sequ*or* *–ī* secūtus sum

food cib*us* *–ī m*

foot pēs pedis *m*; **go on foot** īre pedibus; **at the foot of** sub (*+ abl*)

footprint vestīgi*um* *–ī n*

for *prep* (*for the purpose of*) ad (*+ acc*); (*on behalf of*) prō (*+ abl*); *conj* enim, nam

force cog*ō* *–ĕre* coēgī coāctus

forehead frōns frontis *f*

foreigner aliēn*us* *–ī m*

forest silv*a* *–ae f*

forever in perpetuum

forget about omitt*ō* *–ĕre* omīsī omissus

fork furc*a* *–ae f*

fortify mun*iō* *–īre* *–īvī or* *–iī* *–ītus*

fortunate fortūnāt*us* *–a* *–um*

fortune fortūn*a* *–ae f*

found cond*ō* *–dĕre* *–didī* *–ditus*

fountain fōns fontis *m*

fourth quārt*us* *–a* *–um*

fratricide frātricīdi*um* *–ī n*

free līber*ō* *–āre* *–āvī* *–ātus*

frequent frequēns; frequentis

friendly amīc*us* *–a* *–um*

frighten terr*eō* *–ēre* *–uī* *–itus*; **frighten away** dēterr*eō* *–ēre* *–uī* *–itus*; **frightened** territ*us* *–a* *–um*

frightening formīdābil*is* *–is* *–e*

fringe marg*ō* *–inis m*

from ā, ab (*+ abl*); **from now on** ex hōc

fruit fruct*us* *–ūs m*

fugitive fugitīv*us* *–a* *–um*

full plēn*us* *–a* *–um*; **full of** plēnus (*+ gen*)

funny cōmic*us* *–a* *–um*

furnace furn*us* *–ī m*

furthermore porrō
future futūra –ōrum n pl

gamble aleā lūděre
game lūdus –ī m; **public games** lūdī
　–ōrum m pl
garden hortus –ī m
garland serta –ae f
gate porta –ae f
gather colligō –ěre collēgī collēctus;
　conveniō –venīre –vēnī –ventus
Gaul Gallia –ae f
generous līberālis –is –e
genocide genocīdium –ī n
gentle mitis –is –e
Germans Germānī –ōrum m pl
Germany Germānia –ae f
germicide germicīdium –ī n
germinate germinō –āre –āvī –ātus
get (*become*) fīō fierī factus sum; **get**
　away effugiō –ěre effūgī; **get up** surgō
　–ěre surrēxī surrēctus
gift dōnum –ī n
girl puella –ae f
girlfriend amāns –antis f
give dō dare dedī datus
gladiator gladiātor –ōris m
gladiatorial gladiātōrius –a –um
gladly lībenter
globe orbis –is m
glory glōria –ae f
glow ardeō –ēre arsī arsus
go eō īre īvī *or* iī itus; **go away** abeō –īre
　–iī *or* –īvī, –itus; **go away!** abī abhinc!;
　go into ineō inīre iniī *or* inīvī initus
　(in + *acc*); **go on** prōcēdō –cēděre –cessī
　–cessus; **go out** exeō exīre exīvī *or* exiī
　exitus; **go to** adeō adīre adiī aditus
goat caper –rī m
gold–plated aurātus –a –um
golden aureus –a –um
good bonus –a –um; **good deed**
　beneficium –ī n; **be good for** prōsum
　prōdesse prōfuī (+ *dat*)
government rēs (reī f) pūblica
grandfather avus –ī m

grandmother avia –ae f
grass herba –ae f
grateful grātus –a –um
great magnus –a –um
Greece Graecia –ae f
greedy avārus –a –um
Greek Graecus –a –um
greeting salus –ūtis f; **send greetings**
　salūtem dīcěre
grieving maestus –a –um
grip occupō –āre –āvī –ātus
grocery store macellum –ī n
grow crescō –ěre crēvī crētus
guess conīciō –ěre coniēcī coniectus
guest convīva –ae m/f
guild collēgium –ī n
guilt culpa –ae f
gymnasium gymnasium –ī n

hail grandinat –āre –avit; grandō
　–inis m
hair coma –ae f, capillī –ōrum m pl
half–bull sēmitaurus –ī m
half–man sēmihomō –inis m
hammer malleus –ī m
hand manus –ūs f; **on the other hand**
　contrā; **be at hand** adesse
hand over trādō –ěre trādidī trāditus
handcuff manica –ae f
handle tractō –āre –āvī –ātus
handsome pulcher –chra –chrum
hang down dēpendeō –ěre –ī
happen accidō –ěre –ī, **if I happen to see**
　you sī forte tē vidēbō
happy laetus –a –um
hard dūrus –a –um; *adv* (*strenuously*)
　vehementer; (*diligently*) dīligenter
hardware store taberna (–ae f) ferrāria
harm noceō –ēre –uī (+ *dat*)
harvest metō –ěre messuī messus
hate odī odisse
have habeō –ēre –uī –itus
hay faenum –ī n
haystack meta –ae f
he is m
head caput –itis n

headache dolor (–ōris m) capitis
heal sānō –āre –āvī –ātus
health sānitās –ātis f
healthy sānus –a –um
hear audiō –īre –īvī –ītus
hearing audītus –ūs m
heart cor cordis n
heaven caelum –ī n; **by heaven!**
    mehercule!
heavy gravis –is –e
heel calx calcis f
hello! salvē! (*pl*: salvēte!)
helmet galea –ae f
help iuvō –āre iūvī iūtus; **so help me!**
    mehercule!
helpless inops; inopis
her eius; **her own** suus –a –um
herbicide herbicīdium –ī n
here hīc; (*to this place*) hūc; **from here**
    hinc
hide occultō –āre –āvī –ātus; lateō
    –ēre –uī
hide pellis –is f
high altus –a –um; celsus –a –um
higher superior –ior –ius
highest summus –a –um
highway via (–ae f) strata
hill collis –is m
his eius; **his own** suus –a –um
hit icō icĕre īcī ictus
hobbyhorse eculeus –ī m
hoe sariō –īre –uī; sarculum ī n
hold teneō –ēre –uī tentus; **hold it!**
    dēsiste!; **hold back** retineō –ēre –uī
    retentus; **hold together** contineō –ēre
    –uī contentus
hole forāmen –inis n; (*of a mouse, ant*)
    caverna –ae f
holiday fēstus diēs (–ēī) m
home domus –ūs f; **at home** domī
homicide homicīdium –ī n
honey mel mellis n
honor: your honor! vir illūstris!
honorable honestus –a –um
hoodlum grassātor –ōris m
hook hamus –ī m

hoop trochus –ī m
hope (for) spērō –āre –āvī –ātus; **hope**
    spēs speī f
horn cornū –ūs n
horoscope horoscopium –ī n
horrible horribilis –is –e
horse equus –ī m
hospitality hospitālitās –ātis f
hostile infēstus –a –um
hot-headed cerebrōsus –a –um
hot room caldārium –ī n
hour hōra –ae f
house tēctum –ī n; domus –ūs f; casa
    –ae f
household familia –ae f; domus –ūs f;
    household gods Larēs –um m pl
how quōmodo; **how long** quōūsque;
    how many quot; **how often** quotiēns;
    how proud quam superbus
however autem
huge grandis –is –e
humid hūmidus –a –um
hunger famēs –is f
hungry: be hungry ēsuriō –īre
hunt vēnor –ārī –ātus sum; vēnātiō
    –ōnis f
hunter vēnātor –ōris m
hunting dog canis (–is m) vēnāticus
hunting spear vēnābulum –ī n
hurl conīciō –ere coniēcī coniectus
hurler iaculātor –ōris m
hurry properō –āre –āvī –ātus
husband marītus –ī m
hut casa –ae f

icicle stiria –ae f
idea cōnsilium –ī n
if sī
immediately statim
importance momentum –ī n
important magnus –a –um
in in (+ *abl*); **in front of** ante (+ *acc*)
industrious industrius –a –um
infanticide īnfanticīdium –ī n
inflamed īnflammātus –a –um
influence afficiō –ere affēcī affectus

inhabit inhabit*ō* –*āre* –*āvī* –*ātus*
inn caupōn*a* –*ae f*
innkeeper caupō –*ōnis m*
innocent innocēns; innocentis
insect īnsect*um* –*ī n*
insecticide īnsecticīdi*um* –*ī n*
insert inser*ō* –*ěre* –*uī* –*tus*
inside intus
instead of prō (+ *abl*)
instruction mandāt*um* –*ī n*
intellect intellect*us* –*ūs m*
intelligent intellegēns; intellegentis
intently intentē
into in (+ *acc*)
invent inveni*ō* –*īre* invēnī inventus
invisible invīsibil*is* –*is* –*e*
invite voc*ō* –*āre* –*āvī* –*ātus*
irritable irrītābil*is* –*is* –*e*
island īnsul*a* –*ae f*
Italy Ītali*a* –*ae f*
it is *m*; ea *f*; id *n*
its eius; its own su*us* –*a* –*um*

jail carc*er* –*ěris m*
javelin iacul*um* –*ī n*
jilt repudi*ō* –*āre* –*āvī* –*ātus*
join iung*ō* –*ěre* iūnxī iūnctus
joint articul*us* –*ī m*
joke ioc*us* –*ī m*
joy gaudi*um* –*ī n*
judge iūd*ex* –*icis m*; **judge's bench**
    tribūn*al* –*ālis n*
jump sali*ō* –*īre* –*iī* –*tus*; **jump rope** ad
    fūnem salīre; **jump up** exsili*ō* –*īre* –*iī*
juror iūd*ex* –*icis m*
just iūst*us* –*a* –*um*; *adv* modō; **just as**
    sīcut, perinde ac; **just now** modō; **just**
    what? quidnam?

keep retine*ō* –*ēre* –*uī* retentus; **keep in**
    mind in memoriā tenēre
kidnap rapi*ō* –*ěre* –*uī* –*tus*
kill nec*ō* –*āre* –*āvī* –*ātus*; caedēs –*is f*
kind benign*us* –*a* –*um*
kindness beneficī*um* –*ī n*
king rēx rēgis *m*

kingdom rēgn*um* –*ī n*
kiss ōscul*um* –*ī n*
knead subig*ō* –*iğěre* –*ēgī* –*actus*
knee gen*ū* –*ūs n*
knife cul*ter* –*trī m*
knock at puls*ō* –*āre* –*āvī* –*ātus*
know sciō scīre scīvī scītus; (*a person,*
    place) cognōscō –*ěre* cognōvī cognitus;
    not know nēsci*ō* –*īre* –*īvī* or –*ii* –*ītus*
knowledge scienti*a* –*ae f*
known: **well known** nōt*us* –*a* –*um*

label titul*us* –*ī m*
labyrinth labyrinth*us* –*ī m*
lady of the house domin*a* –*ae f*
last dūr*ō* –*āre* –*āvī*
last novissim*us* –*a* –*um*
late sēr*us* –*a* –*um*; *adv* sērō
later post(eā); **a little later** paulō post;
    later on posteā
latest novissim*us* –*a* –*um*
lathe torn*us* –*ī m*
Latin Latīn*us* –*a* –*um*; **learn Latin** Latīnē
    discěre; **teach Latin** Latīnē docēre;
    speak Latin Latinē loquī
laugh rīd*eō* –*ēre* rīsī rīsus
lava pum*ex* –*icis m*
law iūs iūris *n*; **law and order** iūs et
    ōrdō
lawyer advocāt*us* –*ī m*
lazy pig*er* –*gra* –*grum*
lead dūc*ō* –*ěre* dūxī ductus; (*a life*) agěre,
    dūcěre; **lead back** re*dūcō* –*dūcěre*
    –*dūxī* –*ductus*
learn disc*ō* –*ěre* didicī
least: **at least** utique
leave relinqu*ō* –*ěre* relīquī relictus; abe*ō*
    –*īre* –*iī* or –*īvī* –*itus*
lecture hall auditōri*um* –*ī n*
left sinis*ter* –*tra* –*trum*
leg crūs crūris *n*; (of chair, table) pēs
    pedis *m*
legion legi*ō* –*ōnis f*
leopard leopard*us* –*ī m*
letter epistul*a* –*ae f*
lettuce lactūc*a* –*ae f*

liberate līberō –āre –āvī –ātus
liberty lībertās –ātis f
library bibliothēca –ae f
lictor lictor –ōris m
lie (down) iaceō –ēre –uī; lie next to
    adiacēre
life vīta –ae f; lead a life vītam agĕre,
    vītam dūcĕre
lift levō –āre –āvī –ātus
light incendō –ĕre –ī; lūx lūcis f
lighten fulminat –āre –āvit
lightning fulmen –inis n
like placet –ēre –uit; I like the city urbs
    mihi placet; prep sīcut, tamquam
lily līlium –ī n
line līnea –ae f
listen to audiō –īre –īvī –ītus
litter lectīca –ae f
little parvus –a –um; a little paulō; a
    little later paulō post; little by little
    paulātim
live vīvō –ĕre vīxī victum; (dwell) habitō
    –āre –āvī –ātus
load onerō –āre –āvī –ātus
located situs –a –um
lock up inclūdō –ĕre inclūsī inclūsus
long longus –a –um; adv (for a long time)
    diū; for a longer time diūtius; long
    ago iamdūdum, iam prīdem; long and
    hard (adv) diū et ācriter
look m aspectus –ūs m; (on the face)
    vultus –ūs m; looks habitus –ūs m
look spectō –āre –āvī –ātus; look! ecce;
    look at aspiciō –ĕre aspexī aspectus;
    look for quaerō –ĕre quaesīvī
    quaesītus; look over lustrō –āre –āvī
    –ātus
loot praeda –ae f
lose amittō –ĕre amīsī amissus
loser victus –ī m
lot: a lot multum
loud magnus –a –um
lovable amābilis –is –e
love amō –āre –āvī –ātus; amor –ōris m
lover amāns –antis m/f
low dēmissus –a –um

lowest īmus –a –um
lucky fēlīx; fēlīcis
lunch basket sportula –ae f
lurid lūridus –a –um

madam domina –ae f
magnificent magnificus –a –um
maid ancilla –ae f
mailed datus –a –um
make faciō –ĕre fēcī factus; fabricō –āre
    –āvī –ātus; make one's appearance
    appareō –ĕre –uī
man vir –ī m
mane iuba –ae f
many multī –ae –a; many more multō
    plūrēs
mark down dēnotō –āre –āvī –ātus
marketplace forum –ī n
marriage mātrimōnium –ī n
married woman mātrōna –ae f
marry: marry a husband nūbō –ĕre
    nūpsī nūpta (+ dat); marry a wife in
    mātrimōnium dūcere
massage unctiō –ōnis f
massage room unctōrium –ī n
master dominus –ī m; master craftsman
    magister –trī m
mathematician mathēmaticus –ī m
matricide mātricīdium –ī n
matron of honor prōnuba –ae f
matter rēs reī f
maybe forsitan, fortasse
maze labyrinthus –ī m
meadow prātum –ī n
meal cibus –ī m
mean sigificō –āre –āvī –atus
meet occurrō –ĕre –ī occursum (+ dat);
    go to meet obvius (–a –um) īre
    (+ dat)
melt liquefaciō –facĕre –fēcī –factus
memory memoria –ae f
mention mentiō –ōnis f
messenger nūntius –ī m
method modus –ī m
mild mītis –is –e
mile mille passūs –uum m pl

milk mulgeō –ēre mulsī mulsus; lac
  lactis *n*
Milky Way Via (–ae *f*) Lactea
millstone mola –ae *f*
mind animus –ī *m*
Minotaur Mīnōtaurus –ī *m*
miracle mīrāculum –ī *n*
mirror speculum –ī *n*; **mirrorlike**
  speculāris –is –e
miss dēsīderō –āre –āvī –ātus
mist nebula –ae *f*
mistress domina –ae *f*
mob turba –ae *f*
moment momentum (–ī *n*) temporis
mommy mamma –ae *f*
money pecūnia –ae *f*
month mēnsis –is *m*
moon lūna –ae *f*
more *adv* magis, plūs; **more and more**
  magis et magis; **more time** plūs
  temporis; **the more . . . the more** quō
  magis . . . eō magis
moreover praetereā
morning: in the morning māne; **early in
  the morning** bene māne
mortality mortālitās –ātis *f*
most plērīque plēraeque plēraque
mother māter –tris *f*
mount, mountain mōns montis *m*
move moveō –ēre mōvī mōtus; (*change
  residence*) migrō –āre –āvī –ātus; **move
  into** immigrō –āre –āvī –ātus
movement motiō –ōnis *f*
much multus –a –um; *adv* multō; **much
  too slow** multō nimis lentus
mulberry tree mōrus –ī *f*
murder caedēs –is *f*
murky obscūrus –a –um
muscle mūsculus –ī *m*
mutual mūtuus –a –um
my meus –a –um

nail clāvus –ī *m*
name nōminō –āre –āvī –ātus; nōmen
  –inis *n*
narrate nārrō –āre –āvī –ātus

narrow angustus –a –um
native city patria –ae *f*
native land patria –ae *f*
near *prep* prope (+ *acc*)
neck cervīx –īcis *f*
need dēsīderō –āre –āvī –ātus
neighbor vīcīnus –ī *m*
neighborhood vīcīnitās –ātis *f*
neighboring vīcīnus –a –um
neither neque; **neither . . . nor** neque . . .
  neque
nervous trepidus –a –um
net rēte –is *n*
netman rētiārius –ī *m*
never numquam
nevertheless tamen
new novus –a –um
next (to) proximus –a –um (+ *dat*)
nice bellus –a –um
night nox noctis *f*; **at night** noctū
nightmare somnium (–ī *n*) tumultuōsum
no minimē, minimē vērō, nōn; **no
  longer** nōn iam; *adj* nullus –a –um;
  no one nēmō –inis *m*
nobility nōbilitās –ātis *f*
nonsense nūgae –ārum *f pl*; **nonsense!**
  nūgās!
noon merīdiēs –ēī *m*
North (*the*) septentriōnēs –um *m pl*
northern septentriōnālis –is –e
not nōn; **not only . . . but also** nōn
  modō. . . sed etiam; **not yet** nōndum
noted nōtus –a –um
nothing nihil
notice notō –āre –āvī –ātus
nourish nūtriō –īre –īvī or iī –ītus
now nunc; autem; **by now** iam
nurse nūtriō –īre –īvī or iī –ītus
nuptial nūptiālis –is –e

oar rēmus –ī *m*
obedient obēdiēns; obēdientis
obey obēdiō –īre –īvī or –iī (+ *dat*)
oblige obligō –āre –āvī –ātus
oblong oblongus –a –um
observe observō –āre –āvī –ātus

occupy occupō –āre –āvī –ātus; (*live in*)
teneō –ēre –uī –tum

occur ēveniō –īre ēvēnī ēventum

occurrence ēventus –ūs m

ocean oceanus –ī m

odor odor –ōris m

of course (*adv*) nempe

offend offendō –ere –ī offēnsus

office honor –ōris m

often saepe

old lady anus –ūs f

older māior māior māius (nātū)

oldest maximus –a –um (nātū)

Olympic Olympicus –a –um

omen ōmen –inis n

on in (+ *abl*), suprā (+ *acc*)

one ūnus –a –um

once ōlim, quondam; (one time) semel

only tantummodo

open apertus –a –um; **in the open** in
apertō

opinion opiniō –ōnis f

opponent adversārius –ī m, competītor
–ōris m

or an

orangey flammeus –a –um

order iubeō –ēre iussī iussus; **in order
to** ut (*with subjunctive*)

other alius –a –um; **one after the other**
alius ex aliō; **the other** alter altera
alterum

otherwise aliōquīn

ought oportet –ēre –uit; **I ought to**
oportet mē (+ *inf*)

our noster –tra –trum

out ahead ante

out of ē (ex) (+ *abl*)

outdoors forīs

outside forīs; **outside of** extrā (+ *acc*)

oven furnus –ī m

overcast nūbilus –a –um

overcome superō –āre –āvī –ātus

owe dēbeō –ēre –uī –itus

own: his/her/its/their own suus –a –um

owner dominus –ī m

ox bōs bovis m

pace passus –ūs m

pain dolor –ōris m

paint pingō –ere pīnxī pictus

painting pictūra –ae f

palace aula –ae f

pale pallidus –a –um

palestra palaestra –ae f

palm palma –ae f

panther panthēra –ae f

parent parēns –entis m/f

part pars partis f

participate (in) intersum –esse –fuī
(*dat or* in + *abl*)

party, dinner party convīvium –ī n

path sēmita –ae f

patience patientia –ae f

patient patiēns; patientis

patrician patricius –a –um

patricide patricīdium –ī n

pavement pavīmentum –ī n

pay pēnsitō –āre –āvī –ātus

peace pāx pācis f

peacock pāvō –ōnis f

people hominēs –um m pl; populus
–ī m

perhaps forsitan, fortasse

perish periō –īre –iī

person persōna –ae f, homō –inis m

personal persōnālis –is –e

pertain (to) pertineō –ēre –uī

pesticide pesticīdium –ī n

philosopher philosophus –ī m

picky fastidiōsus –a –um

picture pictūra –ae f

pierce perforō –āre –āvī –ātus

pig porcus –ī m

pillow cervīcal –ālis n

pirate pīrāta –ae m

place locus –ī m

plainly plānē

plaintiff accusātor –ōris m

plan cōnsilium –ī n

plane runcīnō –āre –āvī –ātus; runcīna
–ae f

planet planēta –ae f

plant planta –ae f

play lūdō –ĕre lūsī lūsus
player lūsor –ōris m
please placeō –ēre –uī –itum (+dat);
    please! quaesō
plebeian plēbēius –a –um
plough arō –āre –āvī –ātus; arātrum –ī n
pluck ēvellō –ĕre –ī ēvulsus
point out indicō –āre –āvī –ātus
poisonous venēnātus –a –um
policeman vigil –is m
polite polītus –a –um
politics rēs (reī f) pūblica
pond stagnum –ī n
pony mannus –ī m
poor (unfortunate) miser –era –erum;
    (moneyless) pauper –eris –ere
popular populāris –is –e
pound pulsō –āre –āvī –ātus
pour fundō –ĕre fūdī fūsus; to pour into
    īnfundĕre
power potestās –ātis f
practice exerceō –ēre –uī –itus; sē exercēre
praetor praetor –ōris m
praise laudō –āre –āvī –ātus
pretrial hearing praeiūdicium –ī n
precede praecēdō –ĕre praecessī
    praecessus
predict praedīcō –ĕre –dīxī dictus
prefer praeferō –ferre –tulī –lātus
presence: in the presence of coram
    (+ abl)
present mūnusculum –ī n
present: be present adsum –esse –fuī;
    be present at intersum –esse –fuī
    (+ dat or in + abl)
preside praesideō –sidēre –sēdī
prestige auctōritās –ātis f
prevent dēterreō –ēre –uī –itus
previously ante(ā)
pride superbia –ae f
prisoner (of war) captīvus –ī m
prison farm ergastulum –ī n
private privātus –a –um; private citizen
    privātus –ī m
proceed prōcēdō –cēdĕre –cessī –cessus
procession pompa –ae f

produce market macellum –ī n
prohibit prōhibeō –ēre –uī –itus
promise prōmittō –mittĕre –mīsī –missus
pronounce prōnuntiō –āre –āvī –ātus
prosecutor accusātor –ōris m
protect prōtegō –tegĕre –tegī –tēctus
proud (of) superbus –a –um (+abl)
prudent prūdēns; prūdentis
prune amputō –āre –āvī –ātus
pruning knife falcula –ae f
public pūblicus –a –um
public baths thermae –ārum f pl
pull trahō –ĕre trāxī tractus; pull off
    dētrahō –ĕre dētrāxī dētractus; pull
    out extrahō –ĕre extrāxī extractus
punish pūniō –īre –īvī or –ii –ītus
pupil discipulus –ī m
pursue persequor –sequī –secūtus sum
put pōnō –ĕre posuī positus; put down
    dēpōnō –ĕre dēposuī dēpositus; put
    on (impose) impōnō –ĕre imposuī
    impositus (+ dat); (clothes) induō –ĕre
    –ī indūtus

quaestor quaestor –ōris m
question quaestiō –ōnis f
quick-tempered īrācundus –a –um
quickly citō

racetrack circus –ī m
rain pluit –ĕre pluit; pluvia –ae f
rainbow pluvius arcus –ūs m
raise (children) ēducō –āre –āvī –ātus
rake ērādō –ĕre ērāsī ērāsus; rastellus –ī m
rapid rapidus –a –um
rarely rārō
ray radius –ī m
razor novācula –ae f
reach perveniō –venīre –venī –ventus ad
    or in (+ acc)
read legō –ĕre lēgī lēctus
realize sentiō –īre sēnsī sēnsus
really quidem
reap metō –ĕre messuī messus
reason ratiō –ōnis f
rebellious rebellis –is –e

receive accipiō –ěre accēpī acceptus
recent recēns; recentis; **recently** nūper
recline accumbō –ěre accubuī accubitum
recognize recognoscō –ěre recognōvī recognitus
red ruber –bra –brum
refined polītus –a –um
refuge asȳlum –ī n
refuse recūsō –āre –āvī –ātus
region regiō –ōnis f
regret paenitet –ēre –uit; I **regret** mē paenitet
remain maneō –ēre –uī; (be left over) restō –āre restitī
remaining cēterī –ae –a
remember in memoriā tenēre
repair reparō –āre –āvī –ātus
republic rēs (rēī f) pūblica
respectable honestus –a –um
rest of cēterī –ae –a
restaurant popīna –ae f
restless inquiētus –a –um
retain retineō –ēre –uī retentus
retire sē recipěre
return (go back) redeō –īre –iī –itus
reveal revēlō –āre –āvī –ātus
review recognitiō –ōnis f
rich dīves; dīvitis; **the rich** dīvitēs m pl
rid: get rid of dēmittō –ěre dēmīsī dēmissus
ride equitō –āre –āvī
ridiculous rīdiculus –a –um
right dexter –tra –trum; **right up to** ūsque ad (+ acc)
ring ānulus –ī m
rise surgō –ěre surrēxī surrēctus; ascendō –ěre –ī ascensus
rising oriēns; orientis
river flūmen –inis n
road via –ae f
roar fremō –ěre –uī –itum
roast assum –ī n
robber latrō –ōnis m
robust rōbustus –a –um
rock saxum –ī n
rod virga –ae f
roll volvō –ěre –ī volūtus

Roman Rōmānus –a –um
roof tēctum –ī n
room cella –ae f
rope fūnis –is m; **jump rope** ad fūnem salīre
rostrum rostra –ōrum n pl
rough dūrus –a –um
row remigō –āre –āvī; ōrdō –inis m
rule (over) regnō –āre –āvī –ātus (+ dat)
run (a shop, company) exerceō –ēre –uī –itus; currō –ěre cucurrī cursus; **run away** effugiō –ěre –ī; **run into** occurrō –ěre –ī occursus (+ dat); **run low** deficiō –ěre –fēcī –fectus
runner cursor –ōris m
rush festīnō –āre –āvī –ātus

sad tristis –is –e
safe salvus –a –um
safety salus –ūtis f
sail nāvigō –āre –āvī –ātus; **sail by** praeternāvigāre; **set sail** vēla dare
sake: for the sake of causā (+gen)
same īdem eadem idem
sand arēna –ae f
sandal sandalium –ī n
sanity sānitās –ātis f
sauna laconicum –ī n
sausage tomāclum –ī n
save cōnservō –āre –āvī –ātus
saw serrā secō –āre –uī –tus; serram dūcěre; serra –ae f
sawdust scobis –is f
say dīcō –ěre dīxī dīctus
scared territus –a –um; **scared stiff** perterritus –a –um
scene scaena –ae f
scepter sceptrum –ī n
school schola –ae f; lūdus –ī m
science scientia –ae f
scorpion scorpiō –ōnis m
sculptor sculptor –ōris m
scythe falx –cis f
sea mare –is n; adj. marīnus –a –um, maritimus –a –um; **sea monster** cētus –ī m

seashore or*a* (*-ae f*) maritim*a*
season temp*us* (*-oris n*) annī
secret sēcrēt*us* *-a* *-um*; sēcrēt*um* *-ī n*
security sēcurit*ās* *-ātis f*
sedan chair sell*a* (*-ae f*) gestātōri*a*
see vide*ō* *-ēre* vīdī vīsus; see to it that
    cūrāre ut
seed sēm*en* *-inis n*
seem videor vidērī vīsus sum
seize rapi*ō* *-ĕre* *-uī* *-tus*; occup*ō* *-āre*
    -āvī *-ātus*
self ([*he*] *himself*) ipse; ([*she*] *herself*)
    ipsa; ([*it*] *itself*) ipsum; to wash
    oneself sē lavāre
senate building cūri*a* *-ae f*
senator senāt*or* *-ōris m*
sense sēns*us* *-ūs m*
serious grav*is* *-is* *-e*
serpent serp*ēns* *-entis m*
serve (*food*) adpōn*ō* *-ĕre* adposuī
    adpositus
set (*hair*) cōm*ō* *-ĕre* cōmpsī cōmptus;
    set in order ōrdin*ō* *-āre* *-āvī* *-atus*
setting occid*ēns*; occid*entis*
sew su*ō* *-ĕre* suī sūtus
shape form*a* *-ae f*
sharp acūt*us* *-a* *-um*
shawl vēlām*en* *-inis n*
she ea *f*
shed prōfund*ō* *-fundĕre* *-fūdī*
    -fūsus
sheep ov*is* *-is f*; sheep fold ovīl*e* *-is n*
shepherd pāst*or* *-ōris m*
shield (*round*) parm*a* *-ae f*; (*oblong*)
    scut*um* *-ī n*
shine lūce*ō* *-ēre* lūxī; shine again
    refulge*ō* *-ēre* refulsī
shinguard ocre*a* *-ae f*
shiny splendid*us* *-a* *-um*
ship nāv*is* *-is f*
shipwreck naufrāgi*um* *-ī n*
shoe calce*us* *-ī m*
shoelace corrigi*a* *-ae f*
shop obsōn*ō* *-āre* *-āvī* *-ātus*; tabern*a*
    -ae f
shore ōr*a* *-ae f*

short brev*is* *-is* *-e*
shoulder umer*us* *-ī m*
shout clām*ō* *-āre* *-āvī* *-ātus*; (*in*
    approval) acclāmāre
shovel rutr*um* *-ī n*
show adhibe*ō* *-ēre* *-uī* *-itus*; spectācul*um*
    -ī n; show up appare*ō* *-ēre* *-uī*
shrine aed*ēs* *-is f*
sick ae*ger* *-gra* *-grum*
side lat*us* *-eris n*; from both sides
    utrimque
sidewalk crepīd*ō* *-inis f*
sight speci*ēs* *-ēī f*; at first sight prīmā
    speciē
sign sign*um* *-ī n*; titul*us* *-ī m*
silence silenti*um* *-ī n*
silent: be silent sile*ō* *-ēre* *-uī*
similar simil*is* *-is* *-e*
simple simplex; simplicis
sincere sincēr*us* *-a* *-um*
sing cant*ō* *-āre* *-āvī* *-ātus*
singer cant*or* *-ōris m*
sir! domine!
sister sor*or* *-ōris f*
sit sede*ō* *-ēre* sēdī sessum; sit down
    cōnsīd*ō* *-sīdĕre* *-sēdī* *-sessum*
situation rēs rēī *f*
skill ars artis *f*
skilled perīt*us* *-a* *-um*
skillful artifex; artificis
skin pell*is* *-is f*
skip omitt*ō* *-ēre* omīsī omissus
sky cael*um* *-ī n*
slave serv*a* *-ae f*; serv*us* *-ī m*
slave dealer mang*ō* *-ōnis m*
slave platform catast*a* *-ae f*
sleep dormi*ō* *-īre* *-īvī* *-ītum*; somn*us*
    -ī m; go to sleep dormītum īre
sleepy somnolent*us* *-a* *-um*
slow lent*us* *-a* *-um*
small parv*us* *-a* *-um*; parvul*us* *-a* *-um*;
    smaller minor minor minus; smallest
    minim*us* *-a* *-um*
smile subrīde*ō* *-rīdĕre* *-rīsī* *-rīsus*
smoke fūm*us* *-ī m*
snack shop popīn*a* *-ae f*

snow ning*it* –*ĕre* ninxit; nix nivis *f*
snowball pil*a* (–*ae f*) nive*a*
so ita, sīc **and so** itaque; **so many** tot
    (*indecl*); **so much** tant*us* –*a* –*um*
soft tener –*eris* –*ere*
soldier mīl*es* –*itis m*
sole plant*a* –*ae f*
some aliquot (*indecl*)
someday aliquandō
someone aliquis alicūius
son fili*us* –*ī m*
song carm*en* –*inis n*
soon mox; **as soon as possible** cum
    prīmum
sooner prius
soothsayer harusp*ex* –*icis m*
sophisticated urbān*us* –*a* –*um*
sorry: **I am sorry** mē paenitet
sound sān*us* –*a* –*um*; **be sound asleep**
    dormīre artē
sow ser*ō* –*ĕre* sēvī sātus
spade pal*a* –*ae f*
speak loquor loquī locūtus sum
spear hast*a* –*ae f*
spectator spectāt*or* –*ōris m*
speech ōrāti*ō* –*ōnis f*; **give a speech**
    ōrātiōnem habēre
spider arāne*a* –*ae f*
spin ne*ō* nēre nēvī nētus
splendid splendid*us* –*a* –*um*
spoke radi*us* –*ī m*
spot cōnspici*ō* –*ĕre* cōnspexī cōnspectus
spot macul*a* –*ae f*
spotty maculōs*us* –*a* –*um*
spouse coni*ūnx* –*iugis m/f*
spring (*water source*) fōns fontis *m*;
    (*season*) vēr vēris *n*
sprout germin*ō* –*āre* –*āvī* –*ātus*
squirrel sciūr*us* –*ī m*
stable stabul*um* –*ī n*
stack mēt*a* –*ae f*
stadium stadi*um* –*ī n*
stand st*ō* stāre stetī status; **stand around**
    circumst*ō* –*stāre* –*stetī*
standing stat*us* –*ūs m*
star stell*a* –*ae f*

state cīvit*ās* –*ātis f*
statue statu*a* –*ae f*
status stat*us* –*ūs m*
stay mane*ō* –*ēre* mānsī mānsūrus
steal clep*ō* –*ĕre* –*sī* –*tus*
step grad*us* –*ūs m*; **go up the steps** per
    gradūs ascendĕre; **step forward** prōde*ō*
    –*īre* –*ī* –*itum*
stick virg*a* –*ae f*
still adhūc; (*nevertheless*) tamen; **still**
    today etiamnunc
sting ic*ō* –*ĕre* īcī ictus; ict*us* –*ūs m*
stone: **little stone** lapill*us* –*ī m*
stop (*doing something*) dēsist*ō* –*ĕre*
    dēstitī; (*stand still*) cōnsist*ō* –*ĕre*
    cōnstitī
store cond*ō* –*dĕre* –*didī* –*ditus*; tabern*a*
    –*ae f*
storeroom cell*a* –*ae f*
stork cicōni*a* –*ae f*
storm tempest*ās* –*ātis f*
straight rēct*us* –*a* –*um*
strange mīr*us* –*a* –*um*
stranger aliēn*us* –*ī m*
stream flūvi*us* –*ī m*
strict strict*us* –*a* –*um*
string līne*a* –*ae f*
stroll dēambul*ō* –*āre* –*āvī*
strong valid*us* –*a* –*um*
stubborn obstināt*us* –*a* –*um*
student discipul*us* –*ī m*
studious studiōs*us* –*a* –*um*
study stude*ō* –*ēre* –*uī*; (*room*) tablīn*um*
    –*ī n*
style mod*us* –*ī m*
success success*us* –*ūs m*
such tāl*is* –*is* –*e*
sudden repentīn*us* –*a* –*um*; **suddenly**
    subitō
suicide suicīdi*um* –*ī n*
sulfur sulf*ur* –*uris n*
summer aest*ās* –*ātis f*
sun sōl –*is m*
superstition superstiti*ō* –*ōnis f*
superstitious superstitiōs*us* –*a* –*um*
supervise cūr*ō* –*āre* –*āvī* –*ātus*

supper cēn*a* –*ae f*; **eat supper** cēnō –*āre*
    –*āvī* –*ātus*

support sustentō –*āre* –*āvī* –*ātus*

supposed: I am supposed to obligātus
    sum (+ *inf*)

surely certē

surround circum*clūdō* –*clūdĕre* –*clūsī*
    –*clūsus*

swear iurō –*āre* –*āvī* –*ātus*

sweat sūdō –*āre* –*āvī* –*ātus*

sweep (*up*) verrō –*ĕre* –*ī* versus

swell tum*eō* –*ēre* –*uī*

swim *intr* natō –*āre* –*āvī*

swim natātiō –*ōnis f*

swimming pool piscīn*a* –*ae f*

swing oscillō –*āre* –*āvī* –*ātus*; oscill*um*
    –*ī n*

swollen tumēns; tumentis

sword gladi*us* –*ī m*

table mēns*a* –*ae f*

tail caud*a* –*ae f*

take (*seize*) capiō –*ĕre* cēpī captus, sūmō
    –*ĕre* sūmpsī sūmptus; (*bring*) ferō ferre
    tulī lātus; **take back** recip*iō* –*ĕre* –*cēpī*
    –*ceptus*; **take care** cūrō –*āre* –*āvī* –*ātus*;
    take to addūcō –*ĕre* adduxī adductus

tall alt*us* –*a* –*um*

tame mīt*is* –*is* –*e*

taste gustō –*āre* –*āvī* –*ātus*

tavern tabern*a* –*ae f*

teach doceō –*ēre* –*uī* –*tus*

teacher magis*ter* –*trī m*, magistr*a* –*ae f*

tear lacrim*a* –*ae f*

tear up (*rip*) laniō –*āre* –*āvī* –*ātus*

tell nārro –*āre* –*āvī* –*ātus*

temple (*building*) templ*um* –*ī n*; (*head*)
    temp*us* –*oris n*

tender ten*er* –*eris* –*ere*

terribly vehementer

terrify terrificō –*āre* –*āvī* –*ātus*

test probātiō –*ōnis f*

testimony testimōni*um* –*ī n*

than quam

that (*demonstrative pron or adj*) ille illa
    illud; iste ista istud; (*relative pron*) quī

quae quod; (*in indirect statement: use*
    acc + *infinitive*)

theater theātr*um* –*ī n*

their eōrum; **their own** su*us* –*a* –*um*

then (*next*) deinde; (*at that time*) tum;
    just then tunc maximē; **then when**
    tum cum

there ibi

thereafter exinde

therefore ergō

thick dēns*us* –*a* –*um*

thigh fem*ur* –*oris n*

thing rēs rēī *f*

think cōgitō –*āre* –*āvī* –*ātus*; **think to**
    oneself cōgitāre sēcum

third tertius –*a* –*um*

this hīc haec hōc

three trēs trēs tria; **three times** ter

thresh dēterō –*ĕre* dētrīvī dētrītus

threshing floor āre*a* –*ae f*

threshold līm*en* –*inis n*

thrive vigeō –*ēre* –*uī*

through per (+ *acc*)

throw iaciō –*ĕre* iēcī iactus; **throw down**
    dēiciō –*ĕre* dēiēcī dēiectus; **throw into**
    iniciō –*ĕre* iniēcī iniectus; **throw out**
    ēiciō –*ĕre* ēiēcī ēiectus

thumb poll*ex* –*icis m*

thunder tonō –*āre* –*uī*; tonitrus –*ūs m*

thus ita, sīc

tide aest*us* –*ūs m*

tie ligō –*āre* –*āvī* –*ātus*

tiger tigr*is* –*is f*

till now adhūc

time temp*us* –*oris n*; **at that time** tum

timid timid*us* –*a* –*um*

to ad (+ *acc*); ut (*with subjunctive*)

today hodiē

toga tog*a* –*ae f*

together ūnā; **together with** ūnā cum
    (+ *abl*)

toilet latrīn*a* –*ae f*

tomorrow crās

too (*excessively*) nimis; (*also*) quoque

tool īnstrūment*um* –*ī n*

tooth dēns dentis *m*

top: **at the top of the page** in summā
pagīnā; **on top of** suprā (+ *acc*)
torch taeda *–ae f*
toss iactō *–āre –āvī –ātus*
totter nūtō *–āre –āvī*
touch tangō *–ĕre* tetigī tāctus
tough dūrus *–a –um*
toward erga (+*acc*)
town oppidum *–ī n*
townspeople oppidānī *–ōrum m pl*
track sēmita *–ae f*
train exerceō *–ēre –uī –itus*; sē exercēre
trainer lanista *–ae m*
travel iter faciō *–ĕre* fēcī factus
traveler viātor *–ōris m*
treasure thesaurus *–ī m*
tree arbor *–oris f*
tremble tremō *–ĕre –uī*
tremor tremor *–ōris m*
trial iūdicium *–ī n*
trident tridēns *–entis m*
trip iter itineris *n*; **take a trip** iter facĕre
troubles labōrēs *–um m pl*
true vērus *–a –um*
trust cōnfidō *–ĕre* cōnfidī cōnfisus
(+ *dat*)
try temptō *–āre –āvī –ātus*
tunic tunica *–ae f*
turn convertō *–ĕre –ī* conversus; **turn
out** (*on a lathe*) tornō *–āre –āvī –ātus*;
(*become*) fiō fiĕrī factus sum
twentieth vīcēsimus *–a –um*
twice bis
twin geminus *–ī m*
twine līnum *–ī n*
two duo duae duo
tyrannicide tyrannicīdium *–ī n*

uncertain incertus *–a –um*
under sub (+ *abl*)
underbrush frūtectum *–ī n*
understand intellegō *–ĕre* intellexī
intellectus
understanding intellectus *–ūs m*
underworld īnferī *–ōrum m pl*
undress vestēs exuō *–ĕre –ī*

unfriendly inimīcus *–a –um*
unhappy īnfēlīx; īnfēlīcis
unity ūnitās *–ātis f*
unless nisi
unsure incertus *–a –um*
until donec
unusual inūsitātus *–a –um*
unwilling: **be unwilling** nōlō nōlle
nōluī
up till now usque adhūc
urge on incitō *–āre –āvī –ātus*
urn urna *–ae f*
us nōs
use ūtor ūtī ūsus sum (+ *abl*)
usual solitus *–a –um*
utensils ūtēnsilia *–ium n pl*

vain: **in vain** frustrā
valley vallēs *–is f*
vast vastus *–a –um*
vegetable holus *–eris n*
vendor venditor *–ōris m*
verdict sententia *–ae f*
very admodum
veteran veterānus *–ī m*
victim victima *–ae f*
victory victōria *–ae f*
view aspectus *–ūs m*
vinegar acētum *–ī n*
violet viola *–ae f*
visit vīsitō *–āre –āvī –ātus*
voice vōx vōcis *f*; **in a loud voice** magnā
cum vōce
vote suffrāgium *–ī n*; **cast a vote**
suffrāgium ferre
voter suffrāgātor *–ōris m*
vulture vultur *–is m*

wagon plaustrum *–ī n*
wailing ululātus *–ūs m*
wait exspectō *–āre –āvī –ātus*; **wait for**
exspectāre
wake up expergīscor *–ī* experrēctus
sum
walk ambulō *–āre –āvī*; **walk around**
dēambulāre

wall mūr*us* –*ī m*; (*between rooms*) pariēs
–*etis m*

wander err*ō* –*āre* –*āvī* –*ātus*

want vol*ō* velle volu*ī*; **not want** nōl*ō*
nōlle nōlu*ī*

war bell*um* –*ī n*

ward vīc*us* –*ī m*

warm tepid*us* –*a* –*um*; **warm bath**
tepidāri*um* –*ī n*

warmly benignē

warn mone*ō* –*ēre* –*uī* –*itus*

wash lav*ō* –*āre* –*āvī* lautus

watch spect*ō* –*āre* –*āvī* –*ātus*

water irrig*ō* –*āre* –*āvī* –*ātus*; aqu*a* –*ae f*

wave fluct*us* –*ūs m*

way mod*us* –*ī m*; **by the way** obiter; **in
this way** sīc

wear gest*ō* –*āre* –*āvī* –*ātus*

weather tempest*ās* –*ātis f*

weave tex*ō* –*ĕre* –*uī* –*tus*

wedding nūpti*ae* –*ārum f pl*; *adj*
nūptiāl*is* –*is* –*e*

weed herb*a* (–*ae f*) mal*a*

weight on*us* –*eris n*; (*for exercise*) halt*ēr*
–*ēris m*

welcome excipi*ō* –*ĕre* excēp*ī* exceptus

well: **be well** vale*ō* –*ēre* –*uī*; *adv* bene;

wet madid*us* –*a* –*um*

what? quid?

wrestler luctāt*or* –*ōris m*

Grammatical Index

participles 122, 129
  future participle with **ūrus**
    265, 331
  past participle of deponent verbs 204
  past passive participle 204
  perfect passive participle 195–196,
    213–214, 249
  present participle 122, 124,
    249, 324
  present participle of deponent
    verbs 324, 326, 334
passive infinitive 184
passive voice 178–179, 181,
    246–248
  facěre 211, 249
  with intransitive sense 198
  perfect tense 195, 213–214, 248
  pluperfect tense 195–196,
    213–214, 249
  present passive *see* infinitives
past contrary-to-fact conditions
    305–306
past participle of deponent verbs 204
past passive participle 204
past perfect tense, *see* pluperfect
    tense
perfect active infinitive 224, 240
perfect infinitive 250
perfect passive infinitive 227, 240,
    248, 250
perfect passive participles 195–196,
    213–214, 249
perfect passive tense 195, 213–214, 249
pluperfect subjunctive 305–306,
    307–308, 333
pluperfect tense
  active 111, 162
  passive 195–196, 213–214, 249
positive adjectives 58, 63
posse *(to be able)*
  future tense 40
  present subjunctive 281, 332
present active infinitive 184
present infinitive 250
present participles 122, 124, 249
  of deponent verbs 324, 326, 334

present passive infinitive 184
present subjunctive 279, 280–281,
    282, 332
present tense
  active infinitive 184
  passive infinitive 184
pronominal adjectives (**īdem, eadem,
    idem**) 140
pronouns
  demonstrative (**hīc, haec, hoc**) 6–7, 8,
    73
  demonstrative (**ille, illa, illud**) 6–7, 9,
    83
  demonstrative (**iste, ista, istud**)
    11, 74
  indefinite (**quīdam, quaedam,
    quoddam**) 152, 164
  intensive (**ipse, ipsa, ipsum**)
    152–153, 164
  reflexive 235–236, 250
  reflexive (**sē**) 24, 74, 153
  reflexive (**sibi**) 24–25
  relative (**quī, quae, quod**) 90, 91, 92,
    95–96, 161
purpose clause
  with **nē** 279–280, 294, 333
  with **ut** 279, 294, 333

quam *(than)* 65, 77
quī, quae, quod *(who, which, that)*
    90, 91, 92, 95–96, 161
quīdam, quaedam, quoddam
    (a certain) 152, 164

reflexive pronouns
  in indirect statements
    235–236, 250
  sē 24, 74, 153
  sibi 24–25
reflexive verbs 24, 74
relative pronouns (**quī, quae, quod**)
    90, 91, 92, 95–96, 161

sē *(self)* 24, 74, 153
sī *(if)* 295, 333
sibi 24–25

Topical Index